Tolkien on Chaucer, 1913–1959

Tolkien on Chaucer, 1913–1959

JOHN M. BOWERS
and
PETER STEFFENSEN

OXFORD
UNIVERSITY PRESS

OXFORD
UNIVERSITY PRESS

Great Clarendon Street, Oxford, OX2 6DP,
United Kingdom

Oxford University Press is a department of the University of Oxford.
It furthers the University's objective of excellence in research, scholarship,
and education by publishing worldwide. Oxford is a registered trade mark of
Oxford University Press in the UK and in certain other countries

© John M. Bowers and Peter Steffensen 2024

The moral rights of the authors have been asserted

All rights reserved. No part of this publication may be reproduced, stored in
a retrieval system, or transmitted, in any form or by any means, without the
prior permission in writing of Oxford University Press, or as expressly permitted
by law, by licence or under terms agreed with the appropriate reprographics
rights organization. Enquiries concerning reproduction outside the scope of the
above should be sent to the Rights Department, Oxford University Press, at the
address above

You must not circulate this work in any other form
and you must impose this same condition on any acquirer

Published in the United States of America by Oxford University Press
198 Madison Avenue, New York, NY 10016, United States of America

British Library Cataloguing in Publication Data

Data available

Library of Congress Control Number: 2023914151

ISBN 978–0–19–284888–8

DOI: 10.1093/oso/9780192848888.001.0001

Printed and bound by
CPI Group (UK) Ltd, Croydon, CR0 4YY

Links to third party websites are provided by Oxford in good faith and
for information only. Oxford disclaims any responsibility for the materials
contained in any third party website referenced in this work.

Acknowledgements

We would like to begin by thanking Cathleen Blackburn of Maier Blackburn and the Tolkien Estate for permission to publish a variety of writings by J. R. R. Tolkien. The reprints include his 1934 article "Chaucer as a Philologist: *The Reeve's Tale*"; his 1953 article "Middle English *Losenger*: Sketch of an Etymological and Semantic Enquiry"; and excerpts from his 1959 "Valedictory Address to the University of Oxford". The Tolkien Estate has also granted us permission to present a variety of his unpublished writings. These include selections from his Oxford undergraduate notebooks; his letters in the OUP correspondence file, the Morgan Library, and the Bodleian Library; his unfinished edition *Selections from Chaucer's Poetry and Prose*; his 1939 edition of *The Reeve's Tale*; his lecture "Neck Verse" for the Oxford Dante Society; and his Oxford lectures on Chaucer delivered during the academic years 1947–56.

We thank separately OUP archivist Martin Maw and the Secretary to the Delegates of Oxford University Press for permission to publish Tolkien's eight letters in their correspondence files and to reproduce Tolkien's 1951 letter to Dan Davin of OUP; Cornell University Press for allowing us to quote portions of Tolkien's "Valedictory Address" from *J. R. R. Tolkien: Scholar and Storyteller*; the Morgan Library and Museum for permission to quote Tolkien's 1957 letter to Polish professor Przemyslaw Mroczkowski; the Harry Ransom Humanities Center at the University of Texas, Austin, and further the Society of Authors as the literary representative of the Estate of John Masefield, for permission to publish verses composed by Masefield to introduce Tolkien's 1938 performance of the *Nun's Priest's Tale*; and Lutz Marten on behalf of the Philological Society for permission to reproduce "Chaucer as a Philologist: *The Reeve's Tale*" from *Transactions of the Philological Society*. Rights to Tolkien's conference lecture "Middle English *Losenger*", originally published by the Société d'édition Les Belles Lettres, have reverted to the Tolkien Estate, and the piece is reproduced here by permission with copyright notice © the Tolkien Estate Limited, 1953, 2023.

We are grateful to Oronzo Cilli for sending the PDF of the second edition of his *Tolkien's Library: An Annotated Checklist* so that we could update page references before publication of his extremely helpful volume. Further thanks go to Robin Darwall-Smith and Nelson Goering for puzzling out some especially troublesome Latin. We thank also Chris Smith at HarperCollins for providing Tolkien's new 1945 letter about Chaucer prior to the publication of *The Letters of J. R. R. Tolkien: Revised and Expanded Edition*. John Garth and Catherine McIlwaine were generous with their time and expertise on the author's handwriting for help with transcribing Tolkien's manuscripts, particularly his late lectures on the *Pardoner's Tale*. Peter Gilliver provided similar assistance with Tolkien's letters in the OUP files, also offering further insights into Tolkien's work at the *Oxford English Dictionary*.

Our special thanks go to John Garth as OUP's copy-editor, who went above and beyond the call of duty, even travelling to Oxford to check our transcriptions against Tolkien's original manuscripts at the Bodleian. Not only is Tolkien's handwriting a challenge, but he left his papers in such a chaotic state that it is hard to make sense of their original order; John Garth brought much greater correctness to both scores. His insights have enabled us to catch several errors of interpretation, and he identified passages of great interest in the philological segments of Tolkien's lecture scripts on the *Clerk's Tale* and the *Pardoner's Tale*. Final views are our own.

Our final thanks go to the Bodleian Library's Tolkien Archivist Catherine McIlwaine for extraordinary assistance during the Covid-19 epidemic when research facilities in Oxford were locked down. No investigators into Tolkien's original manuscripts at the Bodleian can over-express their gratitude to Catherine McIlwaine. Her expert help continued when University of Nevada Las Vegas, prior to a one-semester sabbatical, generously supported Professor Bowers's June 2022 visit to Oxford to continue in-person research in the Bodleian's special collections. To make this visit possible, the Warden and Fellows of Merton College hosted Professor Bowers as a visiting scholar, with accommodation fortuitously at 20 Merton Street next door to Professor Tolkien's last address at 21 Merton Street.

Contents

List of Illustrations	ix
List of Abbreviations	xi
Introduction	1
1. Chaucerian in Training, 1913–23	9
"The Language of Chaucer" (1913)	10
"Chaucer and his Contemporaries" (1914)	15
Troilus and Criseyde	23
Oxford English Dictionary (1918–20)	30
Tolkien at Leeds: *TLS* and *YWES*	35
2. Editing Chaucer, 1924–28	41
Oxford University Press correspondence (1924–51)	42
Tolkien Editing Skeat's Chaucer	55
The Glossary (1925)	61
The Notes (1928)	66
3. *The Reeve's Tale*, 1928–44	106
"Chaucer as a Philologist: *The Reeve's Tale*" (1934)	106
Oxford's Summer Diversions (1939)	176
The Reeve's Tale for Navy Cadets (1944)	178
4. Merton Professor of Chaucer, 1947–54	215
The Clerk's Tale (1947)	216
The Pardoner's Tale (1947)	224
The Parlement of Foules (1948)	230
The Pardoner's Tale (1951–1954)	233
5. The Middle English *Losenger*	246
"Neck Verse" for the Oxford Dante Society (1947)	246
Letter on *faynights* (1951)	250
"Middle English *Losenger*" (1953)	252
6. The *Pardoner's Tale*: The Story and its Form, 1955–56	267
7. Valedictory to Chaucer, 1959	319
Coda: Tolkien on Chaucer's *Retracciouns*	323
Works Cited	329
Index	339

List of Illustrations

1. Tolkien's 1913 tutorial essay "The Language of Chaucer" (Bodleian MS Tolkien A 21/1, fols. 44v and 45r).   13
2. Lecture notes from Professor Raleigh's "Chaucer and his Contemporaries" (Bodleian MS Tolkien A 21/4, fols. 16v–17r).   21
3. Tolkien's 1915 student notes on *Troilus* and *St. Juliana* (Bodleian MS Tolkien A 21/7, fols. 5v and 6r).   26
4. Letter of 8 June, 1951 to Dan Davin (Oxford University Press Archives).   53–54
5. Title page and Tolkien's handwritten table of contents for *Selections from Chaucer's Poetry and Prose* (Bodleian MS Tolkien A 39/1, fol. 1).   57
6. Galley long-sheet from Clarendon Chaucer's Glossary (Bodleian MS Tolkien A 39/3, fol. 10).   62
7. Typewritten commentary on Chaucer's *Romaunt of the Rose* (Bodleian MS Tolkien A 39/2/1, fol. 6).   67
8. Handwritten introduction to *Canterbury Tales* (Bodleian MS Tolkien A 39/2/2, fol. 83).   92
9. Copy of the *Reeve's Tale* programme with self-censored lines marked for restoration (Bodleian Tolkien VC Pamph (10), pages 12–13).   179
10. Ink notes over erased pencil draft in *Clerk's Tale* lecture (Bodleian MS Tolkien A 13/2, fol. 10).   217
11. First page of 1947 lecture on *Pardoner's Tale* (Bodleian MS Tolkien 13/2/1, fol. 61).   225
12. First page of 1955–56 lectures *The Pardoner's Tale: The Story and its Form* (Bodleian MS Tolkien A 13/2, fol. 39).   273
13. Last page of 1955–56 lectures *The Pardoner's Tale: The Story and its Form* (Bodleian MS Tolkien A 13/2, fol. 60v).   274

List of Abbreviations

Biography	Humphrey Carpenter, *J. R. R. Tolkien: A Biography*. 1977; Boston and New York: Houghton Mifflin, 2000.
Cilli	Oronzo Cilli, *Tolkien's Library: An Annotated Checklist*. Edinburgh: Luna Press, revised 2nd ed. 2022.
CT	*Canterbury Tales*.
EETS e.s.	Early English Text Society, extra series.
EETS o.s.	Early English Text Society, original series.
Ency	*J. R. R. Tolkien Encyclopedia: Scholarship and Critical Assessment*. Ed. Michael D. C. Drout. New York and London: Routledge, 2007.
Essays	J. R. R. Tolkien, *The Monsters and the Critics and Other Essays*. Ed. Christopher Tolkien. 1983; London: HarperCollins, 2006.
FR	J. R. R. Tolkien, *The Fellowship of the Ring*. 1954; Boston and New York: Houghton Mifflin, 1988.
Hobbit	J. R. R. Tolkien, *The Annotated Hobbit: Revised and Expanded Edition*. Ed. Douglas A. Anderson. Boston and New York: Houghton Mifflin, 2002.
Letters	*The Letters of J. R. R. Tolkien: Revised and Expanded Edition*. Ed. Humphrey Carpenter with Christopher Tolkien. London and New York: HarperCollins, 2023.
LotR	*The Lord of the Rings*.
M.E.	Middle English
NED	*New English Dictionary*, original name for *Oxford English Dictionary*.
O.E.	Old English
OED	*Oxford English Dictionary*.
O.N.	Old Norse
OUP	Oxford University Press.
RES	*Review of English Studies*.
RK	J. R. R. Tolkien, *The Return of the King*. 1955; Boston and New York: Houghton Mifflin, 1988.
SAC	*Studies in the Age of Chaucer*.
SH	Christina Scull and Wayne G. Hammond, *J. R. R. Tolkien Companion and Guide: Revised and Expanded Edition*. London: HarperCollins, 2017: Vol. 1, *Chronology*; Vol. 2, *Reader's Guide, Part I: A–M*; Vol. 3, *Reader's Guide, Part II: N–Z*.
Skeat	Walter W. Skeat, ed., *The Complete Works of Geoffrey Chaucer*. 6 vols. Oxford: Clarendon Press, 1894.

TLC	John M. Bowers, *Tolkien's Lost Chaucer*. Oxford: Oxford University Press, 2019.
TLS	*Times Literary Supplement* (London).
TT	J. R. R. Tolkien, *The Two Towers*. 1954; Boston and New York: Houghton Mifflin, 1988.

Introduction

Scholarship is another form of autobiography, and some academics have lived more than one life. Best known for his scholarly work on the Old English poem *Beowulf*, J. R. R. Tolkien began as a schoolboy reading Chaucer in the original Middle English and ended in his retirement address by summoning Chaucer as the ever-present subject of English study. During the intervening years, he taught Chaucer, he edited Chaucer, he published criticism on Chaucer, and he even dressed up as Chaucer and recited from memory the *Nun's Priest's Tale* and the *Reeve's Tale*. Lecturing on non-religious works such as the *Clerk's Tale* became another ploy to avoid drawing attention to himself as a Catholic at a still-bigoted university. His late published lecture on the Chaucerian word *losenger* became an indirect self-accusation as an "idler" and "deceiver" for wasting his time on fantasy novels instead of devoting himself to serious philological studies. Even his steady interest in Chaucer's descriptive phrase *grey eyes* may have resulted from the fact that Tolkien himself had grey eyes (SH 2:63).

Tolkien's Lost Chaucer (2019) brought to light many of these projects, such as his unpublished edition *Selections from Chaucer's Poetry and Prose* as well as his experimental edition of the *Reeve's Tale*. The current book is a follow-up, reprinting his Chaucerian publications as well as making available for the first time generous samplings of unpublished writings such as his final lectures on the *Pardoner's Tale*. Still, this is only the tip of the scholarly iceberg. Michael Drout points out that the Tolkien canon "leaves out the hundreds and hundreds of pages of unpublished, unfinished material in the Bodleian Library".[1]

Tolkien's Chaucerian enterprises also reflect a personality trait humorously recalled by his friend George Sayer from a visit with him and his wife, when their guest wanted to help in their garden:

---

[1] Michael D. C. Drout, "J. R. R. Tolkien's Medieval Scholarship and its Significance", *Tolkien Studies* 4 (2007), 113–76 at p. 114. For example, Professor Bowers's article "Durin's Stone, Ruthwell Cross, and *Dream of the Rood*", *Tolkien Studies* 20 (2023), 9–28, prints for the first time Tolkien's newly discovered translation of *Dream of the Rood* from Bodleian MS Tolkien A 29 a, fols. 148–9.

He chose an area of about two square yards, part flower border and part lawn and cultivated it perfectly: the border meticulously weeded and the soil made level and exceedingly fine; the grass cut with scissors closely and evenly. It took him quite a long time to do the job, but it was beautifully done. He was in all things a perfectionist.[2]

This anecdote neatly summarizes Tolkien's scrupulous, narrowly focused, even obsessive work upon the *Reeve's Tale* during the years 1928 until 1944, his fixation with the Chaucerian word *losenger* between 1947 and 1953, and his many revisions of lectures on the *Pardoner's Tale* from 1947 through 1956. The phrase "two square yards" keeps coming to mind when describing other preoccupations such as Chaucer's use of Northern dialect in the *Reeve's Tale*.

Tolkien's largely overlooked 1951 lecture "Middle English *Losenger*" recalled: "It was in Chaucer that I first made the acquaintance of that dubious character the *losengeour*. My earliest enquiries about him were addressed to a worthy schoolmaster forty-five years ago."[3] The 2019 biopic *Tolkien* fictionalized him as a new boy at King Edward's School, Birmingham, standing to recite from memory four lines from the *Knight's Tale* beginning, "Whyl that the sege ther-boute lay" (*CT* I, 937-40). Not going back so far as his school days, our book begins its first chapter, "Chaucerian in Training, 1913-23", with his Oxford undergraduate notebooks. These allow us actually to witness Tolkien's earliest engagements with the fourteenth-century poet, first in his precocious tutorial essay "The Language of Chaucer" (fig. 1) and then in his copious note-taking for Professor Walter Raleigh's lectures "Chaucer and his Contemporaries" (fig. 2). After he had earned his First Class degree and returned from the Great War, he secured a job as an assistant lexicographer at the *Oxford English Dictionary* during 1918-20, with responsibility for various "W" words. Besides compiling etymologies, he became aware of the sixty years of quotations that had accumulated as attestations illustrating the uses of these words over time. He also became aware of the wide range of Chaucer editions from which these quotations were drawn, with the result that his later work readily cited early editors such as Thomas Tyrwhitt. When he secured a job as Reader in English Language at Leeds University in 1920, his teaching responsibilities included lecturing on Chaucer. In 1923 he published

---

[2] George Sayer, "Recollections of J. R. R. Tolkien", *Mythlore* 21 (1996), 21–5 at p. 23.
[3] "Middle English *Losenger*: Sketch of an Etymological and Semantic Enquiry", *Essais de Philologie Moderne (1951)* (Paris: Société d'édition Les Belles Lettres, 1953), 63–76 at p. 64. See *Ency* 420–1. Humphrey Carpenter, *J. R. R. Tolkien: A Biography* (1977; Boston and New York: Houghton Mifflin, 2000), 35–6, describes the early influence of the schoolmaster George Brewerton.

a *Times Literary Supplement* review of a new edition of *Hali Meidenhad* in which he managed to insert a reference to Chaucer's *Clerk's Tale*, and in the same year he began a series of three "Philology" surveys for *The Year's Work in English Studies* in which he had occasion to touch upon scholarly topics that would return in his later Chaucerian writings.

Our second chapter, "Editing Chaucer, 1924–28", traces his efforts on the Clarendon textbook *Selections from Chaucer's Poetry and Prose*. We are printing for the first time all of Tolkien's eight extant letters from his Oxford University Press correspondence, to trace his attitude to the project from early optimism to final, bitter resignation (fig. 4). We are including a brief analysis of his editorial work on emending Chaucer's text as inherited from the great Victorian scholar Walter W. Skeat, and we are providing a sampling from his Glossary, which had reached the state of corrected galley long-sheets (fig. 6). The edition floundered on his nearly 200 pages of annotations when only 20 were allowed – another instance of the "two square yards" – and the excesses of these notes have been a challenge for us, too, in providing samples.[4] Sacrificed, for example, are longer notes on Chaucer's Prioress. We have nonetheless included all his headnotes (unless needlessly pedantic) and some of the more interesting remarks, such as the prophetic first sentence from his commentary on the *Canterbury Tales*: "It is easier to plan a big book than to write it" (fig. 8). A single endnote on the *Legend of Cleopatra* inspired Tolkien to compile a four-page excursus on Chaucer's knowledge of the native Alliterative tradition, and we have made room for this mini-essay (minus his complete list of alliterative formulas) since it anticipated important claims by later specialists.

The third chapter, "*The Reeve's Tale*, 1928–44", traces Tolkien's preoccupations with this work from his last, unfinished annotations in his Clarendon Chaucer in 1928 to his major 70-page article "Chaucer as a Philologist: *The Reeve's Tale*" in 1934. He returned to this raucous fabliau in 1939 when invited by Poet Laureate John Masefield to dress up as Chaucer and recite it at Oxford's Summer Diversions. Because the *Oxford Mail*'s review of his previous year's performance of the *Nun's Priest's Tale* mentioned that "the audience were at first a little scared of Chaucer's Middle English" (SH 2:316), Tolkien provided his 1939 audience with a printed programme containing a concise

---

[4] It is tricky calculating the length of the draft annotations. *TLC* gives 160, but this is the number of leaves, many of them written on both sides. The current pagination of the Bodleian's three separate batches totals 187, but this does not include seven pages of "Introduction on Language" or the many scraps of paper scribbled over by Tolkien, many having nothing to do with his Chaucer edition. We have therefore decided that almost 200 better approximates the total pages.

introduction and the text of the *Reeve's Tale*. Though his prefatory remarks claimed that his version did not depart from Skeat's, what he actually did was truly experimental. His text was not based on Ellesmere, or any other early manuscripts, but rather contrived to represent what he believed was Chaucer's authentic personal language. Then five years later during the Second World War, when tasked with teaching Navy cadets at Oxford, Tolkien used leftover copies of the *Reeve's Tale* programme in the classroom and began supplementing it, first with passages previously deleted for the sake of decency (fig. 9), then with a line-by-line glossary of hard words, and finally with his guide "Chaucerian Grammar with Special Reference to the *Reeve's Tale*". He apparently planned publishing this expanded edition, as he did in 1944 with *Sir Orfeo* printed by Oxford's Academic Copying Office, but for some reason, probably the winding down of warfare, he did not. We have assembled these separate components to construct the student edition of the *Reeve's Tale* which Tolkien planned but did not accomplish.

Our fourth chapter, "Merton Professor of Chaucer, 1947–57", follows Tolkien into his appointment as Merton Professor of Language and Literature, when his new duties required him to lecture on the *Clerk's Tale* in 1947 (fig. 10), the *Parlement of Foules* in 1948, and the *Pardoner's Tale* repeatedly from 1947 through 1956, with shifting emphasis upon hard words, editorial cruces, and finally source-studies along with narrative analyses.[5]

Also during this period, Tolkien took a determined interest in the Chaucerian word *losenger*. His student Simonne d'Ardenne had sent him for comments her draft article on *losenger* in November 1946 (SH 1:330). Next, his 1947 lecture "Neck Verse" for the Oxford Dante Society detoured from examining a passage from *Purgatorio* to considering this word from Chaucer's Prologue to the *Legend of Good Women*. Then when he was invited to deliver a paper at a conference in Liège in 1951, he devoted the entire paper to an intense etymological study published in the proceedings volume two years later. In our fifth chapter we are reprinting, with annotations, this largely overlooked 1953 article "Middle English *Losenger*: Sketch of an Etymological and Semantic Enquiry" because, inspired by Chaucer, it represents Tolkien's last strenuous publication in his professional speciality of philology.[6]

---

[5] See John S. Ryan, "J. R. R. Tolkien's Formal Lecturing and Teaching at the University of Oxford, 1925–1959", *Seven: Journal of the Marion E. Wade Center* 19 (2002), 45–62 at pp. 51–2.

[6] Also in 1953, Tolkien published his verse drama *The Homecoming of Beorhtnoth Beorhthelm's Son*; see J. R. R. Tolkien, *The Battle of Maldon, Together with the Homecoming of Beorhtnoth*, ed. Peter Grybauskas (London: HarperCollins, 2023), p. xvii; its accompanying word-study on *ofermod*, confined to a single footnote, did not have much philological heft. Tolkien also delivered his Ker lecture "Sir Gawain and the Green Knight" in 1953, but it was not overtly philological and was not published

Our sixth chapter is devoted solely to Tolkien's lecture series *The Pardoner's Tale: The Story and its Form*, most likely delivered during the academic year 1955–56 immediately following publication of *The Return of the King*. We believe that he was motivated to set aside his habitual word-hopping to engaged in narrative analyses because he had come to realize, probably while preparing *The Lord of the Rings* for publication, that he had told the same story of men driven by greed to fight to the death over a gold treasure. All evidence led to the self-congratulatory conclusion, lost on his undergraduate audience, that he himself had done a better job than Chaucer with this archetypal story. His fair copy (figs. 12 and 13) allows for a complete transcription, here annotated, so that we gain a clearer appreciation for what his Oxford lectures, when carefully revised, might have looked and sounded like.

Our seventh chapter, "Valedictory to Chaucer", reprints excerpts from his 1959 retirement lecture in which Tolkien continued fighting a rearguard action in favour of Language over Literature, and he therefore naturally recruited Chaucer as a medieval author who most benefitted from careful philological study. As a coda by way of conclusion, we quote from a 1957 letter in which Tolkien reflected upon Chaucer's *Retracciouns* appended as his own valediction at the end of the *Canterbury Tales*. We also recall the newly published 1945 letter in which he imagined how Chaucer's risky *Canterbury Tales*, if released during his lifetime, might have landed him "in gaol or at the stake!"[7] Tolkien's remarks upon the medieval poet's anxieties about literary reception can be read also as an expression of his worries about his own unpublished works, particularly his *Silmarillion*.

This survey of Tolkien's career-long engagements with Chaucer has been qualified by the maxim *we don't know what we don't know*. With a medieval poet even as well-documented as Chaucer, a new piece of evidence can change a great deal – most recently, in clarification from legal records that the notorious charge of *raptus* against the poet did not actually mean sexual assault.[8] Careful though Tolkien was at saving his papers, even his undergraduate notebooks, clearly not everything found its way to the Bodleian Library's special collections to give us a full and accurate accounting of his life and career. "The most private of Tolkien's surviving papers remain private," report Scull

---

until 1983. To this list might be added Ida Gordon's 1953 edition of her late husband's *Pearl*, to which Tolkien made contributions over the years, receiving £50 for his efforts from Oxford University Press, though he did not wish to have his name on the title-page.

[7] *The Letters of J. R. R. Tolkien: Revised and Expanded Edition*, ed. Humphrey Carpenter with Christopher Tolkien (London: HarperCollins, 2023), 162.

[8] Mary C. Flannery, "The Case for the Defence: New Evidence Suggests that Geoffrey Chaucer May Be Innocent of Rape", *TLS* (October 21, 2022), 18.

and Hammond, whose *Chronology* can provide references for "no more than a fraction of the personal and professional correspondence".[9] During his Oxford removal from 20 Northmoor Road to 3 Manor Road in 1947, for example, many of Tolkien's papers were lost (SH 1:333–34). Currently missing, for example, are the Chaucer lectures that he delivered at the University of Leeds between 1920 and 1924.

He was also famous for simply giving away his papers to friends and students. George Sayer reported Tolkien handing over a pile of pages with the comment, "If you're interested, have a look at these." After he had a chance to look over these writings in a pub with C. S. Lewis, Sayer quickly returned them to their owner.[10] Not all donations were so fortunate. The great Chaucer critic V. A. Kolve had Tolkien assigned as his B.Litt. supervisor in 1957–58 (SH 1:540, 562) when the professor would sometimes say during meetings in his Merton College rooms, "I wrote something on that subject." Then he would reach into one of the pigeonholes in his desk, pull out a batch of pages, and hand them to his student. Kolve long lamented that these papers were lost somewhere between Oxford and his first faculty position at Stanford University.[11]

And sometimes we have tantalizing hints of what we don't know. In 1955 Derek J. Price published *The Equatorie of the Planetis*, arguing that this astronomical treatise in Cambridge's Peterhouse Library was Chaucer's signed holograph preserving his personal language. In the long list of experts whose assistance Price acknowledged was Professor J. R. R. Tolkien.[12] A variety of material attesting to his involvement, held at the Bodleian, includes twenty-five photostats of the manuscript, with highly glossy surfaces that defeated Tolkien's normal impulse for annotating. This file also contains Tolkien's newspaper clippings of Price's column-long announcement in *The Times* (28 February 1952) and two full-page elaborations of the discovery in the *Times Literary Supplement* (29 February and 7 March 1952).[13] What is currently missing is any letter from Professor Tolkien supporting the claims of the manuscript as a Chaucer holograph. Tolkien should have been very receptive to the notion; his 1934 article "Chaucer as a Philologist" and later lectures on

---

[9] Christina Scull and Wayne G. Hammond, *J. R. R. Tolkien Companion and Guide: Revised and Expanded Edition*. Vol. 1: *Chronology*; Vol. 2: *Reader's Guide, Part I: A–M*; Vol. 3: *Reader's Guide, Part II: N–Z*. (London: HarperCollins, 2017), 1:x–xi.

[10] Sayer, "Recollections of J. R. R. Tolkien", 25.

[11] Permission for this recollection granted in private email.

[12] Derek J. Price, ed., *The* Equatorie of the Planetis *edited from Peterhouse MS 75.I* (Cambridge: Cambridge University Press, 1955), p. xvi.

[13] MS Tolkien VC 277.

Chaucer steadily doubted that the Ellesmere *Canterbury Tales* represented the poet's authentic pronunciation and grammar.[14] Hammond and Scull's weblog records the sale of a three-page letter from Derek Price to Tolkien in 1952, but does not specify whether this was a letter asking for Tolkien's expert opinion on the *Equatorie* or thanking him for it.[15] Missing for the time being, despite searches of the three most likely archives, is any letter from Tolkien that earned him acknowledgment in Price's preface.

The following chapters provide both more and less than Tolkien actually wrote about the fourteenth-century author. For his published pieces "Chaucer as a Philologist: *The Reeve's Tale*" (1934) and "Middle English *Losenger*" (1953), we have added footnotes referencing the primary and secondary sources mentioned in the main texts but not fully explained by Tolkien in his own footnotes. For his unpublished Chaucer editions and lectures, we have perforce cut the great majority of the material because our volume's scope is limited and most of his remarks for beginners offer limited interest. Whereas Christopher Tolkien described making *selections* from his father's literary remains for the 1977 *Silmarillion* and admitted that sometimes "I had had to invent some passages", we are offering only *samplings* and have invented nothing, although sometimes we camouflage cuts in his Oxford notebooks and lectures to give the look of greater continuity. In our transcriptions from Tolkien's manuscripts, his abbreviations have been silently expanded, but the ellipses indicating deleted words are ours, not Tolkien's, and we have italicized what Tolkien underlined in his handwritten copies since he himself italicized these words when producing typewritten versions from the 1920s onward. We have normalized a few eccentric spellings, such as *litterature* for *literature*, and emended some punctuation where necessary for clarity. If Christopher described himself as a "literary archaeologist",[16] we have found ourselves as scholarly archaeologists sorting different layers of the past, especially with his successive lectures on the *Pardoner's Tale*. Tolkien's manuscripts were often hastily written, but rarely in these manuscripts have we been forced to make guesses (marked with a query and in square brackets). Since this is our selection of Tolkien's writings on Chaucer, we have included general illegibility as

---

[14] *TLC* 214–15. See also Andoni Cossio, "Addenda: One Middle English Manuscript and Four Editions of Medieval Works Known to J. R. R. Tolkien and What They Reveal", *ANQ: A Quarterly Journal of Short Articles, Notes and Reviews* (2021), 1–8.

[15] "From Tolkien's Library", wayneandchristina.wordpress.com, 5 May 2018.

[16] Vincent Ferré, "The Son behind the Father: Christopher Tolkien as a Writer", in *The Great Tales Never End: Essays in Memory of Christopher Tolkien*, ed. Richard Ovenden and Catherine McIlwaine (Oxford: Bodleian Library Publishing, 2022), 53–69 at pp. 55, 63–8. Following convention, we refer to Christopher Tolkien by first name to distinguish him from his father.

one criterion for omitting passages.[17] We applaud without imitating Michael Drout's heroic edition of Tolkien's unpublished lectures *"Beowulf" and the Critics* which ends: "It is slow laborious, compact and often taken ???? but full of feeling. ??? ??? what the ???? same time is large and ??????"[18]

Our book strives to approximate the current state of what can be known about Tolkien's engagements with Chaucer, either in published form or in the manuscript holdings of Oxford's Bodleian Library. But nonetheless we believe, as John Dryden said about the pilgrims of the *Canterbury Tales,* here is God's plenty.

---

[17] Stuart D. Lee, "The Manuscripts: Use, and Using", in *A Companion to J. R. R. Tolkien*, ed. Stuart D. Lee (Oxford: Wiley Blackwell, 2014), 56–76 at pp. 62–5, outlines the challenges of working with Tolkien's handwritten materials; see also *Ency* 402–3.

[18] J. R. R. Tolkien, *"Beowulf" and the Critics*, ed. Michael D. C. Drout (Tempe: Arizona Center for Medieval and Renaissance Studies, 2002), p. 78.

1
Chaucerian in Training, 1913–23

Classics was then Oxford's premier degree, but already the schoolboy Tolkien's discovery of Joseph Wright's *Primer of the Gothic Language* had sparked his enthusiasm instead for Germanic philology.[1] Once at Exeter College, Oxford, he attended Wright's lectures, supplemented by tutorials on Greek philology at the professor's home (*Essays* 238). Because he neglected Classical literature in favour of language, Tolkien's lacklustre performance on the second-year Honour Moderations exams jeopardized his plans for an academic career. One examiner pronounced his Latin Prose paper "largely illegible" and his Greek Verse paper written in a "filthy script" – harbingers of challenges to come for scholars struggling to read his hurried handwriting. Wright encouraged a switch to the English Honours School for the third term of the year. Over the next seven terms, then, Tolkien pursued the English syllabus, and in November 1913 we find him writing a tutorial essay on Chaucer's language (SH 1:44–53).

The Middle English works on his reading list included the mainstays *Troilus and Criseyde*, the General Prologue to the *Canterbury Tales*, the *Pardoner's Tale*, the *Clerk's Tale*, and the *Franklin's Tale*. The last of these was Chaucer's version of a Breton lay inspired perhaps by his reading of *Sir Orfeo* in the Auchinleck manuscript.[2] Tolkien probably attended G. K. A. Bell's course on the *Franklin's Tale* as well as the General Prologue, but his notes for these classes do not seem to survive. Though he did not later teach the *Franklin's Tale*, his final lectures on the *Pardoner's Tale* took time to mock the lengthy suicide monologue of its frantic wife Dorigen.

* * *

---

[1] SH 3:1444–45; *Ency* 253–4.
[2] Laura Hibbard Loomis, "Chaucer and the Breton Lays of the Auchinleck MS," *Studies in Philology* 38 (1941), 14-33; Tolkien's translation of *Sir Orfeo* followed the Auchinleck text. He later published his own Breton lay "The Lay of Aotrou and Itroun", *The Welsh Review* 4 (1945), 254–66; see SH 2:645–47.

"The Language of Chaucer" (1913)

His new tutor in 1913 was Kenneth Sisam, a New Zealand Rhodes Scholar only five years his senior, and it seems likely that all his Chaucer essays were written for him (*TLC* 52–60). Many years later Tolkien would recall this "piece of singular good fortune" because Sisam's teaching was "spiced with a pungency, humour and practical wisdom which were his own" (*Letters* 570). This does not mean Tolkien was an ideal pupil. In his earliest published letter, he confessed to his fiancée, Edith Bratt: "I went and saw Mr Sisam and told him I could not finish my essay till Wed" (*Letters* 3). The essays that do survive have the look of last-minute rush jobs tending towards what the Classics examiner had called "largely illegible". Our transcriptions, therefore, are only partial because many words and whole sentences cannot be read with confidence.

Tolkien's undergraduate notebook of essays on philology includes his paper "Scandinavian Influence on the English" (Bodleian MS Tolkien A 21/1, fols. 86–94), which shows an early interest in those Northern features characteristic of the dialect that he would later discuss at length in relation to the *Reeve's Tale*. His paper "Problem of Dialects" (fols. 98–120) shows another early interest that he would explore in so many of his later lectures and writings, notably his 1931 lecture "Chaucer's Use of Dialects", published three years later as "Chaucer as a Philologist: *The Reeve's Tale*".

Joseph Wright's *English Dialect Dictionary*, published in six volumes from 1898–1905, provided a powerful model for Tolkien's interests in native dialects. But his tutorial paper "The Language of Chaucer" (fols. 43–63) transmitted views on the poet's language derived mostly from Walter W. Skeat's "The Dialect of Chaucer" and "Kentish Forms" in his monumental 1894 *Works of Geoffrey Chaucer* (6:xxiii–xxv). This volume also included Skeat's landmark "Glossarial Index" which Tolkien would later mine for his Clarendon Chaucer. The Exeter College library register indicates that Tolkien did not actually check out this volume until Michaelmas Term 1919 (Cilli 53), and so in 1913 he probably studied it in the college library ahead of his fast-approaching appointment with Mr Sisam.

Skeat (6:xxiii) had decided that Chaucer's language "mainly represents the East-Midland, as spoken in London and by the students of Oxford and Cambridge", achieving its pre-eminence not because the dialect of the capital but rather "from its intermediate position" at the centre of the nation. But to Skeat, the Kentish features were a personal characteristic that Chaucer picked up while residing in Greenwich between 1385 and 1399. One of Tolkien's undergraduate notebooks contains twelve pages on Kentish "peculiarities".[3]

Only partly agreeing with Skeat, Tolkien would later emphasize Chaucer's language as the dialect of the capital but with steady assimilation of French-derived words under influence of the court. The South-East dialect of Kentish was not simply part of the poet's idiolect but had been a feature of London documents since the thirteenth century, he would argue. And he would later throw doubt on the notion that Chaucer's usages reflected the language of the universities; his 1934 study of *The Reeve's Tale* notes that the students John and Alain continued speaking their native Northern dialect at Cambridge.[4]

Only a few excerpts from his 1913 essay are reproduced below, interspersed with commentary.[5]

* * *

"The Language of Chaucer"

[43r] Phonology and Accidence (with more especial reference to the native element)
(1) Nov. 5th 1913
(2) Nov. 12th 1913

Before it is possible to make any sweeping assertions as to Chaucer's position in the history of English and his part in determining the dialect of Modern Literature and of modern educated speech, it is really necessary, though not often done, to examine first the actual facts of his language from a study of Chaucer texts without any preconceived notions if possible as to what is to be found there.

The facts however revealed by a careful and minute study of the precise forms used by any writer of large linguistic range are always very complicated and their cataloguing lengthy and difficult. At the very outset we see that in dealing with Chaucer, we are dealing with one author who did not speak or at

---

[3] Bodleian MS Tolkien A 21/3, fols. 50–55.
[4] J. R. R. Tolkien, "Chaucer as a Philologist: *The Reeve's Tale*", *Transactions of the Philological Society* (1934), 1–70 at 6, 53 (pp. 115 and 160 below).
[5] Bodleian MS Tolkien A 21/1, fols. 43–63. Fol. 42v, prior to the essay's start, contained a reminder to himself to consult Richard J. Lloyd, *Northern English: Phonetics, Grammar, Texts* (Leipzig: Teubner, 1899).

any rate did not use a pure dialect. Either from personal study and travelling or simply from the peculiar position of his own dialect he had a large linguistic range, and dialectic doublets of vocabulary, form and pronunciation (so far as rime shows it) abound in his English: rarer dialectic forms being apparently ready to his mind and often substituted for the forms most usual to him when rime or metre required.[6]

> Tolkien inserted a parenthetical comment (44v, fig. 1) on the Northern forms with an *a* where Chaucer usually had an *ō* and cites the same examples *na, swa, gas, fra* (with the addition of *til*) in almost the same order that Skeat (5:121) offered in his one-page commentary on dialect humour in the *Reeve's Tale*. This scholarly aside looks forward two decades to his "Chaucer as a Philologist" where he would return to these same instances, with one whole paragraph devoted to *til* alone (see p. 143 below).
>
> On the reverse side of his title page, he jotted "Examples of dialectal variants...*mery, merie, mury*", which he had found in Skeat's remarks on dialect (6:xxiv). More than a decade later when compiling the glossary for his Clarendon Chaucer, he returned to this point with the entry "**mury**, *Western form of* Mery". Already as an undergraduate, then, he was developing an interest in the dialect peculiar to the West Midlands, the homeland of his mother's Suffield ancestors, and this would lead to his career-long study of *Ancrene Wisse* and related texts of the Katherine Group, arguing for a literary language descended directly from Old English and used with great consistency by scribes in Herefordshire during the early thirteenth century.[7] Farther back in West Midland history lay the Old English kingdom of Mercia which provided the homeland and the language for the Riders of the Mark.[8]

[44v] Deliberate cases of characterisation by dialect (as for example in the case of the Northern students with their long ā in nā, gās, swā, til and frā) of course are not in point though they do show that Chaucer had acquaintance with other dialects: as few persons of any reading or observation could help having, if they lived as Chaucer did in the capital in which thronged speakers

---

[6] Tolkien actually wrote 'when rime is metre required', an evident slip.

[7] See J. R. R. Tolkien, "*Ancrene Wisse* and *Hali Meiðhad*," *Essays and Studies* 14 (1929), 104–26; *Ency* 15–17 and 319–20; and SH 2:58–60.

[8] Tom Shippey, *The Road to Middle-earth: Revised and Expanded Edition* (Boston and New York: Houghton Mifflin, 2003), 123.

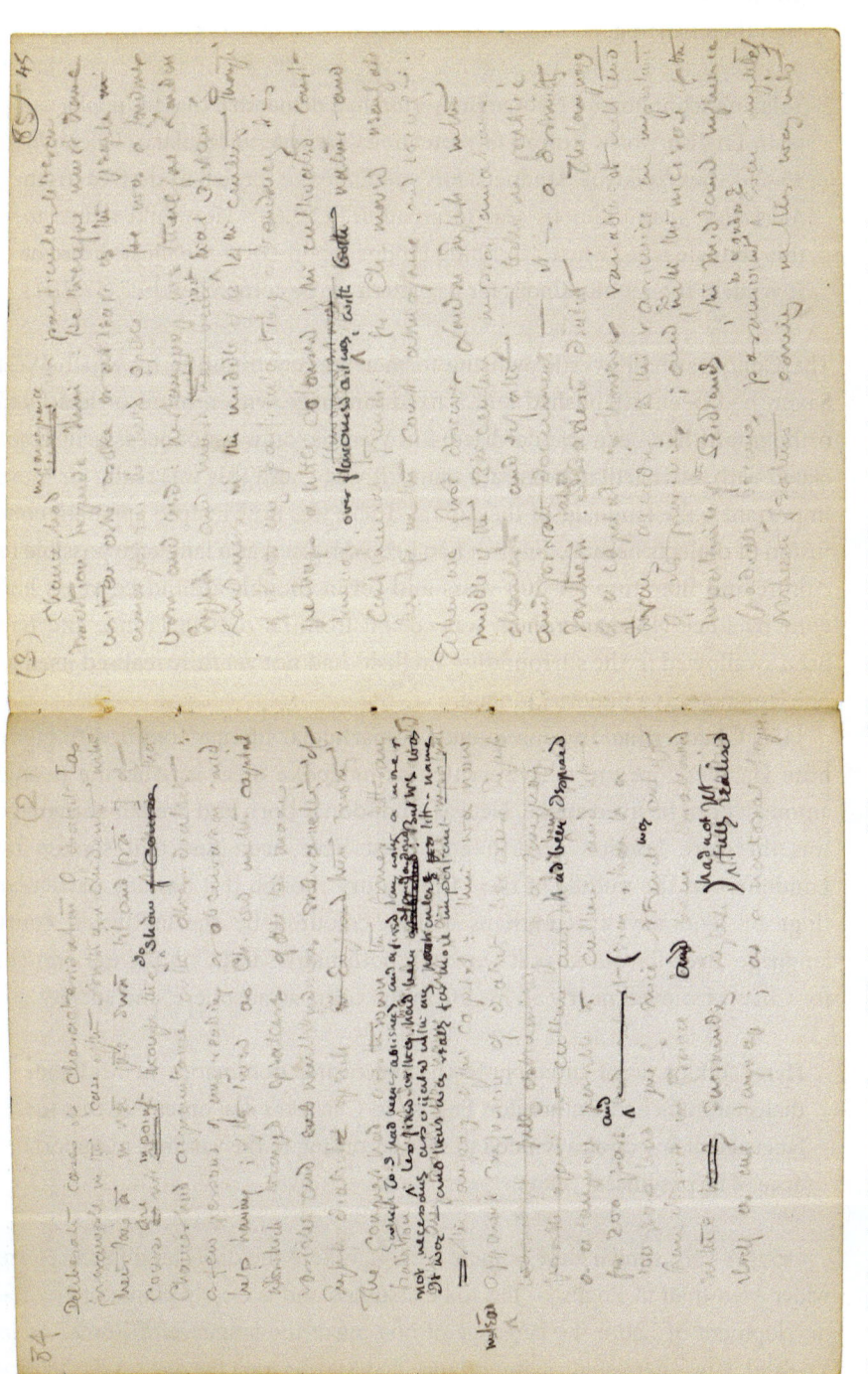

Fig. 1 Tolkien's 1913 tutorial essay "The Language of Chaucer" (Bodleian MS Tolkien A 21/1, fols. 44v and 45r).

of all the many varieties and multitudinous subvarieties of English dialectic speech then existing.

> Tolkien's schoolmaster George Brewerton had demanded that his pupils use plain English words instead of pretentious Latinate vocabulary (*Biography* 35–36), but Tolkien's fondness for *multitudinous* probably derived from *Macbeth*'s "multitudinous seas incarnadine" (2.2.60). He would return to this Latinate word when describing Frodo's rapture over the music heard at Rivendell "too multitudinous for its patterns to be comprehended" (*FR* II/1)

The Conquest had overthrown the former literary tradition by which West Saxon had been established and a fixed language with a more or less fixed orthography had been standardised. But West Saxon was not necessarily associated with any particular literary name. It was – and this was really far more important – the language of the capital. There was now instead apparent confusion of dialects because English had been despised as a language possible to culture and literature for 200 years and (even though a hundred years had gone by since Norman French was cut off from its root in France and had been swallowed in the surrounding English) had not yet fully realised itself as one language; as a national tongue.

[45r] Chaucer had in consequence no particular literary tradition to guide him. He therefore must have written as he spoke or at least as the people among whom he lived spoke. He was a Londoner born and bred: his language was therefore London English and must have been just that spoken by Londoners in the middle of the 14th century though if it has any particular tinge or tendency it is perhaps a little coloured by the cultivated court language, over-flavoured as it was with both native and Continental French: for Chaucer moved nearly all his life in the court atmosphere, and society.

> Here Tolkien went on to note the increasing dominance of Midlands dialectal influences on London English in Chaucer's era, observing that the language of any capital "tended to vary according to the variance in importance of its provinces".

[45v] A very similar development – though here the dialectal differences are wider even than in English – has to be assumed and is clearly pointed to by the development of Latin; the language of one town: the language of Rome. As in England, it was here political importance first that decided the dialect: the literary importance was the inevitable inheritance of the dialect's political influence....

[46v] One of the chief sources of statements concerning vowels is the rhymes. Ten Brink for instance builds a great erection upon them; and of course their general importance cannot be denied, for Chaucer was a good poet, not a cheap jingler, and his rimes are far more careful and usually more accurate than his predecessors'.

As an example of cheap jingling, Tolkien wrote *Havelok* in the margin. Then he drafted an eleven-page discussion of Chaucer's vowels (beginning on fol. 46v) lifted mostly from Skeat's "Pronunciation" (6:xxv–xlvii) and Bernhard Ten Brink's "Die Vocale".[9] With his exhaustive list devoted to open and close vowels, these pages offer a foretaste of two of Tolkien's future failings. Did he realistically imagine that Sisam would listen to all these pages read aloud? In future years he seldom resisted the temptation to over-prepare his lectures with much more information than would fit into a single Oxford term. And the philological details were usually far more challenging than a listening audience could absorb. Even towards the end of his career, this tendency appears in the mind-numbing range of references in his 1951 conference paper "Middle English *Losenger*" – which were especially excessive given that it was delivered to a predominantly French-speaking audience.

"Chaucer and his Contemporaries" (1914)

Tolkien wrote his essays on Chaucer's language a year before he attended Professor Walter Raleigh's lectures on "Chaucer and his Contemporaries" as recorded in a 1914–15 notebook that he called "General Miscellany". Besides Chaucer, this notebook contained lectures on Dr Johnson, particularly the eighteenth-century critic's involvement in the Ossian controversy. Tolkien's jottings included "influence of Ossian on later poetry (Byron)" and "*Fingal* an ancient epic."[10] *Fingal* was published in 1762 as an ancient epic by the legendary Ossian, but it was actually confected by the Scottish poet James Macpherson from Gaelic materials. As such, *Fingal* may have joined with the *Kalevala*, Elias Lönnrot's 1849 assemblage of Finnish legends, as inspirations for Tolkien's own compilation in his *Silmarillion*. "But the beginning of the

---

[9] One of his undated student notebooks (MS Tolkien A 21/9) starts off with reference to "Ten Brink. LM Chaucer, p. 40." That is, he had consulted M. Bentinck Smith, *The Language and Metre of Chaucer* (London: Macmillan, 1901), "Phonology: The Vowels," 1–74, which was a translation of Bernhard Ten Brink, "Die Vocale" in *Chaucer's Sprache und Verskunst* (Leipzig, 1884), 7–63.

[10] Bodleian MS Tolkien A 21/4, fols. 1–11 (quotations 10r, 11r).

legendarium," he would write to W. H. Auden, "was in an attempt to reorganize some of the *Kalevala*" (*Letters* 313). Carpenter reminds us that the year 1914 was also when he read the Old English poem *Crist* and was inspired to write his first poem about Eärendil. "It was in fact the beginning of Tolkien's own mythology" (*Biography* 79).

Raleigh had taught at Glasgow, where one of his pupils was George S. Gordon, Tolkien's future co-editor for their Clarendon Chaucer. Knighted in 1911, Raleigh became Oxford's first Merton Professor of English Literature in 1914. One of his legacies was a momentous one for Tolkien because he championed dividing the English syllabus into Language and Literature, and this would allow Tolkien to specialize on the Language side (SH 3:1050). Raleigh was not himself a medievalist but published books on *The English Novel* (1894) and *Milton* (1900); even his volume *Some Authors: A Collection of Literary Essays* (1923) failed to include Chaucer. But this was still an era when any member of the English Faculty was thought capable of lecturing on any English author. At Tolkien's interview for the Readership at Leeds in 1920, George Gordon turned the conversation to his old teacher, and years later Tolkien recalled: "I did not in fact think much of Raleigh – he was not, of course, a good lecturer; but some kind spirit prompted me to say that he was *Olympian*" (*Letters* 78). Tolkien got the job.

Tolkien's Chaucer notes are dated 15 October to 12 November 1914, and we can forgive the sloppiness of his rapid handwriting when considering how much information he managed to get down on paper – only snippets of which are quoted below.[11] Furthermore, the historical moment is worth recalling. Britain had declared war on Germany on 4 August 1914, and many of Tolkien's friends had already enlisted. There was no conscription yet, and Tolkien took advantage of a scheme which allowed him to join the Officers Training Corps at Oxford with no active duty until he had taken his degree (SH 1:62). With warfare hanging over his head and the future looking uncertain, it is interesting to consider the aspects of Chaucer's life and career which Tolkien wrote down as if anticipating, in some ways, his own ambitions and anxieties.[12] The poets behind *Beowulf* and the fourteenth-century *Gawain and the Green Knight* were entirely anonymous. But Geoffrey Chaucer's biography, gathered in the *Life Records* published by the Chaucer Society between 1875 and 1900, provided a medieval mirror in which a later writer such as

---

[11] Bodleian MS Tolkien A 21/4, fols. 12r–20v.
[12] See "Chaucer and Tolkien: Affinities," *TLC*, 226–41, for fuller comparisons.

Tolkien might search out images for recognition and imitation. He also found a literary father-figure who, later in the 1950s, would provoke from him an Oedipal assault.

* * *

"Chaucer and Contemporaries"

Though Tolkien famously declared in his 1965 Foreword to *The Lord of the Rings*, "I cordially dislike allegory," the next sentence also deserves attention: "I much prefer history, true or feigned." Sir Francis Bacon's *The Advancement of Learning* (1605) had used the term *feigned history* to describe a well-made but imaginative narrative: "The use of this feigned history is to give some shadow of satisfaction to the mind of man in those points wherein the nature of things denies it." Professor Raleigh implicitly critiqued *feigned history* by assessing prior Chaucer biographies which had been based upon dubious facts and notions of the author drawn naively from his writings, even from writings thought wrongly to be his, such as Thomas Usk's *The Testament of Love*. "Birth date *unknown*," Tolkien wrote down in his notebook, then rejected early speculation of 1328: "*Much too early*" (12r).[13] He then added: "If he was born in 1340 then he fell early into the habit of calling himself old." The challenge was to "distinguish between Chaucer Legend dating to 16th century and 'Chaucer' built up from dry evidence". Tolkien had done his homework and consulted Thomas R. Lounsbury's three-volume *Studies in Chaucer: His Life and Writings* (1891) which preserved many of the old legends including the poet's growing hostility to the Church's corrupt practices and his free-thinking heterodoxy, whereas Skeat's "Life of Chaucer" (1:ix–lxi) simply assembled the drier evidence unearthed by the Chaucer Society. Tolkien's note, "Prof. Lounsbury: worthless" (20v) maybe records Raleigh's judgment, or maybe reflects the student's, because Tolkien became notorious for harsh verdicts of this sort. Raleigh's lecture of 20 October drew upon more recent research by James Hulbert: "Chaucer's a perfectly ordinary career not one of industry or exceptional confidence.... Chaucer had varied

---

[13] Speght's "Life of Geffrey Chaucer" says Chaucer died in 1400 at age 72, hence born in 1328. Speght was reprinted in Eleanor Prescott Hammond, *Chaucer: A Bibliographical Manual* (London: Macmillan, 1908), 19–35 at p. 30. See also Derek Pearsall, "Thomas Speght (ca. 1550–?)", in *Editing Chaucer: The Great Tradition*, ed. Paul G. Ruggiers (Norman OK: Pilgrim Books, 1984), 71–92.

life: soldier, diplomatic servant, member of parliament, justice of peace, expert in wines and skins, traveller in foreign countries" (14r).[14]

Raleigh dwelled on Chaucer's father as a wine merchant. "Father's house within vintry of St Martin's parish...Chaucer would see speakers of many tongues. Hence early knowledge of French" (12v). The Shipman in the General Prologue transported wines (Tolkien's notes continue) and the *Pardoner's Tale* proclaimed that "drink has dominacion". This last insight about drunkenness would return years later in Tolkien's own lectures on the *Pardoner's Tale*. Tolkien's next undergraduate note shows his persistent concern for when a literary work had no source-text: "Quite possible that many of Chaucer's stories (for which no original has been discovered) came from tale-tellers within taverns". One wonders if Chaucer's drinking and telling stories with friends provided sanction, however subliminal, for Tolkien's later reading his stories to Inkling friends in Oxford pubs such as the Eagle and Child. Another undergraduate note assumes the vintner's son was "expert in wines" (14r). Tolkien as a student was no doubt improving his own expertise, attending the Freshman's Wine at Exeter College in 1912 and 1913.[15] Years later in 1947 he was appointed a member of Merton College's Wine Committee on which he served until his retirement.

"He tells us he is a great reader," Tolkien wrote when Raleigh was discussing the Prologue to the *Legend of Good Women*. "He had 60 books, an enormous collection for a private person then. Twenty was a large library to the Clerk of Oxenford" (13r). Books were still relatively expensive in 1914 when Tolkien used his £5 Skeat Prize, an Exeter College award for English, to invest in a *Welsh Grammar* as well as three books by William Morris, including his translation of the *Völsunga Saga* (SH 1:58). Grateful to Kenneth Sisam for suggesting the second-hand book catalogues which laid the foundations of his professional library (*Letters* 570), Tolkien would become an aggressive book-collector, often photographed in front of his own crowded bookshelves (*Ency* 361–62).

There follows an ominous note: "Chaucer in early years took part in wars that raged in France (1359). Battles then resembled chivalrous but deadly jousts" (13v). Even a well-managed tournament such as Theseus oversees in the *Knight's Tale* could be lethal for a warrior like Arcite, who dies from an accident suffered in the jousting. Later critics noticed how Chaucer neglected

---

[14] See James R. Hulbert, *Chaucer's Official Life* (Wisconsin: Collegiate Press, 1912).
[15] John Garth, *Tolkien at Exeter College: How an Oxford Undergraduate Created Middle-earth* (Oxford: Exeter College, 2014), 9, and SH 1:333.

the glories of battle without, however, connecting these evasions with his own traumatic experiences as a French prisoner of war in 1359.[16] The young Tolkien took note of these omissions: "He lived in stirring times – Crécy and Sluys in his boyhood, Poitiers in manhood. He mentions or alludes to none of them" (14r). A year later in 1914, the patriotic illusion that England's war with Germany would retain any chivalry would quickly vanish in the trenches of France and Belgium.

Tolkien showed a concern for the kind of family tree that would figure in his own *LotR* Appendix C (*Ency* 188-89), and here he jotted them down for his author: "1366 Chaucer married Philippa (damosel of the Queen's). Philippa Roet daughter of Sir Paon Roet. Sister Kathrine Swynford wed Sir Hugh Swynford, third wife of John of Gaunt. Thomas Chaucer rich…(many properties) lived after death of Geoffrey Chaucer.[17] Speaker of House of Commons. m. Matilda (Burghersh). Owner of Woodstock (1334 died)…If Thomas Chaucer was son, then we nearly had a lineal descendant of Geoffrey Chaucer on the throne, John, Earl of Lincoln (1486 died?)" (13v). Always the monarchist, Tolkien was intrigued that Chaucer's great-great-grandson might have become King of England (much as Aragorn, heir of Elendil after many more generations, would become King of Gondor).

Raleigh recommended that his audience read Trevelyan's *Age of Wycliffe* with its criticism of Roman Catholicism.[18] Tolkien's note objected: "Wyclif no Wyclifite nor Chaucer a Wyclifite. This a mere invention of later Protestantism in looking back: Wyclif a great *medieval Catholic doctor*" (14v). He would remain adamant in this view of an orthodox poet. When an American student came to Oxford in the early 1950s with the intention of writing a thesis on Chaucer and Lollardy, she was assigned Tolkien as her supervisor and he announced abruptly at their first meeting, "Chaucer and the Lollards. Nothing to that!" They did not have a second meeting (*TLC* 17).

A survey of Chaucer's works provided the young Tolkien with warnings. "It is understating it to say that only several of Chaucer's works are lost," he noted (14v) – a thought that would have encouraged his own packrat instincts for keeping everything, including these undergraduate notes on Chaucer. It was a trait remarkable enough for his children John and Priscilla to single out: "As a

---

[16] For a corrective, see John M. Bowers, "Chaucer after Retters: The Wartime Origins of English Literature," in *Inscribing the Hundred Years' War in French and English Cultures*, ed. Denise Baker (Albany: State University of New York Press, 2000), 91–125.

[17] An illegible word stands between rich and *(many properties)*.

[18] George Macaulay Trevelyan, *England in the Age of Wycliffe*, 2nd ed. (London: Longmans, Green, 1899).

family we hoard relics from the past."[19] The challenge for Christopher and other editors (including ourselves) has been to sort through the different versions of his writings – and indeed Tolkien had found an early role-model, noting in these undergraduate writings, "Chaucer continually revised his work." And sometimes Chaucer's reworking took the form of adapting previous pieces for new contexts ("he used up all works in new"), sometimes without making necessary changes: "Signal instance of this: Invocation to 2nd Nonne's Tale, in which, when he embodied it in the Canterbury Tales as told of a Nun, he left in the invocation applying to he himself".[20] Tolkien heeded the warning and later made certain that when he adapted a prior piece, it perfectly fitted its new settings – as with his early 1920s poem *Light as Leaf on Lindentree* recast for Strider's "Song of Beren and Lúthien" on Weathertop (*FR* I/11).

When Raleigh speculated about Chaucer's travels ("Did he visit north of England?"), he summoned as evidence "the marshy Holderness in the Summoner's Tale" and "Reeve's Tale: northern students" (15r). Tolkien's 1913 tutorial essay had already noted the Northern dialect of these students, but here he had the biographical hints later discussed fully in "Chaucer as a Philologist".

"Chaucer's 'chosen attitude' to Love and Love stories: continual (and unconnected) allusions to unrequited love." Hence the poet specialized in unhappy love stories: "His jibes against the married state (many) are part of the stock in trade of the medieval satirist. They must be set against his praises of that state (not so many)". When Tolkien noted Chaucer's rare commendations of marriage, he was already engaged to Edith Bratt and probably entertained happier prospects for himself, not necessarily fulfilled in later life.

Under the heading *Politics*, Tolkien noted: "Chaucer royalist. King one who both reigns and governs" (15v). His own fiction would become steadily royalist, too, for example in *The Hobbit* where King Bard displaces the Master of a mercantile republic like Venice and in *The Lord of the Rings* where King Elessar ascends the throne after the twenty-six generations of Stewards who had ruled Gondor. Tolkien continued about the poet: "Chaucer no political theorist at all; all his observation was expended on individuals; he did not generalize his general truths; he was content to borrow from *olde bookes*" (16r).

---

[19] John and Priscilla Tolkien, *The Tolkien Family Album* (Boston: Houghton Mifflin, 1992), 7.
[20] "And though that I, unworthy *sone* of Eve" (*CT* VIII, 62); see *Complete Works of Geoffrey Chaucer*, ed. Walter W. Skeat. 6 vols. (Oxford: Clarendon Press, 1894), 4:511.

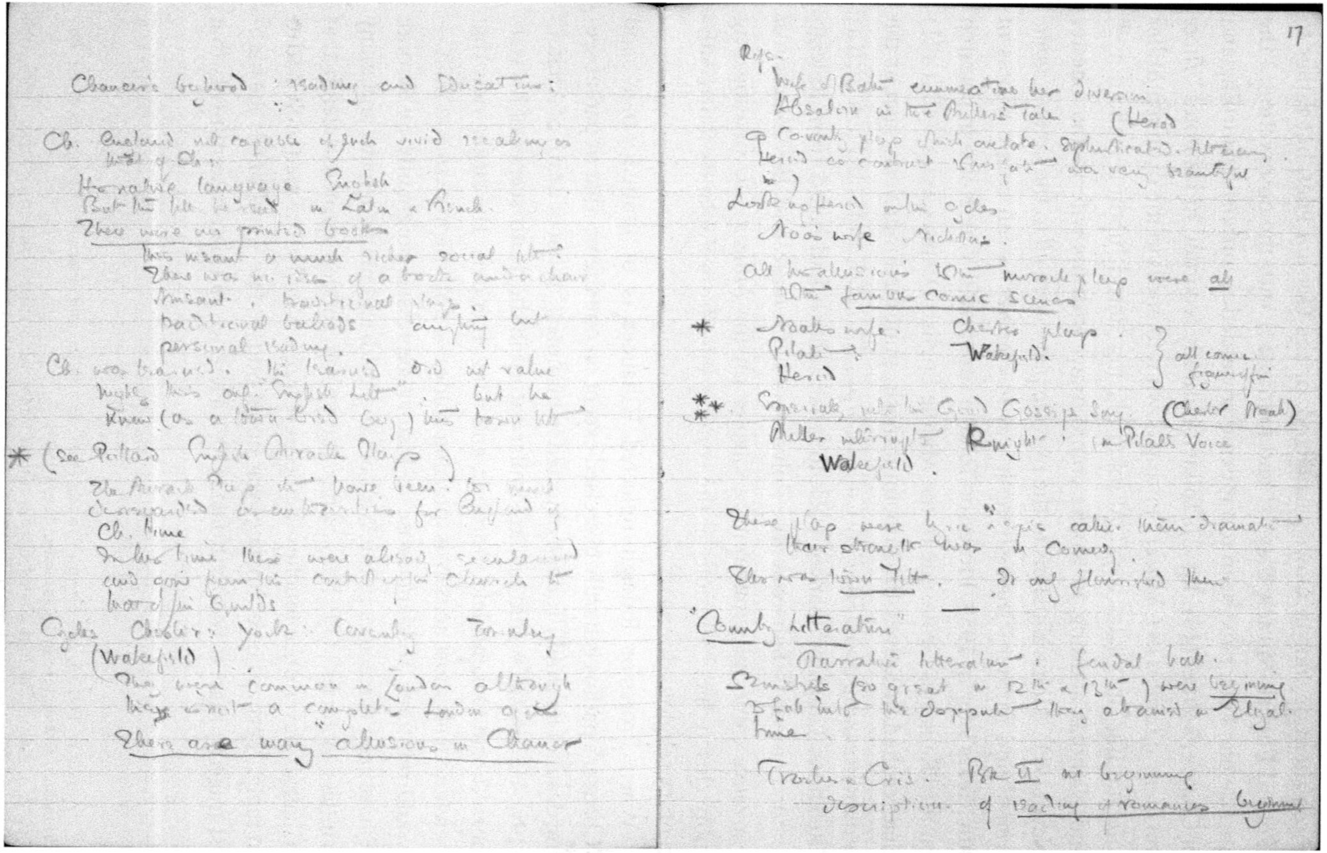

Fig. 2 Lecture notes from Professor Raleigh's "Chaucer and his Contemporaries" (Bodleian MS Tolkien A 21/4, fols. 16v–17r).

To judge by Tolkien's notes, Professor Raleigh neglected Chaucer's "Contemporaries" advertised in the title of his lectures until he drew his audience's attention, not to Gower, Langland, or the *Gawain* Poet, but rather to "Pollard English Miracle Plays"[21] and followed it with the observation: "The miracle plays etc. have been too much disregarded as authorities for England of Chaucer's time" (16v, fig. 2). Tolkien dutifully recorded in his notes "*There are many allusions in Chaucer*", jotting down references to the drunken Miller interrupting "in Pilates voys", Absolon playing Herod "upon a scaffold hye", and Nicholas alluding to Noah's comic brawl with his wife in the Chester plays (17r). "All his allusions to the miracle plays were *all* to the *famous comic scenes*" and further "Their strength was in comedy" – "all comic figures of fun". Years later in 1958, Professor Tolkien supervised V. A. Kolve in research on the "Religious Grotesque in the Middle English Drama Cycles" (Cilli 421) that resulted in Kolve's 1962 doctoral thesis, published four years later as the groundbreaking book *The Play Called Corpus Christi*. Kolve's chapters such as "Religious Laughter" harked back to what Tolkien had heard from Raleigh about comedy.[22] Subsequently Kolve's book *Chaucer and the Imagery of Narrative* came full circle with a chapter on the *Miller's Tale* investigating more closely these allusions to the comic scenes from England's fourteenth-century religious dramas.[23]

When Professor Raleigh reflected "Chaucer is of limited range" and "Chaucer's pathos is hardly exercised except on one theme, that of parent seeing death of its child", Tolkien objected in his notes: "What of death of Arcite?" (19v). He himself would invoke similar pathos in the death-scenes of his warriors Thorin Oakenshield, Boromir, and King Théoden. The larger view that "what he feels most acutely is 'nothing abides'— both happiness and pain"— would reinforce Tolkien's sense of history expressed poignantly by Elrond: "I have seen three ages in the West of the world, and many defeats, and many fruitless victories" (*FR* II/2). After the young Tolkien quoted Raleigh that "Chaucer never once touches the deepest tragic note," he immediately added in reply: "Perhaps true: Chaucer was not at odds at fate – and this is the highest tragedy: man at war with fate" (20r). Here we can detect sentiments that

---

[21] Alfred W. Pollard, ed., *English Miracle Plays, Moralities, and Interludes: Specimens of the Pre-Elizabethan Drama* (Oxford: Clarendon Press, 1909).

[22] V. A. Kolve, *The Play Called Corpus Christi* (Stanford: Stanford University Press, 1966), 146, 262–3, and 205 with references in the *Miller's Tale* to these comic plays.

[23] V. A. Kolve, *Chaucer and the Imagery of Narrative: The First Five Canterbury Tales* (Stanford: Stanford University Press, 1984), 198–216.

will emerge two decades later in his own celebrated lecture "*Beowulf*: The Monsters and the Critics" (*Essays* 20–21).

Troilus and Criseyde

Oxford's *Regulations of the Board of Studies* specified *Troilus and Criseyde* as one of the texts set for examination (SH 1:46–47), and Exeter College's Library Register indicates that Tolkien checked out *Troilus* in volume II of Skeat's *Works of Geoffrey Chaucer* from Michaelmas 1914 until the end of Hilary Term 1915.[24] Already his 1914 note-taking on Raleigh's "Chaucer and his Contemporaries"[25] had taken particular interest in *Troilus* under the heading Courtly Literature (17r).[26] The view that "the realistic background is of course solidly English" leads naturally to the conclusion: "Troilus & Criseyde more a novel than a romance". English literary historians were forever in quest for the origins of the novel, and Raleigh had already published his volume *The English Novel* with early pages on Chaucer's contribution to this history.[27] But the comment "T & C a repository or handbook of poetry" (19r) also looked forward to the debt that Tudor poets owed to this Chaucerian work: "T & C was still in the 16th century, as 15th, Chaucer's most popular".[28] The Trojan origin of the British people that had been traced in many other places, for example the opening stanza of *Sir Gawain*, meant that these Trojan characters represented the audience's "own ancestry" (18r). This sense of kinship between modern readers and very ancient peoples, speaking the same language and sharing cultural values, would also become key to the success of *The Lord of the Rings*.

In addition to lecture notes, Tolkien's private note-taking on *Troilus* survives.[29] There we see him focusing almost exclusively on words, already heading toward the annotating and glossary-making that would become his specialities. At the top of the first page, he jotted a brief reminder (perhaps

---

[24] Cilli 52; see Garth, *Tolkien at Exeter College*, 22, for a photograph of this page from the library's register.

[25] Bodleian MS Tolkien A 21/4, fols. 12r–20v.

[26] Here Tolkien actually wrote "Country Litterature" (using his customary spelling of *literature*). But what this could mean with reference to *Troilus and Criseyde* is unclear. Perhaps "country" as a slip for *courtly* arose from the fact that he had just noted Mystery plays as examples of "town" literature.

[27] Walter Raleigh, *The English Novel: A Short Sketch of its History from the Earliest Times to the Appearance of* Waverley (London: John Murray, 1894), 3–10.

[28] C. S. Lewis, *English Literature in the Sixteenth Century Excluding Drama* (Oxford: Clarendon Press, 1954), 343, would exclaim about Sir Philip Sidney: "Chaucer, unexpectedly but delightfully, is praised not for the *Tales* but for *Troilus*."

[29] Bodleian MS Tolkien A 21/7, fols. 1–7.

from his tutor Kenneth Sisam) to consult Ten Brink's *Language and Metre of Chaucer* as indication that his efforts remained almost exclusively on language.[30] Next he listed the five principal manuscripts discussed by Skeat (2:lxvii–lxxvi): "Oxford Chaucer follows mainly Campsall and Corpus. (These are much alike)." Even as an undergraduate, then, he was becoming aware of the range of fifteenth-century scribal copies that stood behind the printed texts, in contrast to his future specialities *Beowulf* and *Sir Gawain*, which survived in single copies.

He then proceeded to "Notes on Forms" as well as proper names, starting in the first stanza with *Thesiphone* "(Tīsiphŏnē) one of Furies" and remarking that *Priamus* was genitive. He wrote that *sorwful* (line 10) was "disyllabic scansion" and glossed *unlyklinesse* (16) as "unpleasing appearance, character etc.". Some jottings were highlighted and starred in red, probably because he suspected the information would assist with his exams. For the word *temple* he commented: "Chaucer's description of this is drawn (as all his background in T. & C. is) from medieval contemporary London and not from antiquarian ideas of Greece or Troy" (2r). He may have recalled a remark from Raleigh's lecture: "Troilus' description of the Temple was description of St Paul's Cathedral in old London, which was then a public resort and everyone promenaded the aisles daily."[31]

He copied information from Skeat about *Lollius* (2:464): "apparently a mistake owing to Chaucer perhaps seeing quoted out of context 'Troiani belli scriptorem maxime Lolli', Horace *Epistles*" (fol. 2r). He had already noted references to "Dares" and "Dyte" as "the fictitious authors of the spurious Latin chronicles invented in medieval times to connect Troy with the Celtic and Teutonic peoples" – adding that the story was better handled by the "good poet" Benoît de Sainte-Maure as well as the "dull" Guido delle Colonne (fol. 1v). Thus, Chaucer afforded him with precedents for made-up historical sources to lend authority and credibility to his storytelling, much as Tolkien's made-up Red Book of Westmarch would be cited as the historical authority for the War of the Ring in his "Note on the Shire Records" (*FR* Prologue).

With only these few annotations highlighted in red, Tolkien must have realized that his assiduous note-taking on *Troilus* would not much serve him for his exams. This was another early example of overdoing projects with no

---

[30] *The Language and Metre of Chaucer Set Forth by Bernard Ten Brink*, 2nd ed. rev. Friedrich Kluge, trans. M. Bentinck Smith (London: Macmillan, 1901).

[31] Bodleian MS Tolkien A 21/4 fol. 18v. Tolkien had reminded himself on the later notebook's opening page (A 21/7, fol. 1): "See references in own notes of Sir W. Raleigh's lectures on Chaucer. Oxford Michaelmas 1914".

practical application. That the note-taking did not extend beyond single words at the beginning of Book II also looked forward to his tendency to start projects with tremendous energy, only to run out of momentum and leave the jobs unfinished.

Tolkien's study notes on *Troilus* from Hilary 1915 have further interest as representing the template for future efforts, since this leapfrogging from one word to the next would form the basis for his philological practices in the future. Looking back in 1959, his "Valedictory Address" admitted this impulse "to wring the juice out of a single sentence, or explore the implications of one word" (*Essays* 224). This had become his usual approach when lecturing to undergraduates, too, as the distinguished medievalist Derek Brewer recalled, "confining himself entirely to textual cruces (often forgetting to tell us which line he was discussing)".[32] This also became the procedure in his annotations for *Selections from Chaucer's Poetry and Prose* which, cavalierly unconstrained by OUP's page limits, would doom this student edition.

The 1915 student notebook contained another harbinger of things to come. When Tolkien's linguistic notes on Book II of *Troilus* petered out after only four entries (fig. 3), he continued at the top of the page's next column with the large title *St Juliana*. Excerpts from *The Life of St Juliana* were on the required syllabus (SH 1:46), and he proceeded to remark upon some thirty words starting with *munne* until this exercise, too, trailed off after two more pages.[33] He had taken this early interest in a work showing continuity from Old English and written in his own ancestral dialect of West Midlands, although as an undergraduate facing exams and then deployment to the battlefield, he could hardly have predicted how this first encounter with the Katherine Group in MS Bodley 34 would dominate so much of his later career.[34] During his first appointment at Leeds, he published a *TLS* review of the related text *Hali Meidenhad*.[35] Half of his 1925 article "Some Contributions to Middle-English Lexicography" contained examples from *Juliana* including an entry on *munnen*, the first word which he had singled out in his 1915 notebook. Now, ten years later, his word-by-word undergraduate approach extended

---

[32] Derek Brewer, "Introduction", *A Companion to the Gawain-Poet*, ed. Derek Brewer and Jonathan Gibson (Cambridge: D. S. Brewer, 1997), 2. See "Cruces in medieval literature", *Ency* 111.

[33] He probably studied *Ðe Liflade of St. Juliana*, ed. Oswald Cockayne, EETS o.s. 51 (1872).

[34] SH 2:598–99, *Ency* 315–16. His student S. R. T. O. d'Ardenne eventually published her edition *Ðe Liflade ant te Passiun of Seinte Iuliene*, EETS o.s. 248 (1961), respectfully dedicated to Professor J. R. R. Tolkien. Another former student Norman Davis remarked that this edition "presents more of Tolkien's views on early Middle English than anything he himself published" (SH 2:291).

[35] His review of *Hali Meidenhad: An Alliterative Prose Homily of the Thirteenth Century*, ed. F. J. Furnivall, EETS o.s. 18 (1922), appeared in the *Times Literary Supplement* (April 26, 1923).

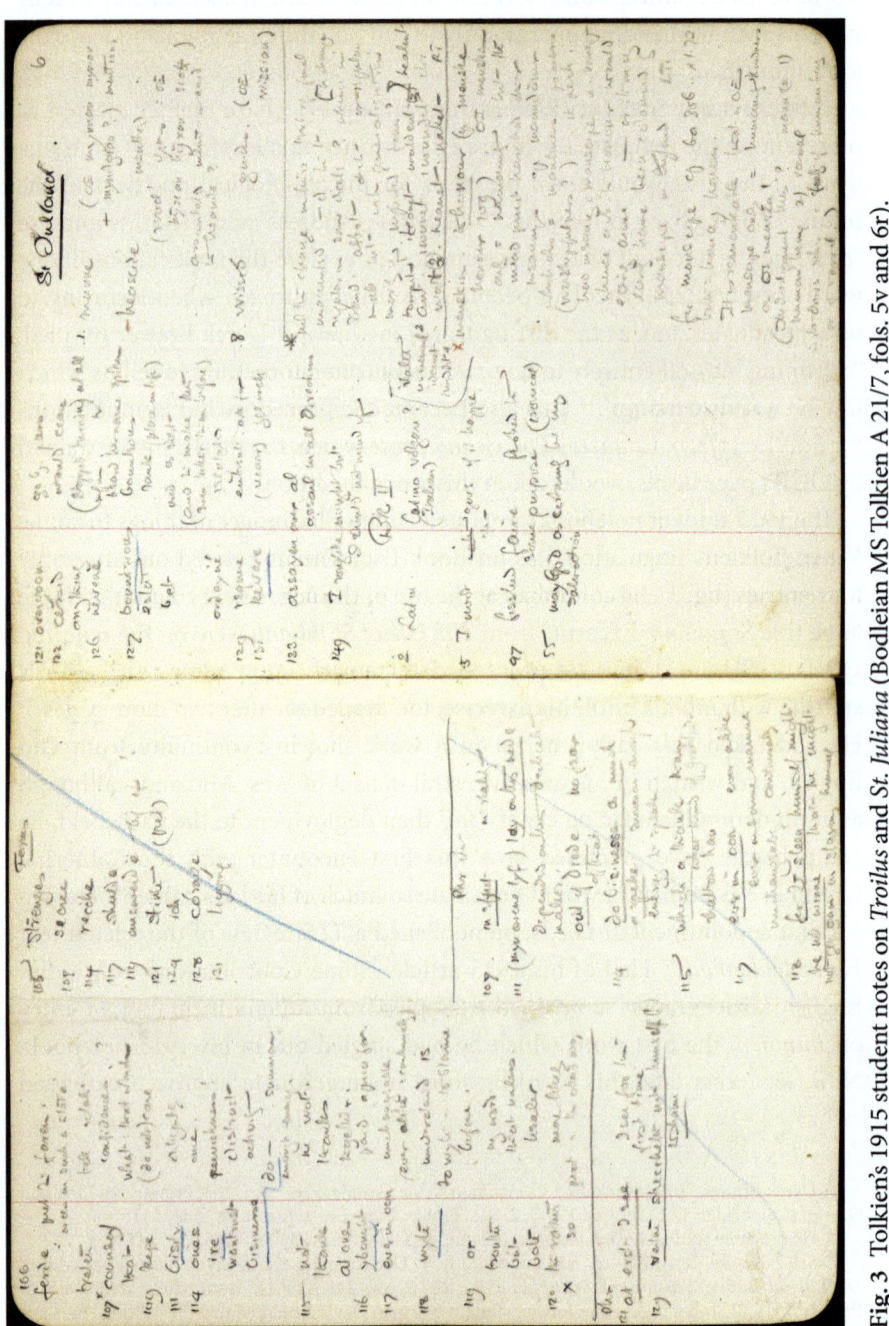

Fig. 3 Tolkien's 1915 student notes on *Troilus* and *St. Juliana* (Bodleian MS Tolkien A 21/7, fols. 5v and 6r).

into this published article, where the first paragraph alerted readers who might be disappointed with what they would find: "scraps of lexicographical and etymological information".[36]

Tolkien's admiration for *Troilus* would surface throughout his career. When drafting commentaries for his Clarendon Chaucer, for example, he devoted the headnote to *The Compleynte unto Pité* mostly to the poem's rhyme-royal prosody, along with an apology for not including any *Troilus* excerpts in their *Selections*:

> The poem is written in the seven-line stanza that Chaucer loved and perhaps invented, and at any rate used so well that it may be called his own. It is known as Rhyme Royal, because it was used in imitation of Chaucer by King James I of Scotland in his *Kingis Quair*. Rhyme Trojan would be a better name, for far the most remarkable example of its use is Chaucer's *Troilus and Criseyde*, at once his greatest achievement and his greatest exhibition of technical metrical skill – a poem whose length and excellence forbade its being laid under piecemeal contribution to the present selection. In *The Compleinte to Pité* this stanza makes its first appearance in Chaucer and in English.
> (Bodleian MS Tolkien A 39/2/1, fol. 9r)

And when commenting on the lovers in the temple of Venus in *The Parlement of Foules*, he remarked on the appearance of Troilus's name among them (line 291):

> In medieval story he loved Criseyde (Cressida) and was forsaken by her for Diomede. They are mentioned together by Gower (*Confessio Amantis* VIII, 2531). The story was later the subject of Chaucer's masterpiece, and only work of first rank that he finished.
> (Bodleian MS Tolkien A 39/2/1, fol. 111)

Troilus would continue asserting influences small and large in his fiction as well as his scholarship. In his lecture to Navy cadets in 1944, Tolkien knew Chaucer's text well enough to pluck a phrase from *Troilus* (V.837) to illustrate Spenser's linguistic misunderstanding in the *Faerie Queene* based on poor Chaucer editions: "From a misreading of *dorring do(n)* as *derring do*, and a misunderstanding of the passage, is derived through Spenser the bogus

---

[36] J. R. R. Tolkien, "Some Contributions to Middle-English Lexicography", *RES* 1 (1925), 210–15.

mediaeval word *derring-do* 'chivalry, knight errantry'."[37] And in 1953 when delivering the W. P. Ker Memorial Lecture on *Gawain*, he concluded by making comparison with Chaucer's masterpiece:

> *Sir Gawain and the Green Knight* remains the best conceived and shaped narrative poem of the Fourteenth Century, indeed of the Middle Age, in English, with one exception only. It has a rival, a claimant to equality not superiority, in Chaucer's masterpiece *Troilus and Criseyde*. That is larger, longer, more intricate, and perhaps more subtle, though no wiser or more perceptive, and certainly less noble. And both these poems deal, from different angles, with the problems that so much occupied the English mind: the relations of Courtesy and Love with morality and Christian morals and the Eternal Law.
>
> (*Essays* 105)

In Chaucer's free adaptation of Boccaccio's *Filostrato*, many readers lose patience with the diffident Trojan prince in his faltering pursuit of Criseyde.[38] In November 1914 just when Tolkien had been taking notes on *Troilus*, he delivered a college lecture on the *Kalevala* where he mocked the hapless lover in contrast to the bold Finnish suitor Kullervo: "There is no Troilus to need a Pandarus to do his shy wooing for him."[39] Tolkien would have felt himself in the superior position to dismiss the crippling shyness of Chaucer's hero. When in January 1913 he had received a letter from Edith Bratt saying that she had become engaged to another man, he promptly caught a train to Cheltenham and took her for a country walk. By the time they returned, he had persuaded her to break her engagement and marry him instead (SH 1:42). In this success, he himself may have more closely resembled the bold, aggressive suitor Diomede in Chaucer's poem.

Tolkien's Lost Chaucer (245–9) suggests that *Troilus* was another medieval text that served as a lens refracting the author's personal experience into a fictional projection with a happier outcome than, in this case, the tragic Chaucerian original. Whereas the lovers Troilus and Criseyde are trapped in Troy, a city besieged and doomed to destruction, Faramir and Éowyn in

---

[37] Bodleian MS Tolkien 14/2, fol. 92, referencing Spenser's *Fairie Queene*, II, iv, 42.

[38] For example, John M. Bowers, "'Beautiful as Troilus': Richard II, Chaucer's Troilus, and Figures of (Un)Masculinity," in *Men and Masculinity in Chaucer's* Troilus and Criseyde, ed. Tison Pugh and Marcia Smith Marzec (Cambridge: D. S. Brewer, 2008), 9–27.

[39] J. R. R. Tolkien, *The Story of Kullervo*, ed. Verlyn Flieger (New York and Boston: Houghton Mifflin Harcourt, 2016), 70. Tolkien delivered this paper at Corpus Christi College, Oxford on 22 November 1914 (SH 1:64).

"The Steward and the King" are confined by their injuries inside Minas Tirith, but even as their wartime romance advances, their apparently doomed city is saved by the successful destruction of the Ring and the collapse of Sauron's power.

Departing from the patterns that C. S. Lewis describes in the opening chapter of *The Allegory of Love*,[40] Faramir's wooing rejects the lover's passive obedience to the lady carried to an extreme by Troilus (and enacted by Gimli in his worshipful love for Galadriel). Instead, Faramir moves forward with the self-assurance embodied in Troilus' Greek rival Diomede and already, in real life, enacted by the young Tolkien. Irritated when readers imagined him as the model for the pipe-smoking Gandalf, Tolkien issued this corrective: "As far as any character is 'like me' it is Faramir" (*Letters* 337n). Faramir understands that his rival is Aragorn and presses his suit by explaining what the author described elsewhere as "the theme of mistaken love seen in Éowyn and her first love for Aragorn" (*Letters* 229–30). Nor is Faramir reliant upon the machinations of a go-between such as Pandarus; instead he simply queries Merry for a better understanding of his lady's "grief and unrest". And unlike Troilus, who accepts Criseyde's insistence on secrecy (to their undoing), Faramir proceeds in full view of the people over whom he currently rules as Steward of the City, standing hand in hand with Éowyn upon the high walls. Tolkien would later explain: "This tale does not deal with a period of 'Courtly Love' and its pretences; but with a culture more primitive (sc. less corrupt) and nobler" (*Letters* 458).

Professor Raleigh's coverage of *Troilus* had drawn upon the medieval notion of Boethian tragedy, pictured in *The Consolation of Philosophy* as the rise and fall upon Fortune's Wheel: "Not Dante even would have conceived of Tragedy as anything but *Fall from High Estate*."[41] Tolkien would have found Chaucer's translation *Boece* alongside *Troilus* in the same volume of Skeat borrowed from his college library. Chaucer's tragic poem explicitly announced this pattern in its opening stanza, "In lovinge, how his aventures fellen / Fro wo to wele, and after out of Ioye"; and he called it by name at its conclusion: "Go, litel book, go litel myn tregedie" (5.1786). But coming in the wake of his *Beowulf* lecture with its description of Northern courage "perfect because without hope" (*Essays* 21), his 1939 lecture "On Fairy-Stories" coined the term *eucatastrophe* to describe an alternative to this fatal outcome as "the joy

---

[40] C. S. Lewis's Preface to *The Allegory of Love: A Study in Medieval Tradition* (Oxford: Oxford University Press, 1936) thanks Professor Tolkien for reading and commenting upon this opening chapter, "Courtly Love".
[41] Bodleian MS Tolkien A 21/4, fol. 15v.

of the happy ending...the joy of deliverance; it denies (in the face of much evidence, if you will) universal final defeat" (*Essays* 153). This is the happy-ending revision of the Trojan tragedy of *Troilus* that Tolkien offered in "The Steward and the King" (*RK* VI/5). Again, Raleigh's outline of medieval genres was helpful: "Dante's Divina Commedia, for instance, is so called simply because it leads *from* Hell *to* Heaven" (15v). If the love of Faramir and Éowyn does not exactly lead them to Heaven, they do live happily ever after in Ithilien, the garden of Gondor.

Oxford English Dictionary (1918–20)

In November 1916, Tolkien was invalided back to England with the trench fever that probably saved his life from the Battle of the Somme, and after stays in various hospitals with recurrences of symptoms, he returned to Oxford in October 1918 still classified as unfit for military duties and recommended only for sedentary employment. He took rooms with his wife and their baby son in St John Street, where he commenced tutorial work. Many students came from the women's colleges because English was one of their more popular subjects—with Chaucer as a fixture on the syllabus. Over the course of his future career, Tolkien continued to work with an impressive number of women students who became distinguished academics in their own right such as Joan Turville-Petre, Ursula Dronke, Mary Lascelles, Celia Sisam, Rosemond Tuve, and Rosemary Woolf.

In November 1918, with no hope of an academic post at a university still scarcely functioning, Tolkien accepted an offer from his former tutor William Craigie to join the staff of the *Oxford English Dictionary*, still then officially called the *New English Dictionary*. He began work as an assistant lexicographer in December, soon joining the staff in the Old Ashmolean building in Broad Street. As the project neared the end of the alphabet, senior editor Henry Bradley supervised his efforts on words beginning with the letter W which took best advantage of his strengths in early English and Germanic languages. His work continued until he was earning enough from tutoring to leave the *OED* at the end of June 1920. Tolkien remained immensely proud of his contributions and retorted imperiously when etymologies were challenged, "The *OED* is me!"[42]

---

[42] John and Priscilla Tolkien, *Tolkien Family Album*, 42.

The lexicographers worked with small "Dictionary slips" approximately 6 by 4 inches – really whatever paper was available, even the wrappers from chocolate bars.[43] This would look forward to Tolkien's own practice of using whatever discarded paper was handy for his own writings. He set to work upon a range of approximately seventy-five words from *waggle* to *wold*, tracing each word's sense development and then researching etymologies, in his first weeks detailing the linguistic histories of *warm, wasp, water, wick*, and *winter (Biography* 108). Once approved by senior editors, the final entries would include pronunciation, variant spellings, etymologies, division of senses and subsenses, definitions, and a selection of quotations to illustrate these meanings. Some Dictionary slips survive in Tolkien's handwriting so that we can see how extravagant his draft etymologies were. For the word *wold*, for example, he assembled long lists of cognates in other European languages, living and dead; speculations about the ulterior origins of Old Teutonic **wilþijaz* and **walþuz*; and some general remarks about the sense developments – few of which remained in the published entries after passing under the editorial pen of Bradley. Tolkien later had opportunity to vent his frustration in print:

> It is arguable that there is not much use in etymologies unless they are fairly full and can have space to hesitate – complete etymologies, complete as they can be made, are of course out of the question, pages could be written on the easiest. Even the *N.E.D.* is obliged often to be too concise to tell the full truth.[44]

It is thus possible to read his thirteen-page article "Middle English *Losenger*" (1953) as an expression of this pent-up ambition for tracing the fullest possible history of a word, unrestrained by editors mindful of the limitations of time and space.

Begun under the auspices of the Philological Society of London in 1857, the "Unregistered Words Committee" evolved into the Dictionary Committee that made the commitment, probably at the urging of Frederick J. Furnivall, to cover *all* English words. They then faced the enormous task of assembling

---

[43] Peter Gilliver, Jeremy Marshall, and Edmund Weiner, *The Ring of Words: Tolkien and the* Oxford English Dictionary (Oxford: Oxford University Press), "Tolkien as Lexicographer," 3–42. Peter Gilliver has generously provided further insights in private emails.

[44] J. R. R. Tolkien, "Philology: General Works," *Year's Work in English Studies* 5 (1926 for 1924), 49–50.

illustrative quotations. When Tolkien arrived, he worked on entries drawing upon quotation slips which had accumulated over sixty years. Of his seventy-five W words listed by Gilliver, Marshall, and Weiner in their book on Tolkien at the *OED* (42), only twelve were provided with Chaucerian attestations, largely because the fourteenth-century writer had no occasion to use words like *waistcoat*, *walrus*, or *wampum*. Here are some of the Chaucer quotations eventually printed for words assigned to Tolkien:

Waist
1. portion of the trunk of the human body that is between the ribs and the hip-bones.

c 1386 CHAUCER *Sir Thopas* Prol. 10 He in the waast is shape as wel as I.

Wake
8. *trans*. To rouse from sleep or unconsciousness.

c 1369 CHAUCER *Bk. of Duchess* 294 I was waked With smale foules a grete hepe That had affrayed me out of my slepe.

Want
2. †g. To fail to recollect. *Obs. rare*.

c 1381 CHAUCER *Parl. Foules* 287 And many a mayde of whiche the name I wante.

Warm *adj.*
†7. Comfortable, comfortably settled.

c 1374 CHAUCER *Troylus* III 1630 Be not to rakel þough þou sitte warme

Water
6. a. *By water*: by ship or boat on the sea.

c 1386 CHAUCER *Prol.* 400 If þat he faught, and hadde the hyer hond, By water he sente hem hoom to euery lond.

Wild *adj.*
8. Fierce, savage, ferocious....

c 1385 CHAUCER *L.G.W.* 805 *Thisbe*, Allas there comyth a wilde lyones.

Winter
2. Put for "year": nearly always *pl.* with a numeral; often in expressions referring to a person's age.

c 1386 CHAUCER *Monk's T.* 69 Fully twenty wynter yeer by yeere He hadde of Israel the gouernance.

Several caveats must be added. Because of evolving collaborations, the final drafting of entries such as the one for *Wield* did not begin until after Tolkien had left the project. It would have been only after drafting in earnest that any significant work was done on the quotation slips. It is therefore uncertain whether Tolkien played any part in the selection of Chaucer quotations, though he may have seen a larger number of them than were finally selected. Therefore, nothing certain can be said except perhaps that the young lexicographer became aware of the range of Chaucer editions from which these quotations were drawn.

A quick look at these Chaucerian citations above, for example, indicates that they are not consistent in spelling practices, some using the thorn *þ* and others *th*. A closer look reveals steady departures from Skeat's 1894 *Works of Geoffrey Chaucer*, which had established itself as the definitive edition by 1918 when Tolkien joined the *OED* staff. Take, for example, this quotation for **Wane**, where *wanye* differs from Skeat's *wanie*:

> c 1386 CHAUCER *Knt.'s T.* 2077 And vndernethe hir feet she hadde a moone Wexing it was and sholde *wanye* soone.
>
> Skeat, *Works* (4:60): "And undernethe hir feet she hadde a mone / Wexing it was, and sholde *wanie* sone."

In the back matter of the *OED*'s final volume, the "List of Books Quoted in the Oxford English Dictionary" clarifies that this wide variance occurred because Chaucer's works were cited in a wide assortment of printed editions. Here are some of the earlier and lesser-known:

> *The Workes of Geffray Chaucer*. Ed. William Thynne. London: T. Godfray, 1532 with reprints in 1542 and 1550.
>
> *The Workes of our Antient English poet, Geffrey Chaucer*. Ed. Thomas Speght. London: G. Bishop 1598 with expanded reprint in 1602.
>
> *The Works of Geoffrey Chaucer*. Ed. John Urry. London: Bernard Lintot, 1721.
>
> Chaucer. *The Harleian Manuscript 7334 and Revision of the Canterbury Tales*. Ed. John S. P. Tatlock. Oxford: Oxford University Press, 1909.

It seems mysterious why so many obsolete editions were quoted when Skeat's edition was available on the shelves of the Dictionary Room where Tolkien and other editors were working. Part of the answer is that quotation slips had already accumulated over the previous sixty years, as mentioned before, and the outside volunteers had consulted whatever editions were available to them in the decades before the standard Oxford edition was published. One would imagine that Tolkien, always punctilious, would have taken the trouble to update whatever Chaucer quotations came across his desk by consulting Skeat, but the reality is that there simply was not time. The *OED* was already many years behind schedule, and everyone operated with a sense of urgency along with their scrupulous attention to details. Here was one situation in which Tolkien's perfectionism allowed for no extensive delays.

Shortly afterwards in his unfinished *Selections of Chaucer's Poetry and Prose* during the mid-1920s, Tolkien included "An Introduction to Language" explaining that even the earliest manuscripts did not faithfully preserve Chaucer's personal language but rather the usages of fifteenth-century copyists: "It must not, however, be overlooked that our extant copies, in varying degrees according to their age and carefulness, have at haphazard altered Chaucer's language, not only in spelling but also in accidence, syntax, and even occasionally in vocabulary, in conformity with the uses of a later century" (*TLC* 279). His two years of *OED* labour had also made him increasingly aware of the long, complicated, and often error-prone tradition of editions representing Chaucer's works. This would encourage his suspicion even of Skeat's authority and, behind it, the trustworthiness of the Ellesmere manuscript for supplying the most reliable texts of the *Clerk's Tale* and the *Pardoner's Tale* which he would teach in the late 1940s and early 1950s. Despite this heightened scepticism, he would nonetheless continue to cite early editions such as Tyrwhitt's and to draw textual lessons from Furnivall's *Six-Text Print of Chaucer's Canterbury Tales* which he had encountered (but did not have opportunity to correct) in his quotations for the W words in the *OED*.

One final note on his time at the *OED*. In June 1920 when he was readying himself to leave the job and the regular salary, Tolkien was paid two guineas by Oxford University Press for a "report on Thomas' Predecessors to Chaucer".[45] Although Tolkien's report does not survive, we can reasonably infer that it was negative, because OUP never published such a volume. Thirty years later, however, the independent scholar Mary Edith Thomas did publish a book subtitled *Chaucer and His Immediate Predecessors*. But the reason for Tolkien's unfavourable response probably lay in the book's main title: *Medieval*

---

[45] *TLC* 16–17; I am grateful to Peter Gilliver for this reference in Publishing Business Cash Book No. 6 in the OUP archives.

Skepticism and Chaucer.[46] Her project had begun at Columbia University under Roger Sherman Loomis, a Rhodes Scholar in the same year as Kenneth Sisam, and he gained notoriety for his articles "Was Chaucer a Laodicean?"— that is, a lukewarm Christian—and "Was Chaucer a Free Thinker?" Thomas's book established fourteenth-century backgrounds for viewing the poet as an unorthodox Christian in an age of widespread unorthodoxy, and Tolkien seems never to have waivered from the belief emphasized in his undergraduate notes from Professor Raleigh's lectures: "Wyclif no Wyclifite nor Chaucer a Wyclifite."

Tolkien at Leeds: *TLS* and *YWES*

Tolkien was at loose ends in June 1920 when his old tutor Kenneth Sisam drew his attention to the advertisement for Reader in English Language at the University of Leeds (*Ency* 350–1). Later that month he traveled northward for an interview and was met at the station by George S. Gordon, the Professor of English who would play a key role in Tolkien's career, both as co-editor of their Clarendon Chaucer and as one of the electors for Oxford's Professor of Anglo-Saxon – which would go to Tolkien in 1925. The Leeds hiring process moved smoothly and quickly, since Gordon was "a master hand at intrigue" (*Biography* 115), and Tolkien's appointment was ratified at the end of July 1920.

Tolkien advanced his scholarly career at Leeds with completion of his *Middle English Vocabulary* for Sisam's anthology *Fourteenth Century Verse and Prose*, his Clarendon edition of *Sir Gawain and the Green Knight* in collaboration with E. V. Gordon (no relation to George Gordon), and early progress on *Selections from Chaucer's Poetry and Prose*. Tolkien's teaching responsibilities included the "Language of Chaucer", "General Prologue to the *Canterbury Tales*", and another class simply entitled "Chaucer". He was assiduous in his efforts on behalf of students. When he began teaching "Language of Chaucer", for example, he produced a mimeographed handout on Kentish dialect features (SH 1:122).

Grateful as Tolkien was for the appointment at Leeds and then the promotion to a new Professorship of English Language in 1924, he did not look back

---

[46] Mary Edith Thomas, *Medieval Skepticism and Chaucer: An Evaluation of the Skepticism of the 13th and 14th Centuries of Geoffrey Chaucer and His Immediate Predecessors – An Era That Looked Back on an Age of Faith and Forward to an Age of Reason* (1950; repr. New York: Cooper Square Publishers, 1971).

with unalloyed fondness upon the undergraduates (*Letters* 565–6). He vented his disappointment satirically in the Chaucerian pastiche *The Clerke's Compleinte*, published anonymously in 1922 and playing upon the opening lines of the *Canterbury Tales*:

> Bifel þat in þat sesoun dim & mat,
> In Leedes atte dores as I sat,
> At morne was come in to þo halles hye
> Wel nygh fyue hondred in my companye
> of newė clerkes in an egre presse,
> langages olde þat wolden lerne, I gesse,
> Of Fraunce or Engelonde or Spayne or Ruce,
> þo tonges harde of Hygh Almayne & Pruce;
> Or historye, or termes queinte of lawe –
> yit nas bot litel Latin in her mawe...[47]

Still later, he emended the poem to replace Leeds with Oxford (SH 1:128, 141) since undergraduates, whatever their university, never measured up to his expectations if they arrived with "litel Latin".

In addition to seeing into print his *Middle English Vocabulary* and *Gawain* edition, Tolkien published a variety of shorter pieces that appeared surprisingly amid so many other responsibilities. "The Devil's Coach-Horses" and "Some Contributions to Middle-English Lexicography" both appeared in 1925. Another short publication was his anonymous 1923 review of Furnivall's posthumous edition of *Hali Meidenhad* in the *Times Literary Supplement*, where he inserted a reference to Chaucer's *Clerk's Tale*:

> With the possible exception of *Sawles Warde*, which approaches the liveliness and picturesqueness, if not the humanity, that make the Anchoresses' Guide so justly praised,[48] these edifying prose-pieces are probably seldom

---

[47] Jill Fitzgerald, "A *Clerkes Compleinte*: Tolkien and the Division of Lit. and Lang.", *Tolkien Studies* 6 (2009), 41-57 at p. 50. See also Anders Stenström. "*The Clerkes Compleinte* Revisited," *Arda* 6 (1990 for 1986), 1–13. The last lines of this excerpt play upon the last lines of the *Epilogue of the Man of Law's Tale* (known by Skeat and in Tolkien's day as the *Shipman's Prologue*): "No phislyas, ne termes queinte of law. / Ther is but litel Latyn in my mawe!" (*CT* II, 1190).

[48] Tolkien knew this "Anchoresses' Guide" from *The Ancren Riwle: A Treatise on the Rules and Duties of Monastic Life*, ed. James Morton, (London: Camden Society, 1853); his personal copy is now Bodleian MS Tolkien E 16/46. He taught selected passages to his Leeds students in October 1920 (SH 1:122).

read even by those interested in the history of English prose. *Hali Meidenhad* is the one that offers the least appeal to modern readers, presenting as it does an extreme example of that ruthless mediaeval concentration on one virtue to the exclusion, for the sake of argument, of all other considerations, which is most widely familiar in the *Clerk's Tale*. From the nature of its subject – an exhortation to perpetual virginity addressed to young women – this homily is often more repulsive to modern feeling than anything in Chaucer's tale, and is in some passages repulsive to the saner feeling of its own period...[49]

The *Second Nun's Tale* would have made a better example of "exhortation to perpetual virginity" since its heroine St Cecilia is so dedicated to lifelong virginity, she warns her newlywed husband Valerian that her guardian angel will kill him if he touches her in any unchaste manner. But the *Clerk's Tale* well represents "concentration on one virtue" since its heroine is such an embodiment of long-suffering endurance at the hands of a sadistic husband that she has been known ever since as Patient Griselda.

Academics have always harboured affection for the Clerk of Oxford praised by the Chaucerian narrator: "And gladly wolde he lerne and gladly teche" (*CT* I, 308). Begun by 1920, Tolkien's poem *Light as Leaf on Lindentree* took its title from the envoy to the *Clerk's Tale* (IV, 1211) where wives were advised to be "light as leef on lynde",[50] and the phrase survived as "light as linden-leaves" in Aragorn's song of Beren and Lúthien (*FR* I/11). When later Tolkien admitted his *Silmarillion* was full of "all that 'heigh stile' (as Chaucer might say)" (*Letters* 343), he was remembering a phrase from the Clerk's Prologue (*CT* IV, 18). And just when he was writing his *TLS* review in 1923, his old tutor Kenneth Sisam, now his OUP editor, was publishing his exemplary student edition *The Clerkes Tale of Oxenford*. Later when Tolkien became Merton Professor and lectured on the *Clerk's Tale* in 1947, he voiced consistent respect for this edition. About Chaucer's phrase *stalked hym ful stille* (525), for example, Tolkien compared endnotes: "Skeat 'comes marching in'. Kenneth Sisam has 'stepped very softly'. Kenneth Sisam is right, I think."[51]

---

[49] His anonymous review of *Hali Meidenhad* appeared in *TLS* on 26 April 1923, 281, and an edited version was reprinted in *TLS* 30 June 2017, 34. Tolkien's review copy is now Bodleian Tolkien VC 186.

[50] SH 1:117; see also Joe R. Christopher, "Tolkien's Lyric Poetry," in *Tolkien's Legendarium: Essays on The History of Middle-earth*, ed. Verlyn Flieger and Carl F. Hostetter (Westport and London: Greenwood Press, 2000), 143–60 at p. 150.

[51] Bodleian MS Tolkien A 13/2, page 32. Compare Skeat 5:347 and *The Clerkes Tale of Oxenford*, ed. Kenneth Sisam (Oxford: Clarendon Press, 1923), 54.

Also during his Leeds years, Tolkien began a little-noticed but very time-consuming series of articles on "Philology: General Works" for *Year's Work in English Studies*. They appeared over three volumes with delays in which one can imagine Tolkien's congenital tardiness played some part. The first volume was promised for 1923, was dated 1924, but appeared only in January 1925.[52] It was a heavy-duty assignment, to be sure; the first volume alone required him to discuss fifteen books, mostly in German and French, as well as many others in passing (SH 1:137). One of the medieval authors mentioned in passing was Chaucer, with tantalizing allusions to topics which Tolkien was facing as editor of *Selections from Chaucer's Poetry and Prose*, launched in 1923. Only a few of these references are mentioned here, though the three journal contributions are worth exploring in greater depth because Tolkien's philological interests were never far removed from his fantasy writings.

In volume 4, Tolkien reviewed German studies, which placed him in an ideal position, almost three decades later, to prepare the Chaucer-inspired lecture "Middle English *Losenger*". He singled out "Watling Street" as another name for the Milky Way which attracted his attention when annotating *galaxýe* in Chaucer's *Parlement of Foules* (line 56) in his Clarendon edition. The importance of Edward Gepp's *Essex Dialect Dictionary* for "students of modern English especially of the South-Eastern dialect forms" (25) would inform his later remarks on the speech of Chaucer's Reeve. George Watson's *Roxburghshire Word-book* held value "for all students whose work takes them to texts in early or modern English hailing from anywhere near the Border" (27). In the *Reeve's Tale*, Chaucer's two Cambridge students speak in the dialect of their elusive hometown of Strother "fer in the north".

In volume 5, Tolkien noted that "traditional Indo-European philology has suffered shocks in recent years" by recovery of the Hittite language:

> The pre-history of Europe and nearer Asia looms dark in the background, an intricate web, whose tangle we may now guess at, but hardly hope to unravel. All this we ought to take account of, however distantly and cursorily. If our present linguistic conceptions are true, there is an endless chain of development between that far-off shadowy 'Indo-European' – that phantom which becomes more and more elusive, and more alluring, with the passage of years… (27–28).

---

[52] J. R. R. Tolkien, "Philology: General Works," *Year's Work in English Studies* 4 (1924 for 1923), 20–37; 5 (1926 for 1924), 26–65; and 6 (1927 for 1925), 32–66.

Questions about the prehistoric linguistic and cultural interplay between East and West, specifically the movements of stories and the directions of those movements, would become recurrent themes when in the 1950s Tolkien considered the earliest Indian analogues for the *Pardoner's Tale*.

In this *Year's Work*, Tolkien also proceeded to his habitual complaint against scribes who inflicted damage on the medieval works that they copied:

> Some person or persons unknown have obviously badly damaged *Layamon* so that its present form falters in its literary and linguistic evidence, though it cries for such curses as Chaucer pronounced upon Adam the Scrivener – curses that cannot be too often called to mind. It is at least arguable that we should sooner cry the mange upon the scalps of scribes than build too loftily upon their laziness. (64)

Here Tolkien alluded to the one-stanza poem *Chaucers Wordes Unto Adam, His Owne Scriveyn* (Skeat 1:379):

> Adam scriveyn, if ever it thee bifalle
> Boece or Troilus to wryten newe,
> Under thy lokkes thou most have the scalle,
> But after my making thou wryte trewe.
> So often a daye I mot thy werk renewe,
> Hit to correcte and eek to rubbe and scrape;
> And al is through thy negligence and rape.

He would have frequent recourse to this poem in "Chaucer as a Philologist", as when he lamented: "Alas! If the curse he pronounced on scribe Adam produced any effect, many a fifteenth-century penman must early have gone bald" (see below p. 111).

In volume 6, Tolkien made only glancing reference to a German *Festschrift*: "A brief note is contributed by W. Fischer on the French of Chaucer's *Prioress*, returning to the older satirical view" (47). At almost this same time, he was drafting annotations on the Prioress for his Clarendon Chaucer and producing what amounted to a mini-essay dismissing this satirical view:

> No special sneer is probably intended at the Stratford nunnery, or at any rate not at its French, which may have been of the highest kind obtainable in England. It is mentioned very likely to fix in the minds of an audience, naturally more alive to topical allusions than we are, precisely the culture

and degree to which the Prioress belonged...(See *TLC* 174 for the full passage).

Regarding Samuel Moore's *Historical Outlines of English Phonology and Morphology*, an American volume under review, Tolkien mentioned slightingly the chapter "Language of Chaucer" (61). His OUP Clarendon Chaucer correspondence, transcribed below (p. 47), would have much harsher things to say about Professor Moore as the potential editor of the *Middle English Dictionary*.

2
Editing Chaucer, 1924–28

Selections from Chaucer's Poetry and Prose represents Tolkien's most extensive, longest-running, and ultimately most frustrating engagement with the fourteenth-century poet.[1] The story begins early in 1922 when George S. Gordon, leaving Leeds for Oxford as Merton Professor of Language and Literature, discussed a student edition of Chaucer with David Nichol Smith, chief adviser on English literature to Oxford University Press. By August of that year, Gordon had compiled a list of contents with precise line counts for this compact textbook, privileging shorter pieces such as *Compleint to his Empty Purse* and dream visions such as *Parlement of Foules* that are often neglected today, but were fixtures in Oxford lectures by Professor Raleigh (and would be key works in the "Chaucer" chapter of C. S. Lewis's 1936 *The Allegory of Love*). Gordon intentionally neglected the *Canterbury Tales* in expectation of separate Clarendon editions such as Kenneth Sisam's *Clerkes Tale of Oxenford* in 1923.

This chapter surveys the Clarendon Chaucer project based on the materials that survived in OUP's correspondence file and much more abundantly, and surprisingly, in a box of materials that had been shoved into a dark corner of the basement archives. We begin with the eight letters dated 1924 through 1951 which trace the faltering progress of the student edition and its eventual demise. Next, we assess Tolkien's work at editing Chaucer's texts based on reprints from Skeat's 1894 *Works of Geoffrey Chaucer*. This phase reached final corrected page proofs ready for publication. Third, we examine Tolkien's glossary, which survives in long sheet galleys corrected, but never retypeset, while he awaited the completion of his notes for cross-referencing. Finally, we approach his almost 200 pages of typed and handwritten draft notes – called "the Chaucerian incubus" in a letter to R. W. Chapman (p. 50) – by transcribing some of his headnotes (so far as legible) and samples from his more interesting annotations. This will include his four-page excursus on Chaucer's indebtedness to the native Alliterative tradition. His typescript "An Introduction on

---

[1] *Tolkien's Lost Chaucer* traces this history in far greater detail in the chapters "Unexpected Journeys", "Tolkien as Editor: Text and Glossary", and "The Chaucerian Incubus: The Notes".

Language" (Bodleian MS Tolkien A 39/2/2, fols. 138–40) was probably planned to fit between the notes and glossary, on the model of his 1925 Clarendon *Gawain* edition (122-9), but it is omitted here because already published in full as "Appendix I" in *Tolkien's Lost Chaucer*.

Oxford University Press correspondence (1924–51)

We are including all eight of Tolkien's letters that survive in the OUP correspondence file for three reasons. They provide snapshots of a project that began in great optimism and ended almost three decades later in resentment and recrimination. They reveal Tolkien in a lesser-known persona, characterized in one of these letters as "a pettifogging scholar rejoicing in the minute and the intricate, and such games as textual criticism". And thirdly they help to fill the notorious twelve-year gap in Carpenter's *Letters* between 1925 and 1937.[2] *Tolkien's Lost Chaucer* provides much more about the principal players George S. Gordon (60–7) and Kenneth Sisam (52–60) as well as their great Victorian predecessor Walter W. Skeat (41–52).

Though no formal contract survives, Tolkien was working on the Clarendon Chaucer's text and word-list by 1923 while still endeavouring with E. V. Gordon to complete their edition of *Sir Gawain and the Green Knight*.[3] This other Clarendon edition, published in 1925, provides a template for organizing the sections that survive from the Clarendon Chaucer: George S. Gordon's introduction followed by Tolkien's text, notes, remarks on language, and glossary. To hasten this project and reduce costs, Kenneth Sisam arranged to pay Skeat's daughter five guineas for reprinting their texts from his monumental *Works of Geoffrey Chaucer*. The printer then typeset passages already agreed upon and sent these pages to Tolkien for any changes. His first extant letter to Sisam, surviving as OUP's typewritten extracts, reveals in his remarks over *buskes/busshe* his ambitions to work as a genuine editor rather than simply reproducing Skeat's text.

---

[2] This hiatus occurs early in the *The Letters of J. R. R. Tolkien*, ed. Humphrey Carpenter and Christopher Tolkien (1981; Boston and New York: Houghton Mifflin, 2000), 13–14, between his acceptance of the Oxford Professorship in 1925 and his correspondence with Unwin & Allen about *The Hobbit* in 1937. The new *Letters of J. R. R. Tolkien: Revised and Expanded Edition* (2023) restores some 150 letters omitted from the original 1981 edition but reduces the chronological gap only from 1925 to 1934 (11). Scull and Hammond have counted some 1,500 letters in private and public hands (SH 2:681), throwing doubt on Carpenter's 1981 statement that "between 1918 and 1937 few letters survive" (*Letters* vii).

[3] See Douglas A. Anderson, "'An Industrious Little Devil': E. V. Gordon as Friend and Collaborator with Tolkien," in *Tolkien the Medievalist*, ed. Jane Chance (London: Routledge, 2003), 15–25, and *Ency* 251-2.

[1]

January 5, 1924

Thank you for your recent letter. You are patient. I now begin the liquidation of my various debts, with the first 21 pages of the text of *Chaucer Selections*. I have only discovered 3 actual misprints in that space. The remainder of my marks are alterations of Skeat, such as *God*, *th'effect* already agreed upon;[4] *pité, attempré* (to which I imagine you will readily assent); restoration of MS e.g., *buskes* (p. 4, l. 102), where Skeat substitutes *busshes* with a note that *busk* is not Chaucerian, although he retains unaltered at l. 54 and elsewhere (notably Knight's Tale, 721); alterations of punctuation.

In the last I have only ventured to ink in a very few corrections, as I have no idea how far I am expected or may be permitted to go. Not far, I suspect. In any case the complete renovation of Skeat's somewhat lavish punctuation is doubtless out of the question. There are a dreadful lot of semi-colons!

In any case I hope that the simplification of such combinations as ;—; ;— etc. will be altered: they give me a pain.

I have also abolished the occasional hyphens that crop up in words like *a-boute, with-oute, a-brayd*, but have allowed Skeat's uniform *y-* (*y-wis* & pps.) to stand, and also *a-* (prep) *a-night* etc. In an effort towards uniformity I have hyphened any *-so* (*what-so, wher-so*) words that are left loose, since Skeat appears to have intended to hyphen throughout, I think rightly.

* * *

Sisam replied immediately, thanking Tolkien for the first batch of page proofs but also warning about unnecessary changes to such things as punctuation: "these trifles will cost us 6d. each." Tolkien responded from Leeds with the next batch of pages including, as will be his habit, an account of family distractions as well as chafing at the limits that require "compression of the glossary, and the jettisoning of all dispensable reference figures".

[2]

February 1, 1924

Dear Sisam,

At last another chunk of "Chaucer" proof. Altered as little as possible, either in punctuation or distribution of hyphens. I propose to restore MS *gnodded* in "Former Age"; Skeat's emendation to *gniden* has prevented its inclusion in NED, s.v. *Gnodde*, but the word appears to be genuine and apposite.

---

[4] Skeat had not capitalized *god* or inserted an apostrophe in *theffect*.

I feel sure that Skeat's contribution, line 56, to the same poem is wide of the mark and that "curtesye" or civilized refinement of manner would not fill the earth in an age of corn-banquets – however I cannot make my ideas rhyme (possibly Chaucer couldn't!) and so we must leave it.[5]

Thank you for 2 extra copies of "Gawain" proofs, which I shall find useful. I can only repeat that I am grateful to you for giving us a specimen, even, of this glossary according to both ways. I am on the one hand not bigoted, and on the other realise that the printer has the whip hand of us, and we shall in the end have to jog down his road – probably willingly. However whatever be his result, "the camel-driver may have his thoughts but the camel his", and at that we may leave it. Certainly whatever small point my arrangement had is now reduced still more in importance, by the compression of the glossary, and the jettisoning of all dispensable reference figures.

My domestic troubles become a tragic-farce. I have had my younger boy laid up with appendicitis, grievously alarming us and seriously upsetting affairs for a week or so – though he suddenly and miraculously got well on the eve of an operation.[6] He is now about again – also, at last, we have found a servant (how long for, is ungrateful to enquire) so things are reviving again. Wone þe bale is alre hecst, þonne is þe bote alre necst, quod Alfred.[7] The further bale also is not far off at times! "Gawain" is now clad in weeds that are pleasant to the eye. It is difficult to realise that it is the same poem, so long have our eyes been inured to the ragged weeds of the EETS. I have absolutely no carp as to form, unless perhaps it be conceded that the title heading on p. 1 looks a bit thin and wan, and is, also, possibly too close down on to the text. These are purely amateur remarks.

I hope you and yours are all well. I am moving, very inopportunely, on March 17th.[8]

Yrs

JRRT

PS. If you have a moment to spare please glance at alterations to Chaucer text proposed *in pencil*. These are I think desirable but not indispensable. I lean in the direction (esp. in a normalized & to some extent modernised text like this) of boldly smoothing out the most apparently stumbling lines in

---

[5] Skeat 1:382 had supplied the missing line 56: ["Fulfilled erthe of olde curtesye".]

[6] This was Michael Tolkien; Christopher was not born until 24 November 1924.

[7] King Alfred is quoted in this couplet from *The Owl and the Nightingale* (685–8); Tolkien owned two copies of the 1907 edition by John Edwin Wells (Cilli 327).

[8] SH 1:134 note that Tolkien moved his family to a three-storey house on the outskirts of Leeds with open fields and cleaner air.

meter also – however rash this may be when set against the uncertainty of our knowledge. PF 445 seems to me a poor line, but it appears like that in all MSS. I should be in favour of *thilke* for *this*, or perhaps more probable *whan that*. I have put in *thilke* in pencil. Have it out if you like.[9]

JRRT

PPS. Mea culpa – I have neglected to thank the Press very much indeed for the copy of Carleton Brown's Religious Lyrics.[10] May I do so through you? I agree the glossary looks messy (but why italics for both parsing and meanings?) – but the text looks delightful except for a few < > abominations.[11] I am most grateful for the book.

JRRT

Already by February 1924, Sisam was complaining about the slow pace, and George Gordon began making excuses for himself as well as Tolkien: "J.R.R.T. has in fact had a hellish time." Soon Sisam was venting to Nichol Smith about Tolkien's dawdling: "If he would put the same time into working that he devotes to writing excuses we might make some progress." Tolkien had offered to resign from the project but, after a dinner with Gordon at the Randolph Hotel in Oxford, he was back at work with a postcard from Leeds.

[3]

October 23, 1924

Thank you for: Gawain frontispiece; Chaucer text proof (2 sets); Gordon's comments; letter – and more of glossary yesterday. I shall now begin to cram Ch. to any cracks of time there are left.

JRRT

In early December 1924, Sisam was nudging Tolkien with reminders to keep the glossary within agreed-upon length: "I see you rely on grace rather than works. Shall we say December 31st for glossary, and January 31st for notes, in view of your illness?" All of these deadlines were overly optimistic. Tolkien's glossary needed to be cut by ten pages – which he did successfully – but his 200 pages of notes outrageously exceeded the maximum of twenty pages, without even reaching the *Nun's Priest's Tale*, and he found himself incapable

---

[9] Becauce Skeat's *Parlement of Foules* (445) reads "Of this formel, *whan* she herde al this" (1:351). Tolkien's *whan that* would smoothen the meter.

[10] Carleton Brown, ed., *Religious Lyrics of the XIVth Century* (Oxford: Clarendon Press, 1924).

[11] Tolkien was complaining about caret brackets < > where missing letters or words had been supplied.

of making the cuts or getting help from his co-editor to reduce them. He transferred his thick manuscript of annotations to Gordon in 1928 and waited two years with no reply, doing nothing himself in the meantime. Tolkien wrote to Sisam referring to Gordon's "elevation" as President of Magdalen College, Oxford, as his excuse.

[4]
November 21, 1930
My dear Sisam,

I put off answering your letter of September until your return, and now I have overshot the mark.

I would like to cooperate in an edition of the *Ancrene Riwle*, as far as I have any equipment for such work – chiefly limited to the possession of rotographs of the Corpus MS, and a pretty close acquaintance with them, more or less in isolation.[12]

But I must clear off *Chaucer*. I am not the sole or even chief culprit in this matter. And all the work so far done has been done by me. I have made one more effort to get back my draft of notes from my "collaborator". So far without success. His elevation is some excuse, but when one thinks of the labour of the glossary disturbed by alteration in selection, the notes, and the text, which have all fallen to my share, there is some justification for my attitude – I will do no more unless I am given some help in the difficult task of selecting notes and reducing them to the somewhat narrow limits which are presumably contemplated.

I have returned again to the attack and demanded my stuff back – two years old now – with comments, from its prison in Magdalen. If I could clear this off this vac, nothing would please me more than to turn to the *Ancrene Riwle*.

Perhaps I could see you and discuss exactly what is contemplated. In the meanwhile what of a plain text – punctuated and perhaps emended (if necessary) – without trimmings *in usum scholarum*. We are going to alter the syllabus and set a special study of the language of *Ancrene* (i.e. CCCC Ms & the Bodley homilies) as well as of *Orm* and D. Michel, instead of a wild floundering in the whole of Middle English philology.[13] A complete text would be a

---

[12] Many years would pass before completion of Tolkien's *Ancrene Wisse: Edited from MS Corpus Christi College Cambridge 402*, intro. N. R. Ker, EETS o.s. 249 (1962).

[13] CCCC refers to Corpus Christi College, Cambridge, home of his favoured *Ancrene* copy. MS Bodley 34 contained works of the Katherine Group which Tolkien had discussed in "*Ancrene Wisse* and *Hali Meiðhad*". The other abbreviations refer to the *Ormulum* (Cilli 237-38) and Dan Michel's *Ayenbyte of Inwit*, ed. Richard Morris, EETS o.s. 23 (1866); see Bodleian's Tolkien VC 188 for Tolkien's copy.

great advantage. Of course a text, plus select glossary, accidence and phonology, and notes directed solely to elucidation of mere sense (as far as this can be separated from wider questions) – i.e. chiefly for students of M.E. *language and prose* – would be still more useful. I am not certain however how far this could be successfully accomplished without involving one in all the wider questions, especially those centring upon date.

I could produce a plain text, accidence and phonology, with a glossary of very unusual, difficult, or exceptionally interesting words only, quite soon – relatively soon that is. I could not promise it before the end of next long vacation.

If the major edition you mention is to be based on CCCC, I imagine in service of M.E. a *complete* glossary would be contemplated, as well as a full "grammar".[14] This is really needed. The Americans are getting ready to produce a M.E. dictionary at enormous cost; but an hour or two's conversation with Prof Sam Moore, who by some freak of fate seems to have been put in charge, reduced me to despair.[15] What he does *not* know seems the most extensive part of his equipment. If there could be a project quite unsuitable to Michigan, I suppose a M.E. dictionary is that project. In the meanwhile if the chief monuments can be provided with real glossaries, we shall get along.

Yrs ever
JRRT

Sisam replied with what encouragement he could muster: "First to say how much I approve your determination to get Chaucer out of hand. It has been eating its head off, and if the Notes could be cleared up to your satisfaction and Gordon's, there is little that stands in the way." His optimism again proved illusory, because we find Tolkien writing more than a year later with the same excuse-making, now compounded with a feigned naivety about the exact ambitions of the edition and its page limits.

---

[14] See Chapter 3's "*Reeve's Tale* for Navy Cadets" where Tolkien provided a full grammar for Chaucer.

[15] Tolkien mentioned passingly Samuel Moore's *Historical Outlines of English Phonology and Morphology* in "Philology" (1927 for 1925), 61. His dire prediction was not unfounded; see Michael Adams, "Phantom Dictionaries: The Middle English Dictionary before Kurath," in *Dictionaries: Journal of the Dictionary Society of North America* 23 (2002), 95–114 at p. 101, claiming that Moore's *Middle English Dictionary* "would have been obsolete almost upon publication." Peter Gilliver, *The Making of the* Oxford English Dictionary (Oxford: Oxford University Press, 2016), 416–17, provides an overview of the *MED* project that included transfer of some 400,000 dictionary slips from Oxford.

[5]

January 22, 1931

My dear Sisam,

Thank you very much for your offprint – I have not yet a moment to look at it, though the week-end may bring one.[16]

I did what I could with a shortened vac. to work at Chaucer, and at last re-extracted my notes from my collaborator (two years old). Nothing in this difficult task of reducing their bulk, for which they went to him, has been done; so I suppose that must fall to my lot. But I am rather appalled at the job, and also feel foggy as to ultimate bulk possible, and precise nature of audience addressed.

Help thou my ignorance and inexperience. If I allow myself even the room you have taken in the two texts you have edited it will add up to a huge bulk on all our texts – and yet it seems to me you have been about as compact as is possible if commentary on this difficult author is to be of any real service to folk (who I take it by the very act of using and buying such a book are newcomers to archaic and Middle English).[17]

I have, of course, been unable to undertake any real "research" – though obscurities or unsatisfactory explanation bristle in one's path. That, and my own general ignorance, are my only safeguards. But the horror of reducing to necessary limits the large book I have, even with such safeguards, written, is such that I must get quite clear as to number of pages allowable, before starting, and avoid any double-work. I have done all now except N. Priest's Tale. You have here smoothed the way, and I imagine you will not object to the inevitable pillage that will take place (within the limit of decency and with suitable acknowledgements).

One method which should enable me to cut down bulk (but not labour) would be to imitate your sections on language and meter, bringing them into line with the texts contained in the *Selections*. I meant in any case to write such sections, but once you have done it, for its purpose so well, the results (especially as I have studied your efforts) will inevitably be very similar.

So much for "Chaucer". I am really endeavouring to clear off this ancient debt, in spite of difficulties that don't grow less. P. Mods and 4 Universities

---

[16] This may have been Kenneth Sisam's just–published "MSS Bodley 340 and 342: Ælfric's *Catholic Homilies*," *RES* 7 (1931), 7–22.

[17] Sisam had by now edited student editions of *The Clerk's Tale* (1923) and *The Nun's Priest's Tale* (1927).

will leave no leisure before August.[18] Chaucer will have to be extracted from time normally given to sleep or study, but I will finish it off, if it is physically possible, before the summer. Any advice you can give would be gratefully received. Since my collaborator has sent in his essay and general introduction, I am again the villain in the piece.

After that I will take thought for A. Riwle on the lines you indicate.

Here is another and quite unconnected S.O.S. I seem to remember you have one (if not two?) complete copies of Finnur Jónsson's corpus of the Scaldic poets.[19] I have tried in vain for years to get hold of one, even in Iceland and Scandinavia, in vain. I am at the moment "flummoxed" for lack of it. Could you possibly lend it me for this term, under due safeguards? I would not let it out of my study. Of course if you really had two copies the thought of attempting to induce you to a sale would cross my mind, though I don't suppose I could afford it.

Yrs sincerely,
J R R Tolkien

PS. Yet another point as Piers might say.[20] What shall I say to Coolidge Otis Chapman (enclosed)?[21] I have said "no press will look at you sans funds in full", but I promised to make further enquiries.

JRRT

In October 1931, Press Secretary R. W. Chapman wrote to George Gordon: "I am investigating derelicts and especially such as seem worth salvage. What about Clarendon English Series Chaucer?" The enquiry reached Tolkien, who replied to Chapman.

[6]
October 25, 1932
My dear Chapman,

---

[18] Tolkien would be occupied with Oxford University's Pass Moderations as well as acting as an external examiner for four other universities. Pass Mods was a first public examination for undergraduates in certain subjects. Those studying English were examined in Latin, Greek and, since 1930 (thanks to a reform campaign led by Tolkien) Old English.

[19] Tolkien went on to use Jónsson's four-volume *Den Norsk-Islandske Skjaldedigtning* in his article "Sigelwara Land," *Medium Aevum* 3 (1934), 95-111 at p. 110.

[20] Tolkien knew William Langland's fourteenth-century *Piers Plowman* well, cited the work often, but never taught or published on it despite its Worcestershire dialect, the language of his mother's homeland, probably because of its heavy Christian (Catholic) contents; see *TLC* 118.

[21] Coolidge Otis Chapman was perhaps trying to find a publisher for *An Index of Names in Pearl, Purity, Patience, and Gawain*, eventually issued by Cornell University Press in 1951.

Chaucer – yes: this must be finished or I shall lose for ever the good will of the Clarendon Press. I am sorry to be your black sheep. You offered me only mechanical assistance. Would this include the typing out of the rather bad and cut-about MS of the notes that are in existence? It would assist me to make a conclusion. The glossary is in existence and corrected, but needs collating with notes. These are written except for the selections from the Prologue and the Monk's Tale, but are nearly all vastly too long, without I fear being new or original.

If I could send in the notes after drastic cuts and have the bits back again typed fairly quickly I think I could soon complete the job, in spite of the burdens of the day and the night.

As soon as this is done I will hearken unto your plea for books. I have in the intervals (and in the process of teaching) learned a good deal in the past few years, and feel that the time is approaching when I not only ought to write out of deference to custom and what is expected of professors, but might even do so with some utility.

But I am (a) a pettifogging scholar rejoicing in the minute and the intricate, and such games as textual criticism; or else (b) which does not concern you, a writer in modern English, a verse-writer and a metrist. I doubt whether I have anything in my head that could be classed as a "masterly treatment of a good theme".

I have (in size already a large volume) a work on Hengest and Finn but that will require a good deal of work to make printable, and is in any case intricate and special.[22] The best thing would be I think the prose version of *Beowulf*, to begin on.[23] It would certainly sell – and from the worst motives. But to justify it (versions of *Beowulf* have never yet performed any good function) it should be preceded by some introductory matters – *not* of the sort given in an edition, but on the diction of O.E. verse, its metre, and so on. Notes should be very few or limited to places which are really hard, and corrupt and divergently treated in the editions. All this stuff is in existence as lectures or papers to societies, & if only I could free my mind & conscience of the Chaucerian incubus might soon be sufficiently polished up to hand over.

I suppose you have not contemplated an actual cheap edition of *Beowulf* aimed at the non-specialist who by the new syllabus now has to read the whole of this poem.

---

[22] See SH 2:433–37 on his long engagements with *Finn and Hengest: The Fragment and the Episode*.
[23] He had written to Sisam about his prose rendering of *Beowulf* completed in April 1926 (SH 1:145); it would be nearly nine decades before the world saw his *Beowulf: A Translation and Commentary*, ed. Christopher Tolkien (Boston and New York: Houghton Mifflin, 2014).

Both *Elene* and *Exodus* will remain set books in the English School. They both need editing. I have commentaries to both.

I should like very much after *Beowulf* to tackle a proper edition of O.E. *Exodus*. The Routledge edn. of MS Junius 11 by Knapp is thoroughly bad, and virtually negligible for our students, though admittedly better than nothing. Sedgefield is of course merely laughable (he does a large chunk of *Exodus* in his miserable Anglo-Saxon verse-book).[24]

"Chaucer" remains, however, as yet unfinished. I will try to see that it does not linger on into another year.

Thank you for your letter. Excuse my delay in answering.

Yrs sincerely,

J. R. R. Tolkien

Chapman wrote back sympathetically: "*Do* get Chaucer off your mind. I know myself that remorse of that kind prevents one from working at anything else, though it does not always lead to constructive repentance. We can help you with typing, if that will help." Tolkien next wrote to Sisam before Christmas 1932 with reference to his recent article "Sigelwara Land".

[7]

December 18, 1932

My dear Sisam,

Thank you very much. Very good of you to bother. I hope the article – now grown to a serial which will extend through 3 numbers of *Medium Ævum* – will not seem to you, and others, a deal of absurd fuss about nothing in particular. I shall not reach the actual *Exodus* passage until the last instalment.[25] Before then I must, if possible, find out the exact spellings of the Paris Psalter Latin, ps. lxxiii 14, 15. The facsimile, apart from internal evidence, shows Thorpe has normalised.[26]

I am also just putting last touches to the "Reeve's Tale" paper you saw, for Phil. Soc. Trans.[27] Then for the disastrous "Chaucer". Nichol Smith is very

---

[24] G. P. Krapp, ed., *The Junius Manuscript* (London: Routledge, 1931), and W. J. Sedgefield, ed., *An Anglo-Saxon Verse-Book* (Manchester: University of Manchester Press, 1928).

[25] Tolkien refers to "Sigelwara Land" in *Medium Aevum* 1 (1932), 183–196, and 3 (1934), 95–111, but he never published the promised third "last instalment" with the key discussion of *Exodus*. This work nonetheless provided his imagination with background for the Balrog; see Drout, "Tolkien's Medieval Scholarship," 117–18.

[26] Tolkien references Benjamin Thorpe, ed., *Libri Psalmorum Versio Antiqua* (Oxford: 1835).

[27] Tolkien had been revising his 1931 lecture "Chaucer's Use of Dialects" for publication as "Chaucer as a Philologist: *The Reeve's Tale*", *Transactions of the Philological Society* (1934), 1–70.

kindly helping me to curtail my overwhelming mass of notes, so that I may get that burden off soon, & so perhaps return to the good books of the Press. *Beowulf* (translation) shall be the next. But life is short & so is the day. I am obliged to examine Oxford (complete new syllabus), Manchester & Reading, for the meeting of ends, this coming year; and probably P. Mods at the end it.[28] Also there are lectures & B. Litts. and goodness knows what. But you are familiar with the tale.

If I can squeeze in a free time from the demands of children and work this vac, I should like to ascend the heights & visit you once again. In any case, perhaps, I may visit you in your ἀνωγέων at the Press[29] – you can always shunt me off, unoffended, if you are too busy.

Yrs sincerely,
J. R. R. Tolkien

Fourteen years later in May 1946 we find Sisam taking stock at OUP as Oxford and the nation emerged from the war years, reflecting ruefully about miscalculations regarding contents of the Clarendon Chaucer: "I should like to leave the Clarendon English Chaucer to lie fallow for a long time: Tolkien is still a Professor. There is too much early poems, and too little Canterbury Tales."

After Sisam's retirement to the Isles of Scilly, Dan Davin took over responsibility for the Clarendon Chaucer at OUP. Though quite a publishing powerhouse, he was still not able to budge Tolkien on his Chaucer edition. After much coaxing and suggesting a new co-editor to replace George Gordon, who had died of cancer in 1942, he finally wrote to Tolkien on 30 May 1951 about retrieving his editorial papers: "When we met last week I suggested that I should let you know when I was proposing to send a car to pick up your C.E.S. Chaucer material." This elicited Tolkien's final grumpy letter (fig. 4), nonetheless valuable for revealing exactly how much material he had to return. The square brackets are his.

[8]

June 8, 1951

Dear Davin,

I sent back today all that might prove useful of *my* material (I know nothing of G. S. Gordon's, which indeed I never saw) for the "Clarendon Chaucer".

---

[28] For Pass Moderations, see footnote 18 above.
[29] Chapman inserted a pedantic jest to Sisam about placement of the accent – "JRRT ought to know that it is ἀνώγεων!" – for the "upper room" where his OUP office was located.

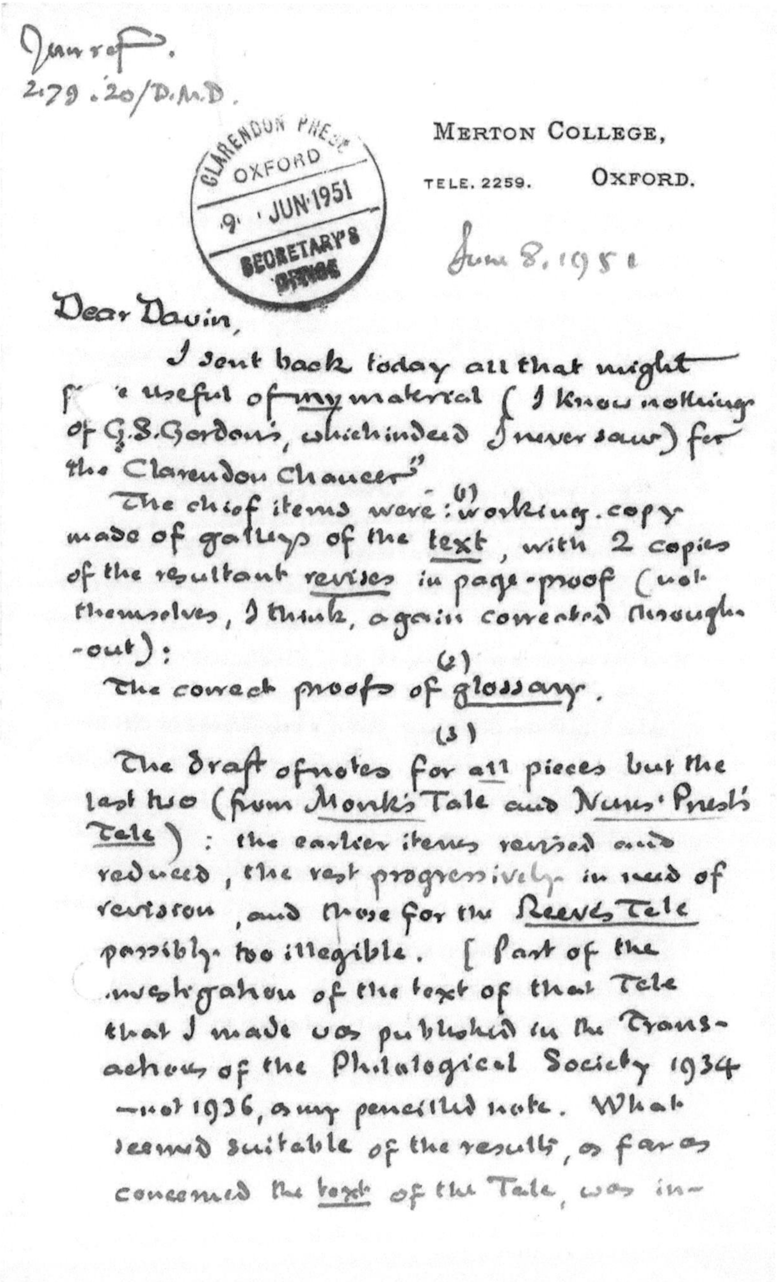

Jun ref.
279.20/D.M.D.

[stamp: CLARENDON PRESS OXFORD 9 JUN 1951 SECRETARY'S OFFICE]

MERTON COLLEGE,

TELE. 2259.   OXFORD.

June 8, 1951

Dear Davin,

I sent back today all that might be useful of my material (I know nothing of G.S.Gordon's, which indeed I never saw) for the Clarendon Chaucer.

The chief items were: (1) working copy made of galleys of the text, with 2 copies of the resultant revises in page-proof (not themselves, I think, again corrected throughout):

(2) The correct proofs of glossary.

(3) The draft of notes for all pieces but the last two (from Monk's Tale and Nuns' Priest's Tale): the earlier items revised and reduced, the rest progressively in need of revision, and those for the Reeve's Tale possibly too illegible. [Part of the investigation of the text of that Tale that I made was published in the Transactions of the Philological Society 1934 — not 1936, as my pencilled note. What seemed suitable of the results, so far as concerned the text of the Tale, was in-

Fig. 4 Letter of 8 June, 1951 to Dan Davin (Oxford University Press Archives).

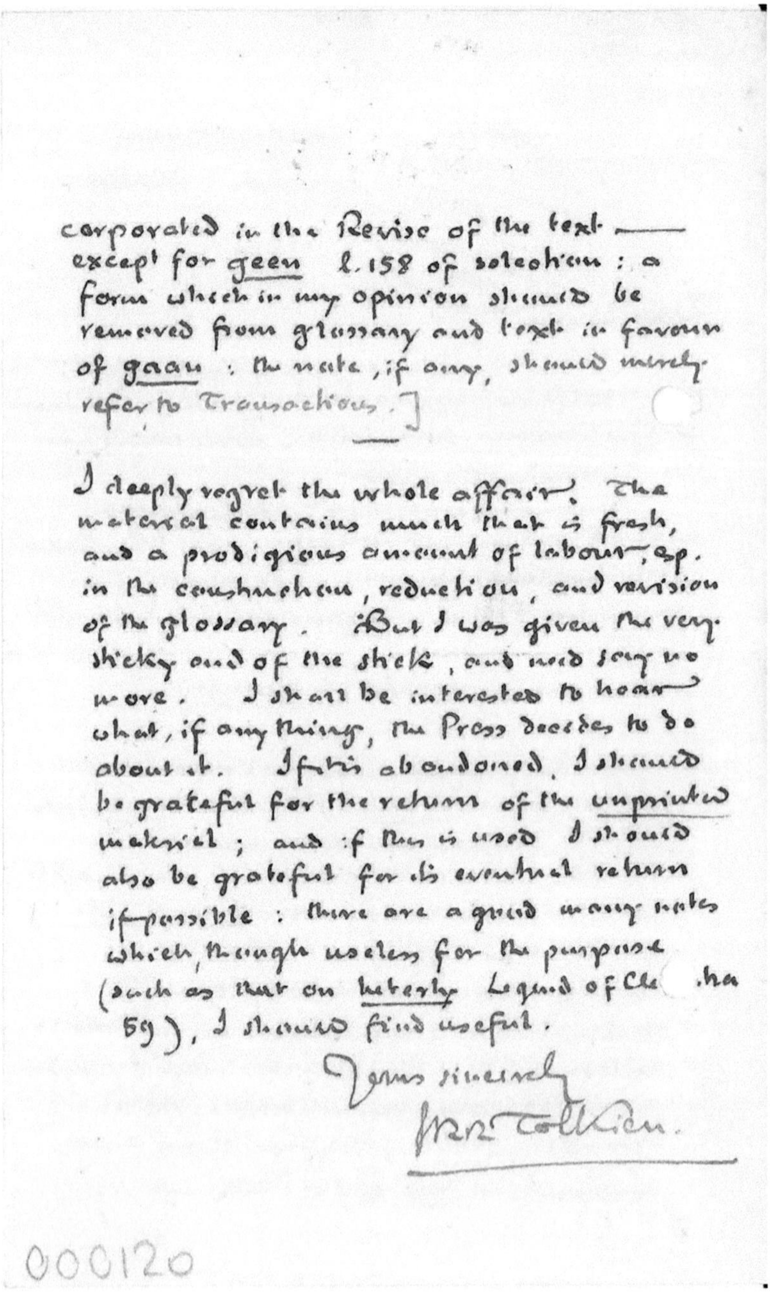

corporated in the Revise of the text — except for geen l.158 of soleohien: a form which in my opinion should be removed from glossary and text in favour of gaan: the note, if any, should merely refer to Transactions.]

I deeply regret the whole affair. The material contains much that is fresh, and a prodigious amount of labour, esp. in the construction, reduction, and revision of the glossary. But I was given the very sticky end of the stick, and need say no more. I shall be interested to hear what, if anything, the Press decides to do about it. If this is abandoned, I should be grateful for the return of the unprinted material; and if this is used I should also be grateful for its eventual return if possible: there are a great many notes which, though useless for the purpose (such as that on hetherly Legend of Cle..ha 59), I should find useful.

Yours sincerely
JRR Tolkien.

Fig. 4 *Continued.*

The chief items were:

(1) working copy made of galleys of the *text*, with 2 copies of the resultant *revises* in page-proof (not themselves, I think, again corrected throughout):

(2) The correct proofs of *glossary*.

(3) The draft of notes for *all* pieces but the last two (from *Monk's Tale* and *Nuns' Priest's Tale*): the earlier items revised and reduced, the rest progressively in need of revision, and those for the *Reeves Tale* possibly too illegible. [Part of the investigation of the text of that Tale that I made was published in the Transactions of the Philological Society 1934 – not 1936, as my pencilled note. What seemed suitable of the results, as far as concerned the *text* of the Tale, was incorporated in the Revise of the text – except for *geen* l. 158 of selection: a form which in my opinion should be removed from glossary and text in favour of *gaan*: the note, if any should merely refer to Transactions.]

I deeply regret the whole affair. The material contains much that is fresh, and a prodigious amount of labour, esp. in the construction, reduction, and revision of the glossary. But I was given the very sticky end of the stick, and need say no more. I shall be interested to hear what, if anything, the Press decides to do about it. If it is abandoned, I should be grateful for the return of the *unprinted* material; and if this is used I should also be grateful for its eventual return if possible: there are a good many notes which, though useless for the purpose (such as that on *heterly* Legend of Cleopatra 59), I should find useful.

Yours sincerely
J. R. R. Tolkien.

"Many thanks for the return of the Chaucer material," Davin replied graciously; "if at any time you would like to have it for consultation we should of course be glad to send it to you." After searching unsuccessfully for a younger medievalist such as John Burrow who might complete the edition – and realizing finally how out of date it had become since 1922 – Davin dropped the project and closed the file in 1960.

Tolkien Editing Skeat's Chaucer

Since Kenneth Sisam had the time-saving idea to pay Skeat's daughter for reprinting from his *Works of Geoffrey Chaucer*, Tolkien's task as an editor did not require him to start anew from the manuscripts, though he steadily consulted Skeat's own textual notes for readings which he felt more likely to be authentic. The lyrics and dream visions were more troublesome because based on later, less reliable manuscripts, whereas selections from the *Canterbury Tales* seemed less problematic because based on the Ellesmere copy. When he found lines that made poor sense or were defective metrically, however, Tolkien was willing to engage in "conjectural emendation" to repair them. He found the selections from *Boece* especially worrying since Skeat had worked from a poor manuscript, and therefore, to restore the author's original renderings, he did the sensible thing and compared Chaucer's translation with the original Latin of Boethius's *De Consolatione Philosophiae*. Sisam was willing to make some (but not all) changes in the edition's verse selections, but he refused to accept Tolkien's alterations of the prose *Boece* because they would have required retypesetting whole pages. As the edited text proceeded through "revises" or corrected galleys, Tolkien continued doggedly to argue in favour of some changes which Sisam had already disallowed. We find him still making a last-ditch argument even in his 1951 letter to Dan Davin, objecting to the word *geen* in the final revise of the *Reeve's Tale* – "a form which in my opinion should be removed from glossary and text in favour of *gaan*".

The following pages provide a condensed overview of Tolkien's efforts as an editor. He corrected 9 misprints, made some 32 emendations (many of them "indifferent" rather than "substantive"), altered punctuation 477 times, and changed 129 spellings. As Michael Drout has pointed out, "he was far, far more attentive to spellings than many scholars of Middle English."[30]

Since there had been no printed table of contents, Tolkien drafted one on the title page (fig. 5). This was later transferred to the headnote of his glossary, with abbreviations and Roman numeral references later used throughout (*TLC* 283–84):

Order of pieces assumed in numbering in glossary

    I. The Romaunt of the Rose (R).
    II. The Compleynte unto Pite.
    III. The Book of the Duchesse (extracts).
    IV. The Parlement of Foules (PF).
    V. The Former Age.
    VI. Merciles Beaute.

[30] "Tolkien's Medieval Scholarship," 117, also 129.

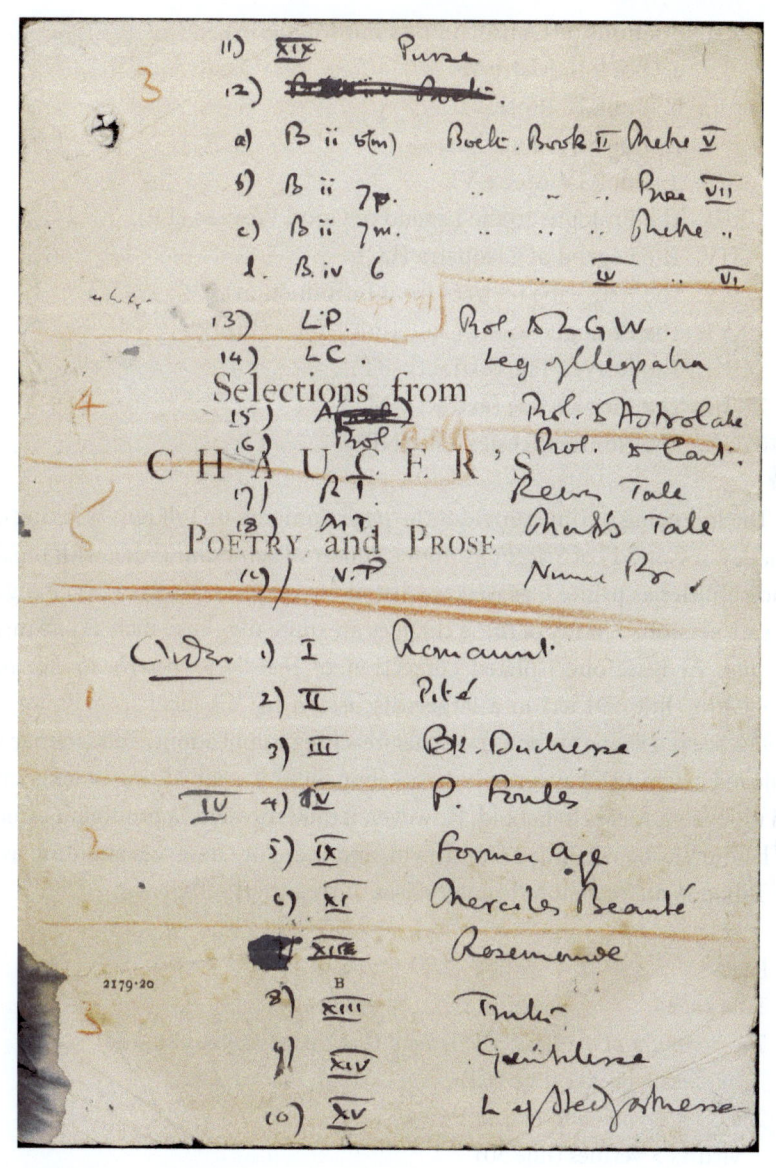

Fig. 5 Title page and Tolkien's handwritten table of contents for *Selections from Chaucer's Poetry and Prose* (Bodleian MS Tolkien A 39/1, fol. 1).

    VII. To Rosemounde.
   VIII. Truth.
     IX. Gentilesse.
      X. Lak of Stedfastnesse.
     XI. Compleint to his Empty Purse.

XII. Boethius de Consolatione Philosophie.
   a. Book II, Metre V.
   b. Book II, Prose VII.
   c. Book II, Metre VII.
   d. Book IV, Metre VI.
XIII. The Prologue to the Legend of Good Women (LP).
XIV. The Legend of Cleopatra (LC).
XV. The Astrolabe (extract from introduction).
XVI. The Prologue to the Canterbury Tales (Prol).
XVII. The Reeve's Tale (extract) (RT).
XVIII. The Monk's Tale (extract) (MT).
XIX. The Nonne Preestes Tale (NP).

The following outline provides the page numbers in Tolkien's working copy (Galley 1, Copy 1) of *Selections from Chaucer's Poetry and Prose*, with the titles and subtitles as printed, as well as a list of many (but not all) of his changes to Skeat's version.[31] Many of these changes are quite niggling, such as *pité* instead of *pite*. At least one isolated correction of *theerly* to *heterly* in *Legend of Cleopatra* (line 59) led to a larger discussion in "Chaucer as a Philologist" (1934, see p. 155 in this book) with far-reaching implications. Tolkien may have enjoyed catching Chaucer in his workshop, but his own editing of texts can be an unlovely process to behold. However, it did represent "a prodigious amount of labour", as he reminded Dan Davin, and therefore deserves attention as one of Tolkien's major scholarly enterprises during the 1920s.

Pages:	
Title page	1
The Romaunt of the Rose: The Dream (Fragment A: lines 21–134)	2
busshes > buskes (line 102)	
The Compleynte unto Pite	7
virtues > vertues (line 50)	
omit [ne] (line 105)	
The Book of the Duchess: The Proem: Of Seys and Alcyone	11
made > make (line 93)	
But good swete herte [look] that ye	
> But swete herte, loke ye (line 206)	

---

[31] Bodleian MS Tolkien A 39/1, fols. 1–120.

The Dream of the Hunt (lines 291–386)	16
ageyn > ayen (line 367)	
The Lover's Portrait of his Lady (lines 817–913)	19
The Parlement of Foules: The Proem	22
The Story	26
mighten > mighte (line 318)	
this > thilk (line 445)	
hath served > served hath (line 476)	
goddesse > quene (line 672)	
The Former Age	45
gniden > gnodded (line 11)	
fantasye > fantasẏe (line 51)	
envye > envé (line 53)	
Merciles Beaute: A Triple Roundel	46
I. *Captivity*	
II. *Rejection*	47
ne availeth > n'availeth (line 15)	
III. *Escape*	
To Rosemounde: A Balade	48
Truth	49
vache > Vache (line 22)[32]	
Gentilesse: Moral Balade of Chaucer	50
Lak of Stedfastnesse: Balade	
Compleint to his Empty Purse	52
Boethius, *De Consolatione Philosophie*	
Book II, Metre V: *Felix nimium prior etas*	53
Book II, Prose VII (lines 31–135)	54
for defaute of unusage and entreocomuninge	
> for defaute and usage of entreocomuninge (line 8)	
Book II, Metre VII: *Quicunque solam mente praecipiti petit*	55
Book IV, Metre VI: *Si uis celsi iura tonantis*	56
The Legend of Good Women: Text A (Earlier Version)	58
The prologe of.ix. goode Wimmen	59
hit > it (line 49)	
dayesye > dayësye (line 55)	

---

[32] Edith Rickert, "Thou Vache," *Modern Philology* 11 (1913–14), 209–26, persuaded Tolkien this referred to Sir Philip de la Vache. He nonetheless included **vache** in his Glossary as "*n.* cow (as beast with earthward gaze)".

>   Somme songen [layes] on the braunches clere / Of love and [May] that Ioye hit was to here >
>   And somme songen on the braunches clere / Of love, and layes that joye hit was to here (lines 127–28)
>   gonnen > gunne (line 134)
>   made > had mad (line 189)
>   ne is > nis (line 326)
>   maked > y-maked (line 403)
>   And > I (line 440)
>   grete > gret (line 499)

The Legend of Cleopatra: Incipit Legenda Cleopatrie, Martiris, Egipti regine   73
>   theerly > heterly (line 59)
>   Unreprováble > Unrépováble (line 112)
>   omit *so* (line 122)

The Astrolabe (lines 1–73)   77

The Canterbury Tales: The Prologue   79
>   Lines 1–100 (Beginning, Knight, Squire)
>   Lines 120–62 (Prioress)
>   Lines 165–207 (Monk)
>   Lines 285–308 (Clerk)
>   Lines 388–410 (Shipman)
>   Lines 445–528 (Wife of Bath and Parson)
>   Lines 545–566 (Miller)
>   Lines 587–622 (The Reeve)
>   Lines 715–858 (Plan of the Tales &c)
>   sette us > sette he us (line 748)

The Reeve's Tale: (A) lines 3921–4148   94
>   Simkin > Simekin (line 21)
>   boës > bos (line 107)
>   in faith > y faith (line 124)
>   drive > driven (line 190)
>   stole > stolen (line 191)

The Monk's Tale: De Hugelino, Comite de Pize (lines 3597–3652)   100

The Nonne Preestes Tale (lines 4011–4636)   102
>   Cometh > Comth (line 107)

The Glossary (1925)

After struggles to shorten it, Tolkien's glossary reached the required scope and was typeset in galley long sheets stamped in batches when leaving the Press in 1925. Tolkien's brief introduction explaining such matters as spelling variations was printed as Appendix II of *Tolkien's Lost Chaucer* (283–84) and is not repeated here. The headnote's second paragraph drew attention to the abbreviation *n.* denoting words "where meaning or form is uncommon or important" and referring readers to the notes. Removing further discussion to his annotations was one tactic for shortening the glossary. Clearly a gap developed between his plans and their execution, however, since many *n.* references point to endnotes not actually written in the draft of the section. Another tactic was to eliminate the bracketed etymologies such as those that he had provided in his glossary to Sisam's *Fourteenth Century Verse and Prose* and in his own *Sir Gawain* edition.

Space precludes presenting our complete transcription of the glossary, but we reproduce a page from Tolkien's galleys (fig. 6) and transcribe its entries of the S and the W words (while omitting other entries in between). This will demonstrate Tolkien's success at conciseness while providing evidence of the Northern dialect words which so much interested him. We then present his corresponding annotations, where they exist. The lengths of his discussions of words like *erne* and *overthwert*, to take only two examples, show how he reduced his glossary by transferring commentaries to his ever-growing body of notes.

These samplings from the glossary for entries from *suster* to *swow* and again from *waat* to *weilaway* come from a galley sheet press-stamped 8 May 1925 (fig. 6):

suster, *n.* sister.
swa, so, RT 110, 120. *Northern.*
swain, *n.* servant.
swerd, *n.* sword.
swere, *v.* swear; *I dar s.*,
   I declare.
swete, *adj.* sweet; *as sb.* III 832;
swetter, *compar.* R 768.
swety, *adj.* sweaty, toilsome.
sweven, swevening, *n.* dream.

swich, *adj.* such; *lo! s. hit is,*
   see what it is, PF 570.
swink, *n.* and **swinke,** *v.* toil.
swithe, *adv.* quickly; *as s.,* at once.
swommen, *pa. t. pl.* swam, teemed.
swo(o)r, *p. a. t. of* Swere; **swore,** *pp.*
swote, *adj.* sweet, lovely.
swoune, *v.* swoon.
swow, swogh, *n.* sough, noise (as of
   wind); swoon; access of grief.

* * *

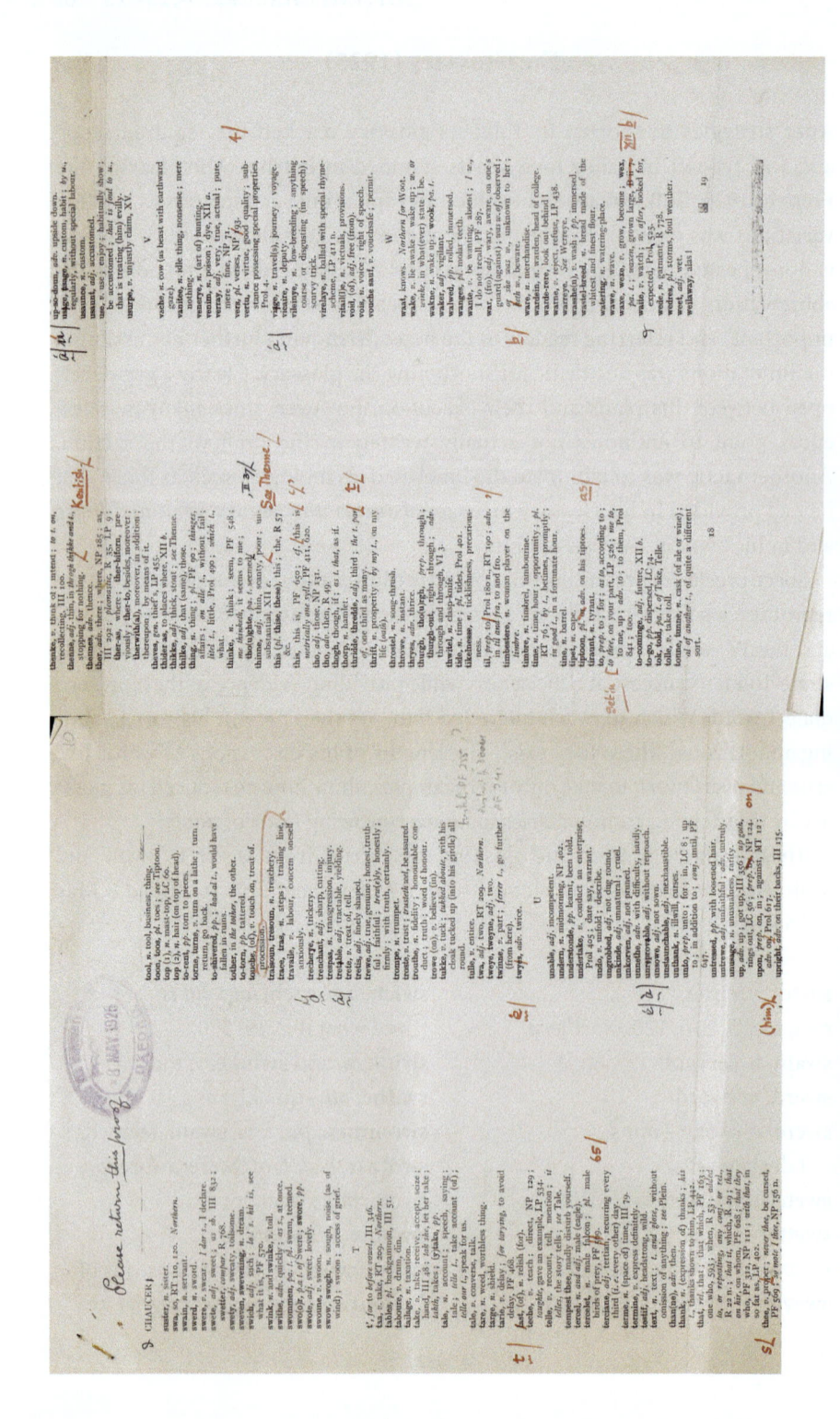

Fig. 6 Galley long-sheet from Clarendon Chaucer's Glossary (Bodleian MS Tolkien A 39/3, fol. 10).

W

waat, knows. *Northern for* Woot.
wake, *v.* lie awake; wake up; *w. or winke*, in what(ever) state I be.
wakne, *n.* wake up; **wook**, *pa. t.*
waker, *adj.* vigilant.
walwed, *pp.* rolled, immersed.
wanges, *pl.* molar teeth.
wante, *v.* be wanting, absent; *I w.*, I do not recall, PF 287.
war, (fro), *adj.* wary, aware, on one's guard (against); *was w. of*, observed; *or she was w.*, unknown to her; *beth w.*, beware.
ware, *n.* merchandise.
wardein, *n.* warden, head of college.
ward-rere, look out behind!

warne, *v.* reject, refuse, LP 438.
warreye. *See* Werreye.
wasshe(n), *v.* wash; *pp.* immersed.
wastel-breed, *n.* bread made of the whitest and finest flour.
watering, *n.* watering-place.
wawe, *n.* wave.
waxe, wexe, *v.* grow, become; **wex**, *pa. t.*; **waxen**, grown large, XII *b*.
waite, *v.* watch; *w. after*, looked for, expected, Prol 525.
wede, *n.* garment, R 778.
wedres, *pl.* storms, foul weather.
weet, *adj.* wet.
weilaway, alas!

Below we list (1) entries from the glossary marked *n.* for *envye, erme, gattoothed, moot, overthwert, spiced, that,* and *virelaye*; (2) the texts cited with the relevant lines from Skeat's Chaucer; and (3) Tolkien's later annotations in Bodleian MS Tolkien A 39/2/1 with folio numbers in brackets:

énvye, *v.* vie (with one another), III 173 n.
Book of the Duchess: "To *envye*, who might slepe best"
to envye: "to vie with one another". The verb, as the modern reduction "vie" still shows, was normally accented *envýe*. *To* is here to be slurred or else to be pronounced merely as *t'*. Compare *t'assaye* l. 346. *envýe* is trisyllabic. [fol. 17]

erme, *v.* grieve, mourn, III 80 n.
Book of the Duchess: "Anon her herte gan to *erme*"
erme. The insertion of the missing passage (ll. 81–96: see introductory note) in MS Tanner and Thynne's edition, our only authorities, give *bigan to yerne*. The emendation (made by Skeat and ten Brink) is certain. Compare the *Pardoner's Prologue* (C.T. C 312) where *thou doost my herte to erme* rhymes, as here, with *terme*. *erme* was a rare word, already obsolescent in the fourteenth century (O.E. *erman* related to *earm*, wretched). The confusion with *yerne* (yearn) was not only easy as an error of copying, but probably also occurred

in the spoken language; *erme* became *erne, yerne* and survives only in the sense of grieving that this blending has imparted to our *yearn*. [fol. 15]

gat-tothed, *adj.* gap-toothed, with teeth set far apart, Prol 468 n.
General Prologue – "*Gat-tothed* was she, soothly for to seye"
gat-tothed: This line appears to be a comment on 467 and to refer to some popular piece of folklore that people with teeth set far apart were destined to travel. Skeat gives evidence, to which the present emendator's own memory could be added, of the survival of this notion down to the present time. [fol. 122v]

moot, *pl.* notes on horn, III 376 n.
Book of the Duchess – "With a gret horne blew three *moot*"
moot: this was a single long note. The fourteenth-century horn had only one note, but various calls were made by combining notes of different lengths, a sort of morse-code. The *moot* was the longest note. *Three moot* (the word was usually unchanged in the plural) was the correct conventional call at the uncoupling. Compare *Sir Gawain*, 1140 f., *vnclosed the kenel dore and calde hem* (their hounds) *theroute, blwe bygly in bugles thre bare mote*. Three long Gs is still used on the military bugle as a similar sort of signal.[33] [fols. 20–21]

overthwert, *adv.* at right angles; challenging, III 863 n.
Book of the Duchess – "Therto hir look nas not a-syde / Ne *overthwert*, but beset so wel"
overthwert: this is usually translated "askance" here, but this sense is given by *asyde*. The lady's chief merit is her *mesure* (881), she steered the golden middle course between all extremes. *overthwert* is then the exact opposite of *asyde*, and refers to a bold and challenging stare straight in the eye. The original sense of the word and its other form *thwertover* is "at right angles" the opposite of *endelong* (cf. the Knight's Tale 1133, and it is especially used of the arms of a cross; it thus got the sense of going clean contrary to any one, right across one's path, and is used figuratively of flat contradiction or the "lie direct" (*þweartouer leasinge* in the Ancren Riwle). In the Romance of the Rose 292 f. *for she (Envy) ne loked but awry, or overthwart, al baggingly* there is certainly no question of Envy looking anything but askance, but this is due to

---

[33] *TLC* 123–4 discusses the author's wartime training in Morse code as well as his brother's experience as a bugler. Here is how Bilbo got people's attention at his birthday feast: "Seizing a horn from a youngster near by, he blew three loud hoots" (*FR* I/1).

bad translation of *ele ne regardast noient fors de travers en borgnoiant*. Two translations, as it were, are offered of *de travers* of which only *awry* is in this case right, though in some cases *overthwert* would be good enough. [fol. 22]

spiced, *pp.* Prol 526 n.
General Prologue: the Parson: – "Ne maked him a *spyced* conscience"
spyced: The same expression occurs in the Wife of Bath's Prol. 435 *a sweet ~ conscience*, where it seems to mean a "scrupulous conscience". The phrase is probably due to French *e(s)pice* in sense (now obsolete) "court-fees", payable to judges. Once paid the judge was scrupulous being inaccessible to anything but large bribes, as unpaid he would have been unfavourable to defaulters. The conjunction of line 526 with 525 suggests that here the sense is not so much "scrupulous" and nearer to the original use – a conscience dependent on circumstances. The Parson was not influenced in his dealings by "spice"; he treated people according to the merits of the case, irrespective of the measure of financial reverence they showed to him. [fol. 125v]

that, *rel.* that; that which, PF 163; one who, 593; when, R 53; *added to, or repeating, any conj. or rel.*, R 22 n.; *that it*, which, R 29; *that on hir*, on whom, PF 628; *that they* who, PF 312, NP 111; *with that*, in so far as, LP 402.
Romaunt: "Whan *that* Love taketh his corage" (22)
whan that: *that* may be added to all conjunctions, or relative words (*which, wher, whom*, R 43), without change of sense; thus it is not to be translated in R 86 or 792, or LP 25 (*if that*). Note also *what maner thing that* = "whatever", II 108; *wherthrough that*, "by means of which", III 120; *theras that*, "where", PF 185. [fol. 7]

virelaye, *n.* ballad with special rhyme-scheme, LP 411 n.
Prologue to the *Legend of Good Women* – "That highten Balades, Roundels, Virelayes"
balades: poems of three stanzas, each ending with the same line (the refrain), to which usually was added a fourth stanza or envoy; see VII–XI, and 203ff. *roundels*: see PF 675 note, and VI. *virelayes*: an example of this metrical form can be seen in lines 256–271, and 317–332 of Chaucer's poem *Anelida and Arcite*. There the rhyme-scheme is *aaabaaab*, after which comes the essential *vire* or "turn," reversing the scheme to *bbbabbba*. Lines 4, 8, 12, 16 are longer than the others. But greater intricacies were also practised. Hoccleve, possibly imitating the last virelayes of Chaucer rather than the French masters direct, is credited with several intricate examples (see his

poems in the Early English Text Soc.). It seems certain that a great many "minor poems" of this sort written by Chaucer are now lost altogether. [fols. 63–64]

The Notes (1928)

Tolkien probably began drafting the notes soon after correcting his glossary's last set of galleys, stamped when leaving OUP on 8 May 1925. In his letter of 23 October 1924, Kenneth Sisam had been prodding him to complete the annotations by the following January, but he was still grinding away at it in 1928 when he sent the bundle to his co-editor George Gordon with an appeal for help in abbreviating his wildly excessive commentary. Certainly Tolkien was in his element; C. S. Lewis described him as "an inspired speaker of footnotes".[34] Yet it is hard to imagine what Tolkien was thinking as he drafted these 200 pages – without getting anywhere near the *Nun's Priest's Tale*, their final selection – after Sisam and Gordon had told him in January 1925 that the modest textbook was allowed only twenty pages of endnotes. It is probably an early example of the obsessive behaviour that George Sayer reported when Tolkien set about trimming "two square yards" of his back garden and not stopping until he had done it to perfection. Here years earlier, Tolkien's pleas for help for saving him from his own extravagances were answered when he reported in his letter of 18 December 1932 (see letter 7, p. 51 above) that "Nichol Smith is very kindly helping me to curtail my overwhelming mass of notes". Our own survey of the cuts proposed in brackets, however, shows that if all of them had been made, the notes would not have been reduced even by half, thus still greatly exceeding the maximum number of pages allowed (*TLC* 31–32).

There is neither space nor need to reproduce all of Tolkien's Chaucer commentary here. We have retained his headnotes for the separate pieces while ignoring his many pedestrian remarks on individual words. We resisted, for example, including his three-page note on *Aprille* from the opening line of the *Canterbury Tales* because it represents an instance of his impulse for overdoing things. We have kept a few longer entries, though, particularly for the Prioress. One especially wayward foray is his four pages on Chaucer's indebtedness to the native Alliterative tradition of English poetry which he inserted into his commentary on the *Legend of Cleopatra*. We have included this

---

[34] Quoted by Sayer, "Recollections", 21.

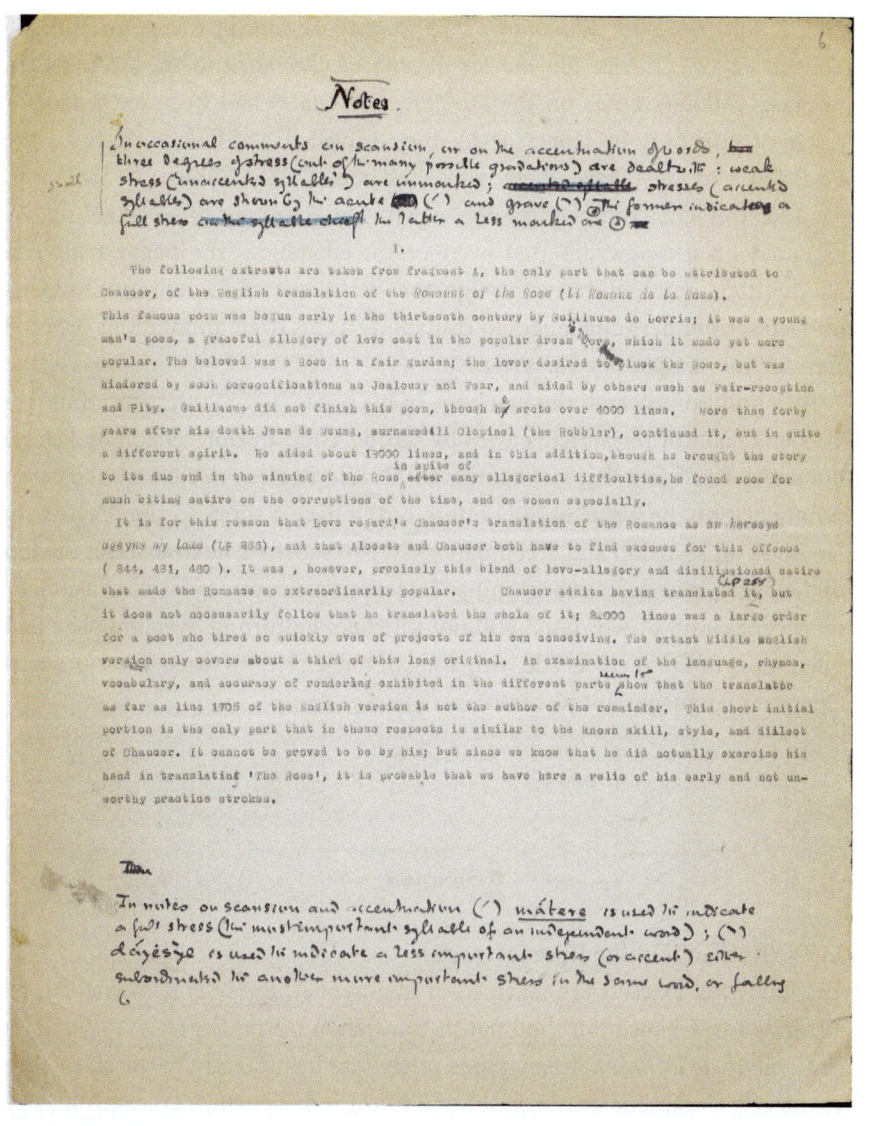

Fig. 7 Typewritten commentary on Chaucer's *Romaunt of the Rose* (Bodleian MS Tolkien A 39/2/1, fol. 6).

digression as a separate "excursus" at the end, though trimmed of Tolkien's full list of sixty-one alliterative formulas gleaned from his own *Selections*. Throughout the commentary, where Tolkien only provided line numbers, we provide the lines themselves in square brackets.

After the main body of notes was discovered in OUP's archives in 2013, they were transferred to the Bodleian Library with shelf marks MS Tolkien A

39/2/1, fols. 6–71 for *Romaunt of the Rose* to *Legend of Cleopatra* and MS Tolkien A 39/2/2, fols. 72–143 for *Legend of Cleopatra* to the *Reeve's Tale*. Because Tolkien's notes on the *Parlement of Foules* had been extracted for teaching purposes in Hilary 1948, they travelled a different route to the Bodleian and now have their own shelf mark, MS Tolkien A 38/2, fols. 96–126. Tolkien's commentary begins with the *Romaunt of the Rose* (fig. 7), executed on a typewriter that even produced italics. The pages switch to handwritten notes midway through the *Parlement of Foules*, and Tolkien's hurried script offers challenges to readability as his draft annotations proceed through the *Canterbury Tales* (fig. 8).

As a point of interest, the first page of his notes (fig. 7) offers in miniature Tolkien's habit of revising his work by setting aside a prior version and starting anew. Realizing that newcomers to Middle English needed guidance on pronunciation, he wrote at the bottom of the page a short section beginning "In notes on scansion and accentuation…" Not satisfied, he inserted at the top of the page a new section beginning "In occasional comments on scansion, or on accentuation of words…" Still not satisfied, he turned over the page and filled most of the reverse side with a much longer handwritten description of Chaucer's language (not pictured).

* * *

Notes

I. The Romaunt of the Rose (extracts)

The following extracts are taken from fragment A, the only part that can be attributed to Chaucer, of the English translation of the *Romaunt of the Rose* (*li Romanz de la Rose*). This famous poem was begun early in the thirteenth century by Guillaume de Lorris; it was a young man's poem, a graceful allegory of love cast in the popular dream form, which it made yet more popular. The beloved was a Rose in a fair garden;[35] the lover desired to pluck the Rose, but was hindered by such personifications as Jealousy and Fear and aided by others such as Fair-reception and Pity. Guillaume did not finish this poem, though he wrote over 4,000 lines. More than forty years after his death, Jean de Meung, surnamed *li Clopinel* ("the Hobbler"), continued it, but in quite a

---

[35] When Tolkien conceived the object of Sam Gamgee's own love, he chose the same flower's name – Rose Cotton.

different spirit.[36] He added 18,000 lines, and in this addition, though he brought the story to its due end in the winning of the Rose in spite of many allegorical difficulties, he found room for much biting satire on the corruptions of the time, and on women especially.

It is for this reason that Love regards Chaucer's translation of the *Romance* as "an heresye ageyns my law" (*Legend* Prologue 255), and that Alceste and Chaucer both have to find excuses for this offence (344, 431, 460). It was, however, precisely this blend of love-allegory and disillusioned satire that made the *Romance* so extraordinarily popular.

Chaucer admits having translated it (*Legend* Prologue 255), but it does not necessarily follow that he translated the whole of it; 22,000 lines was a large order for a poet who tired so quickly even of projects of his own conceiving. The extant Middle English version only covers about a third of this long original. An examination of the language, rhymes, vocabulary, and accuracy of rendering exhibited in the different parts seems to show that the translator as far as line 1,705 of the English version is not the author of the remainder. This short initial portion is the only part that in these respects is similar to the known skill, style, and dialect of Chaucer. It cannot be proved to be by him; but since we know that he did actually exercise his hand in translating "The Rose", it is probable that we have here a relic of his early and not unworthy practice strokes.

731 [*Of mentes ful and fenel grene*]: It is curious that while the birds of the conventional landscape are usually chosen for their strange hues, or merely their strange names, the flowers and trees are almost always chosen for their virtues as spices. At the beginning of *The Pearl*, there is a mound "*with gillyflower (cloves), ginger, and gromwell crowned, and peonies powdered all between*".[37] Here even the peonies owe their place rather to the use of their seeds as a spice in mediaeval cookery than to their colour. This spicy poetic language is made still more appealing to the cook and housewife in the mocking lines of *Sir Thopas*:

> *Ther springen herbes grete and smale,*
> *The lycorys and cetewale,*
>   *And many a clowe-gilofre;*

---

[36] *TLC* 111 suggests "Hobbler" as another ingredient in the author's imagination in the late 1920s when the word "Hobbit" came to him while marking student papers.

[37] Tolkien had glossed a selection from *Pearl* in Kenneth Sisam's *Fourteenth Century Verse and Prose* (Oxford: Clarendon Press, 1921), 56–67; in 1925 he joined E. V. Gordon working on a Clarendon edition of *Pearl*; and by 1926 he had completed his first version of a modern English translation which he here quotes in his endnote for line 127 of the *Romaunt* (see *TLC* 112).

> *And notemuge to putte in ale,*
> *Whether it be moiste or stale,*
> *Or for to lay in cofre.*[38]

Though neither fennel nor mint is particularly fair to look upon, the sweet-smelling path is not entirely unreal. Bacon's essay on gardens may be compared as showing how much more the aromatic odours of flowers and leaves were still valued at a later time than is usual now. The essay ends: "But those which perfume the air most delightfully, not passed by as the rest, but being trodden upon and crushed, are three: that is burnet, wild thyme, and mint. Therefore you are to set whole alleys of them to have the pleasure when you walk or tread".[39]

II. *The Compleynte unto Pite*

Nothing is known of the date of this poem's composition. Speculations concerning its motive and circumstances are equally vain. At least we may feel certain that the love was literary, not real....[40]

14 [*I fond hir deed and buried in an herte*]: that is, in the heart of the lady wherein Pity had once dwelt. The allegory of this poem does not bear close examination. Chaucer has not worked it out well – it was hardly worth it.[41] At any rate *buried* should not be pressed so as to mean "interred", making the *herse* of l. 15 and the *corps* of l. 19 ridiculous. The burial had got no further than Pity's lying in state in her coffin.

92 [*Have mercy on me, thou Herenus quene*]: *Herenus quene*: all the MSS but two have *Herenus* or some further corruption such as *heremus*. The easy reading of the others, *vertuouse, vertous*, is an emendation; it is too easy to have been altered to the difficult *Herenus*.[42] This is (as Skeat first pointed out) a corruption of *Erinyes*. Chaucer himself altered the form of this name no further, at most, than *Herines*; he may have got as near as *Herinyes*. Compare *Troilus and Criseyde* IV, 22: *O ye Herines, Nightes doghtren three*. The strange forms taken by classical names in Middle English are sometimes confusing,

---

[38] Tolkien quotes *Thopas* (1950–55) from Skeat 4:191 with commentary 5:188–9, where the list of trees is compared with the one in the *Romaunt*.

[39] Sir Francis Bacon, "Of Gardens," in *Essays* (London: Oxford University Press, 1902), 129. Sayer, 22, reported that while hiking, Tolkien "liked to stop to look at the trees, flowers, birds and insects that we passed" – much to the annoyance of the Lewis brothers.

[40] The rest of this headnote was already quoted apropos his work on *Troilus* in Chapter 1, p. 27.

[41] SH 2:44–9 traces Tolkien's usually negative attitudes toward allegory.

[42] Tolkien refers to *lectio difficilior potior* (Latin for "the more difficult reading is the stronger") as a major principle of textual criticism.

sometimes charming. They are the product of actual alteration of pronunciation (French), increased by the transference to English, and at the mercy throughout their tradition of mere letter confusion in the copying, not to speak of deliberate variation to make them look more natural or more pleasant or more convenient to the poet. Not only classical names were transmuted: *Ragau* has become *Regan*, and *Medraut, Medrod, Modred, Mordred*... Pity is apparently called *Herines quene* (mistress of the Erīnyes or avenging Furies) because she alone controls the cruelty of vengeance. Chaucer appears to have got the name and the idea from the eleventh book of the *Thebaid* of Statius, where *Pietas* is said to have been created to control even the passions of the gods. Chaucer's *Crueltee* corresponds to the Fury Tisiphone who at the siege of Thebes for once overruled *Pietas*.

95 [*That love and drede you, ay lenger the more*]:... The change from *leng* to *lenger* is a fair example of the slight modernization, neglectful of the finer points of the verse, that has taken place between Chaucer's copy and even the earliest and best extant MSS, and should make us cautious in discussing the details of his metrical practice. We have the words of wrath written by Chaucer to Adam his own scribe. It is only too likely that the texts we now use would enrage him still more; poets are peculiarly impatient of bungled detail. At any rate we would have a good deal "to rub and scrape".[43]

110 [*whether I flete or sinke*]: *Pité* has much departed from a personification of the virtue of pity before she can be accused of not caring whether the lover floats or sinks, or of being likely to slay him by *Crueltee*. Though *your foo* is put in to prop the tottering allegory, it only serves to make the confusion between Pity and the lady worse confounded.[44]

III. *The Book of the Duchess* (extracts)

The poem from which these extracts are taken is one of those whose genuineness has never been doubted, although the manuscript authorities for it are poor. It occurs in three MSS now at Oxford, two of which (Fairfax 16 and Bodley 638) are closely related and both omit lines 31–96, for which our authorities are the remaining MS (Tanner 346) and Thynne's edition of 1532. Chaucer, however, himself alludes to this poem in *Legend* Prologue 406. In many respects it is the most charming of his minor poems, not only because it is complete, but also because through the conventions which he uses there

---

[43] See "Chaucers Wordes unto Adam, His Owne Scriveyn" (Skeat 1:379).
[44] SH 3:989–94 traces "pity" in Tolkien's fictional works, crucially Bilbo's pity for not killing Gollum when he had a chance (*FR* I/2).

runs a real sincerity of feeling – though it may be only art, and the sign of the awakening of his power to give new life to what he borrowed from books and learning, and to join the pieces with cunning into a new whole.

The poem was written to lament the death of Duchess Blanche of Lancaster, wife of John of Gaunt, on September 12th 1369. Chaucer begins by bewailing that he cannot sleep. This leads naturally to the bedside book, convenient machinery for introducing stories. The one related to us, however, is a tale of constant love between husband and wife and is appropriate to the main theme. Nonetheless it is probable that a version of the legend of Ceyx and Alcyone was once made by Chaucer for its own sake separately. It was his way to adapt and rearrange his own work. In the Prologue to the Man of Law's Tale, we are told *in youthe he made of Ceys and Alcion*. But in 1369 he was in the neighbourhood of thirty, so that it is possible that he had treated the original some time before the death of Blanche.

The telling of the tale should be compared with Gower's treatment and with the original of both (Ovid, *Metamorphoses* XI 410 ff.). The comparison with Gower is by no means entirely in Chaucer's favour,[45] but it must be remembered that Chaucer was abridging the tale and fitting it in as an embellishment of a poem of only 1334 lines all told.

63 [*That highte Seys and hadde a wyfe*]: Seys: Cēȳx. He was King of Trachis in Thessaly; his wife Alcyone was a daughter of Aeolus the wind-god. Disaster befell them because they presumed on their great happiness to call themselves Zeus and Hera. It is characteristic of the sentimental treatment in Middle English of borrowed mythology that both Chaucer and Gower omit this essential point. Chaucer has at any rate the excuse that it would have made his tale unsuitable for his purpose to hint at the disaster being a punishment. Perhaps more remarkable is the omission in Chaucer of any reference to the changing of the dead husband and wife into sea-birds, in which shape they renewed their tender love.[46]

68 [*To tellen shortly, whan that he*]: There is another very large class of stock phrases which promise speedy progress in the tale.... They are derived from the minstrels, who had to keep a wary eye on their patrons, and check any incipient yawns. They also had to prevent if possible the chatter of the people

---

[45] Tolkien had glossed the text of John Gower's "Ceix and Alceone" in Sisam's *Fourteenth Century Verse and Prose*, 131–7.

[46] J. R. R. Tolkien, *The Silmarillion*, ed. Christopher Tolkien (1977; London: HarperCollins, 2008), 296–300, mended this omission when Elwing is also turned into a bird and flies over the water seeking her beloved Eärendil; see Kristine Larsen, "Sea Birds and Morning Stars: Ceyx, Alcyone, and the Many Metamorphoses of Eärendil and Elwing," in *Tolkien and the Study of His Sources*, ed. Jason Fisher (Jefferson NC and London: McFarland & Co.), 69–83.

in the back rows from spoiling the best bits, and so we get prayers for silence not only at the beginnings of poems but in the middle when a new part of the tale or an important scene was entered upon. Chaucer himself was not above giving us the hint that his store of knowledge and his skill was greater than the patience of our inattentive minds....

216 [*I may not telle yow as now*]: At this point the sleepless poet makes a vow to Morpheus that he will give him a feather-bed of doves' down covered in gold and black satin, with many pillows, and will paint and upholster his bedchamber to match, if he will send sleep. He immediately falls asleep and dreams – the usual May-day dream.[47]

328 ff [*Of Ector and king Priamus*]:... Poets have at all times been fond of lists of fair names, which are often none the less effective though the audience's knowledge of the legends attached to them was small or vague. Compare *Legend* Prologue 208 ff. In Anglo-Saxon the poem now known as *Widsith* reads today like a bald catalogue of kings and warriors which needs much dry research before we can have even an inkling of why it was ever strung together, but mnemonic list though it may have been, it must once have had power to move the heart with memories or echoes of old tales.[48]

IV. *The Parlement of Foules*

This is a remarkable and on the whole successful poem.[49] In the *Book of the Duchess* Chaucer showed that he could match the masters of grace and charm, and already reveals himself as unrivalled in tender sensibility; his dream is really dreamlike and filled with a soft and gentle air. Now we first get hints of his real originality, and begin to savour his own peculiar temper. Still blending and adapting various sources, French (*Romance of the Rose*), Latin classical and medieval (Cicero and Alanus de Insulis), and Italian (Boccaccio), he constructs a poem that is not only a complete new thing, but is in places very individual and Chaucerian in tone. At last we get the clear touches of Chaucer's humour amid the scenery of the medieval dream and secret garden; in the disclaimer of any personal experience of love; in the description of

---

[47] Tolkien himself was a sleepless writer plagued with what C. S. Lewis described as a "Johnsonian horror of going to bed"; see *TLC* 229–30.

[48] Tolkien indulged his own "bald catalogue" of dead warriors at the end of "The Battle of the Pelennor Fields" (*RK* VI/6).

[49] Tolkien extracted these notes to use for his Hilary 1948 lectures on the *Parlement*, so that they were not returned with the rest of the Clarendon notes in 1951 and, therefore, they have the different shelfmark Bodleian MS Tolkien A 38/2, fols. 96–126. For lecture delivery, these pages accumulated many new blue-ink notes in a smaller, hastier hand difficult to decipher.

the noisy populace of the baser birds, whose comments serve at the same time to poke fun at and to set off courtly manners and fine feeling.

The *Parlement of Foules* is usually assigned to the year 1382 (that is, after Chaucer's two visits to Italy in 1378 and 1379) because it appears probable that it was written as an allegory of the marriage of Richard II with Anne of Bohemia (here represented as the *formel egle*). She had already been betrothed to a Prince of Bavaria and to a Margrave of Meissen (the two tercels of lesser birth). The English ambassadors reached Bohemia in 1381, "when the Princess Anne had already reached the age to choose herself a husband", compare lines 626 ff. The marriage took place a year later on January 14th 1882, compare lines 647 ff.

8 [*For al be that I knowe not love in deed*]: This disclaimer is very Chaucerian. The comic contradiction (at first sight) of the preceding stanza is neatly turned into his favourite description of himself as a book-lover, and so serves to introduce a variation on the machinery of the *Book of the Duchess*, a book and the dreams begotten by it. Humorous self-consciousness, with a touch of vanity – he was well aware of it, Chaucer could mock his own foibles and retain them – prompted many jokes against himself, and disparagement of his own wit and appearance. This is all of a piece with his literary character: if ever the wings of his poetry bid fair to exalt him for a moment in strong flight, they were promptly withered by the flame of his own mockery, and he fell down into (intentional) bathos, a jesting Icarus. This is usually to the delight but sometimes to the despair of the reader.

61 [*That cometh of thilke speres thryes three*]: an allusion to the imagined "music of the spheres". From this harmony the *primum mobile*[50] was probably excluded, and also originally the "firmament". The idea of the harmony of the concentric spheres of the "planets" revolving all in a similar direction was thus bound up with the notion of the excellence of the number seven. Each of these seven planetary spheres emitted one of the notes of the gamut. The music was not consciously heard by mortals because of the blending of these seven primary notes, or because the music never ceased (just as the dwellers by the cataracts of the Nile are unconscious of the noise of the water). A later more "scientific" explanation attributed the inaudibility to the music being made "beyond the air". The "music of the spheres" has in figurative language survived the entire alteration of our astronomic notions, and the discovery of new planets.[51]

---

[50] At exactly this point Tolkien switched from typewritten pages to fairly neat handwritten pages.
[51] Bradford Lee Eden, "The 'Music of the Spheres': Relationships between Tolkien's *The Silmarillion* and Medieval Cosmological and Religious Theory," in *Tolkien the Medievalist*, ed. Chance, 183–93, argues the influence of medieval notions of music for Tolkien's creation myth in his *Ainulindalë*.

80 [*Shul alwey whirle aboute therthe in peyne*]: 'We have here the idea of purgatory' (Skeat). This is not the case.⁵² The souls in purgatory are the souls of the just who have achieved salvation, and are being purified for heaven. Here rather we have the notion of a temporary "hell", and the ultimate salvation of all, which offers to the just only a quicker passage to heaven. Medieval writers seldom troubled to relate such fancies, which they used as the elegant embellishments of a literary theme, to their belief and theology. The idea of the thin shadowy spirits blown about as the sport of the winds is present in Cicero, and in Dante (drawing from the same source) and frequently later.

148 [*Right as betwixen adamauntes two*]: The word is derived from Greek *adamas* (*adamant-*), our "diamond". Partly through a fanciful etymology from Latin *adamans* ("falling in love"), this name became applied to the lode-stone or natural magnet. The product of this verbal confusion was an entirely legendary stone that combined the properties of both. Here only the magnetic properties (which do not really belong to "adamant") are in question.⁵³

176 [*The bilder ook and eek the hardy asshe*]. Chaucer's list of trees is of literary origin; its items show that it comes largely from the Mediterranean. The list has been traced back as far as Ovid (*Metamorphoses*, X, 90) whence, with variation, it appears in Seneca's *Œdipus*, Lucan, Statius; and (from Statius) in Boccaccio and the *Romance of the Rose*. Actually Chaucer is here combining the list in Boccaccio's *Teseide* (XI, 22–24) with one in *Rose* (1338–1368). Chaucer was fond of a descriptive catalogue; the Prologue in the *Canterbury Tales* is an elaborate product of the same partiality. Here the brief characterisation, however, is mainly derivative. Compare the 21 trees in the Knight's Tale (A 2921). The present passage was closely imitated by Spenser (*Fairie Queene* I, i, 8 and 9).⁵⁴

178 [*holm to whippes lasshe*]: "(as the handle) for the whip's lash". Skeat defines this as "holly", but it is probably the *ilex* or "holm-oak", an evergreen with dark pointed leaves, somewhat like holly, and slender shapely acorns. The *ilex* is in Ovid's list (not *holly*, which was probably unknown in Latin). Cf. *holm* = *ilex* in the *Promptorium Parvulorum* (a 15th-century glossary) and *Knight's Tale* 2063. There seems to be no other evidence for the use of either

---

⁵² As a devote Catholic as well as a careful reader of Dante's *Purgatorio* – the subject of his 1947 lecture to the Oxford Dante Society – Tolkien was quick to correct Skeat's theology.
⁵³ Galadriel's Nenya was the Ring of Adamant.
⁵⁴ Mediterranean trees are prominent in the landscape when Frodo and Sam enter Ithilien (*TT* IV/4).

holly or ilex in making whips. *holm* is etymologically the same word as *holly*, O.E. *holegn*, M.E. *holy* and *holin* (surviving dialectally as *hollin*). From *holin* partly by purely scribal confusion *holm* was produced; *holin* is the reading of some MSS here.[55]

309 [*For this was on seynt Valentynes day*]: In Rome the festival of *Lupercalia* took place on February 15th. Some of the customs associated with that day are the probable origin of the giving of "valentines", long connected with the same day in Southern Europe, or transferred to the neighbouring St Valentine's day (February 14th) – deliberately and with the intention of making the original heathen customs more innocent, just as St Francis de Sales (1567–1622) introduced the use of saints' names for the imitation of the receiver on "Valentine's". The idea of mating of the birds on this day is not the origin of the "Valentine" among men, but a fanciful extension of it. In any case, the "birds" here are allegories of men.

330 [*Ther mighte men the royal egle finde*]: *royal*: because he was chosen king of the Birds, as the lion of Beasts....[56] The idea that the eagle could gaze unblinking at the sun is an old one,[57] and is supported by the most undaunted of all etymologists (Saint Isidore of Seville, 7th century) with his derivation: *aquila ab acumine oculorum vocata est*. This is in direct opposition to modern etymological conjecture, which connects *aquila*, the black eagle, with a group of words meaning "dark or blind".

344 [*The crane the geaunt with his trompes soune*]: *geaunt*: derived from the adjective *giganteus* used in Alanus' description (referring to its long legs). Where the bird is still familiar "clangs" or "trumpets" are still used of its cry.[58]

348 [*The stare that the counseyl can bewrye*]: A starling can be taught to talk, but the reference is clearly "mythological", to some story in which a malicious talking starling gave away a secret. Chaucer's Manciple tells just such a story, though it is of a talking crow.[59]

363 [*The raven wys, the crow with vois of care*]: The raven is credited with wisdom because of the great age to which he attains, and his sage appearance.

---

[55] Hollin (Eregion) is the region outside the West Gate of Moria where Frodo and his friends encounter "ancient holly trees" (*FR* II, 3).

[56] In his "Queer Lodgings" chapter of *The Hobbit*, Tolkien pictures this regal status: "the Lord of the Eagles became in after days the King of All Birds and wore a golden crown" (162).

[57] *The Hobbit* partook in this longstanding tradition when introducing the Lord of the Eagles who "had eyes that could look at the sun unblinking" (150).

[58] *TLC* 128–9 connects notions of cranes, herons, and giants with Tolkien's descriptions of the giant Ents walking heron-like.

[59] *The Hobbit* recalls this lore of starlings and crows when talking birds announce the death of Smaug and warn of the army of Elves and Lake-men approaching the Lonely Mountain.

The crow, because of his harsh voice and black feathers, has usually been regarded as ill-omened...[60]

V. *The Former Age*

The title of this piece is modern, and taken from the second line (translating Boethius' *prior etas*). There are only two (poor) MSS of the poem, both defective at the same point, omitting line 56. From one comes the colophon here printed; the other is headed *Chawcer vpon this fyfte metur of the second book*. Boethius Book 5, metre ii is actually only the source of the first four stanzas.[61] The theme is older than Boethius. Chaucer is indebted also to Ovid (*Metamorphoses* I, 89–112). The close and over-literal prose translation of this same metre, p. 53 of this selection, may be compared. It is interesting also to compare the Old English (verse) translation. This can be seen in Cook's *Literary Middle English Reader* or in Sedgefield's *King Alfred's Old English Version of Boethius*.[62]

6 [*Unknowen was the quern and eek the melle*]: *quern*: O.E. *cweorn* "hand-mill", the most primitive apparatus for grinding. In essentials it consisted of two large round slabs of hard stone, pierced and joined by a round peg. The grain was ground between the flattened or hollowed surfaces where the stones met by laboriously revolving the top stone. *Cweorn* is a word that goes back to philological "Indo-European" times, and the thing itself to anthropological "neolithic" times; so that in modern terms Chaucer's "Golden Age" is at latest palæolithic! *melle*: a striking example of the specially Kentish (South-Eastern) forms that are frequent in Chaucer.[63]

11 [*The which they gniden and eete nat half y-nough*]: The manuscripts have *gnodded*, which in earlier and better spelling would be *gnoddede, gnuddede* (with elision of the final *e*). This is a genuine word, used for precisely this action of roughly crushing and rubbing corn in the hands, already before Chaucer. We should therefore retain it, since the trisyllabic third foot is not

---

[60] Skeat 1:520–1. "The Gathering of the Clouds" chapter in *The Hobbit* has the old raven Roäc, "a most decrepit old bird," consulted for "secret news" because ravens "live many a year, and their memories are long" (315). In "On the Doorstep," crows were "black and ominous" and Balin distrusted them: "they look like spies of evil" (258).

[61] Tolkien nodded: the correct reference is to Book II, meter 5 of *Consolation of Philosophy* (whereas he rightly cites Book V, meter 2 in his headnote for the poem *Truth*).

[62] *A Literary Middle English Reader*, ed. Albert S. Cook (Boston: Ginn & Co., 1915), and *King Alfred's Old English Version of Boethius'* De Consolatione Philosophiae, ed. W. J. Sedgefield (Oxford: Clarendon Press, 1899).

[63] Tolkien's 1913 tutorial essay had already taken notice of Chaucer's mixed dialect: "Kentish, that is South Eastern, influence is still naturally important" (Bodleian MS Tolkien A 21/1, fol. 45v).

impossible, even if we suspect that Chaucer really wrote the smoother *gnīde(n)*, pa. t. pl. of *gnīde(n)* (O.E. *gnīdan*), which had the same sense. . . .[64]

59 [*ne Nembrot, desirous/To reynen, had nat maad his toures hye*]: In mediæval accounts Nimrod was made the originator of the disastrous project of building Babel – the only warrant is Genesis 10.10.[65]

VI. *Merciles Beaute*

The title is given as *Merciles Beaute* in the index to the only MS. It is perhaps the most Chaucerian of all the short minor poems, and this is the chief reason for its ascription to Chaucer. The MS in which it is preserved is devoted chiefly to pieces by Chaucer and Lydgate. No one could ascribe the poem to Lydgate, however...

VII. *To Rosemounde*

This little jest of Chaucer's was discovered by Skeat in 1891 on the flyleaf of a manuscript at Oxford, in which it follows a copy of the *Troilus and Criseyde*. To the latter is added the colophon: *Tregentyll / here endeth the book of Troylus and of Crisseyde / Chaucer*... Certainly the comment "Very polished. Chaucer" is just to *Troilus*, and it adds much to the joke of the little piece. Only with regret could we lose it – it reads almost like Chaucer's own signature.

VIII. *Truth*

This well-known ballade occurs in many MSS, but only one of them preserves the *envoy* (see note to l. 22). . . . The title *Balade de bon conseyl* occurs in one MS, with variations in others; one (Shirley) calls it *balade that Chaucier made on his deeth-bedde*, which is not likely to be true.[66] Caxton calls it *The good counceyl of Chawcer*. For so short a poem the number of difficult or uncommon uses of words is large. Chaucer has probably taken hints from more than one passage in Boethius: cf. B ii prose 5 "*for avarice maketh always mokereres* (hoarders) *to ben hated*." But none of them are of importance; the sentiments are mostly commonplaces of unknown antiquity. The piece has been highly praised, but scarcely deserves it.

23 [*Therfore, thou vache, leve thyn old wrecchednesse*]: The previous stanza, and the story of Nebuchadnezzar (cf. Monk's Tale 153 ff.) who "*loste his*

---

[64] Tolkien's obsession with *gnodded* was first mentioned in his 1924 letter to Sisam (p. 43 above).

[65] Tolkien renewed this biblical prejudice with his own wicked towers Dol Guldur, Orthanc, Minas Morgul, Cirith Ungol, the Towers of the Teeth at the Black Gates, and the Dark Tower of Barad–dûr.

[66] John Shirley (c. 1366–1456) was a scribe-editor particularly known for works by Chaucer and Lydgate.

dignitee and lyk a beste him semed for to be, and eet hay as an oxe, and lay theroute" appear to indicate that *vache* is merely the French word for "cow", typical of an enslaved beast of the field with earthward gaze (perhaps softened by being in French). Miss Rickert has since argued that the *envoy* directs the poem to (rather at?) Sir Philip (de) la Vache, who married Elizabeth, daughter of Sir Lewis Clifford – a friend of Chaucer's since it was by his hand that the French poet Deschamps sent a *balade* addressed to the *grant translateur, noble Geffrey Chaucier*.[67] The details of the poem, she also urges, are applicable to the incidents of Sir Philip's life. Nonetheless the strongest argument in favour of the proper name is the absence of any other evidence for the use of the ordinary French *vache* in an English context. The author could not have been innocent or the recipient unobservant of the play on the name implied (which is pointed by the *thou*). The latter can hardly have relished it. If Sir Philip is really meant, the *balade* can hardly be counted a tactful sermon, and it is not altogether surprising that the envoy is found in one MS only. Doubts have been expressed as to its genuineness, for its continuation of the rhyme-scheme proves little. But it may have been written later than the rest, to point lines once written without special aim, perhaps to settle some small score of which we now know nothing.

IX. *Gentilesse*

The title *Moral Balade of Chaucir* is in one of the seven MSS. The poem is also attributed to Chaucer by Shirley, the maker of two of the copies, and acknowledged as Chaucer's by Henry Scogan, who inserted it bodily into a "moral balade" he wrote for his pupils, the sons of Henry IV.[68] Chaucer also wrote a "poetical essay on this subject" in *The Tale of the Wife of Bath*, 253 ff. Though it has been said that the conviction that real nobility lies in virtue was more rare in Chaucer's day than our own, this is not likely to be true. It was a common theme, and doubtless the practice and the preaching accorded as closely then as now. Compare also Boethius III, prose 6, from which Chaucer's treatment is partly derived, direct and through the *Romance of the Rose*. That nobility, both actual worldly eminence and true nobility of character, is by the

---

[67] Edith Rickert, "Thou Vache," *Modern Philology* 11 (1913–14), 209–26. Tolkien (who later discouraged delving into his own biography to interpret his writings) seldom brought forward Chaucer's personal life to explain the contents of his poetry.

[68] For Scogan as an early reader of Chaucer, see John M. Bowers, *Chaucer and Langland: The Antagonistic Tradition* (Notre Dame IN: University of Notre Dame Press, 2007), 87–92. These royal pupils included the future Henry V, a plausible model for Aragorn leading his outnumbered troops through enemy territory to the Black Gates, much as King Henry had led his outnumbered English forces to Agincourt.

grace of God, is clearly the personal conviction of Lydgate in his *Fall of Princes* (whatever his originals thought), a book much praised, and much read by the "noble".

X. *Lak of Stedfastnesse*

Attributed by Shirley, to whom two of the several copies are due, to Chaucer's last years, and said to have been sent to the king at Windsor. Consequently it has been placed between 1393 and 1399, when Richard II was rapidly degenerating. Yet it would seem rash of one depending on royal favour, and not unwilling to curry it (as in XI), to have actually sent such a poem to the king at this period. It would have been clean contrary to the advice given in VIII 8–11 (especially 11). That it was ever sent we may doubt, unless, as has been thought, its composition should rather be referred to 1389, and the period when the young king first began to govern, and might not have taken advice hardly.

6 [*Is al this world for mede and wilfulnesse*]: *for mede*: because of (the love of) gain and pecuniary rewards – especially as shown in taking bribes; cf. *PF* 228. In *Piers Plowman* Mede is bribery and corruption personified. See C Passus IV, 127 ff. There Richard is told that Mede and her allies 'haue maked almost…that no lond loueth the, and yut leest thyn owene.'[69]

XI. *Compleint to his Empty Purse*

The unpleasing *envoy* to this poem, if not the whole, is *probably* the last thing Chaucer ever wrote. The other stanzas may have been written for some other occasion of poverty; one MS at any rate says that the poem is "a supplicacion to King Richard by Chaucier." This does nothing to increase our respect for the language in which Henry IV the conqueror of his former patron Richard II is addressed by Chaucer. Nor can Chaucer have wasted much time in changing sides. The answer (presumably) to the complaint, a grant of an additional forty marks a year, came only a few days after Henry's "election" on September 30th, 1399. About a year later, traditionally Oct. 25th, 1400, Chaucer died. The contrast between the first stanzas and the last is not a happy one to end on – between the elvish Chaucer[70] who could still turn a

---

[69] *TLC* 118, 139, 179 discusses Tolkien's general avoidance of *Piers Plowman* despite its Worcestershire dialect, the language of his mother's ancestors.

[70] Tolkien took the phrase *elvish Chaucer* from the Host's description of the pilgrim-narrator as "elvish by his contenaunce" (*CT* VII, 1893); see J. A. Burrow, "Elvish Chaucer", in *The Endless Knot: Essays on Old and Middle English in Honor of Marie Borroff*, ed. M. Teresa Tavormina and R. F. Yeager (Cambridge: D. S. Brewer, 1995), 105–11.

begging occasion to a witty mockery of his own need, and Chaucer, now probably ailing as well as in need, forced to go begging once more, and scraping lower than ever.

23 [*O conquerour of Brutes Albioun*]: *Brutus* or *Brut* was in mediæval tradition a descendant of Æneas of Troy, and founded the kingdom of *Britain* in this island. Name and tradition probably go back to early Welsh tales ascribing the name of the island to an eponymous founder, whose name was assimilated to Latin *Brutus* when he was connected later with Æneas and Vergil. Since mediæval chronicle histories usually began with *Brut*, this name acquired also the sense of "chronicle", now obsolete in English, but surviving to-day in Welsh *brut*. *Albion* was a traditional name in such chronicles for Britain before the Roman occupation – it is probably an old name, derived from the white southern cliffs; according to plausible conjecture, this may also be the etymological sense of Welsh *Prydain* (Britain).

Henry IV proclaimed himself king by conquest, inherited right, and election. One ground was sufficient in theory. The first was the most real. Chaucer puts them all down in the same order, whatever he may have thought.[71]

XII. *Boethius de Consolatione Philosophie*

Anicius Manlius Torquatus Severinus Boethius was in A.D. 524 cruelly executed (on a probably unfounded charge) by Theodoric the Gothic King, who at that time ruled Italy from Ravenna, on the whole very well.[72] At his death Boethius was, at an age of about 44, in spite of a long tenure of high office, renowned also as a philosopher, theologian and astronomer, probably the most learned man of his day. In a tower at Pavia, where for a year he awaited death, he wrote his last and most famous book, *The Consolation of Philosophy*, in the form of discourse between himself and Philosophia, who appeared to comfort him in his dungeon, in the course of which such metaphysical problems as eternity, free will, and the existence of evil are explored.[73] Gibbon remarks that "such topics of consolation, so obvious, so vague, or so abstruse are ineffectual to subdue the feelings of human nature; and the sage, who

---

[71] *TLC* 153–4 notes that Aragorn, unlike Henry IV, assumes the kingship of Gondor by combination of inheritance, conquest, and election.

[72] We present Tolkien's fair copy of his much-revised observations on *Boece*, but restore two interesting passages from the draft.

[73] The passage from "in the course of..." to the end of the next paragraph comes later in Tolkien's draft. See *TLC* 150 on Lady Philosophy heading a genealogy of wise teachers including Beatrice and the *Pearl* Queen leading to Galadriel. Tolkien around 1959 wrote his own Boethian dialogue *Athrabeth Finrod ah Andreth* ("Debate of Finrod and Andreth"); see *Morgoth's Ring: The Later Silmarillion, Part I*, ed. Christopher Tolkien (Boston and New York: Houghton Mifflin, 1993), 303–60; SH 2:73–80; and *TLC* 143.

could artfully combine in the same work the various riches of philosophy, poetry, and eloquence, must already have possessed the intrepid calmness which he affected to seek."[74]

Even if they affect also to find there moral guidance and comfortable words, it is the eloquence of this artful mixture that in reality recommended it to the Middle Ages. So powerfully moving is this eloquence that it is felt through even a poor prose translation, while translation of Boethius in his verse has been described as poetry made easy. Among the poor translations Chaucer's version must in many respects be reckoned.

This work was divided into five books, each subdivided into alternate proses and metres (in verses of various kinds); the metres were poetical interludes, embellishments of the main arguments of the proses. After the Scriptures no other work was so studied or so quarried by writers of the "Dark" and Middle Ages. Boethius was the teacher of Dante before Chaucer. Jean de Meun (see I) used it freely, so that Chaucer's debt is often indirect, through *The Romance of the Rose*. There (5052–6) it is declared that a translation of the *Consolation* into a tongue understood by the unlearned would be a worthy deed. Jean perhaps took his own advice (a French translation exists that is associated with his name), but we need not attribute Chaucer's version directly to the inspiration of these words. The book was sufficiently famous. Translations are to be found both before the *Romance* and after Chaucer. In English, however, there appears before Chaucer to have been only one, a free rendering by King Alfred in the ninth century, unless we count separately a translation into (poor) Old English verse of the metres only, which was once also ascribed to Alfred. Contemporary with Chaucer, or little later, there were at least two more English translations. Between 1550 and 1800 some ten more were made (mostly unprinted), not including the fragments of Queen Elizabeth's Englishing.[75] There have been others since.

Chaucer's version was perhaps written round about 1380, and close to the time of *Troilus and Criseyde*. The two works are mentioned together in his words to his scribe Adam (*Adam scriveyn, if ever it thee befalle* / Boece or Troilus *to wryten newe*).

Chaucer's translation is often faulty, through sheer mistakes in latinity (for instance in one place he takes *clauus* as *clauis*, though it may be his MS copy that is to blame), errors which more would make to-day but for the

---

[74] Tolkien's quotation from *Decline and Fall*, ch. xxxix, was lifted from Skeat 2:ix.
[75] Tolkien's footnote: "The most accessible is the translation and text in *Loeb Classical Library* (Heinemann), where the *Consolation of Philosophy* is represented by an Elizabethan (1609) version." He refers to the translation in *Queen Elizabeth's Englishings of Boethius*, ed. Caroline Pemberton, EETS o.s. 113 (1899).

dictionaries which did not then exist.[76] To help him he apparently had a MS with glosses and comments on the hard words, drawn probably from Nicholas Trivet's Latin commentary (which he may actually have had, and possibly his French translation). Still more often he may be accused of slavish adherence to the idiom or word-order of his text, or of using words of Latin origin that were no longer good renderings of their etymological ancestors – faults to be met in all periods of English.

It has taken many centuries for English to shake off the trembling awe of the slave in the presence of Lord Latin; if the Latin mode of expression was not natural to the vernacular, so much the worse for the nature of the vernacular. Even so, weighted as he is by respect for his original (and hindered by inadequate equipment for translating an author whose matter and vocabulary is often difficult) Chaucer continually reveals the poet in finely chosen words and phrases....[77]

XIII. *The Prologue to the Legend of Good Women*

The title is that given in the MSS, though in the headlink to the *Man of Law's Tale* the work is referred to as *The Seintes Legend of Cupyde*. Actually ten ladies are dealt with: Cleopatra, Thisbe, Dido, Hypsipyle and Medea (in one piece), Lucretia, Ariadne, Philomela, Phyllis, and Hypermnestra (unfinished). The number Chaucer intended to write (if he ever made up his mind) is unknown. There are nineteen ladies in the train of Love, but the plan need not have included all of these or have been limited to the number. In Chaucer's "Retraction" there is a reference to "The Book of the XXV Ladies".

The prologue and legends are preserved in several MSS. In one of these only is the prologue in the form here printed (the so-called A version of 545 lines). The others have a slightly longer form (B version of 579 lines).[78] The number of lines does not indicate the differences. A has 90 lines not in B; B 124 not in A. The similar or identical matter is in a different order in B, which also shows the following variations: the vision occurs on May 1st; Alceste's name is introduced late (B 432, A 179); the *balade* is not sung by the company, but is offered as Chaucer's own, and later criticized by Love for the absence of Alceste's name. (*My lady comth* appears for *Alceste is here*.)

---

[76] *Letters: Revised and Expanded Edition*, 162, includes a new 1945 letter in which he spoke slightingly of Chaucer as a translator: "He had some Latin (not too much as 'Boethius' shows), but no talent for prose (as 'Boethius' and other efforts show)."

[77] This paragraph is from Tolkien's draft. In his fair copy, he replaced it with the pithier, "Nonetheless he often reveals his talent in finely chosen words and phrases."

[78] F. N. Robinson, ed., *Poetical Works of Chaucer* (Boston: Houghton Mifflin, 1933), 953, established the current designations of "G" for the A version, extant solely in Cambridge University Library Gg 4.27, and "F" for the B version, best represented by Fairfax 16 in Oxford's Bodleian Library. The F version is now almost unanimously considered the earlier and G the later.

Even if we could reach certainty as to the order in which A and B were made, the chief importance of this would lie in the chance offered of observing Chaucer in his workshop, not in the interpretation of the allegory and contemporary allusion – which is hotly debated, and of little ultimate importance, except in so far as it may help to fix the order of A and B. But no certainty has been achieved. A long debate, still in progress, which has produced some sound and ingenious (and some absurd) arguments on either side, leaves the balance still fairly even, though there is a tendency at present to put B before A. But it has not finally dismissed the natural suspicion that the isolated variant (A) represents an earlier form, that has somehow escaped destruction; and the commoner (B), a revised version for some reason – though often asserted, it is by no means agreed that B is the better of the two – favoured by the author.

That the God of Love and his queen were intended for Richard II and his queen, Anne of Bohemia (see *PF*), is often argued, but not proved. In B (496 ff.) occur the words: *And whan this book is maad, yive hit the quene / On my behalf, at Eltham or at Shene*. But this does not prove that Alceste to be Anne. Nor is the absence of the words from A certainly due to excision; they may equally well have been an addition. Anne died in 1394 and the king, whose grief was extravagant, forsook the palace of Shene for good; it had been their favourite house. The lines must have been written therefore before 1394. But this does not tell us much concerning the date of the rest. Since the *Canterbury Tales* were begun about 1387 the beginning of the *Legende* must be earlier still; though the weariness that is very visible in the legends themselves, in contrast to the prologue, may well be due to the beginning of work on the *Tales*. It seems generally agreed that the earlier Prologue (whichever that may be) must be assigned to about 1385–6.

43 [*Swiche as men callen daysies in our toun*]: *daysies*: This is an old name, O.E. *dæges ēage*, literally "eye of day", as Chaucer rightly says (B. 182–4: "*that wel by resoun men hit calle may the dáyesỳe or elles ye of day*"). The name is probably connected with ancient riddles and "kennings" (conventional poetic descriptive compounds) and enshrines a double comparison, a riddle once removed. The sun is the "eye of day" in old terms; as the sun shines in the heavenly fields, so does the daisy, with its golden centre and surrounding rays, shine from the grass below.[79] Chaucer's words here and later do not imply that the name was not widely known and understood; their precision is due to

---

[79] The daisy figures in precisely these terms in the riddle-exchange between Bilbo and Gollum; see *The Hobbit* 122 and *TLC* 150–1.

special imitation of French praise of the daisy.... Nor, of course, does he think the name peculiar to any "toun"; *in our toun* means "by men round about me" and is similar to the common use of *toun* (O.E. *tūn*) in the sense of "world, dwellings of men"....

62 [*Of making ropen and lad awey the corn*]: *making*: "verse-making, poetry". So in Greek the literary sense of *po(i)ētēs* "poet" is "maker", but the English use of *make(r)* probably arose quite independently. Parallel developments are found in many languages....[80]

97 ff [*And in a litel erber that I have*]: These lines... occur in both A and B, and so refer to Chaucer's house at the time of the first writing of the prologue. Chaucer gave up the lease (received in 1374) of his house above the city gate of Aldgate in October 1386.[81] It is thought that an *erber*, which was a green space with shady walls of trained trees and climbing plants, would hardly be connected with such a house, and that we should look in Kent for his dwelling when he wrote this. He was appointed Justice of the Peace for Kent in October 1385, and so perhaps left his Aldgate house even before the date when he relinquished the lease. But then, as now, town-dwellers could doubtless (if they could afford it) have an *erber* detached from their house. The *erber*, and the servants strewing flowers, need not be much closer to reality than the ensuing dream. The sense of freedom which runs through the prologue is, however, unmistakable, and it may be connected with the privilege granted to Chaucer in February 1385 of performing his duties as Controller of the Customs and Subsidies through a deputy. He thus had unwonted leisure, without loss of income, until by a sudden twist of "hir that turneth as a bal" he lost his appointment in December 1386.[82]

179 [*Hir name was Alceste the debonayre*]: Alcestis was wife of Admetus of Pherae in Thessaly (not Thrace, as here). Apollo obtained of the Fates a promise that he should be delivered at the hour of death if father, mother, or wife would die for him. Alcestis died for her husband, and so is taken as a type of pure love and of devotion.[83] Gower tells her story in *Confessio Amantis*.

---

[80] "The Battle of the Pelennor Fields" (*RK* V/6) ends with a lament for the fallen warriors: "So long afterward a *maker* in Rohan said in his song..."

[81] This perk for Controller of the Customs was assumed as Chaucer's residence during these years, but mistakenly: its tiny 14 x 16 foot dimensions lacked light, heat, sanitation, and accommodation for servants and was hardly a "house"; see Paul Strohm, *Chaucer's Tale: 1386 and the Road to Canterbury* (New York: Viking, 2014), 52–4. More likely living in his son Thomas Chaucer's future residence in Golding Lane, Chaucer probably used this strong, well-guarded stone room as storage for his books and literary papers, much as he later used the tenement in the precincts of Westminster Abbey; see Bowers, *Chaucer and Langland*, 183–90.

[82] Tolkien alludes to Chaucer's *Truth* with its image of Fortune's wheel: "In trust of hir that turneth as a bal" (9).

[83] *TLC* 149 describes how Lúthien makes similar sacrifice for Beren.

273 [*Yis, god wot, sixty bokes olde and newe*]: *sixty*: a big library for the time, if the number is to be taken as approximately true to reality.[84]

329 [*For in your court is many a losengeour/And many a queynte totelere accusour*]: *totelere* (MS A *totulour*), also spelt *tutelere*. A rare word derived from *totelen, tutelen* "to speak close in the ear, whisper", an "imitative" word made up in similar fashion to our *tittle-tattle*. Here it is used almost as an adjective "tittle-tattling".

queynte is here used in its more original sense "cunning". The modern sense is an example of a common change...[85]

365 ff [*This is the sentence of the philosophre*]: This probably refers to Aristotle, who was supposed to have educated Alexander the Great, and taught him all his philosophy (under three heads: *Theoric, Rhetoric*, and *Practic*). *Practic* deals with the ordering of a king's life, of his person, household, and realm. Gower sets out all this "education of Alexander" in the seventh book of the *Confessio Amantis*. There Aristotle says that a king must govern all classes in the realm, clerk, knight, merchant, and common people alike: *o lawe must governe hem alle*. The third "point of Policy" after Truth, and Liberality with Discretion, is Justice.[86]

408 ff [*And al the love of Palamon and Arcyte*]: a much discussed passage. "The love of Palamon and Arcyte" is, of course, the subject of the *Knight's Tale*. This is usually held to have been written fairly early (at earliest about 1382–3), and before the idea of the *Canterbury Tales* was born. Therefore it was probably in existence already when Chaucer wrote this prologue. In spite of contrary arguments it is probable that in the *Knight's Tale* we have the actual work here referred to (with but slight alteration to adjust to the later scheme of the *Canterbury Tales*). The *is knowen lyte* is not Chaucer's complaint against an unappreciative world (he seems to have been very fortunate in this respect). It probably is an assertion of copyright in advance; though he had written (or nearly written) it, he had not "published" it, or shown it to many.

491 [*But pitee renneth sone in gentil herte*]: Chaucer's favourite line. It occurs in the same form three times elsewhere, and once in a similar form (all in the *Canterbury Tales*).[87]

---

[84] *TLC* 54 recalls how Kenneth Sisam advised the young Tolkien on using second-hand catalogues for building his own sizable library.

[85] Tolkien glosses this couplet's *queynte* and *totelere* but neglects *losengeour*, a word to which he would devote his last substantial article "Middle English *Losenger*" (1953) reprinted below in Chapter 5.

[86] *TLC* 153–4 discusses how Tolkien's representatives of kingship in Middle Earth, particularly Aragorn's, draw upon Aristotle's standards.

[87] Tolkien echoes this line when Faramir says to Éowyn: "Do not scorn pity that is the gift of a gentle heart" (*RK* VI/5).

514 [*As telleth Agaton for hir goodnesse*]: apparently *Agathōn* (in Dante *Agatone*), an Athenian poet (c. 447–400 B.C.) who wrote a tragedy called *To Anthos* ("The Flower"), only known to us because Aristotle mentions it in his *Art of Poetry* as an example of a drama with entirely unhistorical names and incidents.[88] The passage would seem to have been known in some way to Chaucer, as well as Dante's reference to Agathon (*Purgatorio* xxii, 106). Chaucer's citation of the Athenian is undoubtedly a cutting (and humorous) deception; some authority for this pseudo-classical myth had to be given.

Froissart's poem perhaps provided some hints for it. There we are told how Jove turned the tears of Heres for her husband Cephey into daisies upon the grass. Mercury sent a garland of them to Seres (Ceres). Ceres may have suggested *Cibella*. But the fact that the name *Cephey* is properly *Cepheus* (who in classical mythology was "stellified", as well as his wife and daughter, *Cassiopēa* and *Andromeda*) is a remote suggestion. It still remains uncertain whether the stellification and the change with a daisy are Chaucer's own fabrication, or whether he found either, or both, in predecessors now lost.[89]

519 [*Cibella made the dayesy and the flour*]: *Cybele*, the Phrygian Mother Goddess, of the earth and of fertility. Producing flowers is thus properly attributed to her; her functions were similar to those of the Latin *Ceres*.[90]

XIV. *The Legend of Cleopatra*

The sources of this legend are probably various, and Chaucer has certainly not presented the "naked text" of any one authority. He seems clearly to have used the *Epitome Rerum Romanarum* of L. Annæus Florus (c. 115 A.D.). Though he probably knew the story in Orosius' history (*Historiæ adversus Paganos*, c. 417 A.D.) and also in Boccaccio's *De Claris Mulieribus*, his use of them for this brief tale cannot be proved. He may also have had access to Plutarch's life of Mark Antony, in a Latin translation. Gower does not make use of the *Legend of Good Women*. He tells in the *Confessio Amantis* many of the same tales (e.g. Thisbe, Dido, Medea, Phyllis, Lucrece, Ariadne) in a wholly independent manner. But by the time he reached the end of his long work he shows signs of having read Chaucer's *Legend*. Book VIII 2452 onwards is

---

[88] Tolkien gleaned all of this note's information from Skeat 3:xxxii–xxxiv.

[89] Tolkien devised his own stellification of Eärendil, whose sky-ship bears a Silmaril so that Galadriel calls him "Eärendil, the Evening Star" (*FR* II/7). See Tom Shippey, *Road to Middle Earth*, rev. ed. (Boston and New York: Houghton Mifflin, 2003), "Eärendil: A Lyric Core", 244–7.

[90] Tolkien imagined his own female fertility figures: "men learned the crafts of the Entwives and honoured them greatly" (*TT* III/4). There is an even closer parallel with the Valië Yavanna in *The Silmarillion*.

plainly influenced by it; the description of Love with his train of ladies is there imitated and enlarged. Note especially 2573 ff.:

> Among thise othre upon the grene
> I syh also the wofull quene
> Cleopatras, which in a cave
> With serpentz hath hirself begrave
> Al quik, and so sche was to-tore
> For sorwe of that sche hadde love
> Antonye.[91]

Here the form of the name recalls Chaucer's distorted rhyme-form *Cleopataras*, and the curious account of her death is taken from Chaucer...

1 [*After the deeth of Tholomee the king*]: Ptolemæus, Ptolemy. Ptolemy XI (Aulētēs) died in B.C. 51. Cleopatra was his daughter. The intricacies of the family history were rendered obscurer by the fact that both of her brothers bore the same dynastic name, Ptolemy. She reigned jointly with each in turn (nominally as their wife, according to Egyptian custom), until she got rid of them both, the last by murder.

The medieval forms of classical names are not solely due to ignorance. Both here and in Boethius II prose 7 *Tholomee* may well have been the actual form written by Chaucer, although he knew the classical form well enough, indeed he had it in front of him. And it is no further from the original than our pronunciation of *Ptolemy*, even if our spelling has been a little emended by the schoolmaster. Actually most of the curious forms of classical names have a long history. They came usually through French. In that language many of the best-known were already naturalized, and altered in pronunciation, spelling following suit. These French forms, usually, and not the antecedent Latin ones, were then once more accommodated to English. Their pronunciation and spelling were thus far removed from their originals, but they had become familiar and survived the acquaintance of men with their forms in Latin texts. Some still do. We cling to Homer, Aristotle, Virgil in spite of our knowledge that these people were really named *Homēros*, *Aristotélēs*, *Vergilius*. There were corruptions, of course, especially of less familiar names, some deliberate because pedantic exactitude was not in fashion, some accidental because copyists will always stumble when faced with unfamiliar words. But such

---

[91] Tolkien quotes *The English Works of John Gower*, ed. G. C. Macaulay, EETS e.s. 81 and 82 (1900 and 1901), 2:456. His copy of Macaulay's *Selections from Confessio Amantis* (Oxford: Clarendon Press, 1903) is now the Bodleian's Tolkien VC 258.

distortions and errors were not a disease peculiar to classical names. *Ragan* has become *Regan, Medrod Mordred*.[92]

58. [*With grisly soun out goth the grete gonne*]: *gonne* also spelt *gunne*. It is our word "gun". The etymology is unknown. It is commonly applied to the siege-catapult for casting huge balls or stones, but it also was applied to the heavy missiles. This is the sense here. The change to the sense of "cannon" is already seen in Chaucer's *House of Fame* (1643-4): *as swift as pelet out of gonne/Whan fyr is in the poudre ronne*.[93]

59 [*And heterly they hurtlen al at ones*]: *heterly*.[94] This word only occurs here in Chaucer, and elsewhere it belongs only to the alliterative tradition, whether the alliterative prose of the life of *St Katharine*, and related works,[95] or to such poems as *Sir Gawain and the Green Knight, Wars of Alexander, William of Palerne*. It is foreign to the South East of England, and belongs to the North and West, a blend probably of Old Norse *hatrliga* and Old English *hetelīce*. Almost certainly *heterly they hurtlen* is a reminiscence of some of Chaucer's miscellaneous reading in contemporary English, more lively than the foreign learning he is more proud to parade.[96] In addition to hints of this sort, the style and rhythm of Chaucer, when attempting to describe scenes of action, sometimes becomes very similar to that of the alliterative poets. This passage should be compared with the tourney in the *Knight's Tale*, 1744-1762. There the vague resemblance becomes almost identity. Alliteration is frequent, and sometimes used exactly as in a professedly alliterative poem (e.g. 1747, 1750, 1753, 1754, 1758); while metrically these lines (and others) would seem natural in such poems, and some (e.g. 1758) are the same as the normal lines of Old English verse.

70 [*With pottes ful of lym they goon togider*]: Quick-lime was cast in the eyes of a boarding party to blind them, or else as a fine powder flung down the wind, a primitive sort of "gas-attack".[97]

---

[92] Provoked by such corruptions, Tolkien grew scrupulous about adding diacritical marks to ensure correct pronunciation of proper names like Ilúvatar, Fëanor, and Nazgûl.

[93] Gunpowder would turn the tide of battle in favour of Saruman's Orcs at Helm's Deep, just as Sauron's catapults would inflict serious damage at Minas Tirth.

[94] The word *heterly* became something of an obsession and is discussed at length in Tolkien's 1934 article "Chaucer as a Philologist" (1934, page 155 in this book) and referenced in his 1951 letter to OUP editor Dan Davlin (p. 55 above).

[95] The year after suspending work on his Clarendon Chaucer, Tolkien published "*Ancrene Wisse* and *Hali Meiðhad*" on the literary dialect of the Katherine Group.

[96] At this point Tolkien wrote a four-page 'Note on alliteration and alliterative tradition in Chaucer' (fols. 76r–77v), which he later excised but which we present separately as an excursus, below. The remainder of this paragraph is his replacement.

[97] As a combatant in the Great War, Tolkien knew about these attacks from when the Germans first effectively used tons of chlorine north of Ypres on 22 April 1915.

100 [*And alle the serpents that she mighte have*]: *serpents*: Plutarch mentions only one serpent, or asp. Shakespeare makes it two. Florus says *serpentibus*. Chaucer makes Cleopatra, as lavish in death as in life, collect all the serpents she could. Actually this form of suicide was adopted as relatively pleasant, not as an extravagant expression of grief. The poison of the *aspis*, a small hooded snake of North Africa, had a numbing effect, causing a drowsy sleep before death. But the crowd of serpents, and the pit (99, 118), are probably due to Northern ideas of burial, and to the legendary use of serpents in a pit as a cruel and horrible death. Of this the death of Gunnar, king of the Burgundians, in the snake-pen of the Hun king, is the most famous example. King Ælla of Northumbria in legend gave the same death to Ragnar Loðbrók.[98]

XV. *The Astroloabe* (extract from Introduction)

The *Treatise on the Astrolabe* was first printed in Thynne's edition of Chaucer, 1532.[99] There are twenty or more MSS of it now existing, in two of which it is given the curious title *Bred and mylk for childeren*. The chief interest of the treatise now, for those not specially concerned with the history of mathematics, astronomy, and scientific instruments, lies in the example it offers of Chaucer in a prose not so directly under the direction of a Latin original, and in the affectionate and familiar prologue, part of which is given here.

Lydgate tells us that Chaucer wrote a treatise on the Astrolabe "to his sonne that called was Lowis",[100] but beyond this and what is said in the prologue nothing is known of "litel Lowis". He was ten about the year 1390, and beginning to show tastes of a mathematical kind like his father. His Latin was not precocious. The calculations are directed to be made after the latitude of Oxford (cf. also Prologue, l. 9), so that presumably he was living there. Hardly as a student: fourteen would have been possible, ten was a too "tendre age".

---

[98] Tolkien included Gunnar in the snake pit in his own *Legend of Sigurd and Gudrun*, ed. Christopher Tolkien (Boston and New York: Houghton Mifflin Harcourt, 2009), 297–9. On the execution of Ragnar Loðbrók, see *Sagan om Ragnar Lodbrok och hans söner* (Stockholm: Norstedts, 1880), 82. Beren and Lúthien face reptilian terrors at Morgoth's stronghold: "Black chasms opened beside the road, whence forms as of writhing serpents issued" (*Silmarillion* 211). In *The Hobbit* the Great Goblin ordered the dwarves taken away to "dark holes full of snakes" (110).

[99] For this first "collected works," see James E. Blodgett, "William Thynne", in *Editing Chaucer*, ed. Ruggiers, 35–52. Skeat 3:lxxiii–lxxx took particular interest in the instrument's workings, since he had originally trained as a mathematician.

[100] Tolkien quotes from *Lydgate's Fall of Princes: Part I*, ed. Henry Bergen, EETS e.s. 121 (1924), 9. Tolkien's youngest son shared this interest in astronomy and was given a telescope "which he used constantly", as recalled by Priscilla Tolkien, "A Personal Memory," *Essays in Memory of Christopher Tolkien*, ed. Ovenden and McIlwaine, 46–52 at p. 47.

March 12th 1391 is twice used as an example for calculations in Part II of the treatise. This part must therefore have been written about that date. The prologue was written before the treatise, but after 1387, for it mentions the calendar of Nicholas of Lynne (written in 1386 for use in 1387). Also the table of contents it gives is more in the nature of a forecast of hopes than an account of what actually appears; and it employs the future tense. At the end of it Chaucer speaks of "other noteful thinges, yif God wol vouche sauf and his modur the mayde, mo than I behete".[101] He seems aware of his own tendency to alter plans or abandon them. Actually of the five parts of the prologue's table of contents only two have been preserved; the others were probably never written. As to Part V, in which his son was to "lerne a gret parte of the general rewles of the theorik in astrologie", Chaucer may have had some qualms, in spite of his own half-skeptical interest in the science. In Part II, at any rate, where matters astrological are alluded to, he describes "rytes of payens in which my spirit ne hath no feith".

XVI. *The Prologue to the Canterbury Tales* (extracts)

It is easier to plan a big book than to write it. Chaucer had found this out already, but he had not learned to be less ambitious.[102] Somewhere about 1387 he hit on the very thing he had been looking for, a scheme that would allow him to exercise his humour on contemporary life – the journalistic side of his talent – and give scope also for his skill in tale-telling and his learning. He made his plan, and wrote his prospectus. Filled with the zest of his new idea he made this one of his most famous pieces – but he overdid the estimates. He contracted for about 120 tales, in addition to the connecting account of the adventures and conversations of the pilgrims on the way to Canterbury and back, and an epilogue with supper. He would never have carried this out, even if he had lived in vigour long after 1400. Actually he left us just over a score of tales, not all written specially for the new scheme, and the links are often missing or confused. The study of Chaucer was doomed by the dusty debate of clerks over the proper order of his stories.[103] This is a sign of reverence, but it does not assist much in the appreciation of his art, nor does it make up at all for the absence of his hand. The pilgrimage sets out on a fine

---

[101] Tolkien quotes Skeat 3:177 sympathizing with Chaucer as a writer who altered and abandoned plans.
[102] Tolkien refers to the *Legend of Good Women*, which advertised a larger number of Cupid's "saints' lives" than were actually written.
[103] See Skeat 3:371–88 "The Nine Groups." [Tolkien]

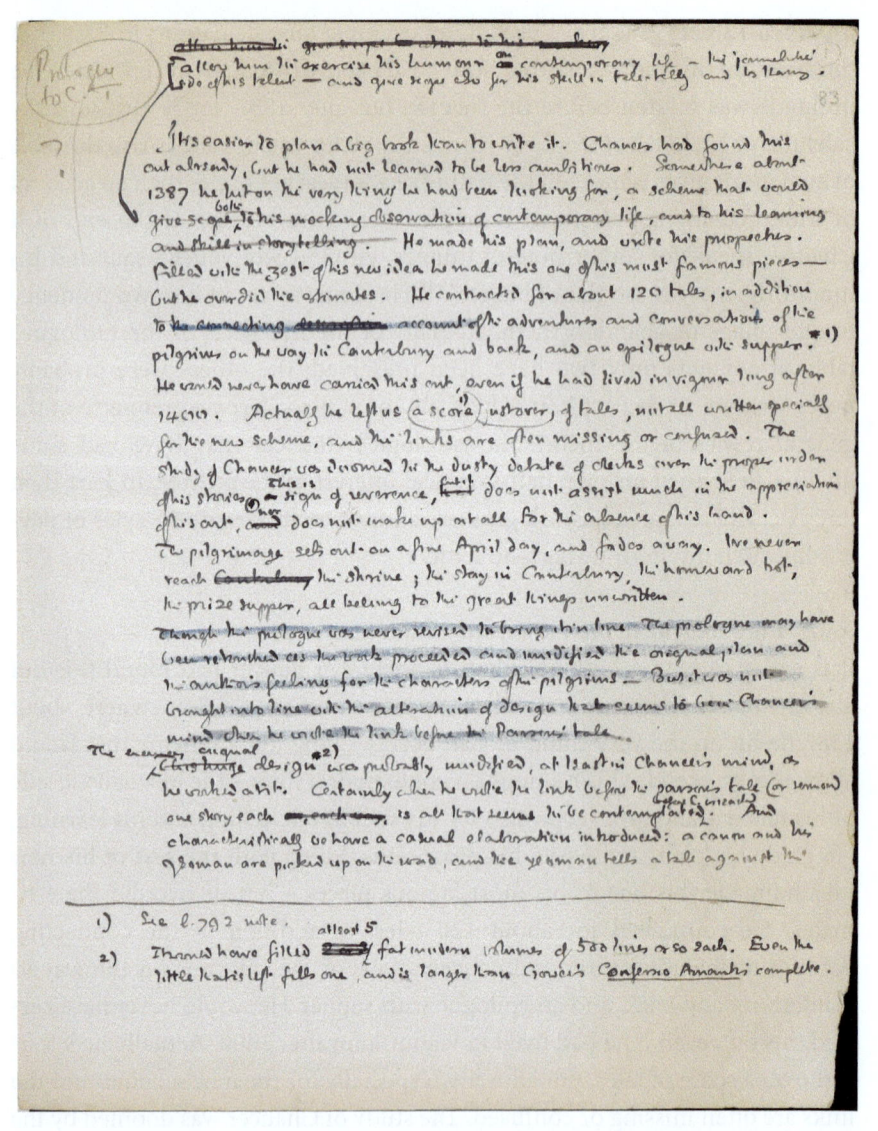

Fig. 8 Handwritten introduction to *Canterbury Tales* (Bodleian MS Tolkien A 39/2/2, fol. 83).

April day, and fades away. We never reach the shrine; the stay in Canterbury, the homeward trot, the prize supper, all belong to the great things unwritten.

The huge original design was probably modified, at least in Chaucer's mind, as he worked at it. It would have filled at least five fat modern volumes of 500 pages or so each. Even the little that is left fills one, and is larger than Gower's *Confessio Amantis* complete. Certainly when he wrote the link before the *Parson's Tale* (or sermon), one story each is all that seems to be contemplated before Canterbury is reached. And characteristically we have a casual elaboration introduced: a canon and his yeoman are picked up on the road, and the yeoman tells a tale against the frauds of Alchemy, the first breath of which sends off his master, an alchemist, in a rage.

There is nothing in English before Chaucer quite like the plan of the *Canterbury Tales*. Collections of tales were, however, common. They owed their origin partly to the assembly of similar matter into a composite manuscript: collected sermons, legends of saints, moral tales, or recipes. Strings were also devised of various kinds for these loosely connected items, and we get them strung into chronicle histories, or hung at intervals, for illustration and enlivenment, in moral treatises on the sins. Chaucer's own *Legend of Good Women* is an example of a collection of tales illustrating a common theme, explained in a prologue. So is the *Monk's Tale* within the larger scheme of the *Canterbury Tales* themselves.[104] In Gower's *Confessio Amantis*, too, we have an immense collection of tales illustrating a large theme, and here there is both prologue and connecting narrative. Even closer is the once very popular *Seven Sages of Rome*, of oriental origin, that began its career in western Europe in the 12th century, and was already in English before Chaucer's day. Here we have a tale that is not merely a connecting device, but which encloses fifteen tales told by characters in the main story. Chaucer could have bridged the gap between such things as these and the *Canterbury Tales* by his own invention unaided. Just as he touched old stories to new life, so he could have made the convention of prologue and setting new and individual. In Italy he would have found more suggestive models, as the *Decameron* of Boccaccio whose hundred tales are united in a single story of lords and ladies of Florence, or Sercambi's *Novelle* in which a miscellaneous company go upon a journey and elect a leader who proposes tales – but these are all told by one man, Sercambi, the equivalent of Chaucer. But that he ever saw them is not proved. Nor does it much matter. He differs from them as much as he resembles them. He would have had to exercise as much originality in reshaping the suggestion they afforded and adapting it to England, as in thinking out the device for himself.[105]

As far as collections in English go, the most original departure of the *Canterbury Tales* is that it offers a *miscellaneous* collection of stories, sermons

---

[104] Tolkien's *Selections* included the tragedy of Ugolino from the *Monk's Tale*; he edited it and included its vocabulary in the glossary, but he never reached it in his draft commentary.

[105] Tolkien himself had written his *Book of Lost Tales* as a frame-narrative containing a series of stories, begun in 1917; see SH 2:176-94.

to ribaldry.[106] There is no more necessary connexion between them than between the chance-gathered pilgrims: the first are typical stories of the day (Chaucerized), the doers ordinary mortals of the day (seen through Chaucer's eyes, humorous and sharp if not seeing very far and deep). The notion that Chaucer thought (or even that his audience would certainly have imagined) that he was continuing the old tradition and deliberately offering groups of tales illustrating *motifs*, love or the Seven Deadly Sins, may be dismissed as clerkly *fantasye*. Chaucer would indeed have been hard put to it to write a single tale (let alone 20 or 120) of interest to men and women of his day that did not deal with Love, or any of the deadly sins, or study conjugal relations!

That the germ of the prologue and the scheme was an actual pilgrimage is perfectly possible. It is the way that books are begun. One April 16th, perhaps 1387,[107] Chaucer may in fact have been at the Tabard. There also he may have noted down a thing or two for the sketches written later – excellent little pictures, if a little external and superficial. But we cannot prove this and he could have written the Prologue without it. He had ample opportunity for observing all the types elsewhere, types of nearly all classes in the land, except the highest and lowest.

Attempts, interesting enough, have been made to identify the pilgrims.[108] But Chaucer's sketches do not suggest, usually, that they are portraits of individuals except, perhaps, Harry Bailey and the Wife of Bath (into whose description in the Prologue we read what we learn of her elsewhere). There is little that is really individual about most of them. Mormals upon the shin may not be typical of cooks, but the grey eyes of the Prioress are shared by most of the ladies of Middle English literature from Guinever to nameless lovers. *Grey as glass* are the eyes of the miller's daughter in the *Reeve's Tale*. And it is difficult to believe in the strange luck that should preserve record or trace of Chaucer's originals among the many gay forgotten things of the dusk of the 14th century.

More probably he has given us a glimpse of the people of his time – typical of many a little chance cavalcade in London. His sketch is in bright and lively colours, here and there suggested it may be by figures he knew well. This is an

---

[106] Tolkien's penmanship, already challenging (see fig. 8), deteriorates in these pages, but we are fairly confident in our transcriptions.
[107] The Man of Law's headlink gives April 18th as the second day of the journey. [Tolkien]
[108] Tolkien may have thought specifically of John M. Manly's *Some New Light on Chaucer* (New York: Henry Holt, 1926).

achievement. To have attempted a gallery of portraits of actual individuals and have failed with most of them is not.

Time has seen to it that the Prologue is now one of the hardest things in Chaucer to really understand. It was meant to be read lightheartedly by men familiar with the clothes and foibles of the day. But clothes change while *hearts* remain much the same. And we can only partly understand the significance of the descriptions now, and that only after a research which the author never intended us to endure. Our casual references to our sports and dress will pass on the problem to the bookworms of future ages....

Prologue
17 [*The holy blisful martir for to seke*]:[109] St Thomas a Becket, born 1118, became Chancellor under Henry II. He succeeded Archbishop Theobald in the see of Canterbury in 1162, largely owing to the king's favour; but he spent the next eight years in a struggle with Henry. In the end he was driven into banishment in France, and had not long returned to Canterbury, after a reconciliation with the king, when he was murdered at the foot of an altar in his own cathedral (Dec. 29 1170) by four of the king's knights. His canonization took place in 1173. The king did public penance for the crime.[110] The frequenting of Canterbury by pilgrims lasted down to the 16th century, by which time the shrine and its treasures of gold and silver and jewels were of great value and magnificence.

[**Squire**] 79 [*With him ther was his sone, a yong Squyer*]: *squyer*: an esquire (Old French *esquier*, Latin *scūtārius*, shield-bearer) was technically one who waited on a knight, and carried his spear and shield. It was a man of gentle birth and himself an aspirant to knighthood, a form of apprenticeship.[111] With the use of the term as the name of rank in the gentry next below the knight (which has ultimately dwindled to our *Esq.* on envelopes) we are not here concerned, though *eldest sons of knights* were later among those supposed to be specially entitled to the name.

[109] The clarity of Tolkien's handwriting much improves in these notes to the text of the *Canterbury Tales*, perhaps based on an early rougher draft, not extand. Still, we have produced only a small sampling of the notes fols. 83-130 for the General Prologue.
[110] Tolkien's Beregond commits sacrilege for spilling blood in the Hallows of Minas Tirith, and Aragorn is obliged to punish him, but with nothing harsher than exile to Ithilien in the service of Faramir (*RK* VI/5).
[111] In Middle-earth's royal households, Merry became esquire to Théoden and Pippin an esquire to Denethor. Having completed these apprenticeships, Merry and Pippin served as well-armed warriors defeating Saruman's ruffians in the Shire.

[**Prioress**] 120 [*Hir gretteste ooth was but by seynt Loy*]:[112] St Eloy or *Eligius* (of which the French form is a regular development) rose to favour under the Frankish kings Clotaire II and Dagobert I (7th century) largely because of his skill as a goldsmith.[113] He gave away his wealth lavishly to the poor, became a priest, and ultimately Bishop of Noyon, an office which he used to evangelize a large part of Flanders, especially the parts about Antwerp and round Ghent and Courtray. Because of his skill he became the patron saint of goldsmiths, and so of smiths, farriers and carters. The use of his name by the carter in the *Friar's Tale* is therefore quite in order.

Why he was selected as the sole oath of the Prioress is not clear. That Chaucer intended a joke of some sort and was not just "drawing from nature" may be confidently assumed. That he glances at her love of gold trinkets (160), or that it is a way of saying that she really hardly swore at all, are suggestions – not very satisfactory. A tale was told of St Eligius (retold by Maitland, *Dark Ages* p. 83)[114] that the saint once refused to take an oath on relics when pressed by King Dagobert, and his unsupported word was ultimately accepted. But there is no evidence that such a tale was well enough known at the end of the fourteenth century to allow even the brightest of Chaucer's audience to mark the subtle point (suggested by Skeat) that she swore by a non-juror, and so at second hand did not swear. This makes the carter in the *Friar's Tale* a bit mealy-mouthed, which he was not. Most likely St Loy, a name originally revered in Northern France and Belgium (especially among craftsmen), whence it travelled among the similar folk of England, had lost most of its association even with the rather high-class art of the goldsmith, and was chiefly an oath of people very little genteel. Herein may be the jest. The Prioress with her *par Saint Eloy* (a little old-fashioned) is not aware that this is perilously like the *by seynt Loy* of blacksmiths, ostlers, carters and the hangers-on of the inn-yard.

125 [*After the scole of Stratford atte Bowe*]: There was a Benedictine nunnery at Stratford-at-Bow, an ancient foundation dating back probably as far as about 1100. Presumably it was where the Prioress had been educated, or had been a novice and young nun. Doubtless the French spoken by the ladies there was good enough, but it is useless to deny that Chaucer is mocking or to

---

[112] We have cut this very long note's first two-thirds, which deal with scansion.

[113] Tolkien's Middle-earth is well populated with Elven smiths, such as Celebrimbor of Eregion who forged the Rings of Power. The Gwaith-i-Mírdain or "People of the Jewel–smiths" was a brotherhood of Elven craftsmen during the Second Age.

[114] Tolkien lifted from Skeat 5:14 this reference to S. R. Maitland, *The Dark Ages: Essays Illustrating the State of Religion and Literature in the Ninth, Tenth, Eleventh and Twelfth Centuries* (1853).

assert that he is merely jotting down facts without comment or malicious motive. This would leave precious little point in the next line. The rather old-fashioned, and indeed at the end of the fourteenth century very provincial, disintegrating, and decadent French of the gentry of England probably still satisfied many of them, who felt its use to mark them off plainly from the common folk (more plainly than the command of *h* does now). But people of larger wealth or wider travel and reading were only too well aware of the inferior position which their transplanted and anglicized dialect occupied with regard to the literary language of Paris. Gower (who wrote French probably a deal better than the Prioress could) is full of apologies for his idiom.[115] The fact that at this time books were made to teach people to speak French, who by descent should have needed no teacher but the conversation of their homes, shows that all was not well with domestic French in England. Many in fact were abandoning it in daily life, even if they made efforts to have their children taught continental French as an accomplishment. No special sneer is probably intended at the Stratford nunnery, or at any rate not at its French, which may have been of the highest kind obtainable in England. It is mentioned very likely to fix in the minds of an audience naturally more alive to topical allusions than we are precisely the culture and degree to which the Prioress belonged: a conservative old-fashioned type, proud of its gentility and traditions, but unconscious of its own narrowness and provinciality and the changing times. Very likely such was the reputation of the house in Chaucer's time. It is not so much the use of French, or even its badness, of course that Chaucer smiles at, as the secure feeling of belonging to a higher order that its use gave to its possessors, unaware (as he knew perfectly well) that a Parisian would esteem their dialect little higher if at all than the patois of country bumpkins.

128-136 [*She leet no morsel from hir lippes falle*]: The jesting drift of the description is that the Prioress behaved like a "copy-book" and was, as might be expected of her, a faithful follower of the rhymes and rules of deportment at table taught to the young. It has been pointed out that this passage is actually very close to a description of good behaviour in *Romance of the Rose* (13,612 ff.),[116] where in much the same order as in Chaucer we learn that the lady did not dip her fingers deep in broth, carefully handled the morsels (bits

---

[115] Unlike Chaucer who wrote exclusively in English, John Gower composed his *Mirour de l'Omme*, as well as some lyrics, in French; see F. R. Yeager, "John Gower's French," in *A Companion to Gower*, ed. Siân Echard (Cambridge: D. S. Brewer, 2004), 137–51.

[116] Skeat 5:16 notes that Tyrwhitt first pointed out Chaucer's debt here to the *Rose*.

of bread neatly cut for the purpose) she had dipped in sauce, lifted them circumspectly so that no drops of broth or condiment fell on her breast, and drank so daintily that she spilled no drops on herself. She was supposed also to wipe her mouth, especially her upper lip, carefully so that no grease was left there.

Chaucer, of course, had read this passage, but need not have been thinking specially of it here. The rules were common form, and continued to be instilled into the young long after his day – and are still, though change of apparatus (especially the later vogue of the fork) have altered some of the details, but not the spirit, of polite observance. But even to-day if one was to relate in detail of a lady that she behaved as ordinary refinement demanded, it would produce a slightly comic effect, a vision of an anxious gentility.

152 [*Hir nose tretys; hir eyen greye as glas*]: The Prioress is described now in terms as conventional, if less obviously burlesqued, as Sir Thopas. She is the romance fair lady, slightly spoiled in a gently malicious manner fitting to the author speaking in his own elvish person. In the *Reeve's Tale* we see the same conventional portrait rudely and coarsely parodied, as is more fitting to Chaucer pretending to be a reeve (who is in a rage with millers). There even his duller readers must have perceived the inversion of the familiar picture of the lady "gent and small",[117] with only her grey eyes left undamaged, a malicious comment on the pretended gentility of the maiden's mother. In the description of the Prioress the joke is milder and dawns on us more slowly. The original of the picture (if there was any single one) may indeed have had "grey eyes", not uncommon, and those who wish may see in this line one of those happy touches on the canvas, taken direct from life, which give individuality to Chaucer's portraits.[118] It is far more probable (and more amusing) to believe that English literary tradition and convenient rhyme (and a jesting purpose) dictated the colour of the eyes and found the alliterative phrase. The latter is one of those familiar things, embedded in everyday language, which are very difficult to track, and which escape glossaries of hard words and learned commentaries alike. Actually Chaucer, here and in the *Reeve's Tale* 54, provides the only two examples of *grey as glas* we can find in Middle English...But nonetheless the coupling is probably ancient, going back to Old English, for we find preserved in our fragments of Old English verse (representative of a tradition more highly wrought than Middle English, and even

---

[117] Chaucer used this phrase to describe Alisoun in the *Miller's Tale* (*CT* I, 3234).
[118] Tolkien gave the same color eyes to many of his attractive characters such as Arwen, "her bright eyes, grey as a cloudless night." The stray page Bodleian MS Tolkien E 16/45, fol. 116, contains a similar list of literary references to grey eyes including those in Shakespeare. Tolkien himself had grey eyes.

farther removed from the current phraseology of everyday life) what appear to be literary elaborations of a simple *græg swā glæs*...The comparison originally made was to primitive and duller glass,[119] but clarity and brightness are certainly implied in the Middle English and already in Old English *glæs-hlúttor*.

Not only Great Ladies, such as Guinevere, all fair ladies' standard (if we do not begin with Olympian Athene *glaukōpis* of the Greeks!), had grey eyes – or blue, for such was the range of the sense, the colour of the sea in most of its northern moods[120] – but almost all fair ladies and maids beside, wherever the colour (besides their size, clearness and their arching brows) is specially mentioned, down to the nameless "lemmen" of love-lyrics...[121]

[**Monk**] 170 [*Ginglen in a whistling wind as clere.*] It was the fashion to hang small bells on the harness of horses. It became especially the custom of pilgrims to Canterbury to use bells. The "Canterbury bells" must have given the name to the clustered bells of campanulas, and which could at one time be heard ringing merrily as a small cavalcade went by on the eastward road. But it is not alluded to here, if the custom yet existed, for the Monk is singled out by his bells, which are meant to point to his copying of the gear and ways of secular people of rank.[122]

[**Clerk**] 285 [*A Clerk ther was of Oxenford also*]: *clerk*: one whose studies had fitted him (or were fitting him) for orders, and ecclesiastical office. This clerk was probably a young man, but at any rate he was already qualified to have a benefice, though he had not secured one. He appears also to have come of a poor family, that had made sacrifices to send him to Oxford – as many do still, if not as much as they did in days before pious benefactors had somewhat eased the way, but when the democratic church offered an avenue of advancement through the hedges of birth and privilege to learning, to artistic talent, and to administrative ability.

This clerk was a sober fellow. Contrast the gay Nicholas of the *Miller's Tale*, who redeems Oxford's reputation.

---

[119] *glæs, glass*, is itself originally probably a colour name, closely related to Celtic *glass* – blue, green, blue-grey. [Tolkien]

[120] When Éowyn confronts the Lord of the Nazgûl, "Her eyes grey as the sea were hard and fell" (*RK* V/6).

[121] There are two draft notes on Merton College postcards addressed to C. S. Lewis concerning Chaucer's use of *lemman* in the *Manciple's Tale* (Bodleian MS Tolkien E 16/45, fols. 106–7).

[122] Glorfindel's horse has a harness ringing with bells because he is an Elf-lord, but the horses of the austere Dúnedain warriors are not thus decorated.

[**Shipman**] 401 ff. [*But of his craft to rekene wel his tydes / His stremes and his daungers him bisydes / His herberwe and his mone, his lodemenage*]: This description is meant to have a nautical air and a smack of genuine sailors' language. It contains some words used in what are now their chief or sole senses, though these are still rare in Middle English, which suggests that they represent contemporary nautical talk, and that our uses have been influenced by the language of the ports, especially London. *tydes* still normally "times". Since the times specially observed by a coastal navigator were those of ebb and flood, this use is probably older among sailors than in ordinary language[123] – it is not recorded in Old English, and is uncommon in Middle English. *daunger* "power (to harm)"[124] – for a sailor possessed chiefly by shoals, currents, reefs and the like, which are here meant by the rare modern-looking plural. *herberwe* is Middle English "lodging" or accommodation, cf. Prol. 765; here "harbourage" approaching modern "harbour"....

[**Parson**] 486 [*Ful looth were him to cursen for his tythes*]. He did not like doing this – he probably did it officially nonetheless. On tithes the parish priest was normally dependent for his support; failure or refusal to pay them, or any fraud in their payment, was a serious sin – usually enumerated under the fruits of avarice in treatises on the sins such as *Ancren Riwle* (C. Soc. p. 208) or *Ayenbite of Inwyt* (p. 41 EETS).[125] There was an excommunication service – somewhat similar to the Commination Service – which was directed to be pronounced before the whole parish two or three times a year "with cross, candle and bell"....

[**Plan of the Tales**] 792 [*In this viage shal telle tales tweye*]. In addition to the *ten* pilgrims represented in this selection, the Prologue also describes a yeoman, friar*, merchant*, lawyer*, franklin*, haberdasher, carpenter, weaver, dyer, tapicer, cook*, physician*, ploughman (the parson's brother), manciple*, summoner*, pardoner*; and mentions a nun* (the prioress' *chaplain*) with her three priests, one* of whom tells a story (NP).

This makes 30, or 31 with Chaucer* – the Host as umpire is not to be included in the storytellers. *Wel nyne and twenty* (l. 24) was probably intended as exact when written (*one and thirty* would have fitted the line as well). It is

---

[123] One such older speaker is Gandalf the White in Fangorn Forest: "We meet again. At the turn of the tide. The great storm is coming, but the tide has turned" (*TT* III/5).

[124] Tolkien uses this word and its variation *dangerous* 170 times in *LotR*.

[125] *Ancren Riwle*, ed. Morton, and *Dan Michel's Ayenbite of Inwyt*, ed. Richard Morris, EETS o.s. 23 (1866).

possible that the *three* priests, only one of whom is ever heard of again, is an unrevised error, or a later confusion. The original plan is thus for 31 (or 29) × 4 = 124 (or 116) tales.[126]

Actually a single story is extant (each probably belonging to the outward journey) for the *ten* characters of the selection, and for those marked * above. Chaucer recites the parody of contemporary verse *Sir Thopas*, and when this is cut short by the Host, gives a long sermon (*Tale of Melibeus*). The Cook's tale and the Squire's were never finished. Thus we have, with the Canon's Yeoman's tale, 20 tales, 2 fragments, and a little parody, out of a projected total of 124 or 116 tales – tales modified perhaps to 58.

XVII. *The Reeve's Tale* (extract)

The Reeve's name was Oswald (*Osewold*, Miller's Prologue A. 3151, Reeve's Prologue A 3860, 3909) and we have learned already that he came from Baldeswell in Norfolk. In his own words in the prologue to his tale there are dialect traces as *so thee'k, ik am* (compared with the *so theëch* used elsewhere by the Host).[127] Having decided on this localization of the Reeve, Chaucer proceeds to make him localize the tale he tells also in the Eastern districts, in Cambridge, although the story is probably an adaptation of an earlier *fabliau* of French origin. Whether Chaucer took it from French direct, or found or knew of it already adapted in English, is not now known, and no version close enough to be regarded as his direct source is extant. But in any case his is certainly one of the tales made specially for his *Canterbury Tales* and for the supposed narrator....[128]

94 [*Of o toun were they born that highte Strother*]. *Strother*: the next line is of course a jest – a Southern shrug of the shoulders at the unknown geography of the barbarous North (which Chaucer had nonetheless visited).[129]

---

[126] Skeat 3:374 and 384 discussed the altered format without struggling with the precise number of tales intended. Robinson, ed., *Poetical Works of Chaucer* (1933), 2, reckoned 120 projected tales but only 23 completed, numbers which have been largely accepted ever since.

[127] Skeat 5:113 had remarked on these dialect features which Tolkien's student Norman Davis, in his review of J. A. W. Bennett's *Chaucer at Oxford and at Cambridge*, *RES*, n.s. 27 (1976), 336-7 at p. 336, called "the *ik* which everybody notices". See Simon C. P. Horobin, "Chaucer's Norfolk Reeve," *Neophilologus* 86 (2002), 609-12, and Philip Knox, "The 'Dialect' of Chaucer's Reeve," *Chaucer Review* 49 (2014), 102-24.

[128] In the left margin, Tolkien inserted in pencil: "These in so far as legible need revising in light of my study of Reeve's Tale, Philol. Soc. 1936." He had revisited the draft commentary sufficiently long afterwards to forget that his study "Chaucer as a Philolgist" was published in 1934, not 1936.

[129] "Chaucer as a Philologist" pp. 161-2 below: "Once at least he is believed to have been in Yorkshire; and though a residence at Hatfield as a very young man would not provide even an inquisitive person, less biassed than usual by southern prejudices... with much opportunity for observation of the local vernacular."

Cf. Trevisa in Sisam XIV etc. p. 150.[130] But it also implies that the village was thought of as the extreme North of England. Skeat says there is no such town now, but there are two villages in Northumberland of the name.... The element is in any case very common in Northern England and in Scotland and appears frequently in names like Anstruther. It appears to have meant "marsh" and to have been related to OE *strōd* "marsh", which has also generated several place-names further south.

The names *Aleyn* and *John* are so common that not much importance can be attached to the occurrence of *de Strother* as last name of a Northumberland family of whom in 1381 *Alan de Strother* was a recorded member, and his son *John de Strother*.[131] This family was fairly important in the North, Alan de Strother being constable of Roxburgh Castle. There was nothing at this time of course against members of such a family speaking dialectically, but these were young clerks of no particular wealth and not likely to have belonged to it. Nor are they relatives or thought of as having (de) Strother as a surname. They are simply boys from a village of the name. The fact that *Strother* is a common Northern element is significant: Chaucer probably chose it for that reason.

* * *

Tolkien's increasingly hasty annotations end here, not continuing for the remaining 134 lines of the edition's truncated *Reeve's Tale*, but below his last notes he jotted the phrases "Chaucer at Hatfield" and "The dialect is Yorkshire". These two dangling thoughts would then become the impetus for his 1931 lecture "Chaucer's Use of Dialects" published as his major 1934 article "Chaucer as a Philologist: *The Reeve's Tale*". This in turn led to his 1939 experimental edition of the *Reeve's Tale* and his 1944 teaching materials for Naval cadets at Oxford – all of which form the subjects of the next two chapters, after we consider Tolkien's four-page digression on the Alliterative tradition.

Excursus: Chaucer and the Alliterative Tradition

Tolkien halted his commentary on the *Legend of Cleopatra* at line 59's *heterly* to write four pages on Chaucer's alliterative practices (Bodleian MS Tolkien

---

[130] Tolkien alludes to John Trevisa's famous remarks on England's regional dialects in his 1387 translation of Hidgen's *Polychronicon* – "Al þe longage of þe Norþhumbres, and specialych at ʒork, ys so scharp, slyttyng, and frotyng, and vnschape, þat we Souþeron men may þat longage vnneþe vndurstonde" – which he knew in Sisam's *Fourteenth Century Verse and Prose*, 150, where he himself had glossed *scharp, slyttyng, frotyng*, and *vnschape* as "harsh", "piercing", "grating", and "formless".
[131] Skeat 5:120 provides information about Alan de Strother and his son John.

A 39/2, fols. 76r–77v) and later inserted a pencil note at top of the first page by way of explanation. He took the trouble to review all the texts of the *Selections* and list sixty-one alliterative doublets starting with "*fressh floures*, PF 259" and ending with "*blood and bones*, NP 607". We have omitted the other fifty-nine examples for considerations of space. Tolkien's insights in these notes sent in 1928 to his co-editor, George Gordon, anticipated Robinson in his *Works of Chaucer* (1933), 783, and Dorothy Everett in "Chaucer's 'Good Ear'", *RES* 23 (1947), 201–8. Tolkien's 1940 essay "On Translating *Beowulf*" concludes with two helpful sections summarizing the tradition of Old English "Meter" and "Alliteration" (*Essays* 61–71).

* * *

Note on alliteration & alliterative tradition in Chaucer
Originally written to follow on as part of note on "heterly" in Legend of Cleopatra, 59.

Chaucer's vocabulary rarely affords hints of this sort; and though he uses alliteration, he does so, usually, no more than is natural in any writer of good verse (e.g. III 337–338, PF 190–3, Prol 591, NP 578–9).[132] The frequent alliterative phrases to be found in his work are mainly due to the language itself, not the poet. They are there partly as an indication of the liking for alliteration in everyday speech, partly as traces of the drill which the language had received from countless alliterative poets. Such are *fressh floures*, PF 259… *blood and bones*, NP 607.

Many of these seem obvious and inevitable, but these are often very old both in the language and alliterative verse: such as *telle with tonge, hevene and helle*, or even *gadre togidre* Prol 824. Alliterative verse, even in its conventions, was really more closely linked with natural speech than rhyme and its artifices. Some are new, but on old models, such as *month of May, pert as is a pye*. Some survive today ("brown as a berry," "proud as a peacock," "through thick and thin.") Sometimes indeed the old phrase is altered by the poet or the changing language, and falls out of our list. Compare NP 242 with PF 458. The old and still very common *swete and swinke* appears as *swinken and laboure* in Prol 186 (and elsewhere in Middle English). Compare also the note to NP 436.

Apart, however, from these phrases embedded in the language, or echoes through minstrel's verse of ancient nearly forgotten traditions, it is noticeable

---

[132] Tolkien's abbreviations such as PF for *Parlement of Foules* and NP for *Nun's Priest's Tale* are keyed to the titles listed at the head of his glossary; see *TLC* 283-4.

that where Chaucer is describing scenes, such as battles, that require a forcible and graphic method, his style and rhythm approaches close to that of the alliterative poets. The passage here (*Legend of Cleopatra* 56–74) should be compared especially with the tourney in the *Knight's Tale* (A 2602–2620). There the resemblance passes beyond a mere hint or echo, and becomes so great that it is impossible to deny that English reading has played a significant part in this adaptation of an Italian original. Not only is the alliteration frequent, but it is used in some lines exactly as in an alliterative poem; and metrically, while it is still perfectly possible for us (and Chaucer) to carve up the lines into the approved five feet, they fall naturally into the alliterative line, having two main accented syllables in each half, with the caesura in between.

```
2605   ther | shívėrėn | sháftės || upon | sheéldės | thíkkė
2608   óut goon the | swérdės || as the | sílvėr | bríghtė
2611   with | míghty | mácės || the | bónės they to-|bréstė
2612   he | thúrgh the | thíkkeste || of the thróng | gan thréstė
2616   And | hé him | húrtleth || with his hórs | adóun
```

The arrangement of the alliteration in these examples may be paralleled from professedly alliterative poems. In 2605, 2608, 2616 it is correctly arranged even according to the strictest Old English principles. Metrically 2616 would be correct in an Old English poem, where we should say it had *and* as "upbeat" and was for the rest composed of two halves, the first of A type (falling rhythm $\acute{-}\;\smile$), the second of B type (rising $\smile\;\acute{-}$).

Chaucer was writing at a time when alliterative verse, preserved unrecorded in popular use, doubtless often rude enough, was being written once more (for gentle audiences) in large quantities and sometimes of great merit – to judge even by what chance has saved of it.

He never wrote any verse himself that was alliterative, except by way of adornment, or reminiscence. That he despised the work of alliterative poets as provincial is improbable. They were as dependent on French matter and sentiment as he was. But the practice of alliterative verse was associated with a region (the North and West Midlands) removed from the places he normally lived in, and especially with an unfamiliar vocabulary. Also it needed its own early training, and Chaucer's had been in rhyme. In any case it was not (though it might by a master have been made) an instrument for the lighter kinds of music; and no master could make it as easy to write as rhyme.

Chaucer makes his Parson say:—

> But trusteth wel, I am a Southren man
> I kan not geestë 'rum ram ruf' by lettre,
> Ne, God woot, rym holde I but litel bettre.

But this (as is sometimes forgotten) is spoken in character, and the Parson by these very words (and his later tale!) shows himself no poet or judge of poetry. His words have not the weight of Milton's censuring of rhyme, after first showing his mastery of it.[133] What Chaucer himself thought of *rum ram ruf* is better to be gauged, delicate matter though it be, from his own work set against the background of Middle English. The just conclusion probably is that he read it, liked it when it was good, but knew that his own taste and talent were different.

---

[133] John Milton's note on "Verse" in the 1668 second edition of *Paradise Lost* defended his use of blank verse, instead of iambic pentameter couplets, though even as a 15-year-old student at St. Paul's, he had shown his mastery by translating Psalm 114 into heroic couplets.

3
The Reeve's Tale, 1928–44

When Tolkien's co-editor George Gordon and his OUP editor Kenneth Sisam dropped the *Prioress's Tale* from their Chaucer textbook because of its anti-semitism, they decided to replace it with the first half of the *Reeve's Tale* stopping, however, before the double rape of the miller's daughter and wife. This truncated tale nonetheless obliged Tolkien to engage with Skeat's text and change six spellings, with the alternatives *bos/boës* causing him repeated doubts. Out of the excerpt's 228 lines, Tolkien's draft annotations reached only line 94, where he remarked upon *Strother* as the hometown of the "poor clerks" John and Alain, before sending his nearly 200-page bundle of notes off to George Gordon in the hopes that he might help with reducing its excessive length. Largely untouched, these pages would remain with Gordon at Magdalen College for two years before Tolkien again took possession, but without making further progress either abbreviating what he had drafted or annotating the final two selections, the *Monk's Tale* and the *Nun's Priest's Tale*.

As unfinished business, Tolkien's work with the *Reeve's Tale* would lead to his 1931 lecture "Chaucer's Use of Dialect" published in 1934 as his weighty article "Chaucer as a Philologist: *The Reeve's Tale*". When invited to dress up as Chaucer and recite for Oxford's Summer Diversions in 1939, Tolkien chose to perform the *Reeve's Tale* from memory and, to help his audience, prepared a programme with the poem's text which he had newly edited. But he was not finished with this fabliau. When teaching Navy cadets at Oxford in 1944, he used leftover copies of the programme in the classroom and supplemented it with various paratexts, notably his typed-up "Chaucerian Grammar (with special reference to the *Reeve's Tale*)". The following sections trace this sixteen-year engagement with a work where the Northern dialect features had first attracted his attention in his 1913 tutorial essay "The Language of Chaucer".

"Chaucer as a Philologist: *The Reeve's Tale*" (1934)

Tolkien's last two cryptic jottings on the *Reeve's Tale* in his Clarendon notes – "Chaucer at Hatfield" and "The dialect is Yorkshire" – planted the seeds for further consideration of the teenage Chaucer in the Countess of Ulster's retinue at Hatfield House in Yorkshire in 1357. Here the young Londoner would have heard the regional speech which he later employed for his two Cambridge students (Skeat 1:xvii). That Chaucer used the Northern language in a very expert manner in their dialogue, not casually "to amuse us" as Skeat had thought (5:121–22), received its first airing in Tolkien's lecture "Chaucer's Use of Dialects", delivered on 16 May 1931 to the Philological Society in Oxford. Since this lecture would be published as a matter of course in *Transactions of the Philological Society*, Tolkien worked very hard, as he explained in his opening apology for the delay, to supplement the delivery text with a critical edition of the dialect passages, textual notes, footnotes, and appendices on particular words.[1]

It is a mystery why Tolkien's "Chaucer as a Philologist" has been mostly overlooked from the time of its appearance in 1934. Thomas Honegger has remarked how the scholarly pieces selected by Christopher Tolkien for *The Monsters and the Critics* "have by now achieved canonical status among Tolkien scholars, whereas most of the other academic essays have sunk into oblivion."[2] A few suggestions come to mind why "Chaucer as a Philologist" sank. First, Tolkien had been Oxford's Professor of Anglo-Saxon since 1925 and therefore was not expected to publish significant work on Chaucer. He might indeed have been viewed as encroaching upon the professional turf of Chaucer specialists such as John M. Manly and John Livingston Lowes. And later, of course, Tolkien's fame as author of *The Lord of the Rings* eclipsed his scholarly output except for those pieces which Christopher had promoted.

But Chaucer's editors had an obvious reason to ignore the argument, because it reached the unsettling conclusion that no modern edition, not even Skeat's, faithfully reproduced the poet's authentic texts because no early manuscript, not even the Ellesmere copy of the *Canterbury Tale*, accurately preserved his original language, only the languages of the fifteenth-century scribes. He dismissed even Chaucer's personal copyist: "Adam and his offspring have fortunately kept copies, it is true, but unfortunately they are unreliable on the very points we wish to scrutinize, less so perhaps in vocabulary, more so certainly in grammar, dialectal forms, and spellings" (p. 119). Tom

---

[1] Many of Tolkien's notes for this lecture and its revisions for its publication can be consulted in the Bodleian: MS Tolkien A 14/1, fols. 84, 88; MS Tolkien A 17/2, fols. 112–14, 116, 118–22, 126, 128–31; MS Tolkien A 30/2, fols. 39–40, 42, 140–2, 144–6; MS Tolkien A 32/2, fols. 2–6, 9–16; MS Tolkien E 16/45, fols. 4–5.

[2] Thomas Honegger, "Academic Writings", in *Companion*, ed. Lee, 27–40 at p. 27.

Shippey pinpointed the source of dissatisfaction when compared with the high standard set by his AB copyists in the Katherine Group:

> Professor Tolkien's scribes were reliable, accurate, punctilious. The rest – well (so it seemed), they wrote the way they felt, and every time some new copier came along, he copied what was in front of him, imitated a bit, spelt a few words his own way, produced a garble, and then handed it on to the next garbler.[3]

The unreliability of Chaucer's fifteenth-century scribes would have undercut F. N. Robinson's just-published *The Poetical Works of Chaucer* (1933) as well as the massive Chicago edition of the *Canterbury Tales* ongoing since 1924 by Manly and Rickert.[4] Specialists who have given the article any scrutiny tend to see Tolkien exaggerating Chaucer's accuracy with the Northern dialect,[5] siding instead with the scribes who transmitted, albeit imprecisely, what the poet wrote.

To return to the article's lack of impact, much of the published version of the study, apart from the core lecture, is so dense in linguistic evidence that it makes for difficult reading even for someone with philological training, but is nearly impenetrable for others interested in poetry and storytelling.[6] But if the data-dense "Chaucer as a Philologist" was a flop in 1934, Tolkien appears to have learned to do better two years later when targeting "*Beowulf*: The Monsters and the Critics" for a listening audience, stashing more technical questions such as "Grendel's Titles" in the Appendix (not always reprinted), with the result that it became his most widely read and most influential scholarly publication.

"Chaucer as a Philologist" has been previously reprinted in *Tolkien Studies* 5 (2008), 109–71, without commentary. Our transcription also follows the original 1934 text but includes corrections that Tolkien inserted in his own

---

[3] Tom Shippey, "Tolkien's Academic Reputation Now", in *Roots and Branches: Selected Papers on Tolkien* (Zollikofen, Switzerland: Walking Tree Publishers, 2007), 203–12 at p. 209, refers to the AB language's scribes praised by Tolkien in "*Ancrene Wisse* and *Hali Meiðhad*" (1929). See *Ency* 1–2.

[4] John M. Manly and Edith Rickert, eds., *Text of the Canterbury Tales Studied on the Basis of All Known Manuscripts*, 8 vols. (Chicago and London: University of Chicago Press, 1940). Bodleian MS Tolkien 14/2, fol. 99, indicates Tolkien was aware of their heroic project: "Manly & Rickert have studied 84 MSS".

[5] N. F. Blake, "The Northernisms in *The Reeve's Tale*", *Lore and Language* 3 (1979), 1–8; Simon Horobin, "J. R. R. Tolkien as a Philologist: A Reconsideration of the Northernisms in Chaucer's *Reeve's Tale*", *English Studies* 2 (2001), 97–105; and *Ency* 93–4.

[6] Drout, "Tolkien's Medieval Scholarship", 125.

copies (supplied by Christopher for *Tolkien Studies*, 158) and in a presentation offprint (Cilli 306–07). To avoid confusion with editorial annotations, we have removed his square brackets from around his introductory comments and from several of his entries on sounds and forms (*tulle* line 214, *gar* 212, *greiþen* 389). For ease of reference, we indicate in our own square brackets the start of each new page in the original publication. To supply what Tolkien neglected, we have annotated his numerous references to medieval writers and works, as often as possible in the editions that he himself owned and consulted. Footnotes have been renumbered so that they run consecutively throughout the article; the author's original notes are indicated with [Tolkien] and our editorial notes with [Ed.].

Tolkien seldom consulted actual manuscripts even when available in Oxford. His references are to the texts as published in Frederick J. Furnivall's *A Six-Text Print of Chaucer's Canterbury Tales* and *Harleian MS 7334 of Chaucer's Canterbury Tales*.[7] Tolkien refers to these as follows: C for the Cambridge University Library Gg. 4. 27, E for the Ellesmere, H for the Hengwrt 154, Hl for the Harleian MS 7334, L for the Lansdowne 851, O for Corpus Christi College, Oxford, and P for the Petworth.

We have preserved Tolkien's spelling and punctuation throughout. However, to make this intrinsically challenging text easier to read, we have silently expanded abbreviated compass points ("northern" or "North" for "N." according to context, and so on) and other occasional abbreviations of words and titles (for example, "apparently" for "app.", *Book of the Duchess* for *Bk. Duch.*) The remaining abbreviations include the most familiar grammatical terms (sg. singular, pl. plural, adj. adjective, adv. adverb). We have also italicized titles according to our general conventions and removed periods from initialisms (so that the *New English Dictionary* is *NED*, Old English is OE, Middle English ME, Old Norse ON, and Old High German OHG).

* * *

---

[7] *A Six-Text Print of Chaucer's Canterbury Tales: In Parallel Columns from the Following MSS. 1. The Ellesmere: 2. The Hengwrt 154; 3. The Cambridge Univ. Libr. Gg. 4.27; 4. The Corpus Christi Coll., Oxford; 5. The Petworth; 6. The Lansdowne 851*, 8 vols. (London: Chaucer Society, Trübner, 1869–77); *The Harleian MS 7334 of Chaucer's Canterbury Tales* (London: Chaucer Society, 1885), both ed. Frederick J. Furnivall.

Chaucer as a Philologist: *The Reeve's Tale*

By Professor J. R. R. Tolkien, M.A.

Read at a meeting of the Philological Society in Oxford on Saturday, 16th May, 1931.

The delay in publishing this paper is principally due to hesitation in putting forward a study, for which closer investigation of words, and more still a much fuller array of readings from MSS of the *Reeve's Tale*, were so plainly needed. But for neither have I had opportunity, and dust has merely accumulated on the pages. The paper is therefore presented with apologies, practically as it was read, though with the addition of a "critical text", and accompanying textual notes, as well as of various footnotes, appendices, and comments naturally omitted in reading. It may at least indicate that this tale has a special interest and importance for Chaucerian criticism, even if it shows also that it requires more expert handling.

Line references without any prefix are to the actual lines of the *Reeve's Tale*. Numbers prefixed A or B refer to these groups of the *Canterbury Tales* in the Six-Text numbering.[8]

CHAUCER AS A PHILOLOGIST

One may suspect that Chaucer, surveying from the *Galaxye* our literary and philological antics upon the *litel erthe that heer is...so ful of torment and of harde grace*,[9] would prefer the Philological Society to the Royal Society of Literature,[10] and an editor of the English Dictionary to a poet laureate.[11] Not that Chaucer *redivivus* would be a phonologist or a lexicographer rather than a popular writer – *the lyf so short, the craft so long to lerne!*[12] But certainly, as far as treatment of himself goes (and he had a well-formed opinion of the value of his own work), of all the words and ink posterity has spent or spilt over his entertaining writings, he would chiefly esteem the efforts to recover

---

[8] In the original publication of "Chaucer as a Philologist", the introductory comments above were in square brackets to separate them from the content of his paper. [Ed.]

[9] Tolkien quotes from the beginning of the *Parlement of Foules* (57, 65) where *galaxye* (56) had earned an endnote in his Clarendon Chaucer: "Greek *galaxia*, translated in Latin *orbis lacteus*.... The elder Scipio pointed out the Galaxy as the place of the abode of the blessed" (Bodleian MS Tolkien A 38, fol. 100). [Ed.]

[10] The Royal Society of Literature was founded in 1820 under the patronage of George IV to "reward literary merit and excite literary talent". Tolkien himself became a Fellow of the Royal Society in 1954. [Ed.]

[11] Tolkien himself worked as an assistant editor of the *Oxford English Dictionary* from 1918 until 1920; see Gilliver, Marshall, and Weiner, *The Ring of Words*. England's Poet Laureate from 1930 was John Masefield, who would later invite Tolkien to recite Chaucer publicly in 1938 and 1939. [Ed.]

[12] Tolkien drafted a Clarendon note for the opening line of the *Parlement of Foules*: "ars longa vita brevis." When using these notes to lecture on the *Parlement* in 1947, he added "the first aphorism of Hippocrates" and inserted the original Greek (Bodleian MS Tolkien A 38, fol. 98). [Ed.]

the detail of what he wrote, even (indeed particularly) down to forms and spellings, to recapture an idea of what it sounded like, to make certain what it meant. Let the source-hunter *have his swink to him reserved*.[13] For Chaucer was interested in "language", and in the forms of his own tongue. As we gather from the envoy to *Troilus and Criseyde*, he chose his forms [2] and probably his spellings with care, by selection among divergencies of which he was critically aware; and he wished to have his choice handed on accurately.[14]

Alas! if the curse he pronounced on scribe Adam produced any effect, many a fifteenth-century penman must early have gone bald.[15] We know the detail of Chaucer's work now only through a fifteenth-century blur (at best). His holographs, or the copies impatiently rubbed and scraped by him, would doubtless be something of a shock to us, though a shock we shall unfortunately be spared. In our unhappy case, he would be the first to applaud any efforts to undo the damage as far as possible; and the acquiring of as good a knowledge as is available of the language of his day would certainly have seemed to him a preliminary necessity, not a needless luxury. One can imagine the brief burning words, like those with which he scorched Adam, that he would address to those who profess to admire him while disdaining "philology", who adventure, it may be, on textual criticism undeterred by ignorance of Middle English.[16]

Of course, Chaucer was the last man himself to annotate his jests, while they were fresh. But he would recognize the need, at our distance of time, for the careful exhuming of ancient jokes buried under years, before we shape our faces to a conventional grin at his too often mentioned "humour". Chaucer was no enemy of learning, and there is no need to apologize to him for the annotating of one of his jests, for digging it up and examining it without laughing. He will not suspect us of being incapable of laughter. From his position of advantage he will be able to observe that most philologists possess a sense of the ridiculous, one that even prevents them from taking "literary studies" too seriously.[17]

---

[13] This line comes from the Monk's portrait in the General Prologue (*CT* I, 188). [Ed.]

[14] Chaucer included a stanza near the work's end (*TC* 5:1793-9) fretting over the "greet diversitee / In English and in wryting of our tonge" with the unhappy prospect that scribes would "miswryte" and "mismetre" his text. [Ed.]

[15] Tolkien wittily refers to Chaucer's one-stanza poem (Skeat 1:379) in which he threatens his scribe Adam with scratching out his hair from an itchy scalp if he again copied *Boece* or *Troilus* so carelessly that the poet himself needed to "rubbe and scrape" correcting the text. [Ed.]

[16] In 1923 Tolkien had written to the philologist Elizabeth Mary Wright (wife of Professor Joseph Wright): "Middle English is an exciting field – almost uncharted I begin to think" (*Letters* 8). Tolkien's copy of F. H. Stratmann, *A Middle-English Dictionary*, rev. Henry Bradley (Oxford: Clarendon Press, 1891) can be consulted in the Bodleian as MS Tolkien E 16/38. [Ed.]

[17] Tolkien waged war throughout his career against Literary Studies in favour of Language; see Shippey, *Road to Middle Earth*, "Lit. and Lang.", 1-27. [Ed.]

Of all the jokes that Chaucer ever perpetrated the one that most calls for philological annotation is the dialect talk in the *Reeve's Tale*. For the joke of this dialogue is (and was) primarily a linguistic joke,[18] and is, indeed, now one at which only a philologist can laugh sincerely. Merely to recapture some of the original fun would perhaps be worth the long and dusty labour necessary; but that will not be my chief object. Other points [3] arise from a close study of Chaucer's little *tour de force*, so interesting that we may claim that it has acquired an accidental value, greater than its author intended, and surpassing the original slender jest.

The representation of Northern dialect in the *Reeve's Tale* is so well known that it is taken for granted: its originality and novelty are apt to be forgotten. Yet it is a curious and remarkable thing, unparalleled in Chaucer's extant writings,[19] or, indeed (as far as I am aware), in any Middle English work. Even in our copies the dialect lines stand out astonishingly from the linguistic texture of the rest of Chaucer's work. We may well ask: Is this a most unusual piece of dramatic realism? Or is it just the by-product of a private philological curiosity, used with a secret smile to give some life and individuality to a *fabliau* of trite sort, a depressing specimen of low-class knockabout farce? Or does it just pander to popular linguistic prejudices – ranking with what passes for Scotch, Welsh, Yorkshire, or American in supposedly funny stories of to-day? The answer, of course, requires elaborate enquiry. But I think I would here anticipate and say that to all three questions the answer is "yes".

Chaucer deliberately relies on the easy laughter that is roused by "dialect" in the ignorant or the unphilological. But he gives not mere popular ideas of dialect: he gives the genuine thing, even if he is careful to give his audience certain obvious features that they were accustomed to regard as funny. He certainly was inspired here to use this easy joke for the purposes of dramatic realism – and he saved the *Reeve's Tale* by the touch. Yet he certainly would not have done these things, let alone done them so well, if he had not possessed a private philological interest, and a knowledge, too, of "dialect" spoken and written, greater than was usual in his day.

---

[18] As plainly perceived by Skeat, though his enquiry amid the mass of his general labour in the service of Chaucer did not proceed very far. [Tolkien] To the contrary, Skeat had provided an extensive survey of the dialect issues for more than an entire page (5:121–2). For what Tolkien would call "the most striking characteristic of northern speech in a London ear" (p. 117), Skeat had already listed the long *ā* in words such as *ham*, *gas*, *banes*, *bathe*, and *twa*. His conclusion was nonetheless modest: "the poet merely gives a Northern colouring to his diction to amuse us; he is not trying to teach us Northern grammar. The general effect is excellent, and that is all he was concerned with." [Ed.]

[19] For we can scarcely compare the occasional representation of rustic or ignorant forms such as the *astromye* of the *Miller's Tale*, A 3451 (E H L), 3457 (E H), and *Nowelis* for *Noes* in the same tale, A 3818, 3834 (E H C); nor even *sooth pley quaad pley as the flemyng seith*, in the *Cook's Prologue*, A 4357. [Tolkien]

Such elaborate jests, so fully carried out, are those only of a man interested in language and consciously observant of it. It is universal to notice oddities in the speech of others, and to [4] laugh at them, and a welter of English dialects made such divergences more a matter of common experience, especially doubtless in London, then than now. There was already growing in and with London a polite language (there was a polite idiom available for Chaucer's own work), and a standard of comparison was beginning to appear. Yet this does not make such a joke inevitable. Many may laugh, but few can analyse or record. The Northern speech is elsewhere the subject of uncomplimentary reference before this date: in Trevisa's translation of Higden's *Polychronicon* it is called *scharp, slyttyng, and frotyng, and unschape*; but no examples are given.[20] Dialect was, and indeed is still, normally only embarked on, in full and in form and apart from one or two overworked spellings or phrases thrown in for local colour, by those who know it natively. But Chaucer has stuck in a Northern tooth, and a sharp one, a deal more convincing than Mak's poor little *ich* and *ich be*;[21] and he has done it without a word of warning.

The result is, of course, not of any special importance as a document of dialect. It is dialect only at second hand, and Chaucer has affected to excuse himself from localizing it precisely.[22] We can hardly expect the lines to add anything to our knowledge of the northern speech in the fourteenth century. They have to be judged, and only reveal their interest when carefully examined, in the light of that knowledge such as it is. Almost at once, if we try to examine them in that light (none too clear and bright), we shall be confronted with lexicographical and textual difficulties. Lexicographically we shall observe, as usual, that we cannot walk far in such paths without the massive helping hand of the *New English Dictionary*; yet we shall find quickly, nonetheless, how little knowledge is on free tap concerning English words, if we wish to enquire about their *distribution* at any given time. *NED* answers such

---

[20] Tolkien knew this section of John Trevisa's 1387 translation of the *Polychronicon* because he had glossed a selection in Sisam's *Fourteenth Century Verse and Prose*, 150: "Al þe longage of þe Norþhumbres, and specialych at 3ork, ys so scharp, slyttyng, and frotyng, and vnschape, þat we Souþeron men may þat longage vnneþe vndurstonde." Tolkien's two personal copies of Sisam's anthology are now the Bodleian's MS Tolkien E 16/11 and MS Tolkien E 16/12. [Ed.]

[21] Which is all that survives clearly, at any rate in our Towneley text, of Mak's "Southern tooth" – and that is the nearest parallel to Chaucer's effort that exists. [Tolkien] He alludes to the Wakefield "Second Shepherds' Play" in *The Towneley Plays*, ed. George England and Alfred W. Pollard, EETS e.s. 87 (1897). Tolkien had glossed "The Towneley Play of Noah" in Sisam's *Fourteenth Century Verse and Prose*, 185–203. [Ed.]

[22] The words, I. 95, *fer in the north, I can nat telle wher*, are, of course, actually put in the mouth of the Reeve, and so are partly and justly dramatic. Actually, as we shall see, Chaucer was not so vague. [Tolkien]

questions reluctantly, or not at all. But such questions must be asked: the answers are essential to an estimate of the dialect dialogue, even if we must plough many [5] texts to find them (or hints towards them), and hunt in unglossed verses for a phrase.

Textually we shall not be long in noting, or suspecting, that these dialect passages have been exposed to considerable adulteration – because they are in dialect, and because they are in dialect sandwiched between passages of narrative in Chaucer's ordinary idiom. In compensation we may reflect that usually it is difficult to catch Adam and his descendants at their tricks: we only know "Chaucer's language" (confidently though we set examination-questions on it)[23] through the copies of scrivains, who were certainly not his contemporaries, and who would usually have thought no more of altering a spelling or a form than of brushing a fly off the nose – less, because they would notice the fly, but often hardly observe the spelling. We are to a certain extent at their mercy, and they interfere confoundedly with our prosody and our grammar. But here we may have a little revenge. We know something of northern dialect independent of them.[24] What have they made of it? I believe that a close examination of all the manuscripts of the *Canterbury Tales* with respect to the northernisms in this tale would have a special textual value – and that some reputations for fidelity would be damaged. In fact, purely accidentally, the *Reeve's Tale* is of great importance to the textual criticism of the *Canterbury Tales* as a whole.[25]

But for the moment we can reserve these important points, lexicographical and textual, and take what we have got for a preliminary glance. The first thing to recollect, of course, is that (accurate or inaccurate) this northern dialect was intended not for Northerners, but for Chaucer's usual audience. Now "dialect" is seldom amusing in a tale, unless the audience has some actual experience of it (and can in effect laugh at private memories). Modern writers may often forget this, but Chaucer is not likely to have done so. And in any case, jesting apart, the dialect must be more or less intelligible. The talk of the two clerks had to be understood without a gloss: the *Reeve's Tale* when written

---

[23] Preparing for his own undergraduate examinations, Tolkien wrote an essay on "The Language of Chaucer" in November 1913. [Ed.]

[24] Regional dialectology was still in its infancy when Skeat founded the English Dialect Society in 1873, paving the way for Joseph Wright's *English Dialect Dictionary*, 6 vols. (London: Henry Frowde, 1898–1905). [Ed.]

[25] Especially if combined with a study of the forms in the *Tale of Gamelyn*, where a piece not originally in Chaucerian language is treated often by the same scribes. [Tolkien] *Gamelyn* appears in twenty-five manuscripts of the *Canterbury Tales*, including some important early copies such as Lansdowne, Harley 7334, and Corpus Christi 198, typically as a replacement for the unfinished *Cook's Tale*, making it the most widely copied Middle English romance. Its predominantly East Midland dialect would have made it a test case for scribes normalizing to a more familiar dialect. Tolkien would have known *The Tale of Gamelyn*, ed. Walter W. Skeat (Oxford: Clarendon, 1884). [Ed.]

was no place for explanatory footnotes or asides. [6] We learn therefore from it at once – without considering textual adulteration, for that, if it has occurred, will naturally have tended to leave intact the most obvious and familiar elements – what most immediately struck the London ear as comic and unusual in Chaucer's day among the features of northern speech. At the same time we get a glimpse of how much a Londoner could be expected to understand, what sort of dialect details and words were more or less familiar to him, though not used by him. This is in itself interesting: both what is in the *Reeve's Tale* and what is not (e.g. present participles in -*and*, or indications of a shift in the sound of $\bar{o}$) is instructive.

Chaucer plainly kept some of his knowledge up his sleeve, and even so he put in at least one touch (e.g. *slik*, on which see below) that cannot have been familiar, even if the context made it intelligible; but what has been said is generally true. He showed considerable skill and judgment in what he did: skill in presenting the dialect with fair accuracy but without piling up oddities; judgment in choosing for his purpose *northern* clerks, at *Cambridge*, close to *East Anglia* (whence he brought his Reeve). Indeed, in an *East Anglian* reeve, regaling Southern (and largely London) folk, on the road in *Kent*, with imitations of *northern* talk, which was imported southward by the attraction of the *Universities*, we have a picture in little of the origins of literary English. Too good to be mere accident. Whether fully conscious of this or not, it cannot be denied that Chaucer has shown an instinctive appreciation of the linguistic situation of his day which is remarkable. We shall be justified in paying close attention to the dialect-writing of an author such as this. The whole situation is cleverly contrived philologically. Many of the principal features of northern speech, especially in vocabulary, being largely of Scandinavian origin, were also current in the East; and Chaucer was able to use dialectalisms, recognizable as such, that were at once *correct* for the North, and yet, owing to the growing importance and influence of East Anglia, especially Norwich, not unheard-of in the capital. The reeve is at once the symbol of the direction from which northerly forms of speech invaded the language of the southern capital, and the right sort of person to choose to act as intermediary in the tale. Chaucer could have given a good philological explanation – should any [7] hypercritical modern require one – of the ease with which the teller of the tale negotiates the talk of the clerks.

Perhaps it is for this very reason that he tinges the talk of his reeve also with linguistic elements of the same kind.[26] Slight as the touches are, they are

---

[26] Thus the Reeve, even according to our southernizing MSS, used *ik am, so thee'k* (contrasted with Harry Bailey's *thee'ch*, C 947) in *Reeve's Prologue*, 10 and 13. These forms are under no necessity of

nonetheless unusual, and unlike Chaucer's normal procedure; he makes no effort (as far as our manuscripts show) to touch the talk of the Dartmouth shipman with south-westernisms. In any case, it will be granted that a Norfolk man was well chosen as the teller of a story of Cambridge and of northern men.

On the *fer north* Chaucer's choice fell naturally – apart from possible private knowledge, and apart from the possibility that something in "real life", a meeting with real students of Cambridge that came from the North, lies behind not the *fabliau*, but the colouring given to it (a possibility that does not in the least affect the argument) – because, if dialect was to be attempted at all in a funny tale, one of a marked character, one perhaps already as conventionally comic in London as a Welsh "whateffer" is to-day, was both easier to do and more effective. It is significant of the shift since Chaucer's day, that the *fer West* was not selected. It was peculiar enough in some respects, and it might have been put appropriately in the mouths of students of Oxford. But it was not. Probably, in so far as it then differed from the uses of London, it was too remote from London's ken and not a current joke.[27] The dialect-situation, in fact, jumped neatly with the answer of Cambridge clerks and Trumpington [8] miller to Oxford Nicholas and Osney carpenter. Too neatly to be accidental. It had been well thought out.

If we now leave the generalizations and proceed to a more detailed scrutiny, we need as a preliminary to hear the dialogue passages in their setting. They should be read aloud, as one may fancy Chaucer reading them (if he ever did). In the absence of an accomplished renderer, such as Professor Wyld,[28] each must do that for himself, with such approximate fidelity as philological knowledge allows. This is important because mere statistics, and numerical

---

rhyme or metre. The Reeve also uses *capel* "horse", though this may be mere repetition of its use just before by the clerks (see also below for fuller note on this word); and also the dialectal *greithen* [marginal note in one of Tolkien's copies: but *agraiþi* in the *Ayenbite*]. The rare word *sokene* (1. 67) is also actually put into his mouth, and may be meant as rustic or dialectal. At any rate, outside legal use it is rarely found elsewhere (as far as *NED* records, or I can discover), but it is found notably in the East Anglian *Promptorium Parvulorum*. That he is represented as using on occasion þeir and þeim is also probable (see below). [Tolkien] His Clarendon Chaucer had cribbed information from Skeat (5:113) on the Reeve's regional language: "in his own words in the prologue to his tale, there are dialectal traces as *so thee'k, ik am*." Completed about 1440 as the first English-to-Latin dictionary, the *Promptorium Parvulorum* ("Storehouse for Children") is attributed to the friar Geoffrey the Grammarian, who lived at Lynn in East Anglia, and so it was Tolkien's reliable source for East Anglian dialect forms. See *The Promptorium Parvulorum*, ed. A. L. Mayhew, EETS e.s. 102 (1908); Tolkien's personal copy is now the Bodleian's Tolkien VC 215. [Ed.]

[27] It is interesting to contrast the usual southerly or south-westerly stamp of conventional dialect later, as on the Elizabethan stage, after the partial northernizing of the language of the capital. [Tolkien]

[28] Henry Cecil Wyld became Merton Professor of English Language and Literature in 1920 and was one of the electors for the Professor of Anglo-Saxon when Tolkien was named to the chair in 1925. Upon his death, Tolkien succeeded him as Merton Professor in 1945. Wyld's talent for reciting like "Finnish minstrels chanting the *Kalevala*" figured among Tolkien's Oxford recollections in his 1959 "Valedictory Address" (*Essays* 238). [Ed.]

counting, fail altogether to represent the relative prominence of a linguistic feature to the ear, or to make clear the astonishing effect of the contrast of the dialogue with the narrative setting.

One thing arises from any such reading, that is even approximately correct, arises so clearly that no statistics are needed to support it: the most striking characteristic of northern speech in a London ear was the long *ā* (of OE or ON origin), retained where the southerly forms of speech had an *ō*. The latter was probably in Chaucer's time still a pure, not a diphthongal, sound, the same as, or similar to, that in present southern *awe, or*. But in the North it remained *ā*, without trace of any rounding or tendency to an *o*-sound. The tendency in the North of England was rather to fronting, towards an *ǣ*-sound (that is to the preservation of old *ā* until it fell in with the later post-medieval shift of later *ā*-sounds, seen also in the South, which affected generally in all dialects such *ā*-sounds as those of French *blame, dame*, or of English and Norse *make, cake*). This is a trite phonological fact, but nonetheless remarkable; it was also of special importance, since the number of words affected was very large. The dating of the later fronting (towards *ǣ*) only becomes of importance in dealing with *geen, neen*, the one real problem that we encounter, and one that I reserve for a special note in an appendix. For the moment, though the full development of the shift towards *ǣ* was not, I believe, in Chaucer's day accomplished, later history probably warns us to give a quality to our Northern *ā* which anticipates the change: it was not our present Southern *ā* (in *calm*, say), and the difference between Northern *bān* "bone" and Southern *bǫǫn* was wider than that between modern *barn* and *born*. The sound was, indeed, part of the "sharp [9] slitting" which offended Southern ears – in words where they were not accustomed to hear it.[29]

Statistics actually show (see below) that Chaucer has provided a notably large number of examples of this Northern *ā*: some thirty-nine in the manuscripts here used, probably more in his original version, a number far exceeding that of any other feature represented. So, even if we make allowance for the fact that examples were naturally numerous, we may regard the effect produced (which is even more striking than the statistics suggest) as intentional. The joke about *ā* was one all would appreciate, and this *ā* had the advantage of occurring in common words used in all dialects, which would

---

[29] This is, of course, usually the case. A sound will be dubbed uncouth by speakers of another dialect, owing to its contrast to the familiar sound. It may well be itself current in their own speech in another context. There is no reason to suppose that Northern and Southern speech differed much in the pronunciation of *ā*, in, say, *nāme* "name". [Tolkien]

be thus quite intelligible and yet all the more odd and laughable in alien shape because of their very familiarity.

Nonetheless, it is easy for dialect-imitators to seize on some such general correspondence as this $\bar{a} = \bar{\rho}$, and to apply it to cases where, for some historical reason, it is actually false to the dialect. Thus to the vowel-sound in our word *time* the dialects of modern Yorkshire respond in a very great number of cases with some variety of $\bar{a}$, but not in all cases – *lie, light,* and *eye,* for instance, are usually *lī* (or *lig*), *līt,* and *ī,* though imitators will produce *lā, lāt,* and *ā.* Indeed, such forms are actually heard from "natives", supposed to be speaking dialect. In that case they bear witness to the influence of standard English, under which "dialect" tends to become ordinary language altered in accordance with a few regularized sound-correspondences (and thinly sprinkled with local words and locutions). Traces of the same phenomenon have been observed in Middle English: a probable example (since it comes principally from areas where $\bar{a}$ and $\bar{\rho}$ approached one another geographically) is *tōn* "taken", derived, it would appear, from northern *tān*,[30] by substitution of the southern $\bar{\rho}$, although the $\bar{a}$ of *tān* is a late lengthening of $\breve{a}$, and not an original OE or ON $\bar{a}$ that would naturally have exhibited this southern change.

[10] These things are mentioned here only in illustration of the fact that sound-correspondences are readily appreciated by the unphilological, where contact between closely related forms of language occurs, and in the absence of either historical or practical knowledge of both forms of speech in detail, may be, indeed certainly will be, occasionally wrongly applied. It would be interesting if we could detect Chaucer in a wrong application of his $\bar{a}/\bar{\rho}$ "sound-law" to cases where for some reason northern dialect did not show $\bar{a}$ for southern $\bar{\rho}$. There are no such errors. This would be more significant if there were more chances of error occurring. Southern $\bar{\rho}$ which is not northern $\bar{a}$ is derived mainly from older *o* lengthened (as in OE *hopa*, ME *hǭpe*), or from foreign words, chiefly French (as *cote, hoost*). Mistakes are not likely with the latter class; the former is comparatively infrequent. We have, it is true, *hope* (and in a dialectal sense) in line 109, and *hoste* (O.Fr. *hoste*) in line 211; but this is all.[31] *hope* and *hoste* are correct, of course, for the North; but the distinction observed, even if a much larger number of instances occurred, could not be used as evidence of Chaucer's direct knowledge of northern speech. He may have had a guide either in his own pronunciation or in that of old-fashioned people to aid in distinguishing words of this kind from those

---

[30] This form occurs in the *Reeve's Tale*; see below. [Tolkien]
[31] For "stolen", lines 191, 268, Chaucer here probably used *stoln, stollen* (representing the northern dialect, with retained short *o*); see below. [Tolkien]

whose ǭ was northern ā. It is not certain that *o* in *hope* was in his day yet universally identical with that in *soap* (OE *hopa, sāpe*): the two vowels are still, of course, kept apart in the dialect of some areas that share in the rounding of older ā. His rhyming is strict in *Troilus and Criseyde*, and yet we have the famous case in the fourth stanza of the fifth book, where *lore, euermore* (OE *lār, māre*) are contrasted, and do not according to the system of his stanza rhyme with *forlore, more, tofore* (OE *forlŏren, mŏre, tōfŏran*).[32]

We may conclude, then, that the general correspondence of northern ā to southern ǭ was recognized by Chaucer (and also by his audience), and that it was one of the chief points illustrated in his representation of northern dialect: it was specially suitable for his purpose. But there is more in the dialect passages than these broad and easy effects, and we may now examine them in more detail. A fair initial assumption is that all departures from [11] his normal usage, such words and forms as he nowhere else employs, are here intentional and offered to his readers as samples of northern speech. At least it would be a fair assumption, and on it we might justly put Chaucer through a linguistic examination, but for one grave difficulty: the candidate's scripts have been lost. Adam and his offspring have fortunately kept copies, it is true, but unfortunately they are unreliable on the very points we wish to scrutinize, less so perhaps in vocabulary, more so certainly in grammar, dialectal forms, and spellings. We are involved in the attempt to distinguish between Chaucer and his reporters; and a satisfactory comparison of the candidate's essay at "dialect" with his "normal usage" would require a more careful scrutiny of the individual habits (and the casual inadvertent evidence) of the manuscripts, both in the bulk of his work and in these special passages, than has, I believe, yet been made, at any rate with any such a purpose. The following study is merely tentative. For lack of time and opportunity it is based solely on the facsimile of the Ellesmere MS;[33] and on the Six-Text and the Harleian MS 7334 (Hl) printed by the Chaucer Society.[34]

---

[32] Skeat (2:495) remarked upon "long close *o*" and "short open *o*" since the rhyme royal's pattern of a b a b b c c would require the words *lore* and *ever-more* pronounced differently from *forlore, more*, and *here-tofore* in *Troilus* 5.22–28. [Ed.]

[33] *The Ellesmere Chaucer Reproduced in Facsimile*, ed. Alex Egerton, 2 vols. (Manchester: Manchester University Press, 1911), had been undertaken because the manuscript was leaving England after it was sold to Henry E. Huntington. At a gathering of the Inklings in November 1947, C. S. Lewis's brother reported that Tolkien showed them a copy of this facsimile bought for £55; see Warren Lewis, *Brothers and Friends: The Diaries of Major Warren Hamilton Lewis*, ed. Clyde S. Kilby and Marjorie Lamp Mead (San Francisco: Harper & Row, 1982), 215. Starting in the late 1940s, Tolkien's Chaucer lectures regularly weighed this manuscript's authority, for example announcing in his discussion of the *Clerk's Tale*, "I myself am inclined to accept Ellesmere for the following reasons..." (Bodleian MS Tolkien A 13/2, fol. 34). [Ed.]

[34] Presenting besides Ellesmere (E) the following five MSS: Hengwrt (H), Cambridge University Library Gg. 4. 27 (C), Corpus Christi College, Oxford (O), Petworth (P), Lansdowne 851 (L). [Tolkien]

A more extensive investigation of other MSS is obviously required. No classification or grouping made on other grounds seems to be a safe guide to the readings that any given MS will offer in the dialect parts of the *Reeve's Tale*.[35] The similarity, for instance, often extremely close even in minor details of spelling, that can be observed between E and H does not prevent them from differing in notable points in their report of the clerks' northern English. A full comparison of the readings of these seven MSS alone, even limited to points affecting dialect, would nonetheless occupy too much space. Instead, a preliminary essay towards a critical text of the dialect lines is offered, together with some commentary. It is based on the following considerations. That the idea of making the clerks speak in dialect was Chaucer's is, of course, agreed. It need not be argued. [12] Exceptional though the procedure is, dialectal ingredients are shown, in any case, to have existed in the original by the rhymes in lines 167–8 and 209–210.[36] Nonetheless, it has been held, and may still be, that this idea was variously improved or enlarged upon by individual copyists. An examination of the seven MSS does not, however, bear this out. The general tendency of all has been to southernize the original. A comparison of the small list given below of those northernisms which have been correctly preserved in *all seven*, with the much larger one containing those that have the support of a majority (and so can in the first instance be taken as Chaucerian) is sufficient to show this. Of northern *forms*, as distinct from vocabulary, only *swa* 110 and *ga* 182 are common to all in the middle of a line. There are also the rhyme-words in lines 119–120 *fra, swa* (P *fraye, swaye*), 165–6 (*alswa, ra*), 167–8 (*baþe*), 209–210 (*bringes*).[37] The last two could not be altered. The ends of Chaucer's lines have, in any case, in general survived rough handling best; and here are found most of the forms on which the supposed archaism of his verse-language is founded, in reality a testimony to the fact that rhyme resists modernization. The northernisms of the surviving copies are, in fact, the residue of a gradual whittling away of the individuality of Chaucer's text, a residue naturally different in amount and distribution in each case. This is precisely what might be expected, especially in the treatment of dialect sandwiched between passages more or less in Chaucer's

---

[35] This doubtless indicates that alterations *affecting dialect* are relatively late events in the tradition, and in considerable measure due to the procedure of the actual scribes whose works we possess. [Tolkien]

[36] Certain errors (noted below) dependent on the presence of *northern* forms also show that such forms lie behind the existing copies. [Tolkien]

[37] Also the preservation of *es* or *is* in senses *am, art*, in 111, 166, 169. [Tolkien]

normal language. That Chaucer should trouble to write in dialect is remarkable, but it is hardly credible that each of these scrivains (and their predecessors) should at odd moments have had the fancy to improve his attempt. Actually a comparison of the critical text here put forward with the MSS shows a procedure closely similar to that observable in southernizing copies of genuine northern originals.[38] The variations in reading, and the errors, are most numerous precisely where specifically northern forms are concerned; and the variations consist usually in the opposition of southern [13] equivalents to a northern form or word; occasionally and most significantly there appear mongrel blends between northern and southern whose origin is not linguistic but scribal.[39] Had the northernisms been in any considerable measure due to the enterprise and wit of copyists, we should certainly have had frequent competition between different but equally genuine dialectalisms. No certain case of this appears.[40] We have corruptions which have been treated as genuine (in unjustified deference to E), and have even been intruded into historical grammars, such as *geen*, for instance; and we have occasionally the repetition, suitable or unsuitable, of northernisms certainly provided elsewhere by Chaucer in the dialogue;[41] we have little evidence that the copyists themselves possessed independent information concerning the detail of northern dialect, or could use it intelligently to improve the original. Chaucer's jest required some popular knowledge of the kind of dialect depicted, and this doubtless the scribes usually possessed; but Chaucer's detail was finer than necessary, and this probably as a rule escaped readers and copyists alike. The copyists must, of course, usually have perceived that the

---

[38] The process can be studied, for instance, in the various MSS of *Cursor Mundi* or of the *Northern Passion* as printed in the EETS. These examples have been specially examined for the present purpose. [Tolkien] *Cursor Mundi: A Northumbrian Poem of the XIVth Century*, ed. Richard Morris, EETS o.s. 57, 59, 62, 66, 68, 99, 101 (1874–93), had provided some 30,000 lines from around 1300 by an unknown author, which had been scribally translated into "southernizing copies". Tolkien's volumes of this work are now the Bodleian's Tolkien VC 194–6. For his other reference, see *The Northern Passion: Four Parallel Texts and the French Original*, ed. Frances A. Foster, EETS o.s. 145 and 147 (1913 and 1916). [Ed.]

[39] In our text an example is furnished by the readings in line 251 (q.v.). [Tolkien]

[40] On *swilk slik* 210, 251, 253, see notes on text and appendix on *slik*. On *falles* see notes to lines 107, 255. [Tolkien]

[41] Cases probably are: Hl *wightly* for *whistel* 181 – *wight* occurs in 166, but was, in any case, a literary word (see below); *sal*, probably wrongly in all but Hl, for *suld* 209 – *sal* occurred frequently elsewhere; *es*, *is* for *er* 125, or for *may be* in L 124 – *es* was probably used several times in the original; or the *to and fra* rhyming *alswa* of C 373 (others, *fro*, *also*) in the narrative not in the dialogue – compare C *to and fra* (others more correctly *til*) rhyming *alswa* in the dialogue, 119–120. A case equally derivative, but showing greater corruption, is L 255, *þer sal I haue* (shown to be spurious by *þer*) for *þer tides me*. On *folt*, *fonne*, see note to line 108. [Tolkien]

clerks' lines were abnormal in language (spelling alone in the earlier stages of the tradition probably made it obvious and troublesome enough); but the principal textual effect of this was to render less secure their interpretation of letters, and to weaken respect for the language: the normal checks on the making and accepting of errors were reduced. The notion that "dialect" is a lawless perversion of familiar vowels is no new one.

Accordingly, in the following text as a general rule each "northernism" or dialectal feature offered by the seven MSS [14] as a whole has been accepted, even if such a form is given in only one of them (where other considerations are not, as in 103, against this). In addition, perhaps less defensibly, the text has been normalized. For example, if the evidence is held to justify the inclusion of *sal, na, es* in certain lines, these forms have been used throughout the clerks' speeches. As will be seen, this entails less alteration than might be expected. Even our MSS taken as a whole provide something approximating to a consistent text: the presumption that, within the limits of rhyme and metre, Chaucer's own text was fairly consistent in dialectal character is therefore strong. In any case, with the small words such as *is, shal, no*, scribal procedure was casual and need not be imitated slavishly. This gleaning of "northernisms" has not, all the same, been purely mechanical. The habits and peculiarities of each MS used have to be considered,[42] and the evidence they afford is not of equal certainty. In the note on *dreuen* 190 it will be observed that this form, though frequently found in northern texts, may here show nothing more than the *e* for *ĭ* which is almost the rule in C and common in L. At the same time, it must be remembered that the chance of original dialectal details surviving was much increased if they happened to look familiar to later scribes. Some have been preserved not as "dialect" at all, but as (to the scribe) permissible variants. Thus the preservation of "northern" *es = is* in L only is undeniably connected with the fact that *es* for *is* occurs occasionally in L outside the *Reeve's Tale*,[43] though *is* is, [15] nonetheless, its usual form. But

---

[42] Not necessarily the same thing as each "scribe". The linguistic complexion of each MS doubtless in varying degrees owes something to its predecessors. Some consideration has been given to this: at least the groups A and B of the *Canterbury Tales* have been examined with the forms of the *Reeve's Tale* in mind. The *Tale of Gamelyn* has also been glanced at. It would probably repay closer study for this purpose. It is certainly not by Chaucer, and was originally in an Eastern or North-East Midland type of language in many ways nearer to northern dialect than Chaucer's own natural speech. The behaviour of the MSS in *Gamelyn* and the dialectal places in *Reeve's Tale* deserve comparison. *Gamelyn* also may be taken as a stray specimen of the English writings that Chaucer had read. [Tolkien]

[43] Probably not as a northernism, but in such cases related to the use of *e* for *ĭ* alluded to above. Unstressed *is* was identical, or nearly so, with unstressed (inflexional) -*es*, as is frequently shown in Chaucerian rhymes: e.g. *nones – non es* (O P L), *nonys – noon ys* € in A 524. Examples of *es* in L not

the occurrences of *es* in L are far more frequent in the *Reeve's Tale* than in any other passage of Chaucer of equal length. Moreover L always uses *es* where its special dialectal employment as *am, art, are* is concerned (except in line 319, where it has *am* not *is*). This sudden favouring of *es* therefore has probably some special cause, and may proceed from the original. An instructive example is *til* in line 190. All seven MSS preserve *til* in *til hething*, but in *til scorn* O P Hl have *to*. The universal retention in the first case was due to the fact that *til* was not unfamiliar before *h* or a vowel. See the notes on *til* and *driue* (below).

Weight has been given to errors. P *ytwix* 251 is a mongrel, but it is even better evidence for the Chaucerian origin of the genuine northern *ymel* than the actual appearance of this word in E H. It is also a measure of the intelligence and linguistic knowledge shown in the copying of rare words in the *Reeve's Tale*. In the note to line 267 it is also pointed out that the reading *saule sal* rests securely on the error *God sale* (and similar forms) in some MSS, which finds its explanation only in the original presence in the text of these northern forms and in their comparative unfamiliarity to the copyists which favoured misreading.

The spelling adopted is not extremely northern. The original copy or copies made or corrected by Chaucer, and the elder derivatives, certainly differed in mere *spelling* from the usage of Chaucer when writing his own language. The source of Chaucer's knowledge of dialect was largely literary, and drawn from *written* northern works; also he was considering *readers*. The Miller and the Reeve were *cherles*, and we are expressly told by him to *turne over the leef* (A 3177) if we do not approve of their tales. It is a fair assumption that for readers' benefit Chaucer marked off the dialect lines or words by using certain of the characteristic northern spellings of the fourteenth century.[44] But such details [16] have naturally been least observed in the MSS and can scarcely now be recaptured. One marked peculiarity only has been admitted, tentatively and in illustration of the way in which the dialect could be made

---

due to rhyme-spelling are A 573, 658, 1677 (*na es = nis*, preceding stage possibly *nas*; C has also erroneous past tense *dawede* in preceding line). [Tolkien]

[44] The general impression given (see notes on words below) is that texts similar to those surviving now from the early fourteenth century in northern dialect were familiar to Chaucer. One may dismiss any idea that he attempted phonetic gymnastics or tried to bring his "dialect" right up to date and indicate pronunciations taken straight from the mouth by odd and uncouth spellings. The oddities, such as *geen, heem, neen, swaye, faath, sale* "soul", *slape*, etc., which may be gleaned from the various MSS are the products of copyists, perhaps in some cases in the interests of post-Chaucerian dialect-phonetics (P seems to favour equating *a, aa* and *ai, ay*), most often demonstrably the product of error and the conviction that monstrosities were good enough in barbaric dialect. [Tolkien]

effective to the eye as well as to the ear, namely *qu* for *wh*. The evidence that Chaucer actually used this is very slender; but this might be expected. It is, in fact, the duty of an editor to weigh such gossamer - in cases where mere spelling is important. P has *qwistel* in line 182. This MS is an extreme southernizer, and this spelling is, in it, quite isolated and remarkable.[45] The *q* must therefore be either inherited and by chance preserved,[46] or due to a sudden northernizing whim. The latter is extremely unlikely in view of the general behaviour of P.[47]

It may be observed that the text so produced, possessing in most points direct MS authority, even when only seven MSS have been used, is in contrast with more familiar ones (or with E) very nearly purely and correctly northern. The exceptions, southernisms which cannot be removed, are mainly due to the needs of rhyme and metre; but they are in any case so small a proportion of the whole that even a philological examiner would award Chaucer a fairly high mark for his effort.[48] Chaucer has on the whole avoided putting extreme northernisms into the rhymes, and since his scheme made necessary the linking of dialect lines with lines of narrative not in dialect, he has allowed himself some liberty, especially at these joints, and quite reasonably.

[17] The letters ę and ë are used respectively to mark (*a*) unstressed *e* that seems to have been meant to be slurred or omitted, and in some cases was probably not originally written, and (*b*) unstressed *e* that seems to be a

---

[45] So far as I can discover P uses *qw* frequently for *qu* (a frequent use of its period), but nowhere else *qw*, or *qu* for *wh*. *qu*, *qw* for *wh* are not, of course, purely northern, and also occur in texts of eastern origin. *qw* is, for instance, much used by the Dulwich MS of *Handlyng Synne*. [Tolkien] He would have known Robert Manning of Brunne's fourteenth-century *Handlyng Synne* in Frederick J. Furnivall's two-volume edition for EETS o.s. 119 and 123 (1901 and 1903). But he had encountered it when glossing Sisam's *Fourteenth Century Poetry and Prose*: Manning's "The Dancers of Colbek" came first in the anthology, where it was noted, "An important fragment is in the library of Dulwich College". Andoni Cossio, "Addenda: One Middle English Manuscript and Four Editions of Medieval Works Known to J. R. R. Tolkien and What They Reveal", *ANQ: A Quarterly Journal of Short Articles, Notes and Reviews* (2021), 1-8, at pp. 4-5, discusses Tolkien's personal copy of Furnivall's Volume I of *Handlyng Synne*. [Ed.]

[46] As is the case in P with certain other dialectalisms, elsewhere altered, both in *Reeve's Tale* and *Gamelyn*. [Tolkien]

[47] At the same time it must be noted that Hl has *wikked* for *quilk* 158 and *wightly* for *quistel* 182. While these errors suggest that the word concerned had unfamiliar forms that caused difficulty at some stage in the tradition of Hl, they point rather to *w* as the initial letter at least in the immediate source of Hl. [Tolkien]

[48] Examining students was a routine part of Tolkien's job as an Oxford professor. A month after delivering this paper to the Philological Society, he and C. T. Onions examined Alistair Campbell on his B. Litt. thesis *The Production of Diphthongs by "Breaking" in Old English from 700 to 900*. Campbell too must have earned "a fairly high mark", because he later occupied Tolkien's old chair as Professor of Anglo-Saxon. [Ed.]

metrical syllable. This is done to assist later comment. The italics mark normalizations, that is northern, non-Chaucerian forms which *in the places where they appear* are not given by any of the seven MSS, though they are preserved elsewhere. The irreducible southernisms are underlined – which rather exaggerates their importance; but it serves to mark the curious fact that these certain southernisms and the possible ones (represented by the italics) are largely collected near the end. Chaucer himself probably allowed the linguistic joke to fade away as the knock-about business approached. Or he may have got tired of it before it was quite finished, as he did of other things.

102 (4022) Alain spak first: "Al hail, Simond, i faiþ!
     Hou farës þi fairȩ doghter and þi wif?"
     . . . . .

106 (4026) "Simond," quod Iohn, "bi god ned has na per:
     Him boȩs serue̩ himseluën þat has na swain,
     Or els he *es* a folt as clerkës sain.
     Our manciplë, I hopȩ he wil be ded,
     Swa werkës ai þe wangës in his hed.
     And forþi es I cum, and *als* Alain,
     To grindȩ our corn and carie̩ it ham again.
113 (4033) I prai ȝou spedȩs vs heþen as ȝe mai!"
     . . . . .

116 (4036) "Bi god, right bi þe hoper wil I stand,"
     quod Iohn, "and se hougat þe corn gas in.
     Ȝit sagh I neuer, bi mi fader kin,
     hou þat þe hoper waggës til and fra."
     Alain answerdë: "Iohn, and wiltou swa,
     þen wil I be bineþën, bi mi croun,
     And se hougat þe melë fallës doun
     In til þe trogh. Þat sal be mi desport;
     For, Iohn, i faiþ, I es al of ȝour sort:
125 (4045) I es as il a miller as er ȝe."
     . . . . .

152 (4072) And gan to crie: "Harrow and wailawai! [18]
     Our hors *es* lost! Alain, for goddës banes,
     Step on þi fet, cum of man al at anes!

155 (4075)	Alas! our wardain has his palfrai lorn."
158 (4078)	"Quat! Quilk wai es he gan?" gan he to crie.

. . . .

164 (4084)	"Alas," quod Iohn, "Alain, for cristës paine,
	Lai doun þi swerd, and I sal min alswa.
	I es ful wight, god wat, as *es* a ra.
	Bi goddës hertẹ, he sal noght scapẹ vs baþe!
	Qui nad þou pit þe capel *i* þe laþe?
169 (4089)	Il hail! Bi god, Alain, þou es a fonne."

. . . .

181 (4101)	Wiþ "Kep, kep, stand, stand, Iossa, warderere,
	Ga quistel þou, and I sal kepẹ him here!"

. . . .

189 (4109)	"Alas," quod Iohn, "þe dai þat I was born!
	Nou er we dreuẹn til heþing and til scorn.
	Our corn *es* stoln; men wil vs folës calle,
	Baþë þe wardain and our felawẹs alle,
193 (4113)	And namëli þe miller; wailawai!"

. . . .

207 (4127)	"Nou, Simond," seidë Iohn, "bi saint Cutberd,
	Ai es þou meri, and þis *es* fairẹ answerd.
	I haue herd sai man suld ta of twa þinges
	Slik as he findẹs, or ta slik[49] as he bringes.
	But specialli I prai þe, hostë dere,
	Get us sum[50] metẹ and drink, and mak vs chere,
	And we wil paië treuli at þe fulle:
	Wiþ empti hand man mai na haukës tulle.
215 (4135)	Lo her, our siluer redi for til spende."

. . . .

249 (4169)	He pokedẹ Iohn, and seidë: "Slepest thou?
	Herdë þou euer slik a sang ar nou?
	Lo, quilk a complin es imell *þaim* alle!
	A wildë fir upon þair bodiẹs falle!
[19]	Qua herknëd euer slik a ferli þing?

---

[49] Chaucer possibly here wrote *swilk*; see notes below. [Tolkien]

[50] Tyrwhitt (from MS Unspecified) cited by Skeat, notes p. 121, here gives reading *gar us have*. [Tolkien] Thomas Tyrwhitt, a fellow of Merton College, Oxford, is considered the founder of modern Chaucer editing with his *The Canterbury Tales*, published in 1775–78. See B. A. Windeatt, "Thomas Tyrwhitt (1730–1786)", in *Editing Chaucer*, ed. Ruggiers, 117–43. [Ed.]

	3a, þai sal hauę þe flour of il ending.
255 (4175)	Þis langë night þer tidës me na reste;
	But 3it, na fors, al sal be for þe beste.
	For, Iohn," seidę he, "als euer mot I þriue,
	Gif þat I mai, 3on wenchë sal I swiue.
	Sum esëment has lawë schapën vs;
	For, Iohn, þer *es* a lawë þat sais þus:
	Þat gif a man in á point be agreued,
	Þat in anoþer he sal be releued.
	Our corn *es* stoln, soþli it *es* na nai,
	And we hauę had an il fit al þis dai;
265 (4185)	And sen I sal hauę nan amendëment
	Again mi los, I wil hauę esëment.
	Bi goddës saulę, it sal nan oþer be!"
	Þis Iohn answerdę: "Alain, auisë þe!
	Þe miller *es* a parlous man," he seide,
270 (4190)	"And gif þat he out of his sleep abreide,
	He mightë do vs baþę a vilainie."
272 (4192)	Alain answerdę: "I countę him a noght a flie!"

. . . .

281 (4201)	"Alas" quod he, "þis *es* a wikkëd Iape!
	Nou mai I sai þat I es but an ape.
	3it has mi felawę sumquat for his harm:
	He has þe mill*er* doghter in his arm.
285 (4205)	He auntrëd him, and has his nedës sped,
	And I li as a draf-sek in mi bed;
	And quen þis Iapę *es* tald anoþer dai,
	I sal be haldën daf, a cokenai.
	I wil arisę and auntrę it, bi mi fai!
290 (4210)	"Vnhardi *es* vnseli," þus men sai.

. . . .

316 (4236)	And seidë: "Far wel, Malinę, swetë wight!
	Þe dai *es* cum, I mai *na* lenger bide;
	But euer*ma*, quar *sa* I *ga* or ride,
319 (4239)	I es þin awën clerk, swa hauę I sel!

. . . .

329 (4249)	Alain vpristę and þoughtę: "*Ar* þat it dawe,	[20]
	I wil *ga* crepën in bi mi felawe";	
	And fond þe cradel wiþ his hondę anon.	

	"Bi god," þoughte he, "al wrang I hauẹ misgon;
	Min hed *es* toti of mi swink tonight,
	þat makës me þat I ga noght aright.
	I *wat* wel bi þe cradẹl, I hauẹ misgo:
336 (4256)	Her lis þe miller and his wif also."[51]

. . . .

342 (4262)	He seidẹ: "Þou Iohn, þou swinës-hed, awak
	For cristës saulẹ, and her a noblë game!
	For bi þat lord þat callëd *es* saint Iame,
	As I hauẹ þriës *i* þis schortë night
	Swiuëd þe miller doghter bolt-vpright,
347 (4267)	Quils þou hast as a coward ben agast."

. . . .

389 (4309)	(Reeve) And greiþen þeim and toke *þeire* hors anon,
	And ek *þeire* mele and on þeire wei þei gon.

In the subjoined notes references are given to the sources of the "northernisms" adopted. MSS not mentioned have substituted normal southern forms: thus 106 P *haþ*, L *haþe*.

102. *i*: *yfayth* E, rest *in. hail*, etc., all.

103. *fares* E H C O Hl. *fareþ þi fare* P: *fare* a possible northernism, since confusion, graphic and phonetic, of *ai*, *a* is found in northern texts, already e.g. in Cotton text of *Cursor Mundi* (possibly in rhyme 4141). But it is to be rejected, in spite of other similar spellings in P, as casual error due to influence of neighbouring words (here preceding *fareþ*). This type of error naturally common, but P supplies many examples. Cf. C *grate* and *smale* corrected to *grete* 402; P *cauche* for *cacche* 185 (*caughte* in next line).

106. *has* E H C O Hl; *na* E H Hl.

107. *boes* E only. *bihoues* H O (partial southernizing); *by-*, *behoueþ* P L (southernizing); *muste* C, *falles* Hl (rewriting of extreme dialectalism). The word possibly early received glosses. *falles* is probably not an alternative northernism; the *es* may be due to original, while this use of *falle* is not necessarily northern; *falles* also certainly occurred (in different sense) in original

122. *swain* all.

---

[51] Originally prob. *Misgaa* / *alswa*. [Marginal note in one of Tolkien's personal copies, referring to the end rhymes.]

himseluen: *hymselne* E, rest *-self*. *seluen* (used elsewhere by Chaucer) is better northern, and preferable metrically, since *boes* is monosyllabic; Chaucer probably wrote *bos* as genuine northern texts. All have this word-order, but Chaucer may have written *himseluen serue þat* (or *at*).

[21]

has E H C O Hl; *na* E H O Hl.

108. *folt* O; *fon* Hl; rest forms of *fool*. Attribution of *folt* to Chaucer doubtful; but variety of vocabulary likely to be his; variety of abusive words is in character (see below); while *folt* is a likely, though not necessary, starting point for alternative *fool* in contrast to preservation of *fon*, *fonne* in all 169 (though rhyme there made this necessary), and unanimous *fooles* 191. *fon* Hl probably from 169. Neither word was specifically northern; see notes on vocabulary.

110. *swa* all. *werkes* all but P *worchen*. The latter a good example of the southernizing of P; *worchen* is normal in P, and used elsewhere where others have *werke* (as A 779). The substitution is here made, although this *werkes* is a different verb. *wanges* all.

111. *forþi* E, rest forms of *þerfore*. These cannot be distinguished dialectally. *cum*: *come* monosyllabic all but P *commen*. See notes on grammatical forms below. P *commen* is not a northernism and is frequent generally in P.

es L, rest *is*. This *es* here accepted as original (extreme dialectal) for *is*, *am*, *art*. See remarks above, and below on grammatical forms. *als*: *alswa* L, rest forms of *eek*. It is here suggested that Chaucer wrote *als*: *eek* is a southern equivalent; L preserves trace of original (as not infrequently) but has expanded the dialectal form to detriment of metre (*alswa* occurs in 165). Cf. 240 *eek* all but C *also*. In 14th century *als* "also" was mainly northern or northerly. Chaucer's occasional use of it (proved by rhyme *fals*, *House of Fame* 2071, *Franklin's Tale* 870) is unusual in South, and perhaps literary, cf. his *greithe*, *lathe*, *wight* (below). Cf. *Cursor Mundi* 21, 155; *Handlyng Synne* 2748 (*fals* rhyming with *als* glossed *also*); and *Book of the Duchess* 728. *als* "as" occurs 257, q.v.

112. *ham* E O L Hl. H has the notable form *heem* which goes with *geen*, *neen* of E, but because unrecorded by Skeat has not received same notice as forms of E. See discussion of *geen*. *again* is, of course, necessary for northern. Chaucer may have used both *again* and *aʒein* (L here *aʒeine*) in his own language, both appear at any rate in the MSS elsewhere.

113. *speedes* O, supported by plural pronoun, but rest *spede*, etc. *heþen* L; *hepen* P (error, *p* for *þ*, which supports genuineness of *heþen*); *heythen*, *heithen* E H O, *hene* C, *in al þat* Hl (rewriting). The word would not appear to have

been readily understood (which is against northern scholarship of the scribes). L comes out well as frequently. *Heithen-* forms are possibly due to association with *heþen, heiþen* "heathen" (the *ei* forms in this latter word are curiously widespread in ME), but *eith* for *eth*, for whatever reason, is frequent in E H: e.g. *wheither* A 570, 1157.

116. All have *stande* and rhyme-word 115 *hande*. Cf. 181.

117. *howgates* O P; *how þat* E Hl; *how(e)* H C L. Compare 122 *howgates* O, *howe gates* L, *howe gate* P; rest *how þat*. Fair example of casual preservation of northernisms. The original assumed to have [22] been *hougat (hugat)* on metrical grounds (not conclusive); cf. P 122. Forms with and without *es* are both northern, but *hougat* a more likely antecedent of alternative or corruption *hou þat*. Cf. *Cursor Mundi* 27224 *þis word "hugat"* which refers to a preceding *hu* and provides good example of synonymity of *hu, hugat*. In 119 all have *how þat*, which is therefore retained. It is not impossible for northern. Unanimity in 119 favours *hougat(es)* as due to original where there is disagreement. *gas* E H O Hl.

118. *sagh* P. The normal form for "saw" in P is *seegh, segh*.

119. *hou þat*, see 117. *wagges*: perhaps better *waggis*, so Hl, *wagis* C (but in both flexional *is, ys* is frequent; cf. 122, 153, 167). All *s* inflexion, except *wagged* O, *waggeþ* P. *til and fra* E H O L, *to and fra* C Hl, *til and fraye* (rhyme *swaye*) P (cf. 103).

120, 121. *bineþen*, with preserved *n* required for strict northern not in any MS, but such a point would naturally be neglected (possibly by Chaucer, certainly by MSS); *bineþen* is frequent elsewhere in Chaucer. *wiltou* is a correct northern form; so all but *wist þou* C. Cf. *Cursor Mundi weltu* 20355, but *þou will* in rhyme 8379, 20657. *swa* all but *swaye* P.

122. *hougat*, see 117. *falles* E H O P L, *fallys* Hl.

123. *intil, intill* O L. *sal* E H. *be* all, except *ben* C with southern *n*.

124. *yfaith, yfayth* E C. *in faath* P, *in faaþe* L: cf. *fraye swaye* (?), but see below, 289. *es al* L, rest *may ben*, etc., with southern *n* (Hl *be*): *mai be* is equally likely; further readings are required here.

125. *I es* L, rest *I is. as ere* O Hl; *as ar* E H; *as is* C P; *as es* L. None of these forms are normal in the respective MSS. On choice see notes on grammatical forms. *miller: melner* L.

153. *lost* H O P L Hl; *lorn* E C. *lorn* is a usual Chaucerian form; but also possible in northern *lorn* certainly used in dialect passage 155 as shown by rhyme, but the sense is not there the same and derives directly from OE *forloren*, whereas in 153 OE weak verb *losian* "go astray" is also concerned. The distinction between *I am lost* and *I haue lorn* appears to be observed

elsewhere in Chaucer. *banes* all, except C *bonys*. *goddis* P (flexional *is, ys* also found in P independent of the dialect passages).

154. *com(e) of* H C O P L; *cum on* Hl; *com out* E. *at anes, att anes* all, except *atonys* C.

155. *has* E H C O L. *haþ our palfray* P.

158. *whilk(e)* E H O P L, *whedir* C; (*what*) *wikked* Hl. *gan(e)* H L Hl, E *geen*.

165. Hl has *leg* (for *ley?*). *sal* Hl, rest the normal forms of *will* in each MS *alswa* all.

166. *I es* L, *I is* E H C O P Hl. *wight, wyʒt,* E H C Hl; *swift* O P L. *waat, wat(e)* E H O P L Hl. *raa, ra* all.

167. *god* E H (metre shows this erroneous); *goddes* O L, *goddis* C Hl. *sal* E H O L Hl. *baþe, bathe* all.

168. *nad thow* Hl; *ne had(de) thow (þou)* H O P L; *ne haddist* [23] *thou* C: *nadstow* E; cf. 250. *pit* E H C, rest *put(te)*. *capel* in various forms in all; also *lathe, laþe*.

169. *Ilhayl, il(le) hail,* etc., all (*il a hayle* L). *fonne, fon* all (*grete fonne* L). *þou es* L, rest *þou is*.

181. *stand(e)* all, except *stonde* P.

182. *ga* all. *qwistel* P, a remarkable spelling, perhaps pointing to northern orthography, see above; rest *whistle*, etc. (but *wightly* Hl). *sal* H, Hl (*ga wightly þou sal*).

190. *er* L, *ere* O; *ar* H, *are* E C P Hl. Note distribution of forms differs from 125. *dreuen* L, *dreuyn* C (E Hl have southern form without *n*. *dryue*). These forms are part of "northern" language, but may here be due only to orthographic habits of L and C. In C *e* for *ī* is almost regular, in L same use is frequent: thus C *wretyn*, L *wreten* A 161, 1305; *redyn, reden* 1503; *resyn, resen* 1065, etc. For the form in northern texts, cf. *Northern Passion* (EETS), pp. 150, 178 (Harl. MS); also rhyme *driuen, heuen* in *Cursor Mundi* 22110. Under vocab. it will be seen the sense of *drive* here is Northern. *til heþyng* all; *til scorn* E H O L; *to scorn* C P Hl. It is possible second *til* is derived from first, and that Chaucer wrote *to scorn*; see notes to *til* and *driue* (below).

191. *stoln* E, *stolle* P L, rest *stole*; Cf. 263. *men wil* H O P L, *me wil* E, *men wele* C, *men woln* Hl.

192. *bathe* E Hl.

207. *Cutberd* E H P L (*berde*); *Cutbert* C; *Cuthberd* O Hl.

208. *es thou* L, rest *is* except *art* C. *mery(e)* C O P L Hl, *myrie* E H.

209. *say(e)* O L Hl, *seye* H P, *seyd* E C. *man* E, rest *men*. *suld* Hl, *sal* E H O, *sall* L; *schal shal* C P; Cf. 254. *taa* E; *tan* C; *tak, take(n)* H O P L Hl; Cf. 210. *twa, tua* E H O L Hl.

210. The "such" forms are distributed as follows:—
210. *slyk, slik*, twice. E Hl; *swilk(e)* H O L; *swich* C; *such* P.
250. *slyk(e), slik* E H O L, *sclike* P; *swich* C.
251. *whilk* E; *swilk(e)* H O L; *slik* Hl; *sclike* P; *swich* C.
253. *slyk(e), slik* E O L, *sclike* P; *swilk* H Hl; *swich* C.

This is the only case of competition among northernisms. It is possible that *swilk* = *swich* (analogous to *whilk* = *which*) was well known, and that scribes have actually in this case introduced a new northern feature. But this would not be an example of their improving on Chaucer. Their use of a northern word was due to his initiative, and *swilk* is in effect a toning down of the dialect, since *slik* is a more extreme dialectalism of much more limited currency than *swilk* (though context made meaning of either obvious). But Chaucer may, as did genuine northern texts, have used both *swilk* and *slik* – if so, as far as evidence here given goes, we should select 250 as a place where original certainly had *slik* (only C, which resolutely has *swich* in all cases, differs); and 210 as possible for *swilk*, since P has *such*, but does not otherwise boggle at *slik*. In 251 where idiom allows *swich* or *which* (for *lo swich*, cf. [24] A 4318, P.F. 570), E is possibly right in reading *whilk*; but *whilk* was already provided in 158. See appendix on *slik*.

fyndes E H O; rest southern *fynd* (? trace of original *findes*) C; *fint, fynt* P L Hl. Contrast *bringes* ret. by all in rhyme. *taa* E; *tak(e)* H C O P Hl; L omits; cf. 209.

211. *hoot and dere* C!

212. *sum* C L. If *gar vs haue* (see footnote to text) is Chaucerian, then all our 7 MSS have toned dialect down here.

213. *at þe* C Hl, rest *atte* (*att* L). C has *folle* rhyming *tolle*, but *o* for *ŭ* is characteristic of this MS *tulle* seems, nonetheless, isolated; see Appendix I. All except C Hl have *payen* with southern *n*.

214. *man*: all *men*. *na* Hl, *naan* O; *none* E H C; *not, nouhte*, P L.

215. *for til* O.

249. *slepest þou* L, sim. C O; *slepestow* E H and sim. P Hl. *slepest* is accordingly retained as an original southernism, but Chaucer may well have written correctly *slepes, slepis*. Cf. next.

250. *herd thow* H, *herde þou* P; *herdtow* E (mongrel); *herdist* (*herdest*) *þou* C L; *herdestow* (*-istow*) O Hl. Skeat inexplicably adopted O which represents end of southernizing process sufficiently exhibited here. Cf. 168. On *slik* see 210. *sang* all except *song* C. *ar* O only, rest *er* except *or* L; retention (if it is such) of *ar* by O is connected with fact that O has *ar* occasionally in other pieces (e.g. A 2398), and frequently shows *er* > *ar*.

251. On *quilk* see 210. *compline* L, rest errors (such as *cowplyng* E) ? derived from *cōplin* > *conplin, couplin. ymel* E H; *ytwix* P (mongrel, half-way to) *bitwixe, betwix* O Hl; *betuene* L; *among* C. *þaim*: all *hem*; but *þeym* occurs in L 389 (also *þeire* L 390), probably original and meant for Reeve (see above). Cf. *þair* 252, and see notes on vocab. Retention of *þair* and rejection of *þaim* is due to fifteenth century usage, probably not to original.

252. *þair* O Hl, *thair* E H, *þeire* L.

253. *wha* E H L Hl. On *slik* see 210. *ferly* all.

254. *3a* C, rest *ye*; *3a* occurs in northern texts; but C has *3a* elsewhere, e.g. A 1667; also in *Reeve's Tale* 348 (given to miller). *sal* E H, *sall* O; *schal, shal*, C P L; Hl *sul*; the last probably a hybrid southern *schul(le)* + northern *sal* (*sul* probably not a genuine northern form), but may be amateur "northern" on analogy of *schal* = *sal*: Hl alone has *suld* 209, and though this is a correct northern form, both its *sul* and *suld* are perhaps dubious. *il*, etc. all, except *euel* L.

255. *tydes, -is* all, except *þer sal I haue* (imitated northern) L. *na* E H O L Hl. *lang(e)* E H O P L Hl.

256. *na* E H O P L Hl. *sal* E H L Hl. O has southern *ben*.

257. *als* E H O: *as* C P L Hl. *Als* "as" in fourteenth century is mainly but not solely northern. MSS of Chaucer (and Gower) occasionally use this form elsewhere.

[25]

258. *gif*: all *if*, but cf. 261, 270. *3on(e)* P Hl, *yon* E H O; *þe* C L. *sal* Hl, rest forms of *wil* which may be original.

259. *s(c)hapen* H O P L Hl; wrongly with sourthern prefix *yshapen, Ischapyn* E C. *has* E H C.

260. *says* E H C Hl.

261. *gif* E H; *3if* C, rest *if*. *á* (i.e. long stressed *á*): *a* E H C O Hl; *oon* P, *o* L. *agreued* correctly all but E *ygreued* wrongly with southern prefix.

262. *sal* E H L Hl. C has southern *ben*.

263. *stoln* E H Hl, *stollen* P L; *stolin* C, *stolen* O. *soþly*, etc., in all but *s(c)hortly* E C. *na* H Hl; *ne* E (cf. *geen, neen*); rest *no(n)*.

264. *haue* L Hl, rest *han. il(le), ylle* all, except *euel* P, *yuel* L.

265. *seen* L, rest *syn. sal* E H Hl. *nan* Hl, *naan* H; E *neen* (cf. 267), rest *no, non*, etc.

266. *agayn, ageyn* all. *haue* all.

267. *goddes saule it sal* H P L; rest have errors due to proximity of *saule sal* which support these forms as original: *God sale it sal* E, *godys sale it schal* C. *goddes sale it sal* O, *godde sale it sal* Hl. *nan(e), naan* H O P L Hl; *neen* E (cf. 265).

269. *parlous* L Hl: *perilous* E H O P, *perlyous* C.

270. *gif* E, rest *if. sleepe abreyde* E and sim. rest, but *slape abrayde* O (casual error due to neighbouring *as*).

271. *do* Hl, rest southern *don, doon*, etc. *bathe, baþe* E H L.

282. *say* Hl; *saie* L, *seie* P; *seyn, sayn* E H C O. *I es* L; rest *is*, except *am* Hl.

283. *has* E H.

284. *has* E H C O. All show genitival, *s, is* in *milleris*, but cf. 346.

285. *auntred* all (*auntreþ* P, *auntre* L). *has* E H C Hl.

286. *drafsek* E C, *-sak(ke)* H O P L Hl.

287. *tald* E Hl, rest *told(e)*.

288. *sal(l)* E H L Hl. *be* O P L Hl; *been, ben* E H C. *halden; halden a* H; *halde a* E; *holden a* L, *holde a* O P; *held a* Hl: *told a* C. *daf, daff(e)* all.

289. *auntre*, etc., all. C has rhyme *fay, say*; rest *fayth, sayth* in different spellings E H O L Hl; *fath, sath* P. Though dialect is not correctly restored by *say* (see notes on grammatical forms), this is less violently out of place (or a more natural "error" for Chaucer to make). P *fath, sath* may show later knowledge of *ai > a* (see above), but probably depend on *þ, y*, confusion – illustrated by C *þat* for *yet* A 563, 722, and L *boþe* for *boye* in *Gamelyn* 488.

317, 318: the use of southernisms *no, mo, so, go*, etc., by all the MSS in these two lines is curious. Further readings required; perhaps significant, as southernisms begin at this point to multiply in all. Not ascribable, at any rate, to Alain's using a "southern tooth" for [26] Maline's benefit – that he should be able to is rather out of character: in any case, the next line is full of northernisms.

319. *I is* E H C, rest *am. awen* E H. *swa* E. *seel, sel(e)* all, except O *hele*.

330. *cre(e)pen* with southern inf. in all, except *crepe* C; as line stands *crepen* must be dissyllabic.

332. *wrang(e)* E H L. All have the southern rhyme *mysgon* (Hl *Igoon*) with the *anon* of preceding line (which is narrative and not northern).

334. *makes, ga* Hl.

342. *swines-hed: sweuenyst* C!

343. *saule, sawle* E H O P.

344. *called: cleped* Hl, but this verb also found in northern texts.

346. *þe meller douhter* L, but similar ending of the two words and extreme frequency of omissions of final letters in L make this very doubtful as example of northern uninflected genitive.

347. *hast* all. On evidence of other verbal inflexions and use of *es, is* "art" we may assume Chaucer wrote northern *has* here; but since this has not been preserved in any of the seven MSS *hast* is here retained.

389, 390. *greythen, greyþen*, etc., all, except *hastede* C.[52] *þeym* L; *her horse, here mele*, but *þeire weie* L.

Northernisms preserved intact in all seven MSS: (*a*) vocabulary: *hail* 102, 169; *swain* in rhyme 107; *wanges* 110; *ill* 125, 169; *laþe* in rhyme 168; *fonne* in rhyme (eye-rhyme?) 169; *til* before *h* 190; *heþing* 190; *ferly* 253; *auntre* 285, 289.[53] (*b*) forms: *wanges* 110; *fra* (P *fraye*) rhyming *swa* (P *swaye*) 119, 120; *alswa* rhyming *ra* 165, 166; *baþe* in rhyme 167; *ga* 182; and the 3 sg. *bringes* in rhyme 210; *es, is* am 166. About twenty-four points, many fixed by rhyme.

Northernisms preserved in four or more MSS: Add to the above: *es, is* art 208; *es, is* am 282; *has* 106, 107, 155, 284, 285; other 3 sg. forms in *s* 107, 117, 119, 122, 125, 260; 3 pl. in *s* 110; *a* for *oo* one 261; *na, nan* 107, 255, 256, 267; *ham* home 112; *wha* 253; *gas* 117; *banes* 153; *at anes* 154; *wat* 158; *saule* 343; *til* (scorn) 190; *til and fra* 119; *thair* 252; *sal* 167, 256, 262, 288; *lang* 255; *sang* 250; *whilk* 158; vocabulary: *yon* 258; *il* 254, 264; *seel* 319; *heþen* (accepting *heithen, hepen*), 113. About forty-one additional points.

Ellesmere (E) is sole authority for *boes* 107, *gif* 270, *swa* 319, *taa* 209, 210; and to these can perhaps be added *whilk* 251 and *stoln* 191, *yfayth* 102 (not necessarily northern). In conjunction with H it preserves an otherwise altered *sal* 123, *ymel* 251, *gif* 261, *has* 283, *awen* 319; with Hl *bathe* 192, *tald* 287; with C *drafsek* 286. But it shows over thirty cases of fairly certain error or alteration, of seven of which (such as *ygreued* 261) it alone is guilty.

The above text offers approximately ninety-eight lines put into the mouths of the northern clerks. If we now examine the [27] departures from Chaucer's normal usage that there appear, and which we can assume that he offered as dialect, we shall discover what accuracy and consistency he achieved. The italicized forms which have not in their places, in the seven MSS studied, actual MS authority are omitted. Chaucer's consistency will then certainly not be exaggerated. The abnormal or dialectal features of the lines may be divided into: A. *sounds and forms*, that is, words current in Chaucer's London English are presented in a different shape, due to a divergent development, from a common Old English or Old Norse original, in North and South; B. *vocabulary*, words (chiefly of Scandinavian origin) are used, which were not yet in Chaucer's time, and in some cases have never since been adopted into southern or literary English. Here will be included instances of dialectal senses of words current throughout the country.

---

[52] P *greieþ*. [Marginal note in one of Tolkien's personal copies.]
[53] Tolkien enclosed *auntre* and its citations in square brackets. [Ed.]

A. Sounds and Forms

(i) *ā* for *ǭ*: *na, nan* (OE nān) 106, 107, 214, 255, 256, 263, 265, 267. *swa* (OE swā) 110, 120, 319. *ham* (OE hām) 112. *ga, gan, gas* (OE gā-n) 117, 158, 182, 334. *fra* (ON frá) 119. *banes* (OE bān) 153. *at anes* (OE ānes) 154. *alswa* (OE alswā) 165. *wat* (OE wāt) 166. *ra* (OE rā) 166. *baþe* (ON bāþi-r) 167 (in this case *a* fixed for the original by rhyme), 192, 271. *twa* (OE twā) 209. *qua* (OE hwā) 253. *á* (OE ān) "one" 261. *saule* (OE sāwol) 267, 343. *awen* (OE āgen) 319.

(ii) Similarly in the combinations *ald*: *tald* (OE táld) 287. *halden* (OE hálden) 288.[54]

(iii) *ang* for *ong*: *wanges* (OE wange "cheek") 110; see below on the meaning of this word. *sang* (OE sang) 250. *lange* (OE lang) 255. *wrang* (ON vrang-r) 332. Note that all the words in (i), (ii), (iii), with the exception of *wanges*, would be normal (Chaucerian) English with substitution of *o* for *a*.

(iv) *e* for *ĭ*: *dreuen* "driven" 190; authority doubtful, see note to the line.

(v) *k* for *ch*: *quilk* 158, 251; also possibly *swilk* 210 (and perhaps elsewhere: see notes above). These are derived from OE *hwilc* (*swilc*), whence also normal Chaucerian *which, swich*.

[28] (vi) *verbal inflexions*: (*a*) *es, s* for *eth, th* in 3 sg. present *fares* 103. *has* 106, 107, 155, 259, 283, 284, 285. *boes* 107. *gas* 117. *wagges* 119. *falles* 122. *findes* 210. *bringes* 210 (fixed for original by rhyme). *tides* 255. *sais* 260. *makes* 334. There are seventeen instances. There cannot be any doubt that these *s*-forms are intended as a dialect feature, and this is specially interesting as showing that Chaucer largely made use of points that were to some extent familiar. Not only has this inflexion since become part of ordinary English, but Chaucer himself occasionally uses it in his own work, perhaps only to assist in rhyming (as e.g. in *Book of the Duchess*, 73, 257). He would hardly have done this if the inflexion was in his day entirely unfamiliar and odd to London ears. (*b*) *es* for *eth* in the imperfect pl. *spedes* 113. (*c*) *es* for *e, en* in present pl. *werkes* "ache" 110. These are more distinctively dialectal and not elsewhere used by Chaucer (as far as rhymes and printed texts show). Though they appear later in London English, they never became established. It is therefore perhaps significant that we have only *one* example of the indicative pl. as against 17 of the sg., and in the only other case of a verb in the present pl. the "incorrect" form *sain*[55] fixed by rhyme with *swain* is used. *fares* 103

---

[54] But *ald* occasionally occurs in the MSS elsewhere: e.g. *houshalder* A 339 O P L; *halde* A 414 in L. [Tolkien]

[55] Whether Chaucer used the "incorrect" pl. *sai* or sg. *saith* is not clear in 290. Such forms as *sain* do, of course, occur (in rhyme) in works from some parts of the North (in general this is rather a feature of the debatable North-West). Cf. *Sir Eglamour* 52 *layne* "conceal" / *sayne* inf.; 223 *payne* "pain" /

might be pl. but is probably sg. as reckoned above; cf. 336. (*d*) Here may be observed the monosyllabic forms, with unchanged stems in the plural, of "shall" and "will"; as *wil* 191, 213; *sal* (variant reading *sul*) 254. Monosyllabic forms, with the stem the same as in the singular, are found elsewhere in Chaucer (according to the MSS), but *shal* is rare as compared with *shul*, *shuln*, *shullen*. (*e*) The forms of past participles. These should in northern dialect have no *y*-prefix, and should retain the ending (*e*)*n* in strong verbs – except in a few cases where final *n* is lost in northern forms after a verbal stem containing *m*, *n*:[56] as *cum* "come", *bun* "bound". The following are all correct for northern speech. Strong: *cum* 111, 317. *born* (rhyming *scorn*) 189. *stoln* 191, 263. *dreuen*[57] 190. *lorn* (rhyming *corn*) 155. *schapen* 259. *halden* 288. *gan* 158. *ben* 347. Weak: *lost* 153. *pit* 168. *answerd* 208. *herd* 209. *agreued* 261 (E wrongly *ygreued*). *releued* 262. *had* 264. *sped* 285. *tald* 287. *called* 344. *swiued* 346. Incorrect is *misgo* without *n*, rhyming *also*, 335; *misgon* 332 rhyming *anon* has correct form but southern vowel. The correct forms are in the great majority. But actually in most cases they coincide with variants possible or usual in normal Chaucerian grammar. At the same time most of them represent opportunities for error (as is seen in the southernized forms of some MSS) that have been avoided. Some are additionally marked as northern by vowels, as *gan*, *tald*, *halden* (*dreuen*). *cum* (MSS *come*) only occurs before a vowel where elision is possible. *Stoln*, by metre probably a monosyllable in both instances, may be taken as more specifically dialectal: i.e. as *stŏln* with short vowel contrasted with normal Chaucerian *ystōle*(*n*), *stōle*(*n*), trisyllabic or dissyllabic; *stŏln* and later *stollen* (so P L) are characteristic of northern texts (e.g. *Cursor Mundi* 4904, *Sir Gawain* 1659). (*f*) The 2 sg. of the past tense. *nad þou* 168, *herde þou* 250.[58]

(vi) *Various northern forms and contractions*: (*a*) *es* (*is*) for *am*, 111, 124, 125, 166, 282, 319. *es* (*is*) for *art*, 169, 208. *es*, not *is*, for *is*, 158, 251 (derived from uncertain evidence of L, see above). *er* for *ben* "are", 125, 190. All these are correct and specifically northern forms and uses. The choice among the

---

ye sayne. Under *ra* will be seen a hint that Chaucer had read this poem or things like it. [Tolkien] *Sir Eglamour of Artois* was written about 1350 in a dialect assigned to the North-East Midlands, perhaps Yorkshire. Tolkien believed it was one of the tail-rhyme romances that Chaucer parodied in his *Sir Thopas*. He would have known the work in *Bishop Percy's Folio Manuscript: Ballads and Romances*, ed. John W. Hales and Frederick J. Furnivall, 3 vols. (London: Trübner, 1867–68), 338–89, or *Sir Eglamour: A Middle English Romance*, ed. A. S. Cook and Gustav Schleich (New York: Holt, 1911). It is noteworthy that Sir Eglamour is given a magical ring which grants its wearer protection from death. [Ed.]

[56] A similar development is found in some German dialects. [Tolkien]
[57] In the original publication, page 29 starts here. [Ed.]
[58] *Sir Gawain and the Green Knight*, ed. J. R. R. Tolkien and E. V. Gordon (Oxford: Clarendon, 1925), 51: "Wyth stille *stollen* countenaunce, þat stalworth to plese" (1659). The Bodleian has two of Tolkien's personal copies of this edition, MS Tolkien E 16/34 and MS Tolkien E 16/35. [Ed.]

variants in case of "are" 125, 190, assumes that Chaucer wrote *er* (or *ar*) in 190, where all the MSS have *r*-forms, and that he also did so in 125, where the *is*, *es* of C P L are due to the preceding *I is* (*es*). The *r*-forms are correct in immediate conjunction with a pronoun, *es* (*is*) being only used normally when separated from a pronoun. An instructive contrast is provided by *Cursor Mundi* 354 *thre thinges þam es witjn*, and 356 *four er þai*.[59] Though the more extreme forms *es, er* have been adopted, *is* and *ar* are not necessarily incorrect. *is* varies freely with *es* in any of its uses in northern texts. OE *aron, aro* were both northern and midland, and so were the derived forms in Middle English.[60] [30] *es, er* were due to the influence of ON *es, ero*; they were not, of course, merely "northern" forms, but were also found in the East. The uses of *es, is* were probably due to the association of their *s* with the northern *s*-inflexion of verbs, which caused them to spread beyond the 3 sg. When replacing *am* this dialectal usage was probably found laughable: the specially large number of instances of this in the text may be noted. (*b*) *sal* 123, 165, 167, 182, 254, 256, 258, 262, 265, 267, 288 (all 1 or 3 sg., except 254 pl.); an irregular but well-evidenced form of *shal*, found still in northern dialects and in Middle English confined to northern texts.[61] This detail has been favoured by Chaucer and well preserved by the MSS as a rule – some of the cases may even represent the substitution of *sal* for Chaucerian *wil* (see variants above). The past tense *suld* occurs in 209, a good northern form (but only in Hl). (*c*) *ta* 209, 210: an irregular reduction of *take*, which was specifically northern. Chaucer does not use it elsewhere. It remained dialectal, though the pp. (written *tan, taan, tâne, tain,* and now *ta'en*) later gained some currency, especially in verse. (*d*) *als* (111), 257: a form characteristic of northern texts; but see notes to 111, 257 above. (*e*) *boes* 107: this is written in genuine northern texts *bos, bus*, and is a reduction of *bihoues*. Its preservation in E only is notable. E has not preserved the northernisms particularly well, and shows no tendency or ability independently to improve the dialect with such genuine details as this. (*f*) *gif* 261, 270: an irregular variant of *if*, of obscure origin, but well evidenced in northern language. There can be little doubt that it also appeared in 258. (*g*) To the above may be added *ar* "ere" 250, also current outside the northern area and found in various places in O (which gives it here) and L,

---

[59] *Cursor Mundi* 4847 *es we* cited by Skeat is a passage dubious textually. [Tolkien]

[60] The MSS seem not elsewhere to represent Chaucer as using the now current *are*, certainly not in rhyme, though there are a few cases of *arn* (probably not genuine). The later currency of *ar(e)* probably explains the retention of the dialectal *r*-forms in these two lines. [Tolkien]

[61] Apart, of course, from spellings with *s, ss,* for *sh*. [Tolkien]

for instance. *ʒa* 254 (see note on this line above). *sagh* 118, a familiar form and spelling in northern texts. *i* (for *in*), early found in the north, perhaps partly owing to ON *í*, but here only in *i-faiþ* 102, 124, where *i* probably had a wider currency; cf. *imell* in B, next. *pit* (for *put*) 168, found in modern northern and Scottish dialect, but rare in Middle English, where it is mainly, but not solely, northern.[62] The uninflected genitive *miller* 346 rests on poor evidence (see above). For the forms of *auntre*, *draf-sek* see below.

[31]

B. *Vocabulary*

capel, 168 horse. This word did not obtain a footing in "standard" English, and is plainly intended as dialectal here, though it must have been a fairly familiar word, since Chaucer uses it himself elsewhere. Used by the Reeve in the narrative part of his tale (185), it is probably intended also to be dialectal or rustic; it is also used by the Summoner in his tale, and by the Friar in his, and by the Host in the prologue to the *Manciple's Tale* (none of them examples of elevated speech). Chaucer is right in making it an element of northern vocabulary, though it is found in the West (*Piers Plowman*) and in alliterative verse generally,[63] and was probably also known in the East (East Anglia, which accounts for the Reeve) – it appears at any rate in the *Promptorium Parvulorum*.

daf, 288 fool. This word is dialectal, and is probably quite correctly put into the mouths of northerners; but words of abuse are easily acquired, and have generally a wide distribution. This word is not limited to the North in Middle English (it occurs, for instance, in *Piers Plowman*); nor in modern dialect, where its use is, however, mainly northerly or Scottish.

ferli, 253 wonderful. This word, whether used as a noun, adjective, or verb, is very common in Middle English, both in the North and the West, and is especially associated with alliterative or alliterated verse. After Chaucer's time it is recorded almost exclusively from the North and West, yet it must be reckoned as one of the elements of the vocabulary of verse, with its roots in the

---

[62] *pitte* past tense occurs in Gower, *Confessio Amantis*, viii, 2796 (MS F.). [Tolkien] He cites *Confessio Amantis* in *The English Works of John Gower*, ed. Macaulay: "And as he *pitte* forth his hond" (2:462). [Ed.]

[63] Tolkien knew very well William Langland's *Piers the Plowman in Three Parallel Texts*, ed. Walter W. Skeat, 2 vols. (Oxford: Oxford University Press, 1886), and it remains a mystery why he did not lecture and write about the poem during his long career, since its West Midland dialect was centered upon Worcestershire, which he cherished as the homeland of his mother's family (*Biography* 27). His personal copy of Skeat's 9th edition of *Piers*, inscribed in February 1914, is now Bodleian's Tolkien VC 259. [Ed.]

alliterative verse of the Scandinavianized North and North-West, that has always been widely familiar, if never naturalized, in the South. Chaucer, however, does not himself use the word elsewhere.

folt, 108 fool. This word is perhaps less common than *fonne* but has a similar distribution, being found (with its derivatives *folte* v., *folted, foltisch*) chiefly in northern or eastern texts and writers.

fonne, 169. This is the only occurrence of the word in Chaucer. It is a northern and north-midland word. It did not become part of the "standard" language, though its derivative *fonned, fond*, which was until long after Chaucer's time still dialectal and northerly, has since become current. It is quite correct in the [32] mouth of John, but must also be reckoned among the words that were, if northern, not totally foreign. The derivative *fonned* is found, contemporary with Chaucer, in Wyclif or Wycliffite writings; the simple *fon, fonne* is found in Manning, Mirk, and (after Chaucer) very frequently in the Coventry Plays: it seems thus marked as a widespread midland word.[64]

That in this short vocabulary of dialectal words we should have three words for "fool" and one for jeering (*heþing*, see below), not to mention the universally current *fol* 190, or the words *drafsek, cokenai*, and *swines-hed*, is a perfectly just testimony to the richness of the northern and Scandinavianized dialects in terms of abuse. We have the same observant Chaucer behind the linguistic portraiture of this tale as behind the sketches of the Prologue.

hail in *al hail!* 102; *il hail!* 169. This is the Norse *heil-l* "hale, sound", used in greetings, such as *kom heill, far heill!* But the noun *heill* "(good) luck, omen" also used in greetings doubtless contributed. The adjective, except in the salutation, was and remained dialectal, and chiefly northern, or eastern (e.g. *Bestiary* and *Promptorium*).[65] The noun, especially in such expressions as *il hail*, was always northerly: the most southerly example, older than or

---

[64] Tolkien had ready access to these editions: *The English Works of Wyclif*, ed. F. D. Matthew 2nd ed. rev. EETS o.s. 74 (1902); Manning of Brunne's *Handlyng Synne* in Furnivall's two-volume EETS edition; *Mirk's Festial: A Collection of Homilies*, ed. Theodore Erbe, EETS e.s. 96 (1905); and *Ludus Coventriae or The Plaie Called Corpus Christi*, ed. K. S. Block, EETS e.s. 120 (1922). Tolkien had glossed two English texts attributed to Wyclif in Sisam's *Fourteenth Century Verse and Prose*, 115–28. [Ed.]

[65] It is found nonetheless in Layamon (who has many surprising words), and more curiously in Gower, who uses it at least twice in rhyme, *Confessio Amantis* 703, 2022 (*heil* rhyming *seil, conseil*). [Tolkien] His personal copy of *Layamon's Brut*, ed. Joseph Hall (Oxford: Clarendon, 1924), now the Bodleian's Tolkien VC 260, would have supplied him with the text in a language close to his specialty works *Ancrene Wisse* and *Sawles Warde*. Tolkien probably alludes to the East Midland *Bestiary* available in *An Old English Miscellany Containing a Bestiary, Kentish Sermons, Proverbs of Alfred, Religious Poems of the Thirteenth Century*, ed. Richard Morris, EETS o.s. 49 (1872), 1–25, or *Selections from Early Middle English*, ed. Joseph Hall, 2 vols. (Oxford: Oxford University Press, 1920), 1:176–96. His personal copies of Hall's *Selections* are now Bodleian MS Tolkien E 16/9 and E 16/10. The *Bestiary* was a source of Tolkien's poem *Iumbo, or ye Kinde of ye Oliphaunt* (1927) later faintly echoed by Sam's "Grey as a mouse / Big as a house" (*TT* IV/3). [Ed.]

contemporary with Chaucer, given in *NED* is from Manning (Lincolnshire) in the expression *to wrother-haylle*.⁶⁶ In salutations, however, *hail* either alone or in formulae such as *al hail, hail be thou*, is found widely scattered. It is found, for instance, in *Vices and Virtues*, presumed to be from the South-East (Essex) and dated about 1200.⁶⁷ It is, nonetheless, used little by Chaucer; outside this tale it appears only in the mouth of the somnour, who is a character in the *Friar's Tale*.⁶⁸ We may, therefore, reckon Alain's salutation of [33] the miller among the features intended by Chaucer to be taken as dialect, while recognized by him as familiar. The word later became current and literary, but its earliest record seems to be in the angelic salutation to Mary, in which alone it could still be said to be in general use.

heþen, 113 hence. This is from ON *heðan*, replacing *henne(s)* from OE *heonane*. It is quite rightly offered as a northern word; but was also used in the East from Lincoln to East Anglia (Manning, *Havelok*, *Genesis* and *Exodus*, *Ormulum*).⁶⁹ It remained dialectal, and is not else used by Chaucer, nor by any southern or London writer.

heþing, 190 contumely, scorn. This again is a word rightly ascribed to the North, but in fact widely used, together with its relatives *heþe* jeer at, *heþeli* contemptible *or* contemptuous, in the Scandinavianized areas (North-West, North, and East) It never became part of the literary vocabulary, and is nowhere else used by Chaucer. It is purely Norse in origin: ON *hæða, hæðing* (and *hæðni*), *hæðiligr*, used precisely as in Middle English.

hougat, 117, 122 how. This word (with or without added *es*) seems to have been purely northern, belonging to Yorkshire, Northumberland, or Scotland. Skeat's failure to record its presence in the MSS used for his edition is curious. The similar formation *algates* was frequently used by Chaucer.

---

⁶⁶ Cf. also *Handlyng Synne* 3672, where *wroþerheyl* in one MS is in others altered to *wroþer yn helle*. I have noted an earlier example in the reading of the Corpus MS of *Ancrene Wisse*: *to himmere heile hire to wraðerheale*, which corresponds to the Nero reading *to wrother hele* (Cleopatra *himmere*), Morton, p. 102. Here we have both native *hǣlu* and the Scandinavian word. The *Ancrene Wisse* contains a notable Scandinavian element; and the distribution of *hail* is plainly related to the areas of Scandinavian influence. [Tolkien] He had considered these dialect issues in his article "*Ancrene Wisse* and *Hali Meiðhad*" (1929) and would eventually publish his own edition of *Ancrene Wisse* (1962) where he doubted the reading *himmere heile* (54); his personal copy is now Bodleian Tolkien VC 211. For the Nero and Cleopatra versions, he refers the reader to *The Ancren Riwle*, ed. Morton (1853). [Ed.]

⁶⁷ See *Vices and Virtues*, ed. Ferdinand Holthausen (London: Oxford University Press, 1888). [Ed.]

⁶⁸ See Skeat 4:361: "Sir," quod this Somnour, "hayl! and wel a-take!" (*CT* III, 1384). [Ed.]

⁶⁹ Tolkien would have read these editions: *Havelok the Dane*, ed. Walter W. Skeat, EETS e.s. 4 (1868); *The Story of Genesis and Exodus*, ed. Richard Morris, EETS o.s. 7 (1865); and *The Ormulum*, ed. Robert Holt (Oxford: Clarendon, 1878). The Bodleian has Tolkien's personal copies of Skeat's first edition of *Havelok* (MS Tolkien E 16/17) as well as the 1915 revision by Kenneth Sisam (MS Tolkien E 16/19) and Ferdinand Holthausen's 1910 Heidelberg edition (MS Tolkien E 16/18). [Ed.]

il, 125, 254, 264, and in *il hail* 169, evil bad. This word was characteristic of East and North, and its frequent use (as opposed to its occasional appearance, especially as a rhyme-word) was in Chaucer's day still confined to the language of those areas. The word was later adopted into ordinary and literary English. It now remains current chiefly in uses derived from the ME adverb (*it is me ille*, I am ill). It may be noted that the uses here are adjectival. It is interesting to observe this familiar modern word employed by Chaucer to give an impression of dialect. He does not use it elsewhere, but if only because of its later acceptance, we may reckon this word also among northernisms already fairly familiar to his audience.[70]

[34]

imell, 251 among. This was and remained a characteristically northern word, and is among the more extreme dialectalisms used. It occurs in the forms *e-mell*, *o-mell(e)*, *i-mell(e)*, derived from Old East Norse; cf. Old DInish *i mellae* (modern *imellem*, *mellem*), Old Icelandic *í milli*, *á milli*. It is not used by Chaucer elsewhere. Compare the use in the *York Plays*, xi, 30, and xxxvii, 104, which is very similar to the use in Chaucer's passage.

laþe, 168 barn. This is derived from ON *hlaða* store-house. It is a genuine northern word, still in use in the North. It was also found in the East, and appears as early as *Genesis and Exodus* (probably representing East Anglia). There can be no doubt that it is meant to be one of the dialect features in the clerks' speech, and it has not been adopted in the standard language; yet it must also be reckoned as one of the words Chaucer could assume were familiar, for he uses it once elsewhere (*House of Fame* 2140, rhyming with *rathe*).

sel, 319 good fortune. This is of native origin, a dialectal preservation, not an innovation (OE *sæl*, *sēl*). It is found widely in early Middle English (Western, Northern, and Eastern), but it is certainly not wrong to put it in the

---

[70] This important word is here passed over lightly; it requires more investigation. In distribution it would probably be found to agree with many other Scandinavian words (e.g. *wight*): that is, it would be likely to turn up almost anywhere except in the south, including originally London; while its later currency was probably due to eastern influence (coupled with some literary influence proceeding from the vernacular writings of North and West). It certainly appears in the west (in Layamon, for example). Its early appearance in the south-east – for example in *King Horn* (? Essex), where it seems certainly to be original – is well-known and curious. More remarkable is its occurrence in the *Owl and Nightingale*, 421 (adj.) and 1536 (adv.). Compare *hail*. It is clear, nonetheless, that Chaucer here used the word as a dialect substitute for *yuel*, *euel* (by which some MSS replace it). [Tolkien] See *King Horn: A Romance of the Thirteenth Century*, ed. Joseph Hall (Oxford: Clarendon, 1901); this is considered the oldest surviving romance in Middle English. Tolkien owned two editions of the early Kentish debate-poem, *The Owl and the Nightingale*, ed. John Edwin Wells (Boston and London: Heath, 1907), and *The Owl and the Nightingale*, ed. and trans. J. W. H. Atkins (Cambridge: Cambridge University Press, 1922), now Bodleian MS Tolkien E 16/23 and MS Tolkien E 16/24 respectively. [Ed.]

mouth of a northerner. The word was obsolescent, and after the thirteenth century seems to have been preserved chiefly in the North.

slik, 210 (twice), 250, 253, and as a variant for *quilk* 251, such. This is derived from ON *slík-r*, and competed with rather than replaced OE *swilc* in its regular northern form *swilk*. It was a word of more limited currency than any of the others here used as dialect by Chaucer, and so possesses a special interest. It cannot be counted among the widely known or familiar words, and though context usually interprets it, it is sometimes altered or misunderstood in copies of genuine northern texts. See the special note on this word, Appendix II.

[35]

swain, 117 servant. This is from ON *sveinn*, which usually ousted the cognate OE *swān* (whence rare ME *swon*). It has ceased to be dialectal, though the process has probably been a literary one, and not a development in the colloquial language. Here the sense "servant" (as well as its use in what appears to be a proverb) marks it as colloquial and dialectal, and distinguishes its use from Chaucer's only other employment of the word, *Sir Thopas* 13. There its sense, "young warrior, knight", marks it as a literary borrowing from the vocabulary of the type of poem Chaucer is there ridiculing – a vocabulary that has various connexions with northern and alliterative verse. Compare the notes on *auntre* and *wight* below.

til, 190 (2ce), to; also in *in til*, into 123; and before infinitive *for til*, 215; as adverb in *til and fra*, 119. All these uses are correct for the North. *Til* is found in Old English, only in Northumbrian (Ruthwell Cross, Cædmon's Hymn, Lindisfarne glosses: in senses *to*, *for*, and before infinitive),[71] and in Old Frisian; in Middle English its use and distribution was probably strongly influenced by Old Norse. The competition with the synonymous *to* produced (*a*) specialization of sense, and with reference to time *til* is found early in all parts, and is, of course, normal in Chaucer; (*b*) a tendency to use *til* instead of

---

[71] The Ruthwell Cross is an eighth-century Northumbrian cross engraved with probably the oldest surviving lines of Old English poetry parallel to lines in *The Dream of the Rood*. Here is the passage with *til* that Tolkien probably had in mind: "Krist wæs on rodi. Hweþræ / þer fusæ fearran kwomu / æþþilæ *til* anum." Tolkien lectured on the poem in 1930, 1933, and 1934 (SH 1:165, 178, 187), and he drafted a prose translation (MS Tolkien A 29 a, fols. 147–9). The Northumberland version of *Cædmon's Hymn* was printed in Henry Sweet's *Anglo-Saxon Reader in Prose and Verse* (Oxford: Clarendon, 1879), 196; Tolkien's much-annotated copy of Sweet's *Anglo-Saxon Reader*, 8th ed. (1908), inscribed by him at Exeter College, Michaelmas 1911, is now Bodleian MS Tolkien E 16/40. In the tenth century, Old English interlinear translations were inserted into the Latin Lindisfarne Gospels, now one of the most substantial witnesses to Old Northumbrian. Tolkien's copy of *A Glossary of the Old Northumbrian Gospels (Lindisfarne Gospels or Durham Book)*, ed. Albert S. Cook (Halle: M. Niemeyer, 1894) is now the Bodleian's Tolkien VC 231. [Ed.]

to before a vowel or *h*.⁷² *Til* in such positions appears as a synonym for *to* early and widely, and is well represented in MSS of Chaucer; for instance, in A 180 (*Prologue*): *til a fissh*.⁷³ But *til scorn* (though see *driue*), and more still *for til spende*, and *til and fra* are specifically northern. The last is rarely recorded (as a variant of *to and fro*), and the present passage is the latest of the three instances cited in *NED*. *In til* is probably better not treated as a distinct compound word in Middle English: it occurs before a vowel or *h* with same distribution as *til*. Later *intil* is specifically northern and Scottish. Here the use before þe is northern.

þair, 252 their. This has long since become the standard form, [36] and was no doubt already familiar. It is, however, rare in MSS of Chaucer, and was probably never used by him in normal language. (Had he used it, its later currency, which has assisted in preserving the present instance, would certainly have caused its frequent retention elsewhere.) Here he rightly uses it as a mark of northern speech, though it could in his day, and long before, have been heard, together with *þaim*, in familiar use side by side with the native *h*-forms in the East, certainly as far south as Norfolk – the home of the Reeve. It seems highly probable that this was recognized by Chaucer, and that he allowed the Reeve himself to use casually here and there the forms *þaim*, *þair*. The Lansdowne MS actually represents him as doing so at the end of the tale, lines 339–40: *And greyþen þeym and toke her hors anone, And eke here mele & on þeire weie þei gone.*⁷⁴ The conjunction with the dialectal verb *greyþen* (see below), and also the isolation of such a form in L, are strongly in favour of descent from Chaucer. As far as I can discover, L does not elsewhere use the þ-forms in genuine Chaucerian pieces. Support is given to this view by the occasional occurrence of þ-forms in the *Tale of Gamelyn* in various MSS; for here on other evidence we are dealing with copies of a work originally in language of (North-)East Midland type, where the þ-forms would be likely or certain to appear.⁷⁵ It will be noted that even in *Gamelyn* the form *þair* is better preserved than *þaim*. For this reason, though *þaim* does not occur in any

---

⁷² This probably appears in the earliest examples; all four examples cited in Bosworth-Toller from Old Northumbrian are before vowel or *h*. It is still a feature of dialects that use *till* for *to*. Compare also the quotations under *driue* below. [Tolkien] This standard Old English dictionary was first published in 1838 by Joseph Bosworth – his memory honoured by Oxford's Rawlinson and Bosworth Professorship of Anglo-Saxon – and it was revised in 1898 by Thomas Northcote Toller. [Ed.]

⁷³ E H O P L *til, tille*; C *to*. Other examples are *til a bere* (A 2058 *Knight's Tale*), H C O *til*, E P L *to*; *til a tree* (A 2062), E C O L *til*, H P *to*, Hl *in til*; *til Athenes* (A 2964), E H O P L *til*, C *to*. [Tolkien]

⁷⁴ For *þeym þeire* the other MSS in Six-Text have *h*-forms. In line 71, for *her whete* C has the very unusual spelling *heyre*, which is conceivably a relic of an antecedent *theyre*. [Tolkien]

⁷⁵ *Gamelyn* 49 *þeire* L, rest *h*-forms; 426 *þair* O, *þeir(e)* L Hl, rest *h*-forms; 569 *þeir(e)* O P L, Royal, Harley 1758, *þer* Sloane, *here* Hl. *Gamelyn* 438 *þam* O, *þeim* L, rest *hem*; 485 *þam* O, *þaym* L, rest *hem*. [Tolkien]

of the MSS used in the clerks' speeches, I have adopted it for line 231, instead of *hem*, and not treated this *hem* as an "unremoved southernism".[76] The presence of *paim* in Chaucer's version is very probable. To retain *pair* and substitute *hem* is, in fact, to bring the language into line with the usage of the century after Chaucer's death; it is the usage found in Lydgate.[77] After Chaucer's time *thair, their, ther* quickly established themselves owing to the ambiguity of *her*, but *hem* maintained itself much longer and has never been completely banished.

[37]

wanges, 110. This word is usually explained as "back-teeth, molar teeth". The word is not elsewhere recorded in Middle English (in this sense); in fact, from the whole range of English the *NED* only cites this present passage, and a modern (1901) record of South Lancashire dialect, which gives *wang* as a word for "tooth" or "back-tooth". In favour of the reference to teeth may then be urged (*a*) this modern dialect use, (*b*) the occurrence in Old English of a word *wang-tōþ* "back-tooth", whence ME *wangtooþ, wongtooþ*, the former appearing in Chaucer's *Monk's Tale* 54. The first element is OE *wang(e)* "cheek, especially the lower part, the jaw"; cf. *wang-beard* "side-whiskers". If we accept this interpretation, we must then assume that *wang* "back-tooth" is a shortening of the compound, which would only be likely to take place after *wange, wonge* had become obsolete in ordinary language in the sense "jaw".[78] Against

---

[76] Tolkien here (and elsewhere) engages in "conjectural emendation" to alter the text on the basis of what he considered his better understanding of what Chaucer actually wrote against the unanimous testimony of the manuscripts. [Ed.]

[77] John Lydgate (c. 1370–c. 1451) was a monk of Bury St Edmunds whose relationship with Chaucer's son Thomas – to whom he addressed his poem "On the Departing of Thomas Chaucer" – seems to have given him early, complete access to the poet's literary papers; see Bowers, *Chaucer and Langland*, 202–5. [Ed.]

[78] We must in that case also delete this word from our list of northernisms of vowel above, since its *ang* is then probably to be ascribed to shortening in the first component of a compound. Compare the many names of the type *Langley, Langford* that occur far south where *long* is the normal form of the separate adjective. It may also be noted that the form *wang* is odd in South Lancashire. This area belonged from early OE times to the West Midland (not to the technically Northern or Northumbrian) dialect region, an area specially characterized by *om, on, ong*, independent of lengthening. The original compound from which the word is supposed to be derived should here be *wong-tōþ*, the quality of the vowel being unaffected by composition. Cf. Lancashire names of the type *Longley*. *Wang* then has the appearance of not being originally native to South Lancashire even if recorded there, and its form alone may be some sort of evidence for a former wider diffusion. But Lancashire is a difficult dialect area. North of the Ribble it belonged anciently to the Northumbrian area, and there has been a good deal of shifting and interchange, in addition to the disturbance of the Scandinavian settlements, as far as place-name forms go largely in favour of *an*. Of this Camden's *Lonkashire* compared with the current *Lancashire* may be taken as an illustration. See Ekwall, *Place-Names of Lancashire*. [Tolkien] William Camden (1551–1623) was an English antiquarian whose *Britain, or a Chorographicall Description of the Most Flourishing Kingdomes, England, Scotland, and Ireland* was first published in Latin in 1586 and in English translation in 1610; his *Remaines of a Greater Worke, Concerning Britaine* (1605) often provided the earliest or sole usages for words in the *OED*. See Eilert Ekwall, *The Place-Names of Lancashire* (Manchester: University of Manchester Press, 1922). [Ed.]

the sense "tooth" may be urged the doubtful evidence for its existence, indeed absence of any evidence for Middle English. The usual word for "back-tooth" was evidently *wang-tōþ*, which was in general use in Old English. It occurs in the North and in the southern laws (*Laws of Alfred*, sect. 49);[79] it is fairly widely distributed in Middle English (e.g. Wyclif, Langland, Chaucer, *Promptorium*) and is still preserved in the dialects of recent times (though the last reference in *NED* is from Ray's [38] collection of north-country words, 1674). Apart from the supposed occurrence in the *Reeve's Tale* one would naturally conclude that the scantily evidenced *wang* = tooth was a fairly recent development (*a*) long after the disappearance of *wang* "cheek" (which had not taken place in the Middle English period in the North and West), and (*b*) in connexion with the development of the sense "tooth" for *fang*.[80] One may enquire, then, whether the present passage really supports the sense "tooth". It is not easy to see why the manciple of the Soler-hall was likely to die of toothache – that the ache was in the molars may have made it more painful, but hardly more deadly. The manciple might feel like dying himself, of course, but John is not likely to have shared his fear, and we are expressly told that "he lay sick with a malady and people thought he would certainly die".[81] A violent headache, as a symptom of fever, is in our tale a much more likely explanation of John's words. It may be noted that the word *werke, warke* "ache" is specially associated with headache. The only compound in which it occurs is *head-wark*, found in various forms in Middle English in the North and East, and surviving down to modern times in the North; while *warking* means "headache" by itself and is in the *Promptorium* glossed *heed-ake, cephalia*.[82] It might seem, therefore, that unnecessary trouble has been made about the manciple's *wanges*, and that there is no need to look further than the OE *wang(e)*, a word certainly still alive in the North and West in Middle English. But two difficulties occur. First: the simple *wange* in Old English seems generally to have

---

[79] See the Old English "Laws of King Alfred" in *Ancient Laws of England*, ed. Benjamin Thorpe (London: Eyre and Spottiswoode, 1840), 94–5, on the fines for injuring someone's teeth: "A man's grinder (*wonner tux*) is worth xv. shillings." [Ed.]

[80] The earliest reference in *NED* to sense "tooth" for *fang* is from sixteenth century. The sense was not unknown to the dialects: see *NED* FANG 6, quotation from Cheshire. The form *fengtōþ* once recorded in OE is interesting. It is glossed "canine tooth" by Sweet, but seems to mean the same as *wangtōþ*; see Bosworth-Toller, *Supplement*. *Feng* is the native English form later almost universally replaced by Norse *fang* "seizing". [Tolkien]

[81] Some will say, it is obviously a joke – the petty malady, and the pother about it, and the final comic *I hope he wil be deed*. Unfortunately with an ancient writer it is dangerous to remain content with the findings of one's private sense of humour; verbal jokes cannot be assumed unproved. [Tolkien]

[82] But cf. quotation in *NED* (from Jamieson), apparently Scottish of seventeenth century, where "toothache" seems equated with "head-work". [Tolkien]

been used of the lower cheek and jaw, though the words descriptive of unclearly defined parts of the body are specially liable to shifts of meaning. [39] Second: it is a curious fact that in Middle English the word is almost solely recorded in the alliterative formulae *wete wonges* or *to wete þe wonges* with reference to weeping.[83] To the examples quoted by the *NED* (from *Cursor Mundi*, *Alysoun*, *Sir Tristrem*, Wyntoun, and the *York Plays*, all northern except the second which is probably western in origin) I can only add Layamon, *Brut* 30268: *wete weren his wongen* (the earliest ME instance), and *Joseph of Arimathie* (an alliterative poem) 647: *I wepte water warm and wette my wonges*, both of which show the same formula.[84] This would certainly suggest that, though alive, the word was preserved in the North and West chiefly as part of the equipment of the alliterative poets and in the vocabulary derived from them – which might be reckoned a point in favour of "teeth". But it shows more. The ME *wange*, *wonge*, so far as it survived, was no longer used for the jaw, but for the upper part of the face. This is the sense of the cognate ON *vangi*, which refers to the side of the head from the ear to just under the eyes; and to Old Norse the ME use (in North and West) is probably largely due.[85] This sense would have, moreover, the support of the word *thunwange*, the common Germanic word for the "temples",[86] a word still alive in Middle English in the North and East.[87] We might then assume a use in the North

---

[83] The well-known passage in *Alysoun*, a highly alliterated poem, *forþi my wonges wexeþ won*, refers also to weeping, and is so only a partial exception; though it does supply an example of the word *wong* without the concomitant *wet*. This conjunction is curiously illustrated by the Yorkshire place-name *Wetwang*, though this probably contains the distinct but related ON *vang-r* "field". [Tolkien] The Harley 2253 lyric *Alysoun* was included in *Specimens of Early English, Part II*, ed. Richard Morris and Walter W. Skeat (Oxford: Clarendon, 1873), 43. Tolkien glossed *Alysoun* in Sisam's *Fourteenth Century Verse and Prose*, 165–6. [Ed.]

[84] Tolkien's spelling of the title indicates that he had in mind *Joseph of Arimathie: The Romance of Seint Graal*, ed. Walter W. Skeat, EETS o.s. 44 (1871). [Ed.]

[85] Such a use is actually found in late Old English, e.g. in *wonges loc-feax* glossing *cesaries*; and in Ælfric's Lives of the Saints, St. Mary of Egypt (EETS, iii, 236, line 556): *ic...þa wongas mid tearum ofergeat*. [Tolkien] The Old English *Death of St. Mary of Egypt* was included in Ælfric's *Lives of the Saints*, ed. Walter W. Skeat, EETS o.s. 76, 82, 94, 114 (1881, 1885, 1890, 1901), 2:2–53. [Ed.]

[86] OE *þunwange*, ON *þunnvangi*, OHG *dunwengi*. [Tolkien]

[87] It is found in the *Promptorium* and in the *Catholicon Anglicum* (Yorks). In Robert Thornton's MS (MS Linc. Ai. 17) occurs a medical recipe for a plaster to be put on the *forhede* and *thonwanges* of a sick man (quoted in Halliwell's *Dict. of Archaic and Provincial Words*, where another reference is given to medicinal anointing of the *thounwanges*, taken from MS Linc. Med. f. 280). [Tolkien] Tolkien's personal copy of *Catholicon Anglicum: An English-Latin Wordbook Dated 1483*, ed. Sidney J. H. Herrtage and Henry B. Wheatley, EETS o.s. 75 (1881), is now Bodleian Tolkien VC 197b; many important words in the English language such as *diphthong* first appeared in this early dictionary. Robert Thornton (fl. 1418–1456) was a member of the Yorkshire gentry whose Lincoln manuscript revealed a liking for alliterative verse resulting in his preservation of *The Alliterative Morte Arthure* and *Wynnere and Wastoure*. James Orchard Halliwell, *A Dictionary of Archaic and Provincial Words, Obsolete Phrases, Proverbs, and Ancient Customs from the Fourteenth Century*, 2 vols. (London: John Russell Smith, 1847), could have served as one of Tolkien's sources for Sam Gamgee's proverbial wisdom; see Shippey, "'A Fund of Wise Sayings': Proverbiality in Tolkien", in *Roots and Branches*, 303–19. [Ed.]

and East of *wange* referring to the side of the head, especially in the neighbourhood of the temples and the eyes. This would fit the case of the sick manciple well enough; and though the evidence for the word is chiefly poetic and [40] alliterative – a diction after all based largely on the actual speech of the northerly regions – it is, at any rate, much stronger in Middle English than the evidence for the sense "tooth". The influence upon native *wange* of the cognate and phonetically identical ON *vangi*[88] is a familiar process, very different from the abnormal (and probably recent) reduction of *wangtooth* to *wang*.[89] This discussion of the meaning of *wanges* has led far afield, but is not without point. Whichever meaning we finally decide on, it has been fairly well established that *wang* was dialectal, and correctly ascribed by Chaucer to the North. If the word meant "side of the head", we can also put it back into the list of those showing northern *ang* for *ong*.[90] In either case we can fairly conclude that the word was not a widely known one, and that Chaucer has for once allowed himself to use an oddity (unless an Eastern use of *wange* = *thunwange* existed, but has escaped record, which is unlikely). In fact, suspicion is aroused that Chaucer got this word from northern or western writings, and not from actual talk. There is a similarity both in the alliteration of Chaucer's phrase, and in the situation, to the recorded poetic formulæ in which *wanges* elsewhere appears.

werkes, 110 ache. The native word OE *wærcan* is in Middle English only found (rarely) in the West, or rather North-West, in the form *warche*: for instance, in MS T of the *Ancren Riwle* and in the *Destruction of Troy*.[91] It is

---

[88] Its form at time when Norse influenced English may be represented *wange. [Tolkien]

[89] Whereby the original noun is lost and only the determinative element is retained. [Tolkien]

[90] The simple word should have been *wang* in the North, usually *wong* elsewhere. Actually the form *wong* does occur in northern texts (in the citations in *NED*, for instance from *Cursor Mundi*, *Sir Tristrem*, Wyntoun) – which suggests that we have traces of the (North)-Western influence on alliterative vocabulary that is seen in other words, such as *blonk*. Cf. the corruptions of *wonges wete* in two MSS of *Cursor Mundi* to *wordes swete*, which indicates both *o* in the original, and obsolescence or dialectal limitation of the word; *wanges wete* with *a* occurs, however, in *Cursor Mundi* 25552 (not in *NED*) and in the *York Plays*. [Tolkien] First published by Sir Walter Scott in 1809, *Sir Tristrem* survives in the Auchinleck manuscript and was available to Tolkien in *Sir Tristrem*, ed. George P. McNeill (Edinburgh: William Blackwood, Scottish Text Society, no. 8, 1886). Andrew Wyntoun (c. 1350–c. 1425) was a Scottish poet credited by the *OED* with the first use of the word "Catholic" in English; see *The Orygynale Cronykil of Scotland by Androw of Wyntoun*, ed. David Laing, 3 vols. (Edinburgh: Edmonston and Douglas, 1872–79). Tolkien had glossed "The York Play Harrowing of Hell" in Sisam's *Fourteenth Century Verse and Prose*, 171–84; see also *York Plays*, ed. Lucy Toulmin Smith (Oxford: Clarendon, 1885). [Ed.]

[91] Tolkien refers to *Ancrene Riwle*, also known as *Ancrene Wisse* (found along with *Sawles Warde*, *Hali Meiðhad*, and *Seinte Katerine* in the thirteenth-century BL Cotton MS Titus D XVIII), about which he wrote his 1929 article "*Ancrene Wisse* and *Hali Meiðhad*". Tolkien had glossed a selection from *The Gest Hystoriale of the Destruction of Troy* in Sisam's *Fourteenth Century Verse and Prose*, 68–75; see *The "Gest Hystoriale" of the Destruction of Troy*, ed. George A. Panton and David Donaldson, EETS o.s. 39 and 56 (1869 and 1874). [Ed.]

recorded in the recent dialect of Shropshire. The forms with *k*, *werke*, *warke*, are either derived from or influenced by the cognate ON *verkja* "to hurt" (intransitive) and *verk-r* "pain". There can be no doubt that Chaucer was right in giving this word as a feature of northern [41] dialect, but it is curious that the present passage[92] is actually the earliest record of the verb *Wark*. As far as the evidence goes, this seems to be another word that was in use in the East as well as in the North – it is, at any rate, found in the *Promptorium*.

wight, 166 active. This word is probably of Scandinavian origin.[93] It is, at any rate, common in Middle English in the North and throughout the areas of direct Scandinavian influence, and wherever alliterative verse or the vocabulary related to it is found. Its area might be described as an arch round the South-East and London, from Robert of Gloucester[94] and Layamon through the West and North (including Scotland) and down the East, where it is found, for instance, in *Havelok* and *Genesis and Exodus*.[95] It was clearly in its proper area, that of direct Scandinavian influence, not solely a literary and poetic word, though it is chiefly so in our records. It must be counted among the words widely familiar, though never adopted by the standard language, and as one, moreover, that tended to spread as a *literary* word, favoured in such formulæ as *wight as Wade*, which was last used by Morris in *The Defence of Guinevere*.[96] It was from literature rather than dialect talk that Chaucer took the word, and he could rely on the reading of romances to make the word intelligible to his audience (and readers). Indeed, he uses the word once elsewhere, in the *Monk's Tale* 277: *wrastlen…with any yong man, were he never so wight*.[97] The use in the *Reeve's Tale* is specially interesting, for it occurs in the formula: *wight as es a ra*. The same formula[98] is found in the romance *Sir Eglamour of Artois* 261: *as wyght as any roo* (rhyming *goo* "go"), describing greyhounds, and showing a sense "swift" very apt for our passage. *Sir Eglamour* is one of the northern or northerly romances, in *rime couee*, of the kind ridiculed in *Sir Thopas*: it is indeed particularly ridiculous, but it

---

[92] Not quoted in *NED* s.v. WARK. [Tolkien]

[93] Its usual derivation from the neuter *vígt* of ON *vígr* "able to fight, skilled in arms" presents certain difficulties. [Tolkien]

[94] Robert of Gloucester (fl. c. 1260–c. 1300) wrote a verse chronicle of English history in the late thirteenth century in the same dialect as the *South English Legendary*. Tolkien would have known *The Metrical Chronicle of Robert of Gloucester*, ed. William Aldis Wright, 2 vols. (London: Eyre and Spottiswoode, Rolls Series 86, 1887). [Ed.]

[95] And after Chaucer's time in the *Promptorium*. [Tolkien]

[96] A great favourite with Tolkien, William Morris published *The Defence of Guenevere and Other Poems* in 1858. [Ed.]

[97] *The Tale of Gamelyn* and his *wight yonge men* (893), wherein wrestling plays the same part as in *As You Like It*, is perhaps actually echoed here. [Tolkien]

[98] Not cited in *NED*. [Tolkien]

must have been popular, to judge by the fact that four manuscripts of it [42] survive.[99] Though Eglamour's name is not in the well-known list in *Sir Thopas*, unless it is concealed under Pleyndamour, it is extremely likely that Chaucer had read (and laughed at) this very poem. If he had, he would have seen there *wight as any ra* (or *es a ra*), for our fifteenth-century copies are all more or less southernized, even Yorkshire Thornton's copy, and the original is seen from many rhymes[100] to have been in a dialect with northern $\bar{a}$ for $\bar{\varrho}$.

yon (ʒon), 258 yon. This adjective is only once recorded in Old English,[101] but it may once have been in fairly general colloquial use, for it is the kind of word that easily escapes literary record: it meant "that yonder" accompanied by pointing to some relatively distant object. In the South and East it evidently died out of colloquial speech (as German *jener* has), and where it remained it tended to oust or to compete with *that*.[102] It is clearly intended as dialect by Chaucer, who does not use it elsewhere; but it may safely be counted one of the familiar dialectalisms. Later it became literary again, though not apparently before the end of the sixteenth century, and at first in the form *yond*, due to the influence of the related adverb *yond*, OE *geond*. It was fairly widely distributed in Chaucer's time, and though it is most frequently recorded from the North, with which its living colloquial use is now associated, it is found in *Piers Plowman* and *William of Palerne* representing the West,[103] and in Manning's Chronicle in the East. Adjectival *yond*, *yend*, in uses which still reveal its originally adverbial function, such as *on yond half* or *the yond* "that one yonder", is found both earlier and much further south,[104] and this would,

---

[99] In spite of Mr. Trounce's essay in *Medium Ævum*, i, 2, pp. 86 ff., I remain of opinion that Chaucer was precisely "misusing the gifts of genius to make a cheap caricature of the 'heroic' effects of the old poem". *Sir Thopas* is clever, but in some ways regrettable; but precisely the result to be expected from the contact of a man of Chaucer's temperament with the conventions of the tail-rhyme poems. Here, however, we are principally concerned with the close study which Chaucer gave to these works and their diction: see Trounce, loc. cit., and sequels. [Tolkien] He disparages A. McI. Trounce, "The English Tail-Rhyme Romances", *Medium Ævum* 1 (1932): 87–108, 168–82; 2 (1933): 34–57, 189–98; and 3 (1934): 30–50. [Ed.]

[100] E.g. *oke* "oak" rhyming *wake* "wake". [Tolkien]

[101] In the *Cura Pastoralis* 443, 25; *aris and gong to geonre byrg*. [Tolkien] He likely knew this work from *King Alfred's West-Saxon Version of Gregory's Pastoral Care*, ed. Henry Sweet, EETS o.s. 45 and 50 (1871). [Ed.]

[102] Producing the blended form *þon* seen in some dialects. [Tolkien]

[103] This Middle English Alliterative poem was commissioned by Humphrey de Bohun, 6th Earl of Hereford, and written around 1350. Tolkien would have known *The Romance of William of Palerne*, ed. Walter W. Skeat, EETS e.s. 1 (1867). [Ed.]

[104] *Ormulum, Owl and Nightingale, Ayenbite*. [Tolkien] *The Ayenbite of Inwyt* is a 1340 translation into Kentish dialect of the French *Somme le Roi* by Michael of Northgate, a Benedictine monk at Saint Augustine of Canterbury. Tolkien's copy is now the Bodleian's Tolkien VC 188. He had previously glossed a selection in Sisam's *Fourteenth Century Verse and Prose*, 32–5, and his lectures on it can be consulted in Bodleian MS Tolkien A 10/1. [Ed.]

of course, assist in making the [43] dialectal *yon* intelligible. Chaucer, however, who uses *yond* often, uses it only as an adverb "yonder".

tulle, 214 "entice". On this form, for which there appear to be no parallels, see Appendix I. Chaucer here either contented himself with an eye-rhyme *folle, tolle*, as probably also in *fonne, yronne*, or else the text is corrupt. He uses *tolle* "entice" elsewhere, in translating Boethius.[105]

gar, 212 make. See the note and footnote. This word might easily have been altered to *get*,[106] and would provide another instance of genuine northern vocabulary. *Gar*, meaning "make, do", is used in Middle English chiefly with a following infinitive in the sense "cause one to do something, or something to be done". It is of Scandinavian origin and so found pretty generally, but not universally, in texts written in a language with a considerable Norse ingredient; it belongs especially to the vocabulary of Yorkshire and Northumbria and Scotland, though it is also found further south, as in Nottingham and Lincolnshire (*Havelok* and Manning's *Chronicle*).[107] The use here is, nonetheless, not easy to parallel exactly: *gar* usually approaches "compel" rather than "let".

greiþen, 389 get ready. This is used by the Reeve, since he is the narrator, and not by the clerks; but was probably, together with accompanying *þaim*, intended to tinge his speech with dialect. It is a Scandinavian word belonging to the North-West and East in natural speech, but it is another word that in early English tended to acquire a certain literary currency, though it did not ultimately keep its place in the standard vocabulary. It is notable that Chaucer employs it three times elsewhere, in the first and probably genuine fragment of the translation of the *Romance of the Rose*, in the *Monk's Tale*, and in the translation of Boethius – probably purely as a literary word, borrowed from books.[108]

[44]

To the above words may be added the following: –

auntre, 285, 290 adventure, risk. This is, of course, strictly the same word as *aventure*, and shows what could happen to a French word when thoroughly popularized, and exposed to the reduction caused by stressing it strongly

---

[105] Tolkien enclosed this entry and the next two (*gar, greiþen*) in square brackets. [Ed.]

[106] Cf. not infrequent confusion of *þat* and *þar, þer* in the MSS. [Tolkien]

[107] It seems to be absent from the *Ormulum*. It is found fairly frequently as an alliterating word in versions B and C of *Piers Plowman*; as far as the references in Skeat's glossary go, only in passages where the A version has been remodelled. It does not appear in the A version (?). [Tolkien]

[108] The word does not seem to have been used by Gower, nor by any other writers of London or standard English. The word is bungled by P *greieþ* and altered by C to *hastede*. It may be noted that *fit* 264 is also fairly frequent in Chaucer, but apart from quotations from his works appears in *NED* as chiefly northern; it is apparently not used by Gower. [Tolkien]

on the first syllable only, in English fashion. The reduced form is not solely northern, and the southern *aventure* represents rather the continued refreshment of the word by French than a dialectal divergence in development. Nonetheless, in the fourteenth century the reduced popular form is found mainly in northern texts, and survives to-day in the North and in Scotland. An exception must be made in the case of *paraunter*, which Chaucer himself used occasionally beside *peraventure*.[109] Otherwise he never uses the reduced form (nor makes *aventure* a verb in any form), except once in the adjective *auntrous* in *Sir Thopas* 188 – a significant place; compare the notes on *swain*, *wight* above.

draf-sek, 286 idle lump. The word *draf* "sediment of brewing; husks" is widespread in Middle English. It is not recorded in Old English and may be of Dutch origin.[110] Chaucer uses it, for example, in the prologue to the *Legend of Good Women* 312. The same Dutch origin is possible also for both the literal and figurative senses of *draff-sack* as "sack of refuse" and "idle glutton"; for Middle Dutch *drafsac* is used in both ways. It is noteworthy that the appearance here is according to the *NED* the first recorded, and nearly 150 years earlier than the next quotation for the word in either sense. That Chaucer meant the word as a whole to be dialectal (though comic and very appropriate to a miller's bedroom, certainly) is not clear. But it was made dialectal by the form *sek*. This is not a chance aberration.[111] It is a genuine form of the word "sack", and is found in Hampole and in such a thoroughly northern poem as *Ywain and Gawain*;[112] though, like so many of the northernisms here used by Chaucer, it is also found in eastern texts, such as [45] *Genesis and Exodus*, *Havelok*, or the *Promptorium*. In origin it is ON *sekk-r*, replacing or influencing OE *sæcc*, *sacc*. The early occurrence of the compound in Dutch, and the occurrence of the *sek*-forms of "sack" in the East, may lead one to suspect that Chaucer did not go very far north to pick up this item; at the same time

---

[109] E.g. in *Legend of Good Women Prologue B* 362, and *House of Fame* 1997. [Tolkien]

[110] Middle Dutch *draf*, whence probably also the same word in the later Scandinavian languages. But *draf* and *chaf* occurs in Layamon, which favours perhaps a native origin from an OE **dræf* cognate with the Dutch word. [Tolkien]

[111] It is preserved in both E and C. It may be noted that in line 97, which is outside the dialect speeches, all seven MSS have *sak(ke)*. [Tolkien]

[112] Richard Rolle of Hampole (d. 1349) was an Oxford-educated hermit who ended his life in South Yorkshire. Tolkien owned Richard Rolle de Hampole's *English Prose Treatises*, ed. George G. Perry, EETS o.s. 20 (1866), now the Bodleian's Tolkien VC 187; *The Psalter Translated by Richard Rolle of Hampole*, ed. H. R. Bramley (Oxford: Clarendon, 1884), now the Bodleian's Tolkien VC 267; and Hope Emily Allen, *Richard Rolle, Hermit of Hampole and Materials for His Biography* (New York: Modern Language Association, 1927), now the Bodleian's Tolkien VC 266. He had glossed three Rolle excerpts in Sisam's *Fourteenth Century Verse and Prose*, 36–43. See *Ywain and Gawain*, ed. Gustav Schleich (Leipzig: E. Franck, 1887), for the early fourteenth-century Arthurian romance based on the Old French *Yvain ou le Chevalier au Lion* by Chrétien de Troyes. [Ed.]

the dialectal accuracy of *sek*, which has no general analogy of sound-correspondences between northern and southern speech to support it, is specially interesting.[113]

Here may be added two cases of dialectal uses of generally current words.

hope, 109 meaning "expect without wishing". This sense appears only here in Chaucer, and is, of course, used primarily because it is comic in such a context to those accustomed to *hope* only as implying a wish. The joke was probably a current one and was still alive later: Skeat in his note on this passage quotes from the *Arte of Poesie* the tale of the tanner of Tamworth, who said "I hope I shall be hanged."[114] In Middle English Chaucer is quite right in representing the usage as dialectal and specially northern: *hope* in the sense "expect, suppose, think" is very frequently met in northern texts of all kinds, and though it was probably not confined to the strictly northern dialects, it is seldom recorded elsewhere.[115]

driue, 190 in *dreuen til heþing and til scorn*. This use seems to be definitely northern, though the fact seems not previously to have been noted. The *NED*[116] gives only three examples, all closely parallel to our text and all from *fer in þe norþ*: Cursor Mundi 26455: *his lauerd he driues to scorn*; ibid., 26810 *þai crist til hething driue*; and post-Chaucerian (1470) Henry *Wallace*: *thow drywys me to scorn*.[117]

[46]

We have now examined all the points in the clerks' speeches which can possibly be regarded as dialectal. The examination has shown Chaucer to be correct in his description of northern language in at least 127 points in about 98 lines, in points of inflexion, sounds, and vocabulary: a very notable

---

[113] In fact, it went contrary to the general tendencies. No one could guess that a man from the North or North-East would say *seck* for *sack* without direct experience of this detail (in speech or book). [Tolkien]

[114] Skeat (5:122) quoted an unspecified later edition of George Puttenham's *The Arte of English Poesie* (London: Richard Field, 1589), Book III, chap xxii: "*I hope I shall be hanged tomorrow.*" [Ed.]

[115] It occurs in the North-West Midlands as, for instance, *Sir Gawain*. It occurs once at least (once in Skeat's glossary) in the C version (x, 275) of *Piers Plowman*, which is somewhat northernized in vocabulary as compared with A (cf. *gar* above). [Tolkien]

[116] s.v. DRIVE iii, 17. [Tolkien]

[117] The contrast, here from genuine northern texts, between *til hething* and *to scorn* suggests that it is possible that Chaucer wrote *to scorn* and the second *til* in 190 is derivative from the first. *Til* is, however, found frequently before consonants in northern texts, and the MSS readings and general procedure point rather to the second *to* as a southernization. [Tolkien] He refers to Henry the Minstrel, popularly known as Blind Harry, who composed a long poem commonly known as *The Wallace* recounting the life of the Scottish independence leader William Wallace. See *The Actis and Deidis of the Illustere and Vaiȝleand Campioun Schir William Wallace Knicht of Ellerslie by Henry the Minstrel Commonly Known as Blind Harry*, ed. James Moir (Edinburgh: Scottish Text Society nos. 6, 7, 17, William Blackwood and Sons, 1889). William Dunbar included "Blind Hary" in his *Lament for the Makeris* (69). [Ed.]

result.[118] Further, we have found no proven case of false dialect, words, or forms used as dialectal but wrongly assigned and impossible for the North. In fact, this scrap of dialect-writing is extremely good and more than accurate enough for literary purposes, or for jest. It is quite different from the conventionalized dialect of later drama or novel, where this is not based on local knowledge, or from, say, modern popular notions in the South of "Scotch" or "Yorkshire". At the same time there is little in the lines that is extreme, or altogether outlandish, or, indeed, very definitely localizable more closely than "northern" or usually "northern and elsewhere". But this would be expected in a tale for a southern audience, whatever was the state of Chaucer's private knowledge, and is probably due rather to his skill in selection than to his own limited acquaintance as a Southerner with northern English. He has, in fact, put in a few very definite northernisms, some of limited currency, such as *gif, sal, boes, tan, ymel*, and especially *slik*, that show that his knowledge was not acquired casually in London, and was founded on the study of books (and people). As the primary northern characteristic *ā* for *ō* comes out first with some 37 instances;[119] it is followed by *s*-inflexions of verbs with 19; by *sal, suld* with *s* for *sh* with 12; and by *es* (*is*) for "am, art" with 8. All these were evidently pretty well known. It is interesting and suggestive to note how large a proportion of the dialect features [47] he uses occur also, more or less contemporarily, in the East, usually at least as far south as East Anglia: *hail, heþen, heþing, ill, laþe, sek, swain, þair, werke*; as well as features more widely distributed and found also in the West or North-West, such as *capel, wight, yon*, and the verbal inflexions in *s*. Of the rest *auntre, daf, ferli, hope*, and *wanges* (if not taken as "teeth") were also not limited to the North; *auntre, wight*, and *ferli* were all three doubtless familiar to anyone acquainted with English literature. Indeed, one is tempted, in the middle of an enquiry into mere dialect, to turn aside and emphasize the occasional concomitant *literary* suggestions of some of the words already dealt with. The suggestions are faint and may be perceptible only to philological ears, but those who feel inclined to dismiss them as fancies should consider the description of the battle of Actium in the legend

---

[118] The figure, while including all points and each proved occurrence (so that, e.g. *werkes* counts 2, being northern in inflexion and in sense), excludes (*a*) all doubtful points textually – *dreuen, es* for *is, als* 111, *ar* "ere", *3a, sagh, i* for *in, miller* as genitive sg., *til scorn, þaim*; (*b*) all cases of common forms possible in Chaucerian language as well as North, such as the past participles other than *stŏln, stollen*, or the forms of *wil*; (*c*) *gar* not recorded in the MSS used, or *greiþen* outside the clerks' speeches. None of the northernisms which were probably used by Chaucer, but are in the critical text italicized since all seven MSS have at that point southernized, have been included. The actual total of points achieved by Chaucer was therefore probably a good deal larger even than 127. [Tolkien]

[119] Including the words with *ald, ang*. [Tolkien]

of Cleopatra, especially lines 56 ff.[120] As in the better known tourney in the *Knight's Tale*, it is impossible here to miss the accents of alliterative verse, turned (or thrust bodily) into "decasyllables". And significantly we here come upon *heterly*. This word occurs only here in Chaucer; indeed it probably occurs here alone in Middle English outside actual alliterative writings, whether in the prose of the "Holy Maidenhood" group,[121] or in such poems as *Sir Gawain* or *The Wars of Alexander*.[122] If its source is not *William of Palerne* 1243: *and hetterly boþe hors and man he hurled to þe grounde*, Chaucer's *heterly they hurtlen* has been taken from some now lost piece he once conned and did not forget. *heterly* is dialect, but it is more. There was, after all, a literature of merit, especially in the West, before Chaucer's day, and before anything literary was written that can be ascribed to London. Chaucer was not independent either of the past or of the contemporary, and neither was his audience.

We may now consider a quite different type of "error", one far more excusable in a use of dialect for literary purposes: the failure to remove features of Chaucer's own normal London English, which would not occur in pure northern speech. We have some right to ask, when an author goes out of his way to give us words and forms not natural to his usual literary medium, that these should be what he pretends, fair samples of the dialect he is representing. We do not necessarily demand that the [48] dialect's greatest oddities should be dragged in, or that all its most characteristic features as tabulated in historical grammars should be present, as long as what we do get is genuine.[123] We have no right to insist that a poet, telling a funny story rapidly and economically,

---

[120] *Cleopatra* is the first tragic love story of Chaucer's *Legend of Good Women*; this passage can be found in Skeat 3:107–8 (lines 36–69). The alliterative lines from the battle scene in the *Knight's Tale* appear in Skeat 4:74–5 (*CT* I, 2602–20). Tolkien took time when commenting upon *Cleopatra* in his Clarendon Chaucer notes to compose the excursus "Chaucer and the Alliterative Tradition" transcribed above, pp. 102–5.

[121] More widely known now as the Katherine Group, these five Middle English texts were composed ca. 1182–1198 in a West Midlands dialect dubbed by Tolkien as AB language: *Seinte Katherine*, *Seinte Juliene*, *Seinte Margarete*, *Sawles Warde*, and *Hali Meiðhad*. The Bodleian now houses Tolkien's personal copies of *Life of Saint Katherine*, ed. Eugen Einenkel, EETS o.s. 80 (1884) (Tolkien VC 199); *The Liflade of St. Juliana*, ed. Oswald Cockayne, and trans. Oswald Cockayne and Edmund Brock, EETS o.s. 51 (1872) (MS Tolkien E 16/30); *Seinte Marherete: The Meiden ant Martyr*, ed. and trans. Oswald Cockayne, EETS o.s. 13, (1866) (MS Tolkien E 16/31); and *Hali Meidenhad*, ed. Frederick J. Furnivall, EETS o.s. 18 (1922) (Tolkien VC 186), for which Tolkien provided the *TLS* review. After years of collaboration with him, Tolkien's student S. R. T. O. d'Ardenne finally published *The Katherine Group edited from MS Bodley 34* (Paris: Société d'edition Les Belles Lettre, 1977). [Ed.]

[122] *The Wars of Alexander: An Alliterative Romance*, ed. Walter W. Skeat, EETS e.s. 47 (1886), p. xxiii, placed composition of this alliterative poem in Northumberland during the middle fifteenth century. [Ed.]

[123] Chaucer has given no sample of several well-known northernisms; the present participle in *and*, for instance. This is purely accidental, by chance no opportunity occurs. [Tolkien]

and in rhymed verse, should offer us dialect through and through. If he gives us about 130 correct dialect points to a 100 lines, this is ample to give a proper impression of the clerks' talk, if the southernisms are not too frequent. All the same, an examination of the lines for this kind of "error", unremoved southernism, brings out one or two points of interest and emphasizes the fact that the *Reeve's Tale* is of importance to Chaucerian textual criticism generally, as a measure of manuscript fidelity to details upon which Chaucer lavished so much care. A proper text of the *Canterbury Tales* (or other major works of his), not to mention the recapturing to some extent of Chaucerian spelling and grammar, is not to be obtained from devout attachment to any one MS, certainly not Ellesmere, however attractive it may look.

The textual notes above will have shown that allowance has to be made for frequent but inconsistent southernizing of many details in the course of the tradition between Chaucer's copy or corrected copies and even the best MSS that now survive. Accordingly those "errors" are here first presented which can, with varying certainty, be ascribed to the author, since they appear to be required by metre or by rhyme. Usually we may say, rather, they were dictated by metre or rhyme, and that they were licences not errors; he was well aware of them and gives the correct northern form elsewhere, but felt justified, as he was, in letting them pass.

(i) There is first the rather difficult case of final *e*. Here are omitted from consideration syllabic *e* in inflexions such as *es, en, ed*: these were certainly largely preserved in the North even at this date, though liable to reduction after vowels or sonorous consonants (as in *stoln*, 191, 263, and *quils* 347, where reduction appears actually in the MSS). The examples of the metrical value of these inflexions are numerous in the text, [49] though slurring or omission occurs, besides *stoln* and *quils*, also in *dreuẹn* 190, *spedẹs* 113, *findẹs* 210 (unless L is right in omitting *ta*), as well as in positions where this was normal in Chaucerian English (e.g. in trisyllables such as *felawes, bodies* 192, 252). *Farës* 103 is marked in the text, but possible is *farẹs* slurred with *fairë* syllabic. Also passed over is the usual ignoring of *e* by elision before a vowel or *h*. The slurring or omission of *e* in other positions, none unparalleled in Chaucerian use elsewhere, occurs in *Maline* 316 (probably); in (*I*) *haue* 332, 335, 345; and in the infinitive *haue* 254, 265.[124]

Metrically significant final *e* occurs in (i) the nouns *mele* 122, *hoste* 211, *wenche* 258, *lawe* 259, 260; (ii) in adjectival inflexion: *þis lange (schorte) night*

---

[124] Correct for northern. Chaucer may have used the specifically northern *haf*. [Tolkien]

255, 345; and possibly in *þi faire wif* 103; (iii) in the adjectives where it was part of the stem inflected or uninflected: *a wilde fir* 252, and *swete wight*;[125] (iv) in verbal forms: past tense *herde thou* 250, *mighte* 271; imperative *auise* 262; and infinitive *paie* 213. This is combined probably with retention of southern *n* in *ga crepen in* 330, where the following vowel seems to require *n* to avoid elision. Are we to reckon all or any of these cases as untrue to northern dialect? *Crepen* 330 we certainly must, noting that it occurs in Alain's soliloquy (329–366), which is remarkable for the number of southernisms it contains in all the seven MSS.[126] The loss of final *e* in the infinitive, and in such imperatives as *mak* for *make* (so 212), was specially early in the North, but this does not certainly apply to words of French origin. Scansions such as *changë* are plainly indicated in fourteenth-century poems (e.g. Rolle) where native *stand*, or *luf* (love), are used. We may, then, allow Chaucer *auise* and *paie*. But he ought to have the benefit of the doubt in the remaining cases. The question of final *e* in the North or in general is none too certain. He was not necessarily, in any case, representing dialect right up to date without a literary flavour. The evidence of northern metre is dubious – it was probably syllabically far more irregular than in the South, certainly than in Chaucer, largely owing to the influence of native [50] metrical feeling kept up by alliterative and alliterated verse – but it does at least show that final *e* was in various cases preserved much later than is commonly recognized, at any rate in verse tradition. It is certainly nonsense to say that *at the beginning of our records e was lost about 1300* (*Cursor Mundi*).[127] Whatever be the original date of the composition of *Cursor Mundi*, the best manuscript obviously misrepresents the original in this matter of final *e* (and many other points) in almost every couplet, and, even so, many cases of metrical *ë* are preserved.[128] It is probable, however, that colloquial use in London, even in Chaucer's time, was beginning already to drop final *e*,[129] and we may conclude perhaps that its presence or absence was a point to which he would not give much attention in dialect speech, but would follow mainly the habits of his own language and literary tradition.

(ii) Certain sourthern verbal inflexions appear. The most definite are the infinitive *crepen* 330 already dealt with; and the past participle with southern

---

[125] OE *wilde, swēte*; and cf. ON *villi-eldr* "wild-fire". [Tolkien]
[126] Though it also contains *wrang*; and (on the evidence of Hl only) *makes* and *ga*, 334. [Tolkien]
[127] Jordan, *ME Gram.*, § 141. [Tolkien] Tolkien's copy of Richard Jordan's *Handbuch der mittelenglischen Grammatik* (Heidelberg: Carl Winter, 1925) is now the Bodleian's Tolkien VC 239. [Ed.]
[128] *Flours þar es wit suete smelles* is, for example, a pretty clear case, *Cursor Mundi* 1014. [Tolkien]
[129] Owing to various causes, grammatical and phonetic. [Tolkien]

loss of *n* seen in *misgo* 335 and fixed by rhyme with *also*. Both occur in Alain's soliloquy. In 108 occurs *as clerkes sain* with southern (strictly midland) plural *n*, fixed by rhyme with *swain*. The correct form, at any rate, for Northumbria, whence the clerks hailed (see below), would have been *men sais*.[130] Similar is the "incorrect" *men sai* or *saiþ* (sg.), rhyming *fai* or *faiþ*, 290, where northern English used *sais*, whether singular or plural was intended.

(iii) There are two proven cases of false vowels:[131] *misgon* 332 rhyming with *anon* – the latter is part of the (Reeve's) narrative and so cannot be altered to *anan* (this again is in Alain's soliloquy); and in 272 we have *flie* "a fly" rhyming *vilainie*, where northern English had *fle* or *flei*[132] (Alain again, but in a different place). The case of *hande* Simkin 114, rhyming with *stande* John 115 is rather different. *Stonde* would have been [51] wrong for John, but *honde* more usual where no dialect is intended. But such forms as *hand*, since victorious, are not uncommon in Chaucer according to the MSS, though they cannot be decisively fixed for Chaucer's use by rhyme.[133] At the same time the comparative rarity of *and*-forms, and the absence of variants here, where all the MSS have *hande, stande*,[134] suggest that Chaucer intended *stand* as true to the northern dialect, but was able to link it in rhyme with a non-dialectal line owing to the occurrence of such forms as *hand* already in London English.[135] *Anan* was a different matter and could not be ascribed to the Reeve. Although he obviously knew that *gan, misgan* were the proper northern forms, he evidently did not think it worth while to recast his rhyme in order to avoid *misgon*.

These are the only "incorrect" details in the dialect passages that can be fixed more or less definitely as belonging to the original.[136] The certain cases are only six in number (excluding the debatable final *e*), a number quite insignificant in comparison with the mass of correct details. But this list does not,

---

[130] Cf. *as clerkes sais þat are wis* in *Cursor Mundi* (Cotton) 343 (variant readings G *seis*, F *sayne*, T *say*). On such forms as *sayn* in northern or North Midland texts see above. [Tolkien]

[131] *misgo* 335 is not absolutely fixed since *alswa* (used elsewhere) might have appeared in 336: *misga* would have been, nonetheless, a mistake. [Tolkien]

[132] Both occur in *Cursor Mundi*, for instance. [Tolkien]

[133] Unless one accepts such cases as the rhyme with *gerland* in *Knight's Tale* 1071–2 (the word frequently is written *gerlond* in ME), or with the name *Gerland*, in *Nun's Priest's Tale* 563–4. [Tolkien]

[134] In 181 only P has *stonde*. [Tolkien]

[135] Owing to the doubt in this matter the three occurrences of *stand* have not been included above among the correct northern details. [Tolkien]

[136] *Wiltou* 120 is not incorrect as are the forms *nadstow, sleepestow*, etc., offered by some MSS. In the latter *tow* probably depends on the presence of a *t* in the preceding inflexion which did not appear in the North. In *wiltou* and *saltou* the *t*-inflexion was common to all areas and such forms are found in such markedly northern texts as *Cursor Mundi* (Cotton) or Minot's poems. But such present forms as *hastou* beside *þou has* are found in northern texts of fairly pure dialect such as the Harley MS of the *Northern Passion*. [Tolkien]

of course, exhaust the "errors" actually found in the text of the dialect passages, even as given above, where the northernisms of all the seven MSS are included. There we have (i) eight cases of southern *o* for *a* in all the MSS in *no* 317, *euermo* 318, *wherso* 318, *also* 336, *go* 318, 336, *misgo* 335, *wot* 335. We need not here reckon *lord* 344, for though certainly southern in origin it was early borrowed by northern English. Already the most pure MS (Cotton) of *Cursor Mundi* has frequently *louerd*, *lord* beside the northern *lauerd*, *lard*. The case of *lo!* 215, 251 is interesting. There is no variant *la* here in either place, though this, of course, does not [52] conclusively prove that Chaucer here wrote *lo*. It is, nonetheless, a fact that *lo* would be correct for northern dialect. The word is derived from OE *lā!* and this form can be found in northern texts; from it is derived Chaucer's usual *lo!* (probably *lǭ*, the ancestor of our present pronunciation *lou*). But in the North and West the word developed various forms, as is not unusual with exclamatory words; and *lo* (also *low*, *lowr*, and other oddities) occur in texts which either by reason of region or date have otherwise still *ā* for OE *ā*. The form *lo*, phonetically *lǭ* rhyming with and sharing the later development of such words as *tō*, is good northern English, and cannot be included among the errors. It may be noted that all the examples of southern *o* (in all the MSS) come from the words of Alain to Maline or from his later soliloquy – except *lo* and *lord*. *lo* alone comes from the more carefully written (or faithfully preserved) part before line 250, which strengthens belief that Chaucer actually wrote *lo*, and in one more minute point (like *sek*) showed his accuracy of knowledge. We have also (ii) the false 3 sg. form *lith* 336; and the 2 sg. forms *slepest* 249, *hast* 347. The latter have been retained in the text since by chance no cases of the preservation of the northern 2 sg. in *s* (*has*, *slepes*) occur elsewhere; there cannot be much doubt, all the same, that the *st* here is due to the scribes rather than Chaucer. Finally (iii) *hem* 251 should probably be included though removed from the text, since it is the form here given by all the MSS. This adds another twelve cases of error, none of which can, however, be certainly ascribed to Chaucer.

Before finally dismissing the question of unchanged southernisms two words require brief notice: *wenche* 258 and *cokenai* 289. The former is not dialect, though it now gives that impression. It was still a respectable and literary word for "girl" in Chaucer's time, and was probably in pretty general use[137] all over the country. It is recorded in modern dialects in practically all parts, including Scotland, Yorkshire, Northumberland, and Durham; but in

---

[137] A reduction of OE *wencel*, early ME *wenchel*. [Tolkien]

this tale it contributes nothing to the linguistic characterization of the clerks either as rustic or northern. It was not actually the characteristic word for their dialect: that was probably already in Chaucer's time *lass*. This is well illustrated by *Cursor Mundi* 2608, where Sarah referring [53] to Hagar says to Abram: *Yone lasce þat I biside þe laid*. Even the Göttingen MS Here substitutes *wenche* (as does naturally the southernized Trinity version), while the Fairfax version goes astray with *allas I hir*. *Cokenai* used by John in his soliloquy provides the *NED* with its first quotation for the sense "milksop" – for which sense the only other references given, that can be called Middle English, are northerly or easterly (the *Promptorium* and the northern but related *Catholicon Anglicum*). The only earlier quotation in any sense is taken from the A version of *Piers Plowman*, where the meaning is "a small egg". Later this word was especially associated with London (or Londoners); but as it is never complimentary in its application, one would naturally suppose that this use did not develop in London, but in the East of England, which had the closest connexion with the capital. The word can hardly be true to the dialect of the "far North", except as a loan, even apart from the fact that the North used Scandinavian *egg* for English *eye, aye*.[138] But Chaucer quite justly puts it into the mouth of the Cambridge clerk. He does not wish when he gets back to college to be called a daff, a cockney – he is, as it were, glossing his more rustic *daff* with *cockenai*, the sort of word he would easily pick up in Cambridge; and it would be just the sort of criticism that a *testif and lusty* north-countryman would most resent, to be called a "soft townee". In fact, consideration of this word might lead us to defend all the inconsistencies of dialect, and the intrusion of southern and midland forms among the northernisms of John and Alain's talk, as not ignorant or even negligent, but intentional and true to life, a representation, in fact, of that mixture of speech that went on at the universities and was one of the causes contributing to the propagation of a south-easterly type of language. But such a defence is not necessary; and in general, whatever may be the case with the word "cockney", Chaucer does not seem to have represented a mixed language (unless here and there, and then to help a line or rhyme). The idea is too subtle for the Reeve (though he is made out a clever raconteur), and is probably too philological for Chaucer, though it is not beyond the nicety of his observation of external detail.

The critical text of the lines given above will perhaps prove, [54] then, even when more abundant variants are compared, to be a fair representation of

---

[138] Which seems certainly to be the final element in the word. [Tolkien]

Chaucer's essay in northern dialect. Even if we allow some significance to the curious collection of southernisms, even those easily avoided, towards the end of the speeches (from 316 and especially from 329 onwards), and see in this either Chaucer's negligence or art, the errors will be few, not many more than fifteen, a small proportion set against the correct details. On the other hand, after textual examination, no MS, and certainly not Ellesmere, can escape the charge of casual alterations, careless of the detail of Chaucer's work and its intent.

The evidence offered, though far from complete or fully investigated, is sufficient to establish the claim of the dialect of the northern clerks to be something quite different from conventional literary representations of rustic speech, tempered though it may have been to Chaucer's literary purpose, and superior to ignorant impressionism. When we consider that it appears in a tale in rhymed verse, in which few words are wasted, we find a sufficient reason for the "impurities" that occur; the number of the certain cases is indeed very small. In accuracy and in abundance the dialectal features go far beyond what was merely necessary for the joke, and we can hardly doubt that from one source or another Chaucer had acquired fairly detailed knowledge of the language of the North, and that such linguistic observations interested him.

The problem of *geen* and *neen* has been passed over, but the solution will not radically affect the general conclusion. A more suitable point with which to conclude a laborious annotation of a successful jest would be to consider more narrowly the question of locality. Chaucer may be imagined to have got his ideas about Northern English by applying his observant mind to people (travelling or on their native soil) or to books, or probably to both. But did he – in spite of the Reeve's disclaimer of any special knowledge of such distant regions – really, for his private satisfaction, give his clerks a home in some place he could have indicated, if he had chosen?

Most of the little evidence that can be extracted from words and forms has been glanced at. From accuracy in small details (such as *sek*), from such touches as *wight as es a ra* (and possibly [55] *werkes ai the wanges*), as well as from the spelling, which in so far as it comes through from Chaucer's hand to us, reflects that of northern texts as we know them, *written* works may be put down as in part the sources of his knowledge. Other sources, of course, were open to him. The eastern speech was, as he seems to have recognized from the very setting of his tale, a natural intermediary between London and the North; and he would have many opportunities of hearing English of the eastern kind without straying far from London. Doubtless actual northern dialect could be heard in the same way. But Chaucer did not stay in the study. Once at least he is believed to have been in Yorkshire; and though a residence at Hatfield as a very young man would not provide even an inquisitive person, less biassed than usual by southern prejudices against dialectal *harring, garring,* and *grisbitting,* with much opportunity for observation of the local vernacular, we may probably take this fleeting glimpse of Chaucer in Yorkshire as a reminder that people moved about, especially those of his class and station.[139] On such occasions Chaucer would not shut his ears. He was observant, and even the least curious were necessarily more dialect-conscious than we are now: dialect assailed the ears more often. It also assailed the eyes, in written works. Chaucer's complaint at the end of *Troilus and Creseyde* concerning the *greet diversitee in English and in wryting of our tonge* has already been referred to. He desired his own work to be handed on in detail as he wrote it, for he wrote as he did by choice among divergences, written as well as spoken. When, then, he suddenly departed, even for a few lines of jest, from his chosen language, he did this deliberately and certainly with some care for detail.

Why he should elect to use the observations he had made to enliven and to plant more firmly in native soil a poor *fabliau* of this sort, to use his knowledge just at this point and not elsewhere, though other appropriate occasions occurred in the *Canterbury Tales* where the same dramatic touch would have been useful, can now hardly be guessed. To guess is not, in any case, the province of the philologist. The chance events of the actual lives of authors get caught up into their books, but usually they are strangely changed and intricately woven anew one with another, or with other contents of the mind. To others may be [56] left the geography of the tale, and the mill of Trumpington,[140] and surmises concerning visits of Chaucer to the East, including Cambridge, the identity of the Reeve, and the possibility of meetings with actual undergraduates. Even if all these details were established facts of Chaucerian biography, it would not alter the more important point that in his selection from his varied experiences he showed a linguistic insight that is remarkable.

At any rate, the Reeve's *fer in the north* means what it says: it means not some way north (of Norfolk), but in the remote North; if not Scotland, then

---

[139] Skeat (1:xvii) reported the record placing Chaucer at Hatfield in Yorkshire in 1357 as part of the household of Elizabeth, Countess of Ulster, wife of Edward III's third son: "Perhaps it was at Hatfield that Chaucer picked up some knowledge of the Northern dialect, as employed by him in the Reves Tale." Tolkien alludes to John of Trevisa's translation of Hidgen's *Polychronicon* excerpted in Sisam's *Fourteenth Century Verse and Prose*, 148: "Also Englyschmen...by commyxstion and mellyng, furst wiþ Danes and afterward wiþ Normans, in menye þe contray longage ys apeyred, and som vseþ strange wlaffyng, chyteryng, *harryng, and garryng grisbittyng.*" [Ed., our italics]

[140] Skeat (5:116) has a long note on *Trumpington.* [Ed.]

(we may make a preliminary guess) beyond the Tees.[141] To make this clear it may seem vain to appeal to the dialect – we should be asking a comic poet to indicate in a few lines a narrow localization which our own studious analysis can rarely manage in texts many times the length. There are some indications nonetheless. The non-linguistic may be glanced at first.

In line 94 we are told of the place of John and Aleyn's birth: a "town" called *Strother*. Skeat says there is now no such town in England.[142] This is true, but it has little to do with Chaucer; for his *toun* does not mean "town", but what we should call a village, a place large enough to have a proper name, possibly a church. This is, of course, the sense also in the *Reeve's Tale*, 23 and 57, and in the Prologue to the *Canterbury Tales*, 478. There are at least two villages of the name still existing, both north of Tees: Strother (Boldon) and Strother (Haughton), not to mention Haughstrother, Broadstruthers, and the now lost *Coldstrother*.[143] The name is confined to Scotland and the North of England, and is, in fact, a dialect word meaning "marsh", ME *strōther*,[144] peculiar to the northern region, and [57] there frequent in names. Chaucer could hardly have chosen a name from among all the northern hamlets more local or appropriate. He may, indeed, have known its then still current dialectal meaning; but neither this meaning nor, in the absence of ordnance maps, the existence of such places is likely to have become known to him except by a visit to the North or contact with actual people from those parts.

---

[141] The River Tees in northeastern England rises on Cross Fell in the northern Pennines and flows seventy miles eastward to the North Sea, forming the boundary between the historic counties of Yorkshire and Durham – the latter being "beyond the Tees". [Ed.]

[142] Skeat (5:120) provided a note longer than Tolkien cites: "Mr. Gollancz tells me:— 'The Strother family, of Northumberland, famous in the fourteenth century, was a branch of the Strothers, of Castle Strother in Glendale, to the west of Wooler.'" Sir Israel Gollancz (1863–1930) was a scholar of early English literature and Professor of English at King's College, London. The British Academy established a memorial lecture in his name for which Tolkien delivered "*Beowulf*: The Monsters and the Critics" in 1936. [Ed.]

[143] Mawer, *Place Names of Northumberland and Durham*, pp. 191 and 240. [Tolkien] Allen Mawer, *Place Names of Northumberland and Durham* (Cambridge: Cambridge University Press, 1920). Tolkien was a member of the English Place-Name Society (SH 3:1239). [Ed.]

[144] Representing an OE *strōdor, *strōðor, probably a variant form (originally from a single ancient noun, as OE *salor – sæl*) of OE *strōd* (strōð), OHG *struot*. The sense in E. seems to have been "marshy land (overgrown with brushwood)". The shorter form is found in charters, and probably survives in various southern place-names, such as Strood in Kent and Stroud in Gloucestershire. See W. H. Stevenson, in *Phil. Soc. Trans.*, 1895–8 (p. 537), quoted also in Mawer, op. cit. [*Place Names of Northumberland and Durham*]; and Bosworth-Toller and Supplement, s.v. *strōd*. The existence of this native word should be added to the recent note by Onions and Gordon on *strothe* in *Pearl* 115 (*Medium Ævum*, i, 2, p. 128); it probably disturbed the development of the imported Norse *storð*, similar in meaning, but only remotely related etymologically, if at all. [Tolkien] See W. H. Stevenson, "Some Old-English Words Omitted or Imperfectly Explained in Dictionaries", *Transactions of the Philological Society* 23/3 (1897), 528–42, and E. V. Gordon and C. T. Onions, "Notes on the Text and Interpretation of *Pearl*", *Medium Ævum* 1/2 (1932), 126–36. [Ed.]

The word *strother*, though characteristic of Northumbria (in the narrower sense), is not solely Northumbrian; it is found in Scotland and appears probably in the West Riding name Langstrothdale, for which in the thirteenth century *lange strother* is recorded.[145] But we possess a second indication which points to Durham or Northumberland. In line 207 John swears *by seint Cutberd*. The form of the name is a perversion, produced or favoured by the needs of rhyme, of *Cudbert*, the more natural medieval form of St. Cuthbert's name. It is true that oaths in Chaucer are all too often but valueless fillings of a line; but this comes in neatly and naturally, it is no mere padding like *for by that lord that called is seint Jame*, 334. Chaucer does not elsewhere mention the great northern saint, and mentions him here undoubtedly for local colour. The local colour is that of Northumbria – not of Scotland. There was small friendship between St. Cuthbert and the Scots, at least in the fourteenth century. Lawrence Minot says: –

> þe Scottes with þaire falshede þus went þai obout
> For to win Ingland, whils Edward was out.
> For Cuthbert of Dorem haued þai no dout;
> þarfore at Neuel Cros law gan þai lout.[146]

The author of the *Metrical Life of St. Cuthbert* has similar views (cf. lines 4881 ff.) regarding even the ninth century.[147]

"The Durham area, when first distinguished from the rest of the earldom of Northumberland, was known as *Haliwer(es) folc* or *Haliwersocn* = the people or soke (i.e. jurisdiction) of the holy man or saint, a term which is the equivalent of the common Latin expression *terra* or *patrimonium Sancti Cuthberti*."[148] This term originally included considerable parts of the present county of Northumberland. It was still in use in the fourteenth century, [58] though it went out of use in the next. In the *Metrical Life of St. Cuthbert* (*c.* 1430) the expressions used are *Cuthbert folk* (*men, lande*) and *saint pople*.[149]

---

[145] Smith, *Place Names of the North Riding*, p. 229. [Tolkien] A. H. Smith, *The Place-Names of the North Riding of Yorkshire* (Cambridge: Cambridge University Press, 1928). [Ed.]

[146] Sisam did not include this anti-Scottish poem in his *Fourteenth Century Verse and Prose*; Tolkien would have found it in *The Poems of Laurence Minot*, ed. Joseph Hall, 3rd. ed. (Oxford: Clarendon, 1914), 33. [Ed.]

[147] *The Life of St. Cuthbert in English Verse*, ed. Joseph Thomas Fowler (Durham: Surtees Society Publications, no. 87, 1891). [Ed.]

[148] Mawer, op. cit. [*Place Names of Northumberland and Durham*], introduction. [Tolkien]

[149] Surtees Society, No. 87, lines 4608, 4794, 7098, 7517. [Tolkien] "Surtees Society" refers above to Fowler's *Life of St. Cuthbert*. [Ed.]

But quite apart from this special use the peculiar association of this part of England with St. Cuthbert and the devotion there to him was familiar throughout the country.[150]

There can be little doubt, then, that Chaucer had actually in mind the land beyond the Tees as the home of his young men and of their speech. For philological purposes that is all that is required. Skeat, and Professor Manly since, have pointed to the actual family of *de Strother* from Northumberland.[151] The names Aleyn and John were borne by its members, though the popularity of these names detracts considerably from the interest of this fact. Aleyn de Strother (whose son was John), was at one time constable of Roxburgh Castle; he died in 1381. The family was important in the North. This may indicate one way, at any rate, in which Chaucer could have learned of the place-name, and even, indeed, have listened to the dialect; for in his days members of such a family might speak dialectally enough at home or at court. If so, in addition to other ingenuities here ascribed to him, Chaucer may possibly have added a crowning touch of satire on living persons. As Chaucer has drawn them, his young men, of course, are not relatives; they came from the same village, and were *felawes* (283), and they were clerks and poor. If we must seek for "real life" at the bottom of all Chaucer's characters, this must be a composite picture. But this is beside my present object, and I will end with one more philological point. The narrower localization seems clear: did Chaucer, or could he, make this appear also in the dialect used? It would be difficult to do, and at any rate difficult now to pick up the hints, were they given, in our ignorance of local peculiarities within the generally uniform Northern (or North-Eastern) English of the time.

Among the dialect words used only one holds out any hope: this is the word *slyk*, 210, 250, 253, for "such", which, if we take in 251 the variant *slike* as descending from Chaucer, is also the [59] sole word for "such" in the clerks' mouths. The words and forms of words for *such* in Middle English require an investigation which I have not been able to give to them. I began to pursue *slike* with a light heart, trusting my casual impression that it was a word limited to (Eastern) Yorkshire that occurred only in a few easily examined texts. Here it seemed Chaucer had clearly been careless, and had fobbed off a Yorkshire Scandinavianism on his Northumbrian clerks. It soon became plain that a diligent search through many northern texts (mostly ill-glossed or not

---

[150] A similar case of local colour in oaths is provided by the Oxford carpenter who in the *Miller's Tale* 3449 swears by *seinte Frydeswyde*. [Tolkien] See Skeat (5:105): "The carpenter naturally invokes St. Frideswide, as there was a priory of St. Frideswide at Oxford." [Ed.]

[151] See Skeat (5:120) on Aleyn de Struther and his son John. [Ed.]

at all), and an enquiry into their textual history (mostly tangled and seldom known), and finally a considerable knowledge of the recent northern and Scottish dialects, would be required. But Chaucer would emerge triumphant. I have not been able to do more than give a preliminary glance at the available evidence, but even so one fact, the only one that really concerns this paper or the criticism of Chaucer, comes out plainly: if *slike* was ever anywhere at home, as the usual, or even exclusive word for "such", it was precisely in England beyond the Tees. A more typical word, and yet one that though strange would still be sufficiently interpreted by the context without need of a footnote, could hardly have been found. After that the critic of Chaucer's dialect and his skill in using it may well retire. In fact, one may end by remarking that even this one odd word bears out the general impression: even under the limitations of a comic tale in rhymed verse told to a Southern audience, Chaucer took a private pleasure in accurate observation and was probably far more definite in his ideas, and more interested in such linguistic matters than he admitted, just as he loved digressions while ever declaring that he was pushing on with the utmost speed. A deal of pother may have been made over a few comic lines of his, yet we may feel sure he would appreciate the attention, and have more sympathy with such pother, and with such of his later students who attach importance to the minutiæ of language, and of his language, even to such dry things as rhymes and vowels, than with those who profess themselves disgusted with such inhumanity.[152]

APPENDIX I

Tulle

Tulle, 214 "entice" rhyming *fulle*. On examination this reveals a small problem, difficult to solve. It would seem from [60] the rhyme that Chaucer intended the word to have ŭ, as still in modern *full*. But this form appears to be unparalleled. Has Chaucer made a mistake, or has he provided us with a genuine dialect form which has otherwise escaped record?

Chaucer's *tulle* here is the only evidence given in the *NED* for a ME *tulle* "entice" from OE **tullian*, a supposed variant of *tollian* (also unrecorded in the Old English but assured by the frequent ME *tolli-n, tolle-n*).[153] The latter,

---

[152] Tolkien spent his whole career battling those who espoused the cause of Literature at the expense of Language, still proclaiming throughout his 1959 "Valedictory Address" that "Philology is the foundation of humane letters" (*Essays* 225). [Ed.]

[153] Such a variation is not in itself impossible and might be compared with *pill, pull* "pluck, pull". [Tolkien] Shippey, *Road to Middle-earth*, 20, explains the use of the asterisk by historical linguists speculatively to retrieve a lost word: "The * is the sign of the reconstructed form, proposed by August Schleicher in the 1860s and used widely ever since." [Ed.]

giving modern *toll* "attract, entice, decoy", remained a literary word till the end of the seventeenth century, and is or was till recently used in dialects of the South and Midlands.[154] But *NED* does not give any instances of this verb (at any rate in this sense) from northern texts, and I have not been able to discover any. Neither fact is conclusive negative evidence; but whether any examples are to be found or not, it is plain that the usual northern equivalent was the related form *till*, from OE *tyllan*.[155] This is very frequent and easily found.[156] These words are supposed to have originally meant "pull". This would be intelligible semantically, and provide a possible link with *toll* applied to bells (see *NED* TOLL, v.²);[157] but the evidence is very shaky. As far as *NED* goes, at any rate, it in effect consists of a few citations of modern uses of *tolle*, *tole* in the sense "pull, drag, draw". The ME examples, both under TOLL v.¹ and TO-TOLL are all doubtful, some certainly misplaced. Discrimination is not easy owing to the variety and vagueness of the senses, and of the forms, produced by [61] contact with the foreign word *toil*.[158] The latter exhibits in Middle English the senses "contend, fight, struggle (with), harass, pull about, drag at". See *NED* under the various words, all of the same origin, TOIL, TOLY, TUILYIE.[159] But, in any case, from TO-TOLL must certainly be removed the citation from *Arthour and Merlin* 8531: the form is *totoiled* and the rhyme *defoiled*.[160] The two instances (all that remain) of *to-tolled* from the *Poem on the times of Edward II* are both under suspicion, since there is a variant reading to the former of them: *totoilled*.[161] From TOLL v.¹, sense 3, must be withdrawn the citation from *York Plays*, xli, 58: *þei toled hym and tugged hym*. In this text *o* is a letter of varied uses, and this example cannot be

---

[154] And in USA especially, according to *NED*, used of decoying birds, a sense closely resembling Chaucer's use. [Tolkien]

[155] Found in *for-tyllan*, rel. to *tollian* as *fylgan* to *folgian*, etc. This variation, which is of ancient origin, suggests that the word is old (from a type *tollē-n*), even though there seems to be no record of a cognate form outside English. [Tolkien]

[156] It may be noted that *tylle*, *tyl* occurs four times in rhyme in *Handlyng Synne* (Lincs), 7091, 7614, 7721, 9036, whereas *tolle* occurs (probably) only once, not in rhyme, 9039: this text has been considerably southernized. *Till* is, however, easier to rhyme on than *toll*. But *Havelok* has *tilled* and not *toll*. *Ancren Riwle* and *Hali Meidhad* Group appear to have both *tollin* and *tullen* (= *tyllan*: *u* = *ü*). [Tolkien]

[157] It would also help to explain the senses shown by the foreign word *toil* in English, if these were due to contact with a native *toll* "pull" of similar sound; see below. [Tolkien]

[158] Mere graphic confusion between *toll*, *toil*, *toill* is also obviously likely to occur. [Tolkien]

[159] They are derived, at any rate in form, from O. French *toeillier*, *tooillier*, *touillier*. [Tolkien]

[160] This same rhyme occurs also in same poem 6945. Contrast in same text *tolling* "enticing". [Tolkien] See *Arthour and Merlin: nach der Auchinleck-Hs*, ed. Eugen Kölbing (Leipzig: O.R. Reisland, 1890). The Auchinleck Manuscript consists of forty-three literary texts including *Sir Orfeo* believed to have been produced in London around 1340. [Ed.]

[161] Tolkien had access to "Poem on the Evil Times of Edward II" in *The Political Songs of England from the Reign of John to That of Edward II*, ed. Thomas Wright (London: Camden Society, 1839), 323–31, and *A Poem on the Evil Times of Edward II*, ed. Charles Hardwick (London: Percy Society, 1849). [Ed.]

separated from the following occurrences in the same text: ix, 281, *to tole and trusse* "to struggle (or toil) and pack" (Noah refers to the trouble of getting his goods and family into the Ark); xxviii, 18, *þou [schall] with turmentis be tulyd*;[162] xlii, 168, *ȝe me þus tene and tule*. With the last compare *Destruction of Troy* 10160: *The Troiens with tene toiled ful hard, With a rumour ful roide*.[163] A better example, though not conclusive since the text shows strange vagaries of spelling, is *Wars of Alexander* 3640, where *tolls of þe tirantis* probably means (the passage is not lucid) "they pull down the tyrants off (their horses in battle)".[164] Further, the A version of *Piers Plowman*, Pass. v, 127, has *putte hem* (i.e. strips of cloth) *in a pressour and pinnede hem therinne, Til ten ȝerdes other twelue tolden out threttene*.[165] Here probably *tolden* means "counted", but B has *hadde tolled out*, and C *tilled out*, apparently meaning "(had been) stretched out (to)". Though not entirely clear, and in a re-touched passage, these uses do seem to point to a verb *toll*, varying with *till*, meaning "draw, pull"; and the variation would seem to confirm its identification with *toll*, *till* "entice". A further example is possibly *Destruction* [62] *of Troy* 914: *he tilt out his tung with his tethe grym* (of the dragon attacked by Jason). However, there is a further complication: namely OE *ge-tillan*, *a-tillan* "touch, reach, attain (to)". It is to the descendant of this verb (TILL v.²) that *NED* ascribes the C reading and the occurrence in the *Destruction of Troy*. It seems to me that *out* is against this;[166] and that though we must allow ME *tillen* (*to*) "reach (to)" to be derived from OE *ge-tillan*, and even to have had some influence on the sense and form of other verbs, it would not by itself have developed the meanings "pull (out), extend".[167] Of *tille* "pull, draw, extend" we seem also to see a trace in *tille* used of setting nets and snares or pitching tents. This is taken in *NED* as a special development of TILL from OE *tilian*, *teolian* "labour, care for, cultivate". But this cannot be at any rate its sole origin;[168] certainly not of *tillen* in *Ancren Riwle* (Morton, 334), which is infinitive. OE *tilian* should and

---

[162] *schall*: Tolkien's square brackets. [Ed.]
[163] Which also illustrates the (northern) interchange of *ō*, *ū*, *oi*. [Tolkien]
[164] "Entice" is *tillid* in this text, 5479: so rather than "draw (physically)" as *NED*. [Tolkien]
[165] According to Skeat's text. [Tolkien]
[166] Also *ge-tillan* and its derivatives are either intransitive or have as their object the thing reached, not the thing extended. [Tolkien]
[167] *tillin* "reach" also seems a definitely south-western word, apart from the debatable passages in *Piers Plowman* and *Destruction of Troy*. In the latter poem also occurs in a description of a storm, 3704: *þere takyll was tynt, tylude ouer borde*. But this is probably an error for *tylt-*, introducing yet another complication: *tilt* "tip up" transitive and intransitive from OE **tyltan* [**tultj-* not West-Saxon **tieltan*, **tyltan* from *tealt* "unsteady", as *NED*, for *tilt* (*tult*) occurs in the North-West and North]; see *NED*, s.v. TILT. [Tolkien]
[168] Of the recent south-western dialect forms *teel*, *tile* I cannot judge; but they seem rather formations from *teld-*, *tild-*, like *spene* beside *spend*. [Tolkien]

does in this text (384) yield *tilien*. Here we have rather the blending of *till*-forms meaning "draw" with *tilden* (*teldin*) "pitch a tent or covering".[169]

Out of this tangle we can select the following possibilities in explanation of Chaucer's *tulle*:—

(*a*) A form *tulle* (OE *tullian) actually existed beside *tollian*, *tyllan*, comparable to ME *pill-*, *pull-* "pluck",[170] but has escaped other record.

[63]

(*b*) *Tollen* "entice" also had a sense "pull". Chaucer saw such forms as *tuled*, *tulyd* (possibly even *tulled*, *tullyd*) in uses such as those exemplified in the York Plays, and mistook them for dialectal forms of *tollen*.[171] These forms were, at any rate, northern.

(*c*) Chaucer misused Western *tullen* = *tyllan* = northern *till*. Extremely unlikely. He plainly knew a northern text when he saw it.

(*d*) He was content with a bad rhyme or eye-rhyme, *folle*, *tolle* (as in the Cambridge MS), owing to the difficulty of finding good rhymes to *tolle*. Such spellings as *folle* can be found in northern texts, but were also characteristic of the South-East.[172] Such a procedure is not worse than Chaucer's elsewhere in a careless moment or a difficulty. Though he seems in general to have taken detailed care with the *Reeve's Tale*, and had no need to rhyme on a word that was a nuisance, we can compare *fonne* 169 (which contains ŏ as in the modern derivative *fond*)[173] rhyming with *yronne* 170 (which contains *o* = *u*, modern *ruI*

(*e*) The passage is corrupt in spite of the consensus of the seven MSS (not the only place where this is possibly true), and Chaucer did not write *at þe fulle*, which is not an inevitable expression defying alteration, but something rhyming with *tolle*, or better with the northern *till*. For example, either *as þou*

---

[169] Cf. the variants in *Piers Plowman*, A, ii, 44 (cited in *NED*) *tentes itilled: iteldyde, teldit, teled*. Corpus, Cleopatra, and Titus also all offer *tildeð* for *tillen* in the above passage from *Ancren Riwle*. Cf. the same (Morton 279) *tildunge* "snare". The contact of this *till* with yet another *toil*, TOIL s.² and v.² "snare, ensnare" may be passed over since this *toil* seems post-medieval. [Tolkien]

[170] Perhaps influenced by it. In *pullian* the vowel *u* between a labial and *l* is more normal and can be compared to the vocalism of OE *wull*, *full*, *wulf*. [Tolkien]

[171] He knew *tollen* and used it himself (in sense "attract") in translating Boethius. [Tolkien]

[172] They are a marked feature of MS C, which has many other south-eastern characteristics. [Tolkien]

[173] That a form *funne* existed is, however, possible. See *NED* s.vv. FON, FUN. [Tolkien]

will (a piece of good northern grammar) or at *þi will*.[174] This will probably only be seriously considered, if a reading containing some such version, or trace of it, turns up. If it is rejected we must fall back on (*d*) – the others are all improbable, even if the existence of ME *tolle, tille* "draw, pull" and its identity with *tolle, tille* "entice" is granted.

[64]

APPENDIX II

Slik

I give here a few notes leading to the conclusion expressed above. Since *slīk* is a purely Scandinavian word that has followed a line of development from an older common **swalīk* which is quite different from that seen in native English *swelc* and its variants, and is, moreover, a form for which English possessed a clear brief equivalent, over which the Scandinavian form possessed no advantages, one would expect to find it less widespread than many other well-known Scandinavian loans, and would look naturally to the East. From the East it appears one can immediately subtract the area south of the Humber (for what reason is not clear). But absence of any trace of *slīk* in the *Ormulum* (which shows only *swillc, swillke*), in *Havelok* (*swich, suilk, swilk*), and, as far as I can find in Manning, as well as the absence of other textual or dialectal evidence, seems conclusive, even for the otherwise highly Scandinavianized language of Lincolnshire. The text of *Havelok*, and of Manning's works, especially the latter, has been in places greatly, even violently, southernized; but *slik* has elsewhere contrived to survive, if it appeared in the original, even thoroughgoing attempts at substituting other more usual words for "such". The *Ormulum* at any rate has not suffered this adulteration.

In Yorkshire *slīk* was known, especially it would seem in the North and East Ridings, in the parts, that is, that to this day are classified as belonging to the true Northern dialect area (which includes Durham and Northumberland). But in Yorkshire it was not in exclusive use, and it had to compete even in the East with *swilk* (just as in the West *swilk* competed with such forms as *soche* and *siche*); variant MSS of the same work constantly substitute *swilk* or *soche* for *slik*, or else rhymes and other tests show that the author used both. This is

---

[174] Cf. *at þi will*, rhyming *sal be still*, in *Ywain & Gawain* 1289. Error or alteration could have occurred in either *wille* or *tille* first, preferably the latter, and caused change in the rhyme-word. Cf. *at þe fol* in Trinity, alteration of *ouer all* of Cotton, in *Cursor Mundi* 4008. [Tolkien]

the case with the York Plays and with the rhymes of that admirable text *Ywain and Gawain*. Minot may be said to use only *slīk*, but he by chance uses in his surviving verses a word for "such" only once (viii, 35).[175]

If we turn to the metrical homilies printed by Small,[176] which on non-linguistic evidence appear to have a connexion with Durham, we shall meet *slik sli*, as the usual word for "such", [65] and observe the alien *swylk* appearing wherever, owing to the lacunæ in the best MS (Edinburgh), a piece from a different MS of slightly different linguistic texture is intruded by the editor. The massive *Cursor Mundi* is scantily glossed by Morris, but small search beyond the examples he gives shows that its language knew probably in the original both *slik* (*slic, sli, scli*) and *suilk* (*swilk, squilk*). Both occur in rhyme (e.g. *slike* with *suike, relike, like* in 4371, 8002, 9775, 9854; *suilk* with *milk* 5794). For the *slik*, etc., of the Cotton MS the others usually substitute another word (*suilk* in G, *suche* in FT), or remodel the line to avoid the rhyme. It is interesting to compare 5794, where the rhyme *suilk – milk* is preserved in all, even the southernized T, with 9775 where *slik – lik* has disappeared from FT, and *slik* in G is a correction of *suilk*. *Slik* was the least current of all forms of "such".

If one seeks for a text in which *slik* is used not only frequently but exclusively, one is to be found – namely, the Metrical Life of St. Cuthbert, written in the very *Cuthbert lande* mentioned above. It is a long text, of over 8,000 lines, and *slyke, slike* is extremely frequent, and there is no other form employed at all, save for a single *syke* (5117).[177] This is probably not a casual error, but an actual later form of *slyke* (however developed), and the ancestor of the varying forms, such as *seik, sāk, saik* still characteristic of the extreme northern area of English.

Needless to say, in this text most of the other northernisms of the clerks are to be found, especially *gif* (the sole form of *if*) and *hedewerk*, used of a headache of which a lady was like to die, and *hope* in its dialectal sense – St. Cuthbert says of the land tilled in vain "I hope this erde is noght of kynd whete to ȝelde." There also are *auntir, bus, es, ferly, fra, ȝon, heþin, ill, laþe, sal* (*suld*), *seel, swa, ta, till* and *whilk*.

---

[175] Laurence Minot (c. 1300–c. 1352) wrote eleven patriotic poems in northern Middle English dialect. Tolkien glossed "On the Scots" and "The Taking of Calais" in Sisam's *Fourteenth Century Verse and Prose*, 152–6, drawn from *Poems of Laurence Minot*, ed. Hall (1914). [Ed.]

[176] *English Metrical Homilies from Manuscripts of the Fourteenth Century*, ed. John Small (Edinburgh: William Paterson, 1862). [Ed.]

[177] I read it through for this purpose, so this assertion is probably, but not certainly, true. [Tolkien]

APPENDIX III
Geen *and* Neen *in Ellesmere MS.*

These strange spellings occur as follows: *geen* gone, 158; *neen* no, none, 265, 267. To them should be added *ne nay*, 263. These, *geen, neen, ne*, are the readings of the Ellesmere MS, [66] from which Skeat adopted the first two, not *ne nay*, for his text.[178] On the readings of the other MSS *gan, nan, na*, beside *gon, non, no*, see textual notes above (H has *a*).

The textual problem requires for its solution further evidence – the readings in these places of all other MSS. The linguistic problem is more or less independent of such evidence. As the evidence available to me stands these forms cannot be attributed to Chaucer. Additional readings of the same character (if independent) might shake this opinion, but it would not alter the linguistic situation – these forms are not those of any spoken dialect anywhere in Chaucer's time. Until they are demonstrated as Chaucer's, therefore, we need not attribute to him these fictitious forms; and the evidence for his authorship will have to be strong before such an attribution is made in face of the credit with which Chaucer has in other respects passed philological examination.

The view here expressed that these forms are not genuine is based on the following considerations. (1) *geen* and *neen* are not to be found elsewhere as far as I can discover. It is to dialect texts, not to MSS of Chaucer's dialect imitation (which have demonstrably adulterated this), that we should go for information on this point.[179] (2) *geen* and *neen* do not exist elsewhere in genuine ME dialect, because there is no basis for their formation. The antecedents of all English dialect forms of "gone, none" are OE (*ge*)*gān, nān*. There was no OE *gǣn, gēn*, or *nēn*, nor any sufficient cause for the development of such forms in Middle English.[180] Scandinavian influence which accounts for many dialectal forms, especially in the North, here fails. The East Norse *ē* (for West Norse, *ei, œi*, ME *ei, ai*) is rare in ME loanwords. It cannot occur here, for Norse has not

---

[178] Skeat (4:118) printed "What? whilk way is he *geen*?" and recorded the variants in his footnote for line 4078. Then Skeat (4:122) rejected Ellesmere for "Our corn is stoln, shortly, it is *na nay*" with textual footnote for line 4183; Skeat (4:122) printed "And sin I sal have *neen* amendement". E. T. Donaldson's *Chaucer's Poetry: An Anthology for the Modern Reader* (New York: Ronald Press, 1958) accepted Tolkien's conclusion against "putting the Ellesmere *geen* 158 into a Chaucerian text" (1934, 70), and therefore his edition silently amended *geen* to *gaan* (136) as well as *ne nay* to *no nay* and *neen* to *naan* twice (140). [Ed.]

[179] There is a late northern *geen* = given (cf. Cotton MS 2nd hand of *Cursor Mundi*, EETS, p. 958, line 77, and 962, line 14); but this is not likely to have been erroneously taken as "gone". [Tolkien]

[180] The mutated vowels in *gǣst, gǣþ*, or in *nænne, nænig* might conceivably have spread to other forms, though this would have been contrary to the observed lines of development in Middle English. There is, in fact, no trace of such a development, and the North is marked, actually, by early rejection of the mutated forms. Chaucer uses *goost, gooth* (cf. rhymes in *Canterbury Tales* B. 3123, and *Troilus and Criseyde* iii. 1108) beside archaic *geeth* (e.g. in rhyme *Legend of Good Women* 2125). Modern northern dialect *gēn, giən, nēn, niən*, etc., derive from ME *gān*. [Tolkien]

the word "go" [67] in any form, while E. Norse did not use *nēn (West Norse neinn). (3) The view that geen, neen are representations of real Northern pronunciation of written gan, nan is untenable. Why was this southern phonetic zeal operative only in a few places? In the paper above abundant examples have been given of the preservation of the symbol a for the descendants of OE and ON ā; all of these probably go back to Chaucer, in many of the cases there is, at any rate, a consensus of Skeat's seven MSS (e.g. 106, 107, 117, 182, 255, 256). And why should the amateur phonetician (Chaucer or another) adopt the notation ee? It is a fact of later development that northern ā was "fronted", and moved in a direction ǣ > ē. The orthodox view, however, is that this does not show its first traces until late in the fifteenth century, and cannot be seriously reckoned with until the sixteenth. The view that this process was complete in the fourteenth century is based either on evidence which does not prove the point or on this very supposed Chaucerian geen.[181] But debate on the question is here unnecessary. The shift in the pronunciation of ā was common to the whole country, and proceeded at least as rapidly in the South as in the North.[182] In that case, since the Southerner's own a (in such words as *name, blame, make, fare*, which he shared with the Northerner) was moving in the same direction, the letter a would remain *far and away the most probable symbol for him to adopt to represent the northern sound*, until long after Chaucer's time, whether in words with common English ā or in those with specially Northern ā (as gan). The use of ee, the [68] principal suggestion of which was long tense ē, would be an astonishing choice for any one in a sudden and inconsistent access of phonetic zeal to make. The unlikelihood of such a choice is, in fact, increased by the very attempt to push back the chronology of English vowel changes; for on this theory ee must commonly have been associated with a sound-value ī. In any case the joke about northern a for o depends on

---

[181] Thus Professor Wyld in his *Short History* (2nd ed., p. 107) has doubtless compressed the evidence, but may be supposed to have selected the cream. He adduces as rhymes which show the fronting of OE ā: Rolle *mare – ware* "were" subj.; Barbour *gais* "goes" – *wes* "was"; *mair*, OE *mār* [sic] – *thair*, OE *þēr*. The only other evidence is *geen* from the *Reeve's Tale* (and this is attributed to Scotland). But the first and third of these rhymes are clearly on identical vowels, and so prove nothing. ME *wāre, wǭre* (past tense pl. and subj.) is abundantly evidenced; its origin, at least in part, is ON *váro*. So also is ME *þāre, þǭre* "there", from OE *þāra*. The second rhyme has little evidential value, since it may depend on *was*, the usual form in such rhymes in *The Bruce*. The MSS, long after Barbour's time, cannot be held to represent his distribution of the varying forms of "was", and, in fact, palpably fail to do so. [Tolkien] For John Barbour's *The Bruce*, ed. Walter W. Skeat, EETS e.s. 11, 21, 29, 29, 55 (1870, 1874, 1877, 1889), Tolkien had glossed a selection in Sisam's *Fourteenth Century Verse and Prose*, 107–14. Tolkien's copy of Henry Cecil Wyld, *A Short History of English* (London: John Murray, 1914) is now the Bodleian's Tolkien VC 7. [Ed.]

[182] This seems agreed; for those who would push back the northern development would also see the first traces of the southern as early as the thirteenth century. Wyld, op. cit. [*A Short History of English*], p. 168. [Tolkien]

the occurrence in words like *gon* of the vowel heard in *name* (not that in *been*, for instance), and this is phonetically very much more effective when the *ā*-words are given an *a*-sound, showing at most the first hint of its later fronting, than with a "mid-front" *e*.

If *geen* and *neen* are not genuine dialect, how have they come to stand at any rate in the Ellesmere text? It is clearly unlikely that Chaucer is in that case responsible for them. But we will deal first with this improbable alternative. If Chaucer wrote them, then they are forms he heard somewhere, and his spelling meant *ē* of some variety. We need not suspect him of fobbing off on us arbitrary and pointless perversions. There is only one possible source remaining: the "Low Dutch" dialects. In Low German, Dutch, and Flemish *ē* regularly corresponds in cognate words to OE *ā* and its medieval English sequels; and language of this kind could have been heard, doubtless, by him in London, Norwich, York, or other places. The wool-trade was one of the principal causes of this linguistic contact, which has left its traces in many loan-words.[183] But Chaucer, at any rate, would have known such speech for what it was, and it may be asked why he should casually intermingle it with truly observed Northern English. The question hardly arises, however, because precisely in the case of the words "go" and "none" this source fails us. "Low Dutch" does not possess exact cognates of OE *gān, nān*. For "gone" it employed *ghe-ghaan* (with an *a* of different origin from OE); for "none" derivatives such as *gheen* of O. Saxon *nigēn*; *neen* was used, but only as an adverb "no". If *geen* and *neen* are to be derived from such a source, we have either to assume they are from Frisian dialect (*gēn, nēn*), or produced by [69] a complication of errors – e.g. the taking of *gheen* "none", *neen* "no" as "gone" and "none" by the singularly unfortunate application of an amateur "sound-law" (based on such correspondences as *heem* = *hoom* "home") to two cases where it did not apply.[184] In fact, "Low Dutch" fails as the source of *geen* or *neen* either in Chaucer's own hand or that of any later amateur re-toucher of his trifle.

If Chaucer did not write these forms they cease to have any great importance for this paper – and they lose most of their value for any purpose. The arguments used above are almost equally weighty against *neen, geen* (as real spoken forms) even if we consider them as the work of some later "editor".

---

[183] An example which illustrates the sound-correspondence discussed is ME *no freese* "no risk" = "doubtless" (*Towneley Play of Noah*, 391), which appears to be a loan from this source; cf. Old Saxon *frêsa* danger, Middle Dutch *vreese* (Frisian *frāse, frēse*); related to OE *frāsian*. [Tolkien]

[184] Such "false" applications do occur in mixed languages produced by the contact of cognate tongues. Examples can be found in the history of the relations of Norse and English, or of the German dialects. Cf. the note on Yorkshire dialect above. But for such a Flemish-English jargon there is little evidence. If there were, we should still be remote from Chaucer's town of Strother. [Tolkien]

That these forms are "corruptions" – the products of inadvertence or ignorant whim – may seem difficult to hold in view of their occurring three times, and rash to argue without complete collations. But that this is their origin is not impossible in such a context. The idea that the vagaries of dialect are lawless is old, and this feeling would co-operate in producing and perpetuating anomalous forms – it would allow palæographical similarities to have more effect than when checked by a more familiar or a more respected form of language.

It may be observed that Skeat did not admit Ellesmere's *ne nay* to his text, and rightly. The confusion, whether linguistic or scribal, between *ne* "not, nor"; *na, no* (OE *nā* "no" adverb); and *no(n), na(n)* "none" is well known in Middle English. But it is not very different in kind from *neen* for *noon* (*naan*), and this reduces somewhat the authority of *neen*. I do not speak with confidence on the palæographical point, but confusion (in the absence of normal checks especially) is obviously possible in fourteenth and fifteenth-century hands between *a* and *ee*, and *o* and *e*; *o* and *e* (both formed with two curved strokes, of which the right-hand one in *e* should finish about half-way down the other, but often exceeds this) are often, even in carefully written [70] books, very similar to the eye. Editors are often confronted with *o* for *e*, and vice versa, in familiar words where there is no question of linguistic variation. I note, though this is from a thirteenth-century MS, *to gene* "to go" from *A Song on the Passion* (MS Egerton G 13) in *OE Miscellany*, p. 199. That this is an error is shown, if not by the rhymes with vowels of like origin, *alone*, *one*, at least by the rhyme with *trone* "throne".[185] But one need not go so far afield. The MSS of Chaucer themselves provide abundant evidence of such errors, especially of careless interchange of *e* and *o* (rather misformation of these letters, in many cases). There is no more reason for putting the Ellesmere *geen* 158 into a Chaucerian text, or into grammars, than for doing the same by Hengwrt *heem* 112, which Skeat scorned to record even in his variants; and both are probably as genuine as the *ge* for *go* in the Cambridge MS line 32 (which rhymes with *to* "two").[186] Indeed Chaucerian "Scotch" *geen* has a ghostly look.

* * *

[185] Yet it is from this same piece that the error *meden* for *maden* (or perhaps *makeden*) is taken and used as evidence in the *Short History*, p. 168, for a phonetic change *a* > *e* in the thirteenth century. [Tolkien] *An Old English Miscellany*, ed. Morris (1872), had emended *gene* to *gone* based on the rhyme-scheme cited by Tolkien. His personal copy is now the Bodleian's Tolkien VC 192. [Ed.]

[186] Or as the frequent *woye* for *weye* "way", or other oddities such as *wayko* "weak", *dofende* (MS L, B. 932, 933), *heor* for *heer* "hair" (P at line 56), and so on. Where any assistance is given by words in the neighbourhood such errors take even more bizarre forms; but the *opinioun* in A 337 is quite as far away from *Epicurus* in A 336, which it has in alliance with *o*/*e* similarity turned into *opiournes* in MSS O. and L., as *heþen* is from *ham* in *Reeve's Tale* 112, 113; and *heþen* has doubtless contributed to *heem*, as the adjacent *he* has to *geen*. [Tolkien]

Oxford's Summer Diversions (1939)

Five years after publishing "Chaucer as a Philologist", Tolkien was back to cultivating his "two square yards" of the *Reeve's Tale* by newly editing the text according to his well-educated confidence in the poet's authentic language. Five years later in 1944, he was still tending the patch of garden by adding previously self-censored passages, a glossary, and a grammar analysis. Below is a more detailed timeline.

In 1937, Poet Laureate John Masefield joined Exeter College fellow Nevill Coghill to launch an annual entertainment which they called Oxford's Summer Diversions. Both men had Chaucerian investments. Masefield had done recitations of the *Monk's Tale* which Tolkien attended, and Coghill would publish a verse translation of the *Canterbury Tales* still in print with Penguin Classics. Coghill was also legendary for his theatrical productions, even encouraging the acting talent of his young undergraduate Richard Burton (*Ency* 105). For the 1938 Summer Diversions, to be performed at the Oxford Playhouse, they invited Tolkien to impersonate Chaucer, complete with headdress and forked beard, and to recite from memory the *Nun's Priest's Tale*. Masefield wrote a few lines to introduce Tolkien, a typescript of which we discovered at the Harry Ransom Humanities Center at the University of Texas at Austin:

> Before the speaking of Chaucer. Wednesday Evening
> Saturday Afternoon
>
> Chaucer, most reverend head, our earliest King,
> Who, in the midst of Winter, brought us Spring,
> Who, in the darkness of our northern Night,
> Unbarred the gates and led us to delight,
> Most reverend, most beloved, be it seen
> We bless your ghost and keep your memory green.

As Oxford's Professor of Anglo-Saxon who had delivered his landmark lecture on *Beowulf* in November, 1936, Tolkien took issue with "the erroneous imagination that Chaucer was the first English poet", reminding Masefield that "Chaucer stands rather in the middle than the beginning". He found the medieval poet more autumnal than springlike and more middle-class than kingly, expressing these contrary views in a letter to the Poet Laureate in July, 1938 (*Letters* 50–1). Here, too, he wondered whether they might offer a "modified modern pronunciation" for the benefit of a listening audience, little suspecting that a year later, his 1939 programme for performing the *Reeve's Tale*, rather than modernizing, would attempt restoring the fourteenth-century pronunciation which he believed was Chaucer's own.

Masefield must have taken the rebuke in stride because he held the letter-writer in high regard: "Professor Tolkien knows more about Chaucer than any living man and sometimes tells the *Tales* superbly, inimitably, just as though he were Chaucer returned."[187] Consequently, he joined with Coghill to invite Tolkien for a return engagement the next year to recite Chaucer again. In a prophetic moment in 1934, Tolkien's "Chaucer as a Philologist" had stressed the need for a live performance of the *Reeve's Tale*: "We need as a preliminary to hear the dialogue passages in their setting. They should be read aloud, as one may fancy Chaucer reading them" (p. 116 above).

Tolkien's 1938 letter had worried that Chaucer's medieval verse might not be understood well enough by a listening audience, and the performance's review in the *Oxford Mail* confirmed this suspicion: "The audience were at first a little scared of Chaucer's Middle English" (SH 1:233–34). To avert this problem a year later, Tolkien produced a printed programme with a title page that read: *The Reeve's Tale / Version Prepared for Recitation at the "Summer Diversions" Oxford, 1939*. One of Tolkien's souvenir copies was discovered in OUP's basement archives amidst the large batch of Clarendon Chaucer materials returned to his editor Dan Davin in 1951 (*TLC* 207–16). Tolkien, angry that his hard-won editorial work was being snatched away, must have been in such a hurry to dispatch these papers that he included materials that did not belong (while omitting others that did, for example his notes on the *Parlement of Foules* which he had extracted to use as lecture notes in 1948). His souvenir *Reeve's Tale* programme has served here as the copy-text for our transcription.

The introduction to the printed programme begins by explaining the story as the Reeve's revenge against the Miller for telling a tale at the expense of a carpenter – which had been the Reeve's former profession. Tolkien quickly emphasizes the poet's innovative humor: "He introduced the new joke of comic dialect. This does not seem to have been attempted in English literature before Chaucer." He next gives what is effectively a precis of "Chaucer as a Philologist": "The clerks' talk, as he wrote it, was probably very nearly correct and pure northern dialect, derived (as usual with Chaucer) from books as well as from observation." The next paragraph goes into greater detail, repeating the observation on dialect long before included in his 1913 tutorial essay:

---

[187] John Masefield, *Letters to Reyna*, ed. William Buchan (London: Buchan & Enright, 1983), 72. See SH 2:777–8.

"Chaucer relied for his principal effect on the long *ā*, preserved in the north in many words where the south had changed to *ō*: as in *haam, banes, naa*, for 'home, bones, no'."

The final paragraph of his introduction begins with the apology: "The text given here is slightly abbreviated." Actually Tolkien had bowdlerized the story to eliminate the violence of the two clerks when sexually assaulting the miller's daughter and wife, as well as the less shocking reference to the wife's breast-feeding her baby, and even Chaucer's swipe at the corrupt village priest for embezzling his church's endowment to provide a dowry for his granddaughter. The review in the *Oxford Mail* took aim at this prudish self-censorship:

> It seems an unjust criticism of an Oxford audience to indicate with such bluntness that they are not broadminded enough to accept the distinctly broad humour of Chaucer in a story of his which can least afford to be cut because of the amazingly ingenious way in which the plot is worked out. (SH 1:244)

But the programme's next sentence shows how far Tolkien's candour had failed him: "Only in the words of the clerks is there any material departure from the text printed by Skeat." *Tolkien's Lost Chaucer* (211–13) discussed how he had in fact abandoned Skeat's text altogether, as well as the Ellesmere manuscript from which the Victorian editor had principally worked, to recreate what he believed to have been Chaucer's original language of the 1390s before it was altered by scribes working at the beginning of the 1400s.[188] With an audacity never attempted by any other modern scholar, Tolkien undertook an experimental edition that discarded any medieval copy-text and sought to reconstitute the poet's vocabulary, as well as the spelling and grammar, which he, as a highly trained philologist, believed he knew better than the fifteenth-century scribes who had automatically translated Chaucer's language to their own.

The Reeve's Tale for Navy Cadets (1944)

It was our original plan to reproduce Tolkien's programme with its concise introduction and experimental text just as it was distributed to the Oxford

---

[188] Shippey, "Tolkien's Academic Reputation Now", 210, notes that his (similar) assumption about Old English texts such as *Exodus* was that "they have been copied so much that a sensitive modern editor should feel free to create 'correct' forms and readings".

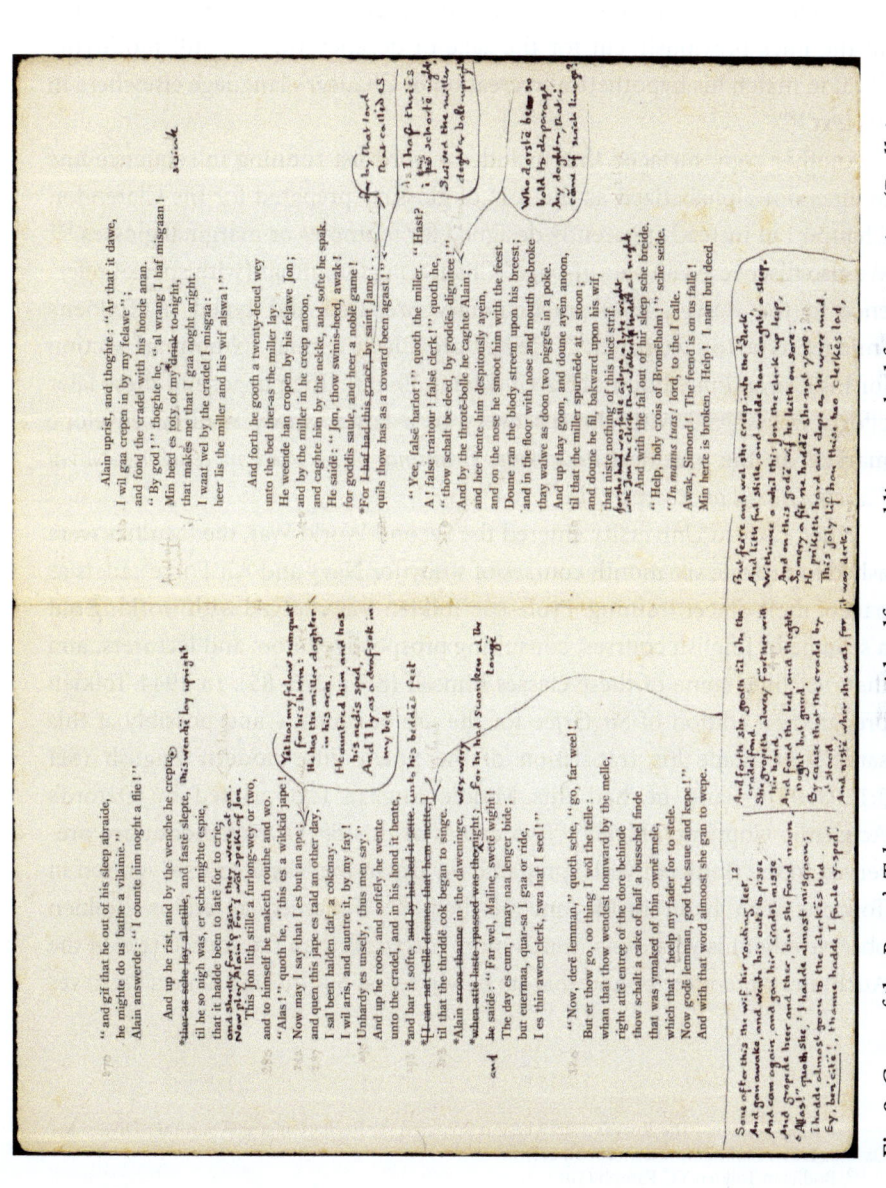

Fig. 9 Copy of the *Reeve's Tale* programme with self-censored lines marked for restoration (Bodleian Tolkien VC Pamph (10), pages 12–13).

audience in 1939, even though a reprint was already available in *Tolkien Studies*.[189] But with the expert help of the Bodleian's Tolkien Archivist Catherine McIlwaine, we discovered programme copies which Tolkien had later subjected to a variety of additions. Is one copy, he very carefully inserted all the lines previously cut for the sake of decency (fig. 9), still modifying Skeat to match his hypothetical recreation of Chaucer's language elsewhere in his text.[190]

Another copy surfaced that includes a word-list running in sequence line by line, not alphabetized as the sort of glossary prepared for his Clarendon Chaucer but instead apparently designed for footnotes or marginal glosses.[191] We also discovered an eleven-page "Chaucerian Grammar (with special reference to the *Reeve's Tale*)" meticulously prepared and typed in Tolkien's "midget" type to save paper.[192] He had provided a similar "Grammar" section for his Clarendon edition of *Sir Gawain* (130–32). The purpose of these later efforts was solved with the discovery of a large, sturdy mailing envelope marked on the outside *Chaucerian Grammar / As used in teaching Naval Cadets / Based on Reeve's Tale*.[193]

When Oxford University entered the Second World War, the faculties were asked to provide six-month courses of study for Navy and Air Force cadets as part of their officer training. Professor Tolkien was charged with working out a scheme of English courses, consulting prospective tutors and lecturers, and then teaching some of these classes himself (SH 1:275–85). In 1944 Tolkien prepared an edition of *Sir Orfeo* for the use of cadets – and possibly at this same time made his translation of the poem into modern English (SH 3:1203–05) – and he had this Middle English text printed by Oxford's Academic Copying Office.[194] Two copies of this *Sir Orfeo* handout are preserved in the Bodleian with "prepared for use in the Naval course" written in Tolkien's own hand inside one of them.[195] Unnamed as editor, Tolkien observes that his version is "much more metrical" than the source-text in the Auchinleck manuscript and that its newly recast South-East dialect retrieves

---

[189] J. R. R. Tolkien, "The Reeve's Tale: Version Prepared for Recitation at the 'Summer Diversions' Oxford: 1939", *Tolkien Studies* 5 (2008), 173–83.
[190] Bodleian Tolkien VC Pamph (10).
[191] Bodleian Arch. He. 176.
[192] Bodleian MS Tolkien a 14/2 (2), fols. 73–119.
[193] Bodleian MS Tolkien A 14/2, fol. 73.
[194] Carl F. Hostetter, "*Sir Orfeo*: A Middle English Version by J.R.R. Tolkien", *Tolkien Studies* 1 (2004), 85–123 at pp. 85–6.
[195] Bodleian's Tolkien VC Pamph (7) and (8).

the poet's original language, which is not represented in any of the three surviving manuscripts.[196] This modest-looking edition shows the same audacity as his experimental 1939 edition of the *Reeve's Tale* in retrieving the poet's original language.

Though Tolkien was still Professor of Anglo-Saxon and therefore had not been lecturing on Chaucer since leaving Leeds in 1925, the poet was never far from his mind during this period. When he wrote to his son Michael in March 1941 about relations between the sexes, for example, he readily quoted the *Wife of Bath's Prologue*: "*Allas! Allas! that ever love was sinne!* as Chaucer says" (*Letters* 67). Tolkien's newly discovered supplements to his 1939 programme – inserting passages previously cut for decency, supplying a line-by-line glossary, and adding a section on "Chaucerian Grammar" at the end – confirm the previous guess that he naturally turned to Chaucer and used leftover copies of the pamphlet as the basis for teaching the *Reeve's Tale* to these cadets (*TLC* 3). Perhaps inspired by Sisam's student editions of the *Nun's Priest's Tale* (1927) and the *Clerk's Tale* (1933), he aimed at assembling a basic textbook – with introduction, text, glossary, and grammar guide – probably to be published by Oxford's Academic Copying Office, which had already produced his handy *Sir Orfeo* edition.

We have therefore decided to produce our own "experimental edition" by assembling all the elements which Tolkien might have combined if the teaching of cadets had not ceased with the end of the Second World War. These elements are as follows:

(1) We begin by offering Tolkien's concise introductory comments for the *Reeve's Tale* in his 1939 programme for Oxford's Summer Diversions.

(2) Next, we provide a complete transcription of his edition of the *Reeve's Tale* from this programme, preserving his breaks between verse-paragraphs and correcting just one error where he gives "Alas! *You* hors gooth" (4080) for Skeat's "allas! *your* hors goth". As part of this text, we insert in brackets the missing lines that Tolkien originally cut as indecent, then himself added in one of his own copies (see fig. 9).[197] We retain even his minor editorial

---

[196] Sisam's *Fourteenth Century Verse and Prose*, 207, had stated the dialect was south-western. Christopher Tolkien, in his edition of his father's translations *Sir Gawain and the Green Knight*, *Pearl*, and *Sir Orfeo* (London: George Allen & Unwin, 1975), 20, says that it originated "probably in the south-east of England" – Tolkien's own view.

[197] Bodleian Tolkien VC Pamph (10). These were Chaucer's lines restored from Skeat's edition: *CT* I (A), 3663–8, 3977–86, 4157–8, 4177–8, 4193–8, 4213–32, 4234–5, 4264–7, 4271–2, 4283–4, 4317–18, 4324.

revisions to Skeat's text, including the removal of hyphens and the addition of diacritical marks to vowels such as ŏ and ë. Tolkien later corrected some errors in personal copies, for example changing "Of o toun *where* thay born" to "Of o toun *were* thay born" (94). We retain Tolkien's line numbers along with the standard lineation of Fragment I (A) of the *Canterbury Tales*.

(3) At the foot of the pages of his *Reeve's Tale* text, we incorporate the line-by-line wordlist that he inserted in the margins of one copy of the 1939 programme.[198] The target audience seems to have been those cadets quite young and poorly prepared, since Tolkien took the trouble to define simple words like *somdel* as "some deal" (43) and *wisly* as "wisely" (74). Though he had restored the two rape scenes, he continued to show prudishness by failing to define *swive* (258). For Alain's assault upon the miller's daughter – "and shortly for to se*i*n, they were at on" (277) – he glossed *at on* modestly as "agreed, good friends" instead of the franker "in sexual union". Not included in our transcription are Tolkien's insertions on the first page, clearly intended for newcomers to Middle English, for example "*nat* = not, *hir* = her, and *hem* = them". His final note shows his devotion to details: "*atte* = at the 16, 92, 137, 227, 323, 385, 391".

It should also be mentioned that a single page survives on which Tolkien used his "midget type" to compile a list of 36 words and definitions for the *Reeve's Tale*, also in order of their appearance in the text.[199] As was his practice, Tolkien had typed a revised version from his handwritten draft wordlist. Many of these entries are fuller, for example the gloss upon the phrase *greye as glas* that steadily interested him in line 54:

> *greye as glas* means what we usually call 'blue eyes', a conventional feature of mediaeval ladylike beauty; by Chaucer also ascribed to the Prioress. In M.E. gray eyes are often ascribed to Queen Guinevere. They are here probably meant to be comically out of keeping with the other features (the broad buttocks and the inherited pug-nose).

But the typewritten list covers only lines 2–79 in this sole surviving page. Because leaves with the remaining entries seem to be lost (or never

---

[198] Bodleian Arch. He. 176   [199] Bodleian MS Tolkien A 14/2, fol. 74.

written), we are using the original handwritten wordlist he added to the old *Reeve's Tale* programme.

(4) Finally, we append his *Chaucerian Grammar*. This is the sort of analytical discussion of morphology and phonology found in other Middle English textbooks and EETS editions of the period. His student Simonne d'Ardenne's EETS edition of *Seinte Iuliene* had a language survey that ran to 73 pages. (Her Prefatory Note thanks Professor Tolkien for his assistance on the grammar section.)[200] Though typed, the lettering is not always easy to read, and we have taken some liberties with punctuation. On separate pages, Tolkien compiled a handwritten list of words under the headings *Negative Forms, Notes on Verbal Forms in Reeve's Tale*, and *Vocabulary of the Reeve's Tale*, this last listing "French words" and "Latin Francized".[201] We omit these lists because they seem like afterthoughts, with no clear placement in his projected textbook.

As evidence of dating, the copy of the *Reeve's Tale* programme in which Tolkien added lines he had previously censored also contained a loose manuscript page for *Lord of the Rings*. It is much faded, but most can be read, and it includes the lines: "You guess I think where we are going Smeagol he said quietly. We are going to Mordor." This is certainly drafting for "The Taming of Sméagol" in *The Two Towers* (IV/1): "You know that, or you guess well enough, Sméagol," he said, quietly and sternly. "We are going to Mordor..." In *The War of the Ring* (92, 96–97, 104), Christopher believed that this chapter had its genesis in April 1944 because he himself had received an airgraph dated April 5, 1944, where his father reported on the progress of Frodo and Sam: "they are just meeting Gollum on a precipice" (*Letters* 103). Tolkien did indeed read a completed draft of "The Taming of Sméagol" on April 12, 1944, to C. S. Lewis and Charles Williams (SH 1:284–85). Of course this stray page could have been inserted earlier or later, but the overall evidence suggests dating his efforts at adapting the *Reeve's Tale* for teaching purposes to spring 1944.

* * *

---

[200] S. R. T. O. d'Ardenne, ed., *Þe Liflade ant te Passiun of Seinte Iuliene*, EETS o.s. 248 (1961), vii.
[201] See Bodleian MS Tolkien a 14/2 (2), fols. 93–5 and fol. 117.

The Reeve's Tale

Version prepared for recitation at the "Summer Diversions"
Oxford: 1939

J. R. R. T.

Among Chaucer's pilgrims was a reeve, Oswold of Baldeswell in Norfolk. The miller had told a story to the discredit of an Osney carpenter and Oxford clerks, and Oswold, who practised the craft of carpentry, was offended. In this tale he has his revenge, matching the miller's story with one to the discredit of a Trumpington miller and clerks of Cambridge.

The story is comic enough even out of this setting, but it fits the supposed narrator unusually well. Nonetheless, "broad" as it is, it probably fits the actual author, Chaucer himself, well enough to justify the representation of him as telling it in person. Apart from its merits as a comic tale of "lewed folk", this piece has a special interest. Chaucer seems to have taken unusual pains with it. He gave new life to the *fabliau*, the plot of which he borrowed, with the English local colour that he devised; and he introduced the new joke of comic dialect. This does not seem to have been attempted in English literature before Chaucer, and has seldom been more successful since.

Even in the usual printed texts of Chaucer the northern dialectal character of the speeches of Alain and John is plain. But a comparison of various manuscripts seems to show that actually Chaucer himself went further: the clerks' talk, as he wrote it, was probably very nearly correct and pure northern dialect, derived (as usual with Chaucer) from books as well as from observation. A remarkable feat at the time. But Chaucer was evidently interested in such things, and had given considerable thought to the linguistic situation in his day. It may be observed that he presents us with an *East-Anglian* reeve, who is amusing *southern*, and largely London, folk with imitations of *northern* speech brought southward by the attraction of the *universities*. This is a picture in little of the origins of literary and London English. East-Anglia played an important part in transmitting to the capital northerly features of language – such as *ill, their* and the inflexion in *brings*, which are in this tale used as dialectalisms, but have since become familiar. The East-Anglian reeve is a symbol of this process, and at the same time in real contemporary life a not unlikely person to have negotiated the dialect in such a tale. The whole thing is very ingenious.

The dialect is, of course, meant primarily to be funny. Chaucer relied for his principal effect on the long $\bar{a}$, preserved in the north in many words where the south had changed to $\bar{o}$: as in *haam, bānes, naa*, for "home, bones, no". But in these short speeches there are many minor points of form and vocabulary which are finer than was necessary for the easy laugh, and show that Chaucer had a personal interest in linguistic detail. For instance: the phrase *dreven til hething* is typically northern in the form of *dreven* for *driven*; in the use of *driven* for *put* in this expression; in the substitution of *til* for *to*; and in the use of the Scandinavian word *hething*, "mockery". Other marked dialectalisms are *slik* "such", *imell* "among", *bōs* "behoves".

Chaucer makes the Reeve disclaim any accurate knowledge of the locality – it is *fer in the north, I can nat telle where*. But Chaucer himself seems to have been less vague: he was thinking of the northernmost parts of England, now Northumberland and Durham. Strother is a genuine village name in that region. The clerk John swears by Saint Cuthbert, just as the Osney carpenter swore by Saint Frideswide. Saint Cuthbert was the patron of Durham, the *terra sancti Cutherberti*, and his name, not elsewhere mentioned by Chaucer, is here certainly a final touch of local colour.

The text given here is slightly abbreviated.[202] Only in the words of the clerks is there any material departure from the text as printed by Skeat. These words are presented here in a more marked and consistently northern form – in nearly every case with some manuscript authority. A star * is prefixed to the two or three lines that the process of abbreviation made it necessary to alter. Unlike many of Chaucer's *Canterbury Tales*, the Reeve's tale is neither easy to shorten nor improved by the process.

J. R. R. T.

> At Trumpingtŏn nat fer fro Cantebrigge
> ther gooth a brook and over that a brigge,
> upon the whichë brook ther stant° a melle.°
> And this is verray sooth that I yow telle:
> a Miller was theer dwelling many a day;
> as any peecok he was proud and gay.
> Pipen he couthe, and fissche, and nettës bete,°
> and turnen cuppës, and wel wrastle and schete;°
> and by his belt he bar a long panade,°
> and of a swerd ful trenchant was the blade.   10 (3930)

---

[202] The original 1939 programme's warning of an abbreviated text no longer applied after he supplied the missing passages in 1944.
° 3 *stant* stands; cf. *uprist* 329
° 3 *melle* dial. (Kentish) form of *mille* "mill"
° 7 *bete* (beet) mend, distinct from *bete* (beat) "beat"
° 8 *schete* shoot
° 9 *panade* long knife

A joly popper° bar he in his pouche;
ther nas no man for peril dorste him touche;
a Scheffeld thwitel° bar he in his hose.
Round was his face and camus° was his nose;
as pilëd° as an apë was his skulle.
He was a market-beter° attë fulle.
Ther dorstë no wight hond upon him legge,
that he ne swoor he scholde anoon abegge°.
A theef he was for sothe of corn and mele,
and that a sligh, and usaunt° for to stele.   20 (3940)

His namë was hoten° deignous° Simkin.
A wif he hadde, ycŏmen of noblë kin:
the persoun of the toun° hir fader was.
With hir he yaf ful many a panne of bras,
for that Simkin scholde in his blood allie.
Sche was yfostrëd in a nŏnnerie;
for Simkin noldë no wif, as he saide,
but sche were wel y-nörissed and a maide,
to saven his estat of yomanrie;
and schee was proud, and pert as is a pie.°   30 (3950)
A ful fair sightë was it on hem two!
on halidaies° beforn hir wolde he go
with his tipet° bounden aboute his heed,
and sche coom after in a gite° of reed,
and Simkin haddë hosen of the same.
Ther dorstë no wight° clepen° hir but dame;

° 11 *popper* dagger
° 13 *thwitel* knife (whittle)
° 14, 54 *camus* flat (pugnosed)
° 15 *piled* peeled, bald; cf. 386
° 16 *market-beter* "market-beater". Not found elsewhere? *beat* often in ME = tramp (beat the streets). "A frequenter of markets"? – "Or a breaker-up of markets" – one who went there and drove hard bargains by beating up the sellers.
° 18 *abegge* dialect (Kent) form of *abigge*, *abye* "pay for it"
° 20 *usaunt* accustomed, in the habit
° 21 *hoten* named: see line 93
° 21 *deignous* haughty, disdainful
° 23 *toun* village cf. 57, 94
° 30 *pie* magpie
° 32 *halidaies* Sundays (and other festivals)
° 33 *tipet* scarf
° 34 *gite* (hard g, probably OFrench *guite*) gown
° 36 *wight* creature, body: cf. 316
° 36 *clepen* call cf. 70

nas noon so hardy that wentë by the weye
that with hir dorstë rage° or ones pleye,
but if he woldë be slain of Simkin
with panade or with knif or boidëkin.°   40 (3960)
For jalous folk been perilous euermo;
algate° thay wolde hir wiues weenden so!
[And eek for she was sŏmdel° smŏterlich,°
she was as digne as water in a dich;°
and ful of hoker° and of bisemare.
Hir thoughtë that a lady shōlde hir spare,°
what for hir kinrede and hir nortelrie°
that she had lerned in the nŏnnerie.]

A doghter haddë thay betwixe hem two
of twenty yeer, withouten any mo°   50 (3970)
sauinge a child that was of half-yeer age:
in cradel it lay and was a proprë page.°
This wenchë thikke and well ygrowen was,
with camus nose and yën greye as glas,°
with buttokes brode and breestës rounde and hie;
but right fair was hir heer, I nil nat lie.
[The person of the toune, for she was feir,
in purpos was to maken hir his heir
bothe of his catel° and his messuage,°
and straunge he made it° of hir mariage.   60 (3980)
His purpos was for to bistowe hir hye
into sŏm worthy blood of auncetrie;

° 38 *rage* romp, play the fool
° 40 *boidekin* (bodkin), small dagger. This the first occurrence.
° 42 *algate* (always) anyway cf. *hougat* 117, 119
° 43 *somdel* "some deal" rather
° 43 *smoterlich* dirty and untidy
° 44 *digne as ditch water* was apparently a 14th century expression = "stinking with pride". *digne* "worthy" often = disdainful.
° 45 *hoker* scorn
° 46 *spare*, show respect
° 47 *nortelrie*. This is not found elsewhere and may be bogus French of the Reeve. It apparently = *norture*, nurture, upbringing.
° 50 *mo* more (in number)
° 52 *page* boy, lad
° 54 *grey as glas* = what we call "blue" evidently a conventional feature of beauty by Chaucer also ascribed to the Prioress. In ME often ascribed to Guenevere.
° 59 *catel* property (chattels)
° 59 *messuage* Anglo-French word = land for dwelling house and its appurtenances
° 60 *made it straunge* "made difficulties, was hard to please"

for Holy Chirches good moot been dispended
on Holy Chirches blood that is descended.
Therfore he wolde his holy blood honoure,
though that he Holy Chirchë sholde devoure.]

    Greet sokene° hath this miller, out of doute,
with whete and malt of al the lond aboute;
and namëliche ther was a greet collegge
men clepen the Soler-halle at Cantëbregge,   70 (3990)
theer was hir whete and eek hir malt ygrounde.
And on a day it happëd in a stounde,°
seek lay the maunciple on a maladie:
men weenden wisly° that he scholdë die.
For which this miller stal bothe mele and corn
an hundred timë morë than beforn;
for ther-beforn he stal but curteisly,
but now he was a theef outrageously.
For which the wardain chidde and madë fare;°
but ther-of sette the miller nat a tare: 80 (4000)
he craketh° boost° and swoor it nas° nat so.

    Than were ther yŏngë pourë clerkes two
that dwelten in this halle of which I seye:
testif° thay were and lusty for to pleye;°
and only for hir mirthe and reuelrie
upon the wardain bisily thay crie
to yeue° hem leuë but a litel stounde
to goon to mille and seen hir corn ygrounde –
and, hardily,° thay dorstë leye° hir nekke
the miller scholde nat stele hem half a pekke   90 (4010)

° 67 *sokene* custom (dialect word)
° 72, 87 *stounde* hour, time, while
° 74 *wisly* (wisely) certainly
° 79 *fare* goings on, to do, fuss
° 81 *crake boost* bluster
° 81 *boost* loud noise
° 81 *nas* was not
° 85 *testif* headstrong, hotheaded
° 85 *lusty* merry, gay; *lusty for to pley* eager for fun, keen on ragging
° 87 *yeue* give
° 89 *hardily* boldly = certainly
° 89 *leye* lay = bet

of corn by sleightë, ne by force hem reue;°
and attë lastë the wardain yaf° hem leue.

    Jon hightë that oon, and Alain hightë° that other.
Of o toun were thay born that hightë Strother:
fer in the north – I can nat tellë where.
This Alain maketh redy al his gere,
and on an hors the sak he caste anoon.
Forth gooth Alain the clerk and also Jon,
with good swerd and with bukeler by hir side.
Jon knew the wey, hem nedëdë no guide,   100 (4020)
And attë mille the sak adoune he leith.

    Alain spak first: "Al hail! Simond, i faith!
How faris thy fair doghter and thy wif?"
    "Alain! Welcŏme!" quoth Simkin, "by my lif!
And Jon also! How now? What do ye heer?"
    "Simond!" quoth Jon, "by god, need has na peer!°
Him bos° himseluen serue at° has na swain,°
or els he es a folt,° as clerkis sain.
Our manciple, I hope° he wil be deed,
swa werkis° ay the wangis° in his heed.   110 (4030)
And for-thy es I cum, and als° Alain,
til grind our corn and carie it haam again.
I pray yow, spedis us hethen° as ye may!"
    "It schal be doon," quoth Simkin, "by my fay!
What wŏl ye doon whil that it is in my hand?"
    "By god, right by the hoper wil I stand,"
quoth Jon, "and see hougat° the corn gaas in!

° 91 *reue* (bereave) rob
° 92 *yaf* gave
° 93, 94 *hightë*, passive was (*or* is) called. The past participle is *hoten* 21.
° 106 *peer* match, equal
° 107 *bos* northern dialectal contraction of *behoues*
° 107 *at* northern dialect = that (as conjunction)
° 107 *swain* (north. dial.) servant
° 108 *folt* (dial.) dolt
° 109 *hope* (north dial.) think
° 110 *werkis* dial. word = "hurt, give pain", with northern plural inflexion.
° 110 *wang* probably means "side of face" here. It has been explained as = *wangtooth* "molar".
° 111, 387 *als* = also
° 113 *hethen* (dial.) hence
° 117 *hougat* how (dial.); *gat* = *gate* "way" as in *algate* 42 "anyway"

Yit sagh I neuer, by my fader kin,
hougat the hoper waggis til and fra."
    Alain answerdë: "Jon! and wiltu swa,   120 (4040)
then wil I be binethen, by my croune,
and see hougat the melë fallis doune
in til the trogh. That sal be my desport.
For Jon, i faith, I es al of your sort:
I es as il a miller as er ye!"

    This miller smilëde of hir nicëtee,°
and thoghte: "Al this nis doon but for a wile:
thay wenen that no man may hem beguile.
But, by my thrift,° yet schal I blere hir yë°
for al the sleighte in hir philosophie.   130 (4050)
The morë queintë crekës° that they make,
the morë wŏl I stelë whan I take.
In stede of flour yet wŏl I yeue hem bren.
'The gretteste clerkës been noght the wiseste men,'
as whilŏm to the wolf thus spak the mare.
Of al hir art I countë noght a tare."

    Out attë dore he gooth ful priuëly,
whan that he sagh his timë; softëly
he loketh up and doune til he hath founde
the clerkës hors, ther-as it stood ybounde   140 (4060)
behindë the mille under a leefsel;°
and to the horse he gooth him faire and wel.
He strepeth of the bridel right anoon;
and whan the hors was loos, he ginneth goon
toward the fen, ther wildë mares renne,
forth with *wee-hee* thurgh thikke and thurgh thenne.

    This miller gooth ayein; no word he seide,
but dooth his note,° and with the clerkës pleide,
til that hir corn was faire and wel ygrounde.

° 126 *nicetee* silliness; cf. *nice* 362
° 129 *thrift* prosperity, profit; cf. *as euer moot I thrive*
° 129 *blere hir yë* "blear their eye": cheat them
° 131 *crekes* tricks (only occurs here in ME)
° 141 *leefsel* arbour, not recorded till 14th century but derived from lost Old E. *leaf-sele* leaf-hall, bower
° 148 *note* "business", OE *notu* (distinct from *note* in modern senses derived from Latin *nŏta* mark)

And whan the mele is sakkëd and ybounde, 150 (4070)
this Jon gooth out, and fint° his hors awey,
and gan to crie: "Harrow!" and "weilawey!
our hors es lost! Alain, for goddis banis,°
step on thy feet! Cum of,° man, al at anis!
Alas! our wardain has his palfray lorn."

   This Alain al forgat bothe mele and corn,
al was out of his minde his husbondrie.
"Quat! Quilk way es he gaan?" he gan to crie.
The wif coom lepinge inward with a ren;
sche saide: "Alas! your hors gooth to the fen 160 (4080)
with wildë mares, as faste as he may go!
Unthank° cŏme on his hond that bond him so,
and he that bettrë scholde han knit the reine!"
   "Alas!" quoth Jon, "Alain, for Christis peine,
lay doun thy swerd, and I sal min alswa.
I es ful wight,° god waat, as es a raa;°
By goddis herte, he sal nat scape us bathe!
Quy nadde thu pit the capil° in the lathe?°
Il hail! By god, Alain, thow es a fonne!"°

   Thise sely clerkës han ful faste yrŏnne 170 (4090)
toward the fen, bothe Alain and eek Jon.
And whan the miller sagh that thay were goon,
he half a busschel of hir flour hath take,
and bad his wif go knede it in a cake.
He saide: "I trowe the clerkës were afeerd.
Yet can a miller make a clerkës beerd°
for al his art. Now lat hem goon hir weye!
Lo, wheer thay goon! Yee, lat the children pleye!
Thay gete him nat so lightly, by my croune!'

  ° 151 *fint* finds; see *stant* 3
  ° 153 *banis* bones (north. dial.)
  ° 154 *cum of* (come off) make haste
  ° 162 *unthank* ill will, a curse
  ° 166 *wight* (dial.) valiant, active, swift. Distinct from *wight* thing, creature 36, 316; *lyte wight* somewhat, a little 363.
    ° 166 *raa* north. dial. "roe-deer"
    ° 168 *capil* horse
    ° 168 *lathe* barn
    ° 169 *fonne* "fool" (whence later *fonned* foolish, doting = mod. *fond*)
    ° 176 *make* a man's *beerd* (beard): trick him

>   Thise sely clerkës rennen up and doune,   180 (4100)
>   with: "Keep! keep! stand! stand! jossa!° warderere!°
>   gaa quistel thow, and I sal keep him here!"
>   But, schortly, til that it was verray night,
>   thay couthë nat, thogh thay doon al hir might,
>   hir capel° cacche, he ran alwey so faste,
>   til in a diche thay caghte him attë laste.
>
>   Wery and weet, as beest is in the rein,
>   cŏmth sely Jon, and with him cŏmth Alain.
>   "Alas!" quoth Jon, "the day that I was born!
>   Now er we dreuen° til hething° and to scorn.   190 (4110)
>   Our corn is stoln. Men wil us folis calle,
>   bathë the wardain and our felaus alle,
>   and namëly the miller. Wailaway!"
>
>   Thus plaineth Jon, as he gooth by the wey
>   toward the mille, and Bayard° in his hond.
>   The miller sittinge by the fir he fond.
>   For it was night, and further mighte thay noght,
>   thay for the lŏue of god han him besoght
>   of herberghe° and of ese as for hir peny.
>
>   The miller saide ayein: "If ther be eny,   200 (4120)
>   swich as it is, yet schul ye han your part.
>   Min hous is streit,° but ye han lernëd art:
>   ye cŏnne by argumentës make a place
>   a milë brood of twenty-foot of space.
>   Lat see now if this placë may suffise!
>   Or make it roum° with speche, as is your guise!"

° 181 *jossa* Old French *jos ça* "down here", this way
° 181 *warderere* "guard rear" look out behind!
° 185 *capel* horse (dial. word, cf. 168)
° 190 *dreven* = driven; *dreven til hething* = put to shame
° 190 *hething* (dial.) mockery
° 195 *Bayard* "The Bay", a horse-name
° 199 *herberghe* harbour, lodging; 225
° 202 *streit* narrow
° 206 *roum* roomy; cf. 225

"Now, Simond," saidë Jon, "by saint Cudbert,
ay es thow mery, and this es faire answerd!
I haf herd say 'man suld taa° of twaa thingis
slik° as he findis, or taa slik as he bringis.'   210 (4130)
But specially, I pray yow, hostë dere,
get us sum mete and drink, and mak us chere;
and we wil payë treuly at thy wille.
With empty hand men may na haukis tille° –
lo, heer our siluer redy for til spende!"

This miller in to toune his doghter sende
for ale and breed, and rostede hem a goos,
and bond hir hors, it scholdë nat goon loos;
and in his ownë chambre hem made a bed
with schetës and with chalons° faire yspred,   220 (4140)
noght from his ownë bed ten foot or twelue.
His doghter hadde a bed al by hirselue
right in the samë chambrë, by and by:
it mightë been no bet° – and causë why:
ther nas no roumer herberghe in the place.

Thay soupen and they speke hem to solace,
and drinken ever strong ale attë beste.
Aboutë midnight wentë thay to reste.
Wel hath this miller vernischëd his heed;
ful pale he was fordrŏnken, and nat reed.   230 (4150)
He yexeth,° and he speketh thurgh the nose,
as he were on the quakke or on the pose.°
  To bed he gooth, and with him gooth his wif;
as any jay sche light was and jolif,
so was hir joly whistel wel ywet.

° 209–10 *taa* take
° 210 *slik* (north. dial.) such; cf. 253
° 214 *tille* draw, allure
° 220 *chalons* (shalloons) blankets, bed-coverings
° 224 *bet* better (adverb)
° 231 *yexeth* hiccups
° 232 *quakke* sore throat; *pose* cold in the head. *quakke* only occurs here in ME; but *quack* or *pose* is found in 16th century.

The cradel at hir beddës feet is set,
[to rokken and to yeve the child to souke.
and whan that drŏnken al was in the crouke,°]
to beddë wente the doghter right anoon;
to beddë gooth Alain and also Jon.   240 (4160)
Ther was namore, hem nedëdë no dwale.°
This miller hath so wisly bibbëd ale
that as an hors he snorteth in his sleep,
ne of his tail behinde he took no keep.°
His wif bar him a burdon, a ful strong:
men mighte hir routinge° herë two furlong;
the wenchë routeth° eek *par cŏmpanie.*

 Alain the clerk, that herde this melodie,
he pokëde Jon, and saidë: "Slepis thow?
Herdë thow euer slik a sang ar now?   250 (4170)
Lo! quilk a cumplin° es imell° thaim alle!
A wildë fir upon thair bodis falle!
Qua herknëde euer slik a ferly° thing?
Ya, thay sal haf the flour° of il ending!
This langë night ther tidis me na reste;
but yit, naa fors,° al sal be for the beste.
[For, Jon," seide he, "als euer moot° I thrive,
gif that I mai, yon wenchë sal I swive.]
Sum esëment has lawë schapen° us.
For, Jon, ther es a lawë that sais thus: 260 (4180)
that gif a man in aa point be agreued,
that in another he sal be releued.
Our corn is stoln, sothly it es naa nay,

° 238 *crouke* jug
° 241 *dwale* delay
° 244 *keep* heed
° 246 *routinge* snoring; cf. 294
° 247 *routeth* snores
° 251 *cumplin* "compline": last of the services (before going to rest) in a church or monastery
° 251 *imel* (north. dial.) among
° 253 *ferly* strange, wonderful
° 254 *flour* "flower" = the most perfect example
° 256 *fors* "force" *naa fors* "no matter"
° 257 *moot: may as euer moot I thriue* "as ever I hope to have good luck", a common asseveration
° 259 *schapen* appointed

and we haf had an il fit al this day;
and sen I sal haf naan amendëment
again my los, I wil haf esëment.
By goddis saule, it sal naan other be!"

This Jon answerde: "Alain auisë° thee!
the miller es a parlous° man," he saide,
"and gif° that he out of his sleep abraide,°   270 (4190)
he mighte do us bathe a vilainie."°
Alain answerde: "I counte him noght a flie!"

And up he rist,° and by the wenche he crepte.
[This wenchë lay upright,°] and fastë slepte,
til he so nigh was, er sche mighte espie,
that it hadde been to late for to crie;
[and shortly for to sein, they were at on.°
Now pley Alein! For I wŏl speke of Jon.]

This Jon lith stille a furlong-wey° or two,
and to himself he maketh routhe° and wo.   280 (4200)
"Alas!" quoth he, "this es a wikkid jape!
Now may I say that I es but an ape.
[Yit has my felaw sumquat for his harm;
he has the miller doghter in his arm.
He auntred° him and has his nedis sped,°
and I ly as a drafsek° in my bed;]
and quen this jape es tald an other day,

° 268 *auise* advise: *auise thee* take thought, have a care
° 269 *parlous* = perilous 41
° 270 *gif* north. dial. = if; cf. 259
° 270 *abraide* should wake up
° 271 *vilainie* low trick; harm, injury
° 273 *rist* rises cf. uprist 329
° 274 *upright* supine, on her back; so also in 346
° 277 *at on* "at one" agreed, good friends
° 279 *furlong-way* (time to walk) a furlong's distance; a short while
° 280 *routhe* (ruth) regret "make ruth and woe" = complain bitterly
° 285 *auntred*, 289 *auntre* reduced form of *auenture, aventure*: "adventure"
° 285 *sped* prospered, furthered
° 286 *draf-sek* "draff" is bran, refuse. *sek* is a (north. dial.) form of sack. A draff-sack was used = idle lump (but the word is specially comic in a miller's bedroom).

I sal been halden daf,° a cokenay.°
I wil aris, and auntre it, by my fay!
'Unhardy° es unsely,'° thus men say."   290 (4210)
And up he roos, and softëly he wente
unto the cradel, and in his hond it hente,
and bar it softe [unto his beddës feet.]
   [Sone after this the wif hir routing leet,°
and gan° awake, and wente hir oute to pisse,
and cam again, and gan hir cradel misse,
and gropede heer and ther, but she fond noon.
"Allas!" quoth she, "I hadde almost misgoon;
I hadde almost goon to the clerkës bed.
Ey, ben'citë!,° thanne hadde I foule y-sped."°   300 (4220)
And forth she gooth til she the cradel fond.
She gropeth alwey förther with hir hond,
and fond the bed, and thoghte noght° but good,
by cause that the cradel by it stood,
and nistë° wher she was, for it was derk,
but feire and wel she creep° into° the clerk,
and lith ful stille, and wolde han caught a sleep.
Withinne a whil this Jon the clerk up leep,°
and on this godë wif he leith on sore:
so mery a fit ne haddë she nat ful yore;°   310 (4230)
he priketh hard and depe as he were mad.
This joly lif han thise two clerkës lad,]
til that the thriddë cok began to singe.
Alain [wex wery] in the daweninge,

° 288 *daf* fool, spiritless fellow
° 288 *cokenay* (cockney): cock's egg, used = townee, gutless fellow
° 290 *unhardy* unbold = nothing venture nothing have
° 290 *unsely* unlucky
° 294 *leet* archaic past tense of *lete* "to let", here used in sense "leave off" (let up)
° 295, 296 *gan* with infin. in verse = did
° 300 *bencité* common exclamation; a corruption of Latin *benedicite* "bless (us)!"
° 300 *y-sped* sped, prospered, fared
° 303 *thoghte noght but good*, had no idea of anything wrong
° 305 *niste* (she) knew not: negative form of *wiste* (past tense of *woot* know) knew; cf. 362, 380
° 306, 340 *creep* archaic past tense of *crepen* "creep" 330; cf. past participle *cropen* 339; and more modern form *crepte* 273
   ° 306 *into*: not into but *in* (sc. into the bed) *to* (beside) the clerk.
   ° 308 *leep* (archaic past of *lepen*, leap) leaped
   ° 310 *yore* for many a long day, (since) long ago

[for he had swonken° al the longë] night;
[and] saidë: "Far wel, Maline, swetë wight!°
The day es cum, I may naa lenger° bide;
but euermaa, quar-sa I gaa or ride,
I es thin awen clerk, swa haf I seel!"°

"Now, derë lemman,"° quoth sche, "go, far weel!   320 (4240)
But er thow go, oo thing I wŏl the telle:
whan that thow wendest homward by the melle,
right attë entree of the dore behinde
thow schalt a cake of half a busschel finde
that was ymaked of thin ownë mele,
which that I heelp my fader for to stele.
Now godë lemman, god the saue and kepe!"
And with that word almoost she gan to wepe.

Alain uprist,° and thoghte: "Ar that it dawe,
I wil gaa crepen in by my felawe";   330 (4250)
and fond the cradel with his honde anan.
"By god!" thoghte he, "al wrang I haf misgaan!
Min heed es toty° of my [swink°] to-night,
that makës me that I gaa noght aright.
I waat wel by the cradel I misgaa:
heer lis the miller and his wif alswa!"

And forth he gooth a twenty-deuel wey°
unto the bed ther-as the miller lay.
He weende han cropen° by his felawe Jon;
and by the miller in he creep° anoon,   340 (4260)

° 315 *swonken* laboured; *swink* 333
° 316 *wight* creature
° 317 *lenger* old comparative of *long*; "longer"
° 319 *seel* luck, happiness "As I hope to prosper"; a variation of *by my thrift* etc.
° 320, 327 *lemman* sweetheart
° 329 *uprist* (cf. *stant* 3) rises; cf. 273
° 333 *toty* totly, tottering, shaky (first recorded occurrence of this word)
° 333 *swink* labour
° 337 *a twenty-deuel wey* "the hell of a way"
° 339 *cropen* crept: see 306
° 340 *creep* crept

and caghte him by the nekke, and softe he spak.
He saidë: "Jon, thow swinis-heed, awak!
for goddis saule, and heer a noblë game!
[For by that lord that callid es] saint Jame
[as I haf thriës i this schortë night,
swived the miller doghter bolt-upright,°]
quils thow has as a coward been agast!"

    "Yee, falsë harlot!" quoth the miller. "Hast?
A! falsë traitour! falsë clerk!" quoth he,
"thow schalt be deed, by goddës dignitee!
[Who dorstë be so bold to desparage
my doghter, that is cŏme of swich linage?"]   350 (4270)
And by the throtë-bolle° he caghte Alain;
and hee hente° him despitously ayein,
and on the nose he smoot him with the feest.°
Doune ran the blody streem upon his breest;
and in the floor with nose and mouth to-broke°
thay walwe as doon two piggës in a poke.
And up thay goon, and doune ayein anoon,
til that the miller spurnëde at a stoon;   360 (4280)
and doune he fil, bakward upon his wif,
that niste° nothing of this nicë° strif.
[For she was falle aslepe a lyte° wight°
with Jon the clerk that waked hadde al night.]

    And with the fal out of hir sleep sche breide.°
"Help, holy crois of Bromëholm!" sche seide.
"*In manus tuas!* lord, to the I calle.

° 346 *upright* cf. 274; *bolt-upright* flat on her back, stretched out straight and flat.
° 351 *throte-bolle* "throat-lump", Adam's apple
° 352 *hente* seized. *despitously* cruelly, fiercely
° 353 *feest* dialectal (Kentish) form of *fist*
° 355 *to-broke* broken (up)
° 362 *niste* see 205, 380
° 362 *nice* foolish; cf. 126
° 363 *lyte* little (in quantity)
° 363 *wight* thing, amount
° 365 *breide* started

Awak, Simond! The feend is on us falle!
Min herte is broken. Help! I nam but deed.°
Ther lith oon up my wombe and up° min heed.   370 (4290)
Help, Simkin! for the falsë clerkës fighte."

   This Jon sterte up as faste as euer he mighte,
and graspeth by the wallës to and fro
to finde a staf; and sche sterte up also,
and knew the estrës° bet° than dide this Jon,
and by the wal a staf sche fond anoon,
and sagh a litel schimmeringe of a light;
for at an hole in schoon the monë bright.
And by that light sche sagh hem bothë two,
but sikerly sche nistë who was who,   380 (4300)
but as sche sagh a whit thing in hir yë;
and whan sche gan the whitë thing espie,
sche weende the clerk hadde wered° a volupeer;°
and with the staf sche drogh ay neer and neer,
and weende han hit this Alain attë fulle –
and smoot the miller on the pilëd skulle.

   Than doune he gooth, and cride: "Harrow! I die!"
Thise clerkës bete him wel and lete him lie,
And graithen° hem, and toke hir hors anoon,
and eek hir mele, and on hir wey thay goon.   390 (4310)
And attë millë yet thay toke hir cake
of half a busschel flour ful wel ybake.

   Thus is the proudë miller wel ybete,
and hath ylorn° the grindinge of the whete,

° 369 *nam* am not; *I nam but dead* "I am nothing but dead", I am dead for certain
° 370 *wombe* stomach; *up* upon
° 375 *estres* "interiors" (way about the inside of the house)
° 375 *bet* old adverb: better; cf. 224
° 383 *wered* worn
° 383 *volupeer* cap, bonnet; apparently here used = nightcap (but usually of a woman's cap)
° 389 *graithe* to prepare, make ready (dial.)
° 394 *ylorn* lost

and payëd for the souper euery deel°
of Alain and of Jon, that bete him weel.
[His wif is swived and his doghter als:
lo, swich it is a miller to be fals!]
    And therfore this prouerbe is said ful sooth:
"him thar° nat wenë° wel that yuel dooth";   400 (4320)
a guilour° schal himself beguiled be.

    And God that sitteth high in magestee
saue al this cömpanië, grete and smale;
[thus have I quite° the miller in] my tale.

° 395 *deel* "deal", bit; cf. *somdel* 43
° 400 *thar* (older *tharf*) need
° 400 *wene* expect
° 401 *guilour* cheat
° 404 *quite* past participle, "requited, paid back"

Chaucerian Grammar
(with special reference to the Reeve's Tale)[203]

1\. Nouns

These show few differences of form from those of Modern English. The nouns that are now "irregular", as *man, men; foot, feet*, show the same irregularities in Chaucer. But some traces of archaic forms (derived from Old English) that have since disappeared were still preserved in the XIVth century. Thus, Chaucer still uses some plurals formed with *n*, besides the still current *oxen, children*. In RT, we have *yën* "eyes" 54; and *hosen* "stockings" 35 (OE *ēgan, hosan*). Elsewhere we find *doghtren* "daughters"; and *toon* "toes", beside the more modern form *toos*.

> NOTE. *Toon* and *toos* both occur in the *Nun's Priest's Tale*, and both in rhyme, which shows that they were both used by the author (NPT 96, 511).

An inflexional *e* (mainly derived from the Old English dative) can still be added to monosyllabic nouns, or adjectives used as nouns, when a preposition precedes them; but the uninflected form can also be used. So, (*of, into*) *toune* 57, 216, beside *toun* 23; *in a diche* 186; *by the weye* (rhyming with *pleye*, where the final *e* is the sign of the infinitive, and cannot be omitted) 37; *to beddë* 239, 240; *with his honde* 381, beside *hir hond* 302.

> NOTE. Of the same origin is the final *e* in certain adverbs or adverbial expressions: as *for sothe* "in fact, forsooth" 19, beside *sooth* 4; *adouns, doune* "down", from OE *of-dune* = "off the hill, downhill, down". Many nouns end in (syllabic) *e* in the nominative sg. or normal form, so that in these cases no such inflexion is possible: thus *whete* 68, *mele* 75, *fare* 79, *mirthe* 85, *tale* 404, etc., etc.

The inflexion of (a) the *plural*, and (b) the *genitive* (or possessive) is still in Chaucer syllabic *-es*. It is reduced to *-s* only where the stem of the noun ends in a vowel, as in *toos* (cited above) or in *shoos, shoon* pl. of *sho* "shoe". This inflexion is derived from (a) OE *-as*, and (b) OE *-es*, the inflexions of regular masculine nouns.

> NOTE. French words, especially those not yet fully naturalized, still occasionally show the plural (not genitive) ending *-s*, as *chalons* 220 (contrast *schetës*). This ending, though so similar in appearance, is quite unconnected with English *-es* in origin, being derived from the Latin accusative plural endings *-os, -es*.

Occasional traces of an "endingless genitive" are seen in Chaucer, that is, survivals of other inflexions than OE *-es*: e.g. *for youre fader kin*, Nun's Priest's Tale 148; *in his lady grace*, Prologue 88.

---

[203] Tolkien's "Chaucerian Grammar" is Bodleian MS Tolkien A 14/2 (2), fols. 73–119.

Chaucer still preserves rather more "endingless plurals" (ordinarily old neuter nouns) than we do; thus not only *swin*, *scheep*, *deer*, but also *hors* (*his hors were gode.* Prologue 74); but always pl. *fissches*, since this is an old masculine noun (OE *fiscas*). *Furlong* is also an old neuter, and we have *two furlong*, 246. But the use of an uninflected plural is frequently found after *numerals* with all kinds of nouns. So in RT, *a hundred time* 76, *ten foot* 221, *twenty foot* 204, *twenty deuel* 337, *of twenty yeer* 50.

> NOTE. This usage, which is a feature of syntax not accidence, is of complex origin. It is partly due to the existence of (neuter) uninflected plurals, such as *furlong* and *yeer* in the examples above. But in Old English nouns preceded by the decades (20, 30, etc.) and by 100, 1000, which were originally themselves nouns not adjectives, were followed by the genitive plural in -*a*, as *twentig fota* (not *fet*); and in expressions of measurement the noun of measure was in the genitive plural. As *six fota lang* "long of six feet".
>
> Different again is the use of the "distributive singular" when the same part or feature of each member of a group is affected. This is seen in *side* 99, *ye* 129. In Old and Middle English the only correct form of expression was *he moved all men's heart* or *they lifted up their hand*. If *hearts* or *hands* were substituted, it would imply that each man had more than one heart, or that they voted by each lifting up both hands. So if Chaucer had written *sides* in 99, it would have meant that Alain and Jon had two swords each.

2. Adjectives

Adjectives were originally inflected even more fully than nouns, but the modern situation, in which they are only inflected for "comparison" (with -*er*, -*est*), had already practically been reached in Chaucer's time. But in his verse *monosyllabic* adjectives, of native or foreign origin, still employ an inflection -*ë* in the following cases: (a) to mark the plural. (b) in the so-called "weak" form, which appeared after a demonstrative (*the*, *this*, *that*), or after the possessives (*my*, *thy*, *his*, *her*, *our*, *your*). (c) in the vocative.

- (a) *plural* are: *greye* 54, *brode* 55, *yongë pourë* 82, *grete and smale* 403.
- (b) *weak* are: *the wichë* 3, *this godë* 309, *the proudë* 398, *his, thin, ownë* 219, 325, *this schortë* 245, *the longë* 315, *the whitë* 382. Both plural and weak is *falsë* in *the false clerkes* 371. The -*e* in *atte fulle* 16, *laste* 92, 186, *beste* 227, is of the same origin (*atte* = at the).
- (c) *vocative* are: *godë* 327, *falsë* 348, 349.

> NOTE. Many adjectives that have since (by loss of final -*e*) become monosyllabic still in Chaucer's day had as their normal uninflected form a final -*e* that was in origin part of their stem. These have -*e* in all positions and cannot show inflexion. So *wilde* 252 (normal), 345, 161 (plural). Other adjectives of this sort are: *dere*, *softe*, *swete*, *thikke*, *thenne* (*thinne*), and many French adjectives like *noble*, *propre*, *straunge*, *nice*.

3. Adverbs

Some adjectives are used as adverbs without inflexion (these were originally neuter accusatives, like Latin *verum*): so *right* 143 etc., *wrang* 332. Some have the old (Old English) inflexion -*e*, that has since been lost, as *harde*, *depe* 311, *sore* 309, *faire* 101, 160, 185, 274, *late* 276, *stille* 279, *hye* 61 (the uninflected adj. is *high*), *foule* 300. When the adjective normally ends in -*e* (see above) the inflected and uninflected forms cannot be distinguished: so *softe*, adj., *softe* adv. 293, 341.

Usually the ending -*ly* is added, as *softëly* 138; also to borrowed (French) words, as: *curteisly*, *hardily*. This -*ly* is a reduction of older -*liche*, which still appears in Chaucer, as in *namëliche* "especially" 69.

In the superlative adjectives and adverbs were already alike in Old English, the ending being -*est*, -*ost* (Chaucer -*est*). In the comparative, adjectives should have had the ending -*re* (OE -*ra*), and the adverbs the ending -*er* (OE -*or*); but the same ending was used in both cases, either usually -*er*, or less commonly -*re*. *bettrë* in 163 is an adverb.

Old English had a few comparative adverbial forms without any -*or* ending: so *betera* "better", *bet* adv.; *mára* "greater", *má* adv.; *lang* "long", *lengra* "longer", *leng* adv. These survive in Chaucer as *bet*, *mo* (*moo*), *leng*. So *bet* adv. "better" 375; *mo* in *euer-mo* 41 (Northern *euermaa* 315). But the adverbial forms were also used predicatively after the verb "to be", as *bet* 224, while the adjectival forms were also used as adverbs as *more* 76. *mo* survives chiefly in adjectival use in the sense "more (in number)", as distinguished from *more* "more (in quantity)"; so *mo* in 50. In this use *mo*, *moe* survived to the XVIIth century. In Chaucer *leng*, which he sometimes uses, is already being replaced by *lenger*, as in 371 (contrast *leng* in the Reeve's Prologue 18); the modern form *longer* with abandonment of the vowel change is post-Chaucerian (*lenger* still survived in the Tudor period).

4. Pronouns

The personal pronouns of Chaucer (apart from a few details of spelling) are the same as those of Modern English, except in the following points:

In the third person plural Chaucer already uses as the nominative form *they* (of Norse origin); but he never, except in representing dialectal speech, uses *th-* forms in the oblique case (modern *them*) or the possessive (modern *their*). For *them* he uses *hem*. For *their* he uses *hir*, *her* identical in form with the feminine singular. It was this awkward similarity which caused the form *thair their* to be adopted in London English, probably when Chaucer was an old man, so that it came into use in the XVth century. The form *thaim* (or, blended with the native form, *them*) was slower in being adopted, and has never actually quite driven out *hem* from our colloquial language. In such colloquial expressions as *give 'em beans* we should really write *hem*; for it is not *th* that is omitted but the *h* of *hem*, as is equally the case in colloquial *him, his, her* (unstressed).

> NOTE. Note that the Northern Clerks use *thair, thaim*; and some of the MSS represent the Reeve as using *thair, theyre* occasionally (e.g. *on thair wey* 390). It was from the Scandinavianized Northern and Eastern regions that first *thay, they* and later *thair, their* invaded the capital.

In the second person plural the nominative is still always *ye*, the form *you, yow* being only accusative and dative (corresponding to *us* not to *we*). When addressing a single person, the forms *thow, thee, thy, thin* were still in normal colloquial use. But the "polite" use of the plural forms in addressing a single person (probably in origin a bad French habit) had long been the custom; so much so that this use was no longer specially polite, and in Chaucer, as in the XIVth century generally, we find *ye* and *thow* used more or less indiscriminately in the same speech. In other words *ye, yow* had become in the singular mere variants of *thow, thee* (which were never used in the plural); and the final result of this tiresome habit was simply that English lost the useful singular form for all practical daily purposes. But the curious (accidental) reversal by which *ou, ow* appeared in the nominative in the singular *thou*, but in the accusative-dative in the plural *you*, probably assisted in producing the modern use of *you* as the normal nominative. Contrariwise Quakers use *thee* as the nominative singular.

In RT, it may be noted that Alain says *thy* to the miller 103, but Jon says *yow, ye* 112; while later Jon 208ff. uses both *thow* and *yow* to the miller, and in 125 Alain uses *ye* even to his fellow clerk, 125, although he had begun with *wiltu = wilt thou*.

who is not used as a proper relative in Chaucer. The relative is *that* (*God that sitteth high in magestee* 402). This is frequently omitted as in modern English: as *a collegge men clepen* 80. So also is the conjunction *that*: as *dorste leye hir nekke the miller scholde nat* 89. *which* (or in imitation of French *li quel*) *the whiche* (as in line 3) is also used, chiefly after prepositions as in 3, 75, 79.

> NOTE. Not represented in RT is the use of *whos* "whose" and *whom* "whom" as relative (possessive and dative).

self has in all number the variants *self, selue, seluen*: as *himseluen* 107, *hirselue* 221.

Before *oon, other* the article may assume the form *that* (originally the neuter form), as in *that oon, that other* 93. Hence modern colloquial *the tone, the tother*.

5. Verbs

The reasons for the variations in Chaucerian verbal forms and their divergence from those now in use can usually only be understood in reference to earlier Middle English and to Old English. In general it is true to say that in the case of variation one form will be older, nearer to Old English, and the other an alteration (often in Chaucer's day a recent alteration) and nearer to modern English: so *legge* "lay" (Old English *lecgan*) 17, beside *leye* (Modern lay) 89. This infinitive *leye* is due to a normalization of the older and in Chaucer's day apparently "irregular" paradigm *leggen* to lay; *I legge, thow leist, he leith* (100); *we, ye, they legge*; subjunctive *legge, leggen*; past tense *leíde*.

Where Chaucer differs from Modern English this is almost always because he preserves an older form that has since been altered or lost. Thus it has been a general tendency for old "strong" (on this see below) verbs to become "weak" (that is, form a past tense with *t d*). So we now say *creep, crept*; *help, helped*. But Chaucer said *crepen* 330, *creep* 306, 340, and past participle *cropen* 339 (nearer to OE *créopan, créap, cropen*); similarly he said *halpen, heelp* 326, *holpen* (nearer to OE *helpan, healp, holpen*).

In *wered* 383 the exception proves the rule. We now say *worn*, a "strong" form; but actually *wear* is a rare example of a "strong" verb in modern English that was originally "weak"; it has been made to conjugate like the old strong verb *bear*, with which it rhymes. Chaucer's *wered* is older and is the same as Old English *wered*.

NOTE. In a few cases Modern English has a form that differs from the one usually found in Chaucer but is equally old. So *fil* 331 beside modern *fell*; *fond* 297 beside modern *found*. These depend either on divergent development from a common older form (the OE for "fell" was *féoll*) or on a variation already present in Old English itself. (OE had both *funde* and *fond, fand* as the pa. t. ag. of *findan* find).

Here are a few notes that will help in the understanding of the verbal system of Chaucer, and of earlier periods, and also explain some of the changes that have since taken place.

Classes of Verbs

The primary division in English verbs, of all periods, is into *Strong Verbs* and *Weak Verbs*. The *Strong* verbs are those which we now consider "irregular"; their chief mark is the formation of the past tense by interior change (a different vowel appears, as in *drive, drove*), not by the addition of any suffix; the past participle in modern English shows either interior vowel-change, or addition of the suffix *en, n* or both (as *drink, drunk*; *shake, shaken*; *write, written*).

The *Weak* verbs are marked by the use of a suffix *ed, d*, or *t* to form both the past tense and the past participle: as *love, loved*; *send, sent*. Vowel-change is also sometimes seen, as in *creep, crept*, but if there is addition of *d* or *t*, the verb is "weak".

The *strong* verbs were anciently divided into about six main "patterns", each having a distinct series of vowel-changes. Some of these were still fairly well preserved in Chaucer's language, and one or two survive today: as *drive, drove, driven; drink, drank, drunk*.

The *weak* verbs can be divided (as far as concerns Middle English and Modern English) into two main divisions: (1) the Contracted verbs; and (2) the Uncontracted.

In Division 1, the suffix *t, d* was added straight on to the stem without any intervening vowel (in Middle and Modern English this vowel is *e*). This addition caused changes in the stem, some very old as in *tell, told*; some more recent as in *creep, crept; leave, left*. In some cases the suffix *t, d* disappeared or was blended with the last consonant of the stem, as in *set, set; send, sent*.

In Division 2, which we now regard as the Regular Conjugation and use as the model for all new or borrowed verbs, the suffix is *-ed*, and the stem remains unchanged throughout the conjugation.

NOTE. Modern spelling may here be taken as a rough guide, as it refers to an older stage of language. The present usage, whereby *ed* is no longer a syllable, except after *t* or *d* (as *graded, imitated*), and sometimes acquires the pronunciation *t* (as in *licked, slipped, kissed, nursed, quaffed, knifed*, etc.) is post-medieval. At an earlier period the suffix *ed* was always a syllable, as it is still where it is used adjectivally as in *wicked, beloved*; and often in the more archaic language of verse.

In Modern English as a rule the Contracted form only survives where some resultant change of stem has also been preserved and the verb has thus become "irregular", as in *hear, heard; weep, wept*; but not in *deemed, kissed*; though these were all originally Contracted Verbs: Chaucerian *heren, herde; wepen, wepte; demen, demde; kissen, kiste*. One of the causes of the confusion, older than the modern contraction of *kissed* to *kist*, was the fact that many old Contracted Verbs had a past participle (*not* past tense) in syllabic *ed*; this was the case actually with most verbs whose stems ended in some other consonant than *t* or *d*: so past tense *demde*, but past participle *demed*. Already in Chaucer we find the tendency to regularize this by having either contracted forms throughout (as *heren, herde, herd* "hear", where the older language had pp. *hered*), or uncontracted throughout (as *demede, demed*). But Chaucer still has *wenen, weenen* "ween, suppose", past tense *wende, weende*, pp. *wened* or *wend*.

Strong Verbs originally distinguished four main stems: 1 the Present Stem; 2 Past Stem (a), used only in the 2 and 3 person of the singular; 3 Past Stem (b), used in the rest of the tense; and 4 Past Participle.

Here are some examples of the main patterns:

	1	2	3	4	Class
Old English	wrĭtan	wrát	writon	ge-writen	I
	write	(I) wrote	(they) wrote	written	
Chaucerian	write (n)	wroot	write(n)	y-write(n)	
Old English	céosan	céas	curon	ge-coren	II
	choose	(I) chose	(they) chose	chosen	
Chaucerian	cheese(n)	chees	chose(n)	y-chose(n)	
Old English	drincan	dranc	druncon	druncen	III
	drink	drank	drank, pl.	drunk	
Chaucerian	drinke(n)	drank, dronk	dronke(n)	y-dronke(n)	
Old English	beran	bær	bǽron	ge-boren	V
	bear	bore	bore, pl.	borne, born	
Chaucerian	bere(n)	bar	bere(n), bare(n) *	y-bore, -born	
Old English	scacan	scóc	scócon	scacen, scæcen	VI
	shake	shook	shook	shaken	
Chaucerian	schake(n)	schook	schoke(n)	y-schake(n)	
Old English	fallan	féoll	féollon	fallen	VII
	fall	fell	fell	fallen	
Chaucerian	falle(n)	fel, fil	felle(n), fille(n)	y-falle(n)	

NOTE. The rare Class IV is omitted above. It was a variety of V in which instead of the vowel *o* in Stem 4 (past participle) the vowel of the infinitive appeared. To this class belong our *eat, eaten*; Chaucer *ete, eten*; OE *etan, eten*.

It will be noticed that though the verbs as a whole distinguish the four stems, they are not all distinct in any one pattern or Class; only Classes II and V distinguish all four. In Classes I and III stems 2 and 4 are alike; in Classes VI and VII stems 1 and 4 are alike. There has in consequence been a tendency in the development of English for the vowels of the past tense plural (and so of the past tense as a whole, when the distinction between sg. and pl. was given up) and past participle to be made alike, even when this was not anciently so. This was assisted by the similarity of the past tense and the past participle in the weak verbs. So we see already in ME in Class II the *o* of the past pple. driving out the older *u* of the Stem 3; while in Modern English it has invaded the whole past tense; similarly in Modern English the *o* of Stem 4 has invaded both Stems 3 and 2 in the case of *bear* (and similarly in other verbs of the same Class, *wear, break, speak*).

* In Old English the vowel of the Infinitive was short, and that of Stem 3 was long; but by Chaucer's day all vowels had been lengthened in dissyllables like *bere(n)*, where the stem-vowel was followed by a single consonant, so *bĕren > bēren*.

The Distinction between Stems 2 and 3 was usually maintained in Chaucerian English, where one had anciently existed, as in Classes I, II, III, (IV), V. But already in Class V (and IV) the *a* of the singular was being transferred to the plural, principally because here the older form *beren* was no longer distinguishable from the infinitive and present plural,* so *baren* for *beren*, *spaken* (after *spak* 102, 341) for *speken*. The distinction was (in Southern Middle English) best maintained in Classes I and III.

The Strong Verbs had in Old and early Middle English four stems: 1(a) the Infinitive Stem used in the whole of the Present Tense, except as in the next; 1(b) the Stem of the 2 and 3 person singular indicative; 2(a) past, 1 and 3 person singular only; 2(b) past; the stem of all the remaining tense, 2 sg. the pl. and the subjunctive.

These newer Middle English forms *bare*, *spake*, *brake* are the ancestors of the earlier Modern English forms of the same spelling, used for both singular and plural; but now in turn replaced in ordinary speech by *bore*, *spoke*, *broke* with vowel of the past participle.

Northern Middle English abandoned the distinction between the two past tense stems earlier than did the Southern language; so in Northern dialect *band*, *drank*, for Chaucer's *bond* and *bounden*, *drank* and *dronken*. In modern standard English the distinction has long disappeared. Sometimes the Stem 2 has survived, as in *sang*, *drank*, *wrote*; sometimes the Stem 3 as in *slung*, *slunk*, *bit*, or archaic *bare*; sometimes a new vowel either derived from the Stem 4, as in *bore*, *chose*; or taken from a different Class, as in our *wove* (weave), *hove* (heave), Chaucer's *haf*, *waf*. The hesitations in earlier modern English, sometimes still preserved today, as between *wrote/writ*; *sang*, *rang/sung*, *rung* are derived from the old distinction of two past tense stems. But the use of *drank* as a past participle or of (say) *done* as a past tense, is a newer development, due to the tendency to regularize the verbal system, so that, whether formed in the "strong" or the "weak" manner, there shall be only one form functioning as both past tense and past participle. *drank* as past tense and *done* as past participle are still considered "incorrect" or vulgar; but they are no different in principle from the now well established use of the past tenses *held* and *sat* as past participles instead of Chaucerian *holde(n)*, *yholde* (archaic modern English *holden*) and *sete*.

Inflexions

The inflexions of *Strong* and *Weak* verbs differed very little. The chief difference was that whereas in Weak verbs the 2 sg. of the past tense had the same inflexion as the present, *-est* (so *herest* hearest, *herdest* heardest), in the Strong verbs the 2 sg. of the past tense took the Stem 3 (as in the plural) and the inflexion *-e* (so *dronke* drankest, *bounde* boundest).

Here are the normal inflexions of Chaucerian verbs, exemplified by *Finde*, Class III Strong; *Here*, Contracted Weak; and *Loue*, Uncontracted Weak:

	Indicative	Subjunctive	Imperative
Present Sg.	1 *finde, here, loue*	*finde, here, loue*	
	2 *findest, herest, louest*	" " "	*find, her, loue*
	3 *findeth, hereth, loueth*	" " "	
Pl.	*finden, heren, louen*	*finden, heren, louen*	*findeth, hereth, loueth*
Infinitive	*finden, heren, louen*	Present Participle	*findinge, heringe, louinge*
Past Sg. 1&3	*fond herde louede*	*founde, herde, louede*	
2	*founde herdest louedest*	" " "	
Pl.	*founden herden loueden*	*founden, herden, loueden*	
	Past Participle	*y-founden; y-herd, y-loued.*	

NOTE 1. In the 2 and 3 sg present indicative, contracted forms, without the medial vowel *e*, are frequently met, in Strong Verbs and Contracted Weak Verbs, *not* in Uncontracted Verbs like *loue*. These forms are commonest when the stem of the verb ends in *t* or *d*, and *t-th*, *d-th* then become *t*, so *fint* for *findeth*, *last* for *lasteth*; *bit* for *bideth* and *biteth* and *biddeth*. Similarly where the stem ends in *s*: *rist* for *riseth*. Other forms are *berth*, *herth*, *comth* for *bereth*, *hereth*, *cometh*. Where the stem ends in *y/i* the contracted form is the usual or only one employed: as *leyen* "lay", *lien*, *lyen* "lie", *seyen*, *sayen* "say", which make *leist*, *leith*; *list* (*lyst*), *lith* (*lyth*); *seist*, *seith*.

These contractions are of ancient origin, and frequently preserve other archaic features, as the change in vowel in *it* "eats" beside *eteth* (cf. German *essen, iszt*); or the strange consonant in *lixt* "thou liest (speakest untruth)", from OE *legan* "to tell a lie", 2 sg. *lígst*, *líhst*. The vowel in these contracted forms was, where it was long in the uncontracted form, shortened. Where the vowel of the uncontracted form was *o* derived from older *ā*, the shortening (which was older than the Southern change of *ā* to *ō*) produces *a*; so *stant* "stands" for *stondeth*; *halt* "holds" for *holdeth*.

NOTE 2. In the imperative singular forms with a final *-e* are found occasionally in all kinds of verbs. In the imperative plural singular forms are often used (cf. the confusion between *thow* and *ye* noted above). So *lat* 205 and *make* 206 although the pronoun used by the Miller is *ye*.

NOTE 3. The 2 sg. of the past tense subjunctive properly has no *-st*, even in Weak Verbs; but in the Weak Verbs (not the strong) the indicative ending sometimes invades the subjunctive.

NOTE 4. The 2 sg. of the strong past tense (represented above by *founde*) was already changing in Chaucer's day, and in the MSS we find monosyllabic forms like *thow took*; and the intrusion of Stem 2, as *thow drank*. The addition of *-st* was probably post-Chaucerian, but already appears in the MSS, as *bigonnest* beside *begonne*. These later forms can seldom be shown, by metre or rhyme to be Chaucerian. Usually they are shown by these tests to be alterations of his text, but he certainly seems, for instance, to have written *thow took* (monosyllable) in the Book of the Duchess, 483.

The above system of inflexions may be taken as the norm, but before the usage of Chaucer can be understood the following points require to be noted:

1. Final *n* can only be used where it appears above: namely in the *plural* of all verbs, in all tenses of the indicative and subjunctive (*not* imperative); in the infinitive of all verbs; and in the *strong* past participle. It cannot be added elsewhere: **I finden*, or **thow founden* are impossible. But it can always be omitted, so that, for instance, *finde* can appear as the plural or the infinitive; or *founde* in the past tense plural or the past pple.

2. Final *-e*, including *-e* standing for *-en*, is omitted (elided) before a following word that begins with a vowel or with *h*. So *couth'* 7, *dorst'* 12, *thay wold'* 42, *to yeu' hem* 87, etc. This final *-e* is also slurred, or omitted, and so does not count as a metrical syllable, in other cases, i.e. even when a consonant follows. The chief cases are:—

(a) Verbal forms in frequent use, especially forms of the verb "to be" and other auxiliaries like *schal, wol, haue*; so *schold'* 66, *wer'* (pl.) 82, 94, *might' thay* 173, *hadd'* 383 (actually written *had* 315, in some MSS).

NOTE. In some words this reduced form has become normal and is usually represented in spelling: so *wol* "will" for older *wole* (also used occasionally), or in the plural *wol* 115, *woln* for older *wollen*; similarly *schul* pl. 201. *Hauen* as infinitive or plural is usually reduced to and written *han* 163, 170, 201, 302, 307 etc.

Other cases occur, as *yeu'* 238, *herd'* 248, *weend'* 381, all before following *th-*. But in such cases corruption of Chaucer's text may often be suspected. Thus in 93 he probably used the forms *hight* or *heet*, which appear elsewhere in his works and are actually older than *highte*. In 80 Chaucer almost certainly wrote *set* "sets", a contracted present (explained above); cf. *craketh*.

(b) In long forms, that is in words of three or more syllables. Thus the present participle is usually scanned as *-ing'* with omitted *e*, and is often so written, as *dwelling* 5.

In verbs whose past tense ends in *-ede* (that is verbs which belong to or have joined the Uncontracted Weak Class) the final *e* of the inflexions is frequently suppressed, and often omitted in writing (as *happed* 72). This is most usual where the stem of the verb is long (i.e. contains a vowel long in Old

English or Old Norse or Old French, or ends in more than one consonant, as *senden*); in such cases trisyllabic forms (according to the metre) are not common: but *nedëdë* appears 100, 241.

Another method of dealing with these trisyllabic verbal forms was to slur or omit not the inflexion but the medial *e*. This occurred most frequently where the stem of the verb ended in a vowel (as *crien*; *criede* > *cride* 387). Other cases, such as Chaucer's past tense *clepte* called, beside *cleped*, are rather to be regarded as transferences of verbs from the Uncontracted *loue*-class to the Contracted *here*-class (so Chaucer has also the past pple. *y-clept* beside *y-cleped*). *Maken* however shows the curious contracted form *made* beside *makede* (and past pple. *y-mad*, *y-maad*, beside *y-maked*). *Made* occurs in RT 60, 79, 219; and *ymaked* in 325.

3. Prefix *y-*. This can only normally be used in the past participle. Its use with the present participle by Spenser (and so derivatively by Milton, as in *ypointing*) is due to ignorant imitation of Chaucer.

> NOTE. But Spenser's mistake is not as bad as is often supposed. There was no essential connexion between the prefix *y-* (derived from Old English *ge-*) and the past participle. The prefix had in OE given the sense of completion, as the modern addition of *up* or *out* may, in *break up*, *find out*. This was specially suitable to the past participle, but could apply to other parts of the verb, and in OE *ge-* was in fact very frequently used in all parts of certain verbs. Some of these survived in Chaucer's language. So we have occasionally *yfinde*, *yhere*, *ysee*, *yknowe* beside *finde*, *here*, *knowe*, *see*; and though it does not actually occur, *yheringe* for "hearing" would not be an impossible Chaucerian form. But it remains true that apart from a few words (the four chief ones are given above), and a few adjectives like *y-nogh* "enough", *y-sene* "visible", the prefix *y-* was in Chaucer's language limited to the past participle. Nonetheless the poets have lost a very useful aid to scansion by its disappearance.

This prefix is not added to verbs that already have another prefix: so *to-broke* "broken up" 355, *for-dronken* 230, *be-soght* 198, *be-guiled* 401, *a-feerd* 175. This applies also to borrowed words with Latin or French prefixes: as *dispended* 63, *descended* 64. The prefix can also be omitted in other cases: so *piled* 15, 386; *sakked* 150, *quit* 404, *knit* 163, *lerned* 202, *vernisched* 229, *set* 238, *bibbed* 242, *caght* 307, *lad* "led" 312, *hit* 385, *waked* 364, *payed* 395, *wered* 383, *said* 399; *hoten* 21, *slain* 39, *founde* 139, *take* 173, *born* 94, *dronken* 238, *swonken* 315, *cropen* 339, *falle* 363, 368, *broken* 369, beside *y-fostred*, 26, *-spred* 220, *-maked* 325, *-sped* 300, *-wet* 235, *-bounde* 140, 150 (but *bounden* 33), *-comen* 22, *-growen* 53, *-ronne* 170, *-grounde* 71, 88, 149, *-bake* 392, *-bete* "beaten" 393, *-lorn* 394.

> NOTE. It will be noted that the forms without the inflexional *-n* mostly have the prefix *y-*; but *founde*, *falle*, *take* occur without either. With strong past participles Chaucer had the

advantage over modern poets; he had four forms to choose from, *yfounde, yfounden, founde, founden,* and he could also elide the final *-e* of *founde* or *yfounde.*

6. Irregular and Auxiliary Verbs

From the point of view of Modern English the principal of these are *be, have, do, go;* and the group known as preterite-presents (because in Old and Middle English their present tenses resembled strong past tenses) *shall* (to which *will* originally of a different sort was assimilated in Middle English); *may, can, dare,* and the obsolescent *wot;* also *must.*

The irregularities that these verbs still show are of ancient origin and so naturally also appear in Chaucer (e.g. *was,* pl. *were*); but Chaucer still preserves a few forms that have since disappeared.

BE. Infin. *been (ben, be).* The present sg. is as in Modern English. The plural, however, was in Chaucer the same as the infinitive; so *been* "are" 41, 134. The MSS (very rarely) present the form *arn;* but Chaucer probably himself only used the forms *been (ben, bee).* The imperative pl. is *beeth.* The plural *-n* can be added in the past tense, which may thus take the form *weren, were* 82, 94, etc., and occasionally *wern.* The past tense subjunctive is *were.* Note that the 2 sg. of the past is *were* (not *wert*).

HAVE. This is conjugated as in Modern English with the substitution of *-th* for *-s (hath* "has" 67, 173, etc.). The imperative plural is *haveth.* In the present, if the inflexion *-n* is used, the contracted form *han* appears, as infinitive 163, 201, 307, 385; and as pl. 170, 302, 312. The past tense is *hadde,* often reduced in pronunciation and sometimes in writing to *had* 315 (as described above).

DO. This is conjugated as in Modern English, but the vowel of the stem was still long in all forms of the present and in the past pple., and the *o* was usually (not always) written *double.* So Chaucerian *doo, doost, dooth,* pl. *doon;* subjunctive *doo, doon;* imperative *doo,* pl. *dooth;* infinitive *doon (doo);* past pple. *doo(n)* and *y-doon, y-do.* The past tense was *dide,* often reduced to a monosyllable (as *hadde*).

GO. This is conjugated like Do, but the stem vowel differed in quality. The *o, oo* of Go was the "open *o*", like that in modern *awe, door, cause.* In the past tense *wente* 37, 239, 291 was already in use; but though it does not occur in RT., Chaucer also commonly uses the now lost form *yede* (OE *éode*).

SHALL. The Chaucerian forms are *schal, schalt, schal;* and in the plural an archaic change of vowel is preserved *schulle(n).* This form, as described above, is often reduced to *schuln schul* 201. The past tense is *scholde.*

WILL. The Chaucerian forms are *wole, wolt, wole*; pl. *wollen*. The *-e* is usually omitted, so *wol* 132–3 etc.; *wollen* (cf. *schullen*) is usually reduced to *woln, wol* 115. In the MSS forms with the vowel *i* as in Modern English also appear. These are the forms usual in the northerly and easterly dialects (they are used by the Clerks 109, 116, 120, etc.). Whether Chaucer himself used both forms cannot now be determined. The *wol-* form survives in the modern colloquial negative form *won't* from Chaucerian *wol nat*. In the negative form the present stem vowel is always *i*: so *nil* 56. In the past tense the vowel is always *o*, *wolde* 32, 39, 42, etc. The past pple. is *wold*.

MAY. This still usually means "can, am able to". The modern sense as in *I may go*, meaning "It is possible that I may (or shall) go", or as a kind of subjunctive auxiliary after *that, so that, in order that*, is derived from the subjunctive of MAY, which had however already in Chaucerian English become indistinguishable in form from the indicative. The Chaucerian forms are: *may, might, may*; pl. *mowen, mowe*. For the old (very irregular) 2 sg. *might*, which had the same form as the past tense without a final *-e*, the newer form *maist, mayst, mayest* is usually substituted (at any rate by the MSS). For the present tense plural the singular form *may* also appears. The infinitive is *mowen*. The past tense is *mighte*, sometimes reduced to *might'* 197 (see the remarks above).

CAN. The proper sense of this verb is "know", a sense that still frequently survives in Chaucer. Another sense is "to get to know, learn", a sense that still survives, though it is given the different form *con*. From the sense "know how to, have the skill or knowledge to" is derived the modern leading sense "can, am able" already developed in Chaucerian English. A good example occurs in RT. 203 *ye conne by argumentes make a place* = "you (being philosophers) have the skill to make".

The Chaucerian forms are: *can, canst, can*; plural *connen, conne* (for which the singular form *can* also appears). The subjunctive is *conne, connen*; and the infinitive *conne(n)*. The past tense is *couthe* 7, for which the newer form (with *de* from more regular past tenses) *coude* also appears. The past pple. is *couth*, chiefly adjectival and only in the sense "known, well-known, familiar"; only the negative form now survives in *uncouth*.

NOTE. The *o* in *conne, connen* is graphic *o* for *u*; cf. the modern derived noun *cunning*, and adj. *cunning*; Chaucerian *conninge* knowledge, learning, skill; skilful.

DARE. This has now become regular. The Chaucerian forms are: *dar, darst, dar*; plural **dorren *durren*, reduced to *dor*, or replaced by the singular *dar* (the plural forms seldom occur). The past tense is *dorste* 12, 17, 36, 38 or *durste*. The infinitive is *dorren, durren*. The verbal noun *durring, dorring* "daring, course" also occurs.

> NOTE. In *Troilus and Criseyde* V 837 occurs the following: *Troilus was never unto no wight. in no degree secounde in dorring don that longeth to a knight*, meaning that Troilus was second to none in daring to perform all deeds proper to a knight. From a misreading of *dorring do(n)* as *derring do*, and a misunderstanding of the passage, is derived through Spenser the bogus mediaeval word *derring-do* "chivalry, knighterrantry".

WOT. To know (facts). The Chaucerian forms are: *woot, woost, woot*; plural *wite(n)*, for which the singular *woot* sometimes appears. The infinitive is *wite(n)*; the subjunctive *wite, witen*; the imperative *wite, witeth*. The past tense is *wiste*; the past pple. *wist, y-wist*. In the negative form *n* is substituted for *w: noot*; past tense *niste* 305, 362, 380.

MUST. The Chaucerian forms are: *moot, moost (most), moot*; plural *mote(n)*. The subjunctive is *mote(n)*. The past tense is *moste*. The sense is usually "must, ought to, am obliged to" but in wishes or imprecations it is rather "may." So *moot* must 63; *moot* may 257.

4
Merton Professor of Chaucer, 1947–54

In June of 1945 when Tolkien was elected Merton Professor of Language and Literature, his lecturing duties shifted from Old English texts like *Beowulf* to Middle English works like *Sir Gawain and the Green Knight*. He had not taught Chaucer since the 1924–25 academic year at Leeds, but in Michaelmas 1947 he found himself scheduled to teach a course combining the *Clerk's Tale* and *Pardoner's Tale* because both works were required for undergraduates (SH 1:343). Neither of these works had been included in his long-stalled *Selections from Chaucer's Poetry and Prose* for the Clarendon Press, and therefore he was starting largely from scratch. But then, when the *Parlement of Foules* replaced the *Clerk's Tale* as a required text in Hilary 1948, he was able to repurpose his endnotes from the Chaucer edition for his teaching. Although Tolkien never again lectured on either work over the course of his career, he did continue lecturing on the *Pardoner's Tale* for a total of ten times until Hilary 1956, revising his notes and even changing his mind about the quality of this Chaucerian work over the years. At a gathering of the Inklings in November 1947, C. S. Lewis's brother Warren reported that Tolkien showed them a very beautiful facsimile of the early Ellesmere manuscript of the *Canterbury Tales* costing him £55, a considerable investment.[1] Skeat had relied heavily upon this manuscript as his base-copy for editing the *Canterbury Tales*, and Tolkien would consult this facsimile for his Chaucer lectures during the 1940s and 1950s, often challenging its authority as he had done already in his 1934 article "Chaucer as a Philologist".[2]

Earlier in 1945 before Tolkien knew that his future duties would include lecturing on Chaucer, he received a letter asking him if the fourteenth-century poet might have participated in the Wycliffite project of translating the Bible into English. A portion of his reply to E. H. Connor is now newly published (*Letters* 162). In the full text of the letter, Tolkien said that while

---

[1] Warren Lewis, *Brothers and Friends*, 215. This was *The Ellesmere Chaucer Reproduced in Facsimile*, ed. Egerton (1911).

[2] Carleton Brown had sent an offprint of his review of "The Text of the Canterbury Tales by John M. Manly and Edith Rickert", in *Modern Language Notes*, 55 (1940), 606–21, where Tolkien found well-documented scepticism of the Ellesmere's authority.

Chaucer had "a gift for narrative poetry", his translation of Boethius demonstrated his shortcomings in Latin and his ineptitude in prose. But in any case, the poet would not have dared to join the Wycliffite enterprise. Tolkien referred Connor to Margaret Deanesly's *Lollard Bible*, a history of the vernacular project and its thorough entanglement with heresy. Chaucer showed "great familiarity with the Old and New Testaments", she concludes, but only as an amateur scholar familiar with "the other great reference books of the age".[3] Terry Jones's book *Who Murdered Chaucer?* has made the case that the poet operated in an anti-Lollard environment of increasing danger that might even have ended his life in foul play: "Lines that read wittily in the 1370s might seem problematic in the 1380s and perilous ten years later."[4] Tolkien was alert to these hazards as well. Chaucer, he wrote, "had not the energy or the time to finish his own proper projects, let alone take on a vast project, which would have broken him, if it did not land him in gaol or at the stake!" (*Letters* 162). During subsequent years when lecturing on excerpts from the *Canterbury Tales*, potentially the poet's most subversive work, Tolkien steadily focused upon a variety of non-political topics such a source studies and editorial cruces, consistent in the position already recorded in his 1914 undergraduate notes (see p. 19 above): "Wyclif no Wyclifite nor Chaucer a Wyclifite."

The Clerk's Tale (1947)

Tolkien began his first lecture notes on Chaucer's *Clerk's Tale* on the reverse sides of pages torn from student exam booklets, and later he supplemented this sketchy pencil-written draft with ink insertions between lines and in the margins (Bodleian MS Tolkien A 13/2, fols. 5–38). Because the English Faculty switched the required Chaucerian text to the *Parlement of Foules* in Hilary 1948, Tolkien was never again assigned the tale of Patient Griselda and therefore never transcribed these lectures in a more legible fair copy. Blue-ink additions and even whole new pages may represent revisions during the 1947 term, or they may have been added in Trinity 1957 if he again used these notes when teaching a class entitled "The Language of Chaucer" for which no independent lecture materials appear to survive. Professors routinely recycle old lectures when they can, revising and expanding them as necessary. For these 1947

---

[3] Margaret Deanesly, *The Lollard Bible and Other Medieval Biblical Versions* (Cambridge: Cambridge University Press, 1920), 224.
[4] Terry Jones with Robert Yeager, Terry Dolan, Alan Fletcher, and Juliette Dor, *Who Murdered Chaucer? A Medieval Mystery* (New York: St. Martin's Press, 2003), 226.

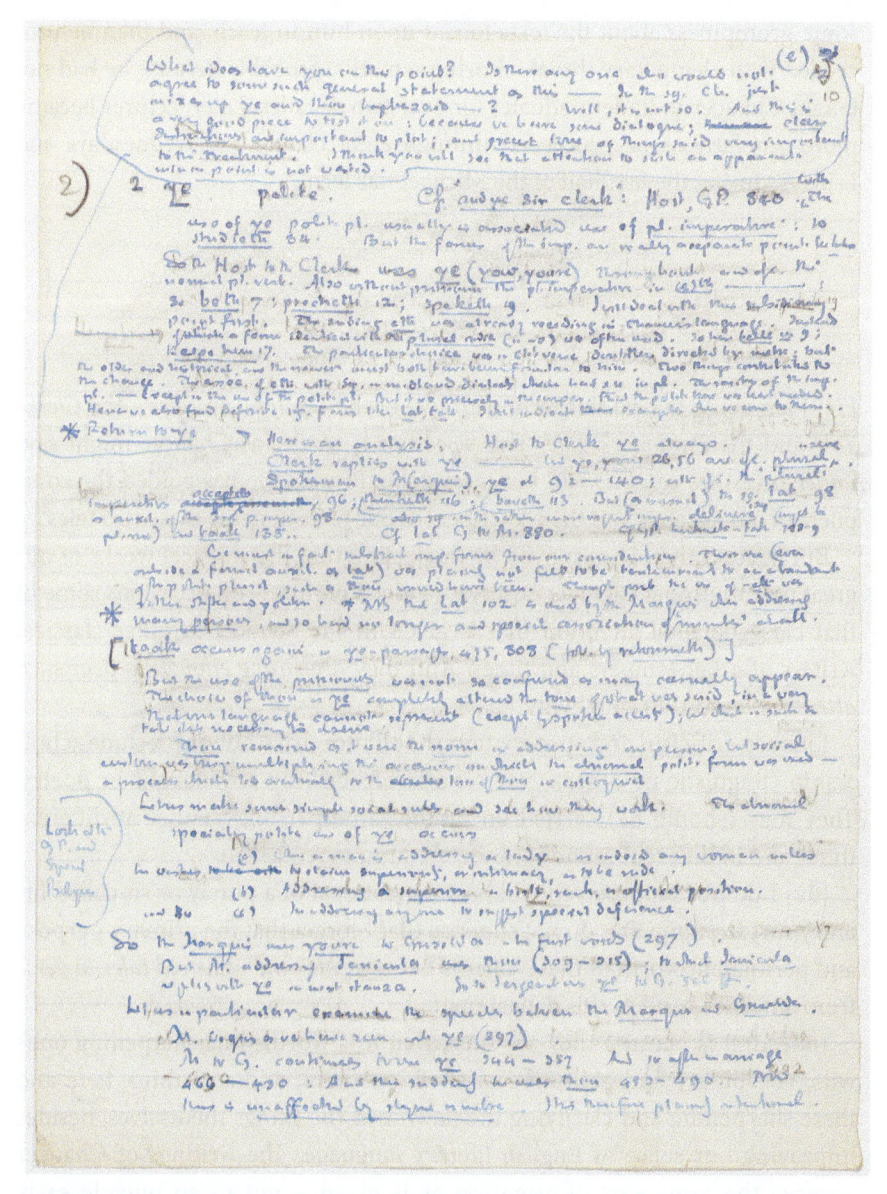

Fig. 10 Ink notes over erased pencil draft in *Clerk's Tale* lecture (Bodleian MS Tolkien A 13/2, fol. 10).

lectures, as with Tolkien's others, readability has been the primary factor in our selection of passages, and his notes are especially challenging when he erased his pencil drafts and overwrote them in ink (fig. 10). Often our ellipses signal the omission of whole pages. For his opening remarks, Tolkien began with some grumpiness about the texts forced upon him to teach, and then he proceeded with elementary throat-clearing remarks, probably because he had not taught Chaucer to undergraduates for over two decades. Later lectures became more scholarly as he proceeded through eight classes, on Wednesdays and Fridays, during the first half of the Michaelmas term.[5]

* * *

The Clerk's Tale

[5r] I am going to deal this term with two of the *Canterbury Tales* – the *Clerk's Tale* and the *Pardoner's Tale*. This selection is made (as Chaucer might say) *under necessitee condicionel*.[6] For inscrutable Providence has guided the compilers of our syllabus and the prescribers of our texts to name these two tales...

But beyond that, I am moved by the feeling that the classical works of our great narrative poet Chaucer deserve – indeed require – on occasions some of that close detailed attention that is given in the Schools to other classical writers of other tempers and times. And they *are strong enough to bear such attention*, indeed to gain by it...

Literary criticism and appreciation should not drive out or preclude scholarship (linguistic or other). Nor scholarship destroy any delight in poetry. They may (should be) carried on by the same personas, either at different times and in different moods – or better simultaneously...

[5v] I do not suppose you will hear a great deal of a purely or so-called literary sort from me. But do not suppose that I forget that the primary purpose and permanent worth of these Tales is because they are *well-told tales in verse* from a master hand in this department.

Indeed, it is because they are such, that it is worthwhile sharpening one's wits, vocabulary and grammatical sense on them; and so I think here and there sharpening and clarifying the flavour of the things themselves, besides improving our sense of English literary language. The writings of Chaucer deserve the same sort of attention as is given – not to go outside early English – to pieces of literary virtue in Anglo-Saxon, either the greater *Beowulf* or say the lesser *Wanderer* and *Maldon*....

---

[5] Tolkien's teaching duties for Michaelmas 1947 were a seminar on Middle English on Tuesdays and Thursdays; "Outline on the History of English" on Wednesdays; and "Chaucer: the 'Clerke's Tale' and the 'Pardoner's Tale'" on Wednesdays and Fridays at noon in the Examination Schools, beginning 15 October (SH 1:343).

[6] See the *Nun's Priest's Tale*: "Or if his witing streyneth nevere a del / But by *necessitee condicionel*" (*CT* VII, 4439–40).

[6r] ...Chaucer is not yet quite a closed book to those unversed in bygone idioms. Yet this has disadvantages. *His difficulty is disguised.* I do not now refer to his, or his supposed, elusive ironic temper except that I think that this is often an illusion caused by lack of precise knowledge of his idiom. I refer however merely to his idiom. *His language is more difficult and tricky than is often supposed.*

This can be tested – by those who really have any feeling for the texture of verse, for exactitude of meaning and connotation. Try to translate him into present idiom. If you take any piece at all extended, and even if you are well versed in Middle English, you will be fortunate if you do not find yourself often in doubt as to the precise meaning, the exact construction and its implications, and the like.

And so I excuse myself at once beforehand if many of my remarks may seem elementary to some of you. For even those who have proffered editions or selection for our use – and should presumably know this language – have shown themselves careless or defective...

[6v] *The Clerk's Tale*: this has of course been edited many times, and some of the separate pieces most well provided for since Mr Kenneth Sisam edited it in 1923.[7] Those that have this little (but well-stuffed) edition will need my assistance less than others...

[7r] Following my usual system, I mean to *run through the Tale* first before talking about it, though it is a piece that presents a great many points of interest in Chaucerian studies. Chaucer was proud of such learning as he had – so that he would (perhaps) have been more pleased than some authors by the analytic attention he has received, and fairly amused even when not particularly flattered. Still he was *primarily* a narrative poet. That is: the first purpose of his tales was to be tales and to be taken as such without research into sources or analogues.

(a) The background of the larger scheme of the *Canterbury Tales* was of course important, and the first thing to look at after preliminary reading.

(b) Yet of all the work expended on him, I fancy he would chiefly value the effort to understand the precise meaning and drift – and to scan him right.

Tolkien spends fols. 8–9 on fourteenth-century spelling and pronunciation of vowels before a series of new pages begins in clearer ink handwriting (see fig. 10). Here on fol. 10 he discusses Chaucer's uses of the second-person

---

[7] Chaucer, *Clerkes Tale of Oxenford*, ed. Sisam (OUP).

pronouns *ye, thou,* and *yow* as indicators of shifting social and emotional relationships between characters, principally Walter and Griselde. Walter initially addresses her as *ye*, used "when a man is addressing a lady, or indeed any women, unless he wishes to claim superiority, or intimacy, or to be rude." Then, when he tells his subjects who are complaining about having to serve her, a peasant, he calls her *thou*. When he switches back to *ye*, it is "a softening of the tone".

[11v] Now there's one *special exception* that I have kept to the last. It is I think an exception that proves the rule. It is meant to stand out – for artistic purposes.

In the speech of Griselda to Marquis 501–511, in spite of the emotion Griselda continues to use *ye*. Save only once: *Save only thee.*

This is meant to be startling – the precise emotional climax or centre of the poem. And apart from the pathos, the sob of the *thee*, it is meant to soften and humanize the story, by suggesting that under the humility and patience of Griselda's character (by nature and by living) which makes her subservient in manner, she had personal affection, love, for her husband.

[22v] *Grisildis*. It is difficult to find out anything about *proper names*, and therefore in notes etc. little attention is paid to them, but they are often very significant.

... Chaucer draws direct from *Petrarch*, and Petrarch direct from Boccaccio, and beyond that nothing is known except that clearly, from the whole inner character of the tale, we have a *folk-tale*, a fairy-story never originally intended to be *realistic* or a description of life at all. In the effective story – whatever branch of the Great Tree it may have grown on – that is where the two main characters have names *Griselda, Walter*. Now these are both Germanic = OE *Grísheld, Waldhere. It is improbable that Boccaccio therefore invented *Gualtieri, Griselda* and the names indicate that the story is descended from *Germanic* folk tale...

[23r Tolkien considers how Germanic *Grísheld* could have first arisen as an alteration of *Grimhild* using "*grís* 'grey' to suggest peasant origin".] It is at least curious that the most famous "Walter" of legend *Waldhere* or W. of Aquitaine had a lover (not at all similar) with a *Hild* name, *Hildegyth, Hiltgunt, Hildegund*.

[23v] I don't mean (of course) that there is the slightest connexion between the stories. Merely that in choosing *names* from a timeless "fairy-tale" two names (long before Boccaccio!) such as Walther and Grimhild could have been taken from hero and heroine of popular language and legend...

[26r] Generally Chaucer's alterations, expansions and contractions are done with skill: sufficient at least to hide the workings from anyone who has not the source open before him. But the total effect, even though Chaucer's own language is simpler and more natural than any Latin (let alone Petrarch's!), is a softening, slowing, a greater diffuseness. (It was far from simple or colloquial except in structure, idiom, and basis: it glistened and bristled with words that were learned, sophisticated or novel – more so than now when these words (or their like) are more familiar in writing, e.g. *Whan she translated was in swich richesse* 385.) Of this a very good example occurs here. Chaucer has again distributed *data michi hac tua filia in uxorem generum velis* so as to form the ends of adjacent stanzas 307–8, 314–15.[8] But this reduces the tension and the surprise. The last trace of the "fairy-story" mode with its sudden change of fortune like the clap of thunder evaporates...

[28r] In Petrarch (and Boccaccio) Griselda's willingness (to fall in with wishes of father and lord) is assumed.... Chaucer has softened the matter *and* greatly increased the courtesy of the Marquis...by making the Marquis first give Griselda a chance of *refusal of his offer* – even suggesting to her a polite formula for refusal "that she will think it over"...

Note the difference of handling of this procedure. For all his firm "insight" into the superiority of *virtue* (240 ff) the Marquis was a proud noble, and wished to sever his wife from her former life.

> For the scene where Griselda is stripped of her peasant clothes by woman villagers and dressed in the finery that the Marquis has brought, Tolkien discusses Boccaccio's treatment ("coarse and brutal as usual") and Petrarch's "more gentle" handling.

[29r] Chaucer (as often) is halfway. He has apparently deliberately reversed Petrarch's picture and inserted the line describing the distaste of the ladies at handling the poor clothes. He has altered Petrarch's words also (...that the Marquis wished her to bring no reminder of her former fortune) to *nothing of hir olde geere*. In fact he has transmuted lordly sentiment into snobbish disdain for mere poverty. It may be "realistic" but it is not good: it is "out of the picture". There is no snobbery in the story – for the "snobbery" which the Marquis alleges as an excuse for his first cruel test is a pure fiction. But I suspect that Chaucer was led astray – or at least had his treatment suggested – by

---

[8] Tolkien refers to the lines: "Thy doghter wol I take, er that I wende, / As for my wyf, unto hir lyves ende.../ If that thou wolt unto that purpos drawe, / To take me as for thy sone-in-lawe."

verecunde [in Petrarch] which he may have taken as *with shame*: the matrons did their task shamefacedly and quickly...

[31r] 459 *sadnesse* hardly needs a note, since this context at least would make clear to all but the most careless readers (not uncommon) that it did not mean "sadness". It never does in Chaucer. Neither does *sad* mean "sad" – i.e. sorrowful. You will find examples quoted from the 14th century of *sad* = *mournful*. For instance, NED quotes Chaucer's Knight's Tale 2127 (A 2985) *And wyth a sad visage he syked stille*. But these are contextual, examples rather of the contexts which caused the shift of sense, rather than of a shift of sense. Thus here certainly Theseus' face was "grave and serious" but not mournful – at least it was probably "sad" but that is not said. The main senses in Middle English were heavy (a) grave, serious – of behaviour, looks, or mood; (b) staid, steadfast. *sadness* here = steadfastness. Note that the phrase sadder and wiser (first in Coleridge's Ancient Mariner "a sadder and a wiser man") originally meant (and occurs in phrase *sad and wise, saddest and wisest*) grave and wise.

[32v] 547 ff. Chaucer increases pathos by making Griselde ask permission to kiss the child – though this makes Griselde too subservient. She may, according to the form of the story, keep her *vow* of acquiescence to her husband, but it is unnecessary (and I think not a good stroke) to make her treat the "sergeant" as a superior. Petrarch only says that "she calmly took up the little girl and looked at her a little, at the same time kissing her, she blessed her and made upon her the sign of the holy cross, and handed her to the retainer." There is no "lulling".

(Also, of course, though the whole scene is made "suspicious", so that Griselda might fear the worst, there is no overt threat of death to the infant. So that Chaucer again by making this express – *that she moste kisse hir child <u>er that it deyde</u>* – has, to increase the immediate pathos, done harm to the portrayal of Griselda...

> Tolkien etymologizes ME *blisse*, "from OE *blipsian, blissian* 'rejoice' or transitive 'gladden, enrich, endow'", and *blesse*, "from OE *blēdsian, bletsian* a word probably descending from heathen times and originally meaning 'to hallow' – with sacrificial blood" but concludes that Chaucer means "bless" whether he says *blesse* or *blisse*, "implying signing the children with the cross".

[33r] In this stanza we have a further puzzle. Ellesmere alone of available MSS has the order *kisse-blisses* (as in 679 where *all* have it). The others have *blisse-kisse* here. It is a pretty puzzle. If we keep Ellesmere here, Mr Kenneth

Sisam suggests that "we must assume, whenever it suits our taste, that Ellesmere (or any other chosen MS) has been corrected quite exceptionally by reference to a superior tradition, now lost".[9] This is too severe. Though Ellesmere is not quite so reliable as has sometimes been assumed, it is at least one of the best MSS we have, and to keep its readings is not the same as willfully adopting that of "any chosen" MS at whim. And surely it is possible to assume not that it has been "corrected" but that it has by chance *preserved* (*ab origine*) Chaucer's text in one point.

This is a chance which does (and is always liable to) occur in any form of tradition down different channels: that a genuine original feature may survive in one single branch only; while all others will alter often in the same direction, yet not necessarily in connexion with one another but because of the similar operation of similar causes. The similar cause might here be the one that Kenneth Sisam suggests that *blisse* was taken as "gladden" and would be felt awkward after "lulling" – of which it was really part...

[34r] I myself am inclined to accept Ellesmere for following reasons.

(1) Petrarch here has the order *kiss–bless*: though this is not a point of much value, as he has no "lulling", and envisages the action as more or less simultaneous – in second passage he has *bless – kiss*.

(2) Chaucer has, on the first occasion of the sergeant's visit, included *lulled*: not in Petrarch and so is giving more thought to the picture. Now it is as a rule very unwise to *kiss* an infant after you have "lulled" it to sleep, if you want it to go on sleeping! A point the commentary does not (I think) observe.

(3) *lulling* (in ME *only* of singing and caressing a child to sleep) is constantly associated with kissing: so that "gan the child to kisse and lulled it" is natural: the other order not. (See quotes with Lull in NED.)

All these points *might* be the ones that caused Ellesmere to "improve" Chaucer. But this would be to make a scribe more perceptive and skilled than Chaucer, a thing I find harder to believe than that one branch of a complex tradition may have preserved a detail unaltered.

Note that by introducing *lulled* Chaucer has as often *slowed* the thing up. The cruel sergeant would hardly have waited for a dandling and lullaby!

In one final test, Walter announces he has a new wife and orders Griselda to go back to her father, taking her dowry with her. According to Petrarch, she

---

[9] Sisam, ed., *The Clerkes Tale*, 55, actually begins "The alternative is to assume, whenever it suits our taste..."

brought nothing as dowry except her virginity. Chaucer repeats a line to the same effect, but also says the dowry included her old peasant smock. Tolkien notes the inconsistency, commenting:

[37r] Some of the French versions... make her say, "As for the dowry, allow me to take my own clothes, which I have preserved." Did Chaucer use a French version? If so he did not use it very skillfully. But the preservation of the old clothes and sudden return to them when all the splendid things are taken away or vanish seems very likely an element of the original fairy-story basis.

[This lecture's notes end a little further, on page 38v, with remarks on line 876 – some 336 lines short of the end of the tale.]

The Pardoner's Tale (1947)

There are many undated notes, in various states of drafting and rewriting, for Tolkien's lectures on the *Pardoner's Tale* in the Bodleian Library. The earliest pages, dating from Michaelmas 1947 and perhaps drafted before the start of term, are certainly Bodleian MS Tolkien 13/2, fol. 61 ff., with continuations on fols. 186–7 and 189–90. This is shown by the language of the opening paragraph (fig. 11), which is almost identical to the opening paragraph of his lectures on the *Clerk's Tale*, which he taught only once in Michaelmas 1947.

* * *

[61r] I am dealing this term with the *Pardoner's Tale*, being, as Chaucer might say, *under necessitee condicionel*. For inscrutable Providence has guided the compilers of our Syllabus and prescribers of our texts to name the *Pardoner's Tale and Prologue* for special study... both as a specimen of mediaeval literature (a text with problems of origin and transmission), and as a specimen of (presumably) fourteenth-century literary language.

It is an innovation that the *same* Chaucerian texts should appear in both places. The primary object of this change is (I am told) to lighten the amount of Middle English prescribed for close study. But it is also a good thing, because the two kinds of study so-called "linguistic" and literary or textual cannot be rigidly separated. Chaucer's language is interesting because of Chaucer: his time, his place, his literary eminence. But no specimen of it can be satisfactorily studied without textual examination. Many practical

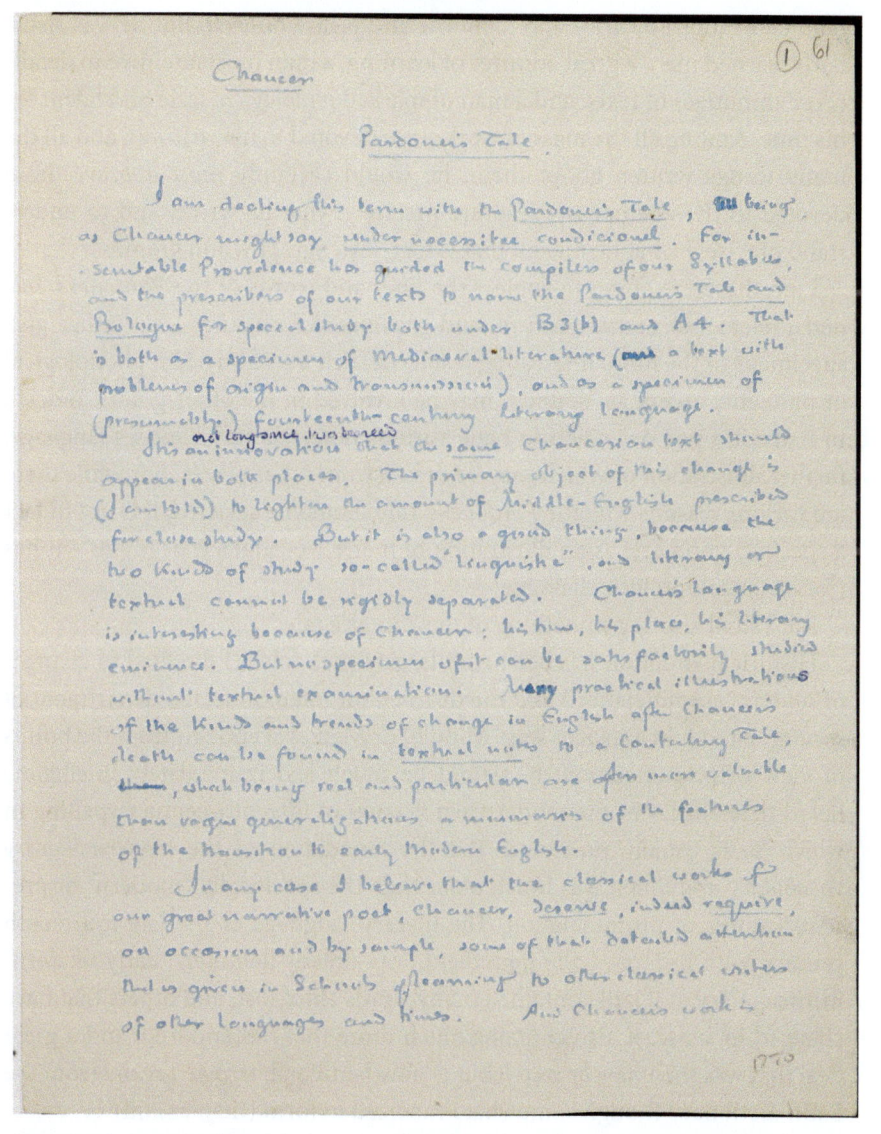

Fig. 11 First page of 1947 lecture on *Pardoner's Tale* (Bodleian MS Tolkien 13/2/1, fol. 61).

illustrations of the kinds and trends of change in English after Chaucer's death can be found in textual notes to a Canterbury Tale, which being real and particular are often more valuable than vague generalizations or summaries of the features of the transition to early Modern English...

By which I mean: that enjoyment of it (or criticism of it) as literature will be in the end enhanced. Chaucer of course wrote to amuse and give pleasure (and edification) by art – and to amuse and please himself. But he was also a fairly learned man, a great admirer of learning, a man most attentive to details (even minutiae) of texts, and a man of marked *philological* taste and talent for his time. Among all the mass of work since devoted to his writings, and all the many things written about them, he would certainly *most approve* those devoted to the attempt to recapture precisely what he wrote, and to understand precisely what he meant: that is text, lexicography, and grammar.[10]

I am therefore going to subject the lines and words of the *Pardoner's Tale and Prologue* to *textual, lexical,* and *grammatical* scrutiny – or rather give specimens of the more interesting results of such a scrutiny. Not phonological or phonetic, except as "sounds" may be involved in the other points. Indeed, to make it a peg on which to hang various notes about Chaucer's language, further illustration of which may be drawn from other places. For while there are various reasons why the *Pardoner's Tale* should be selected, it is not in fact a specially good one as an illustration of metre, vocabulary, or idiom – it has (for instance) too little dialogue.

But I shall also say something of the *Tale* as a tale….

Historical attention has been very largely (not solely!) directed to changes of *sounds* (pronunciation) and the distinct but interconnected department of *spelling*. No doubt Chaucer was "Middle" or Medieval enough from the points of view of pronunciation; he would be much less immediately intelligible heard than read – in the modernized version of fifteenth-century spelling in which he is usually presented. But the foundation of the *modern literary vocabulary and idiom* was much older than the specifically "modern" or present features of pronunciation. The literary language of the late fourteenth century, with its large *Latin* ingredient, was already definitely "early modern" in vocabulary. If it still contained many words since lost, and others that have changed in sense, it also contains much more that has endured, and a great deal that was then *new or recent* but is now familiar, borrowed really from the Latin dictionary though somewhat Francized in form (then as still)…

Tolkien then turns to what he himself calls a "very niggling point" from the *Clerk's Tale* before the lecture script comes to an abrupt stop. Just possibly he had set aside this early sketch of his lectures on the *Pardoner's Tale* and never actually delivered it, since it was too generalizing and too lacking in substance. It was his common practice when revising to set aside his first

---

[10] MS Tolkien 13/2, fol. 61 breaks off at this point. Fols. 186–7 and 189–90, written in the same ink, continue the line of thought and are judged the continuation.

draft and write a completely new one. Many pages further on in the current gathering, though still demonstrably from 1947, Tolkien offers a new beginning with remarks that sound as if following directly from the *Clerk's Tale*. The following may have been the substitute lecture which the undergraduates actually heard:

[86r] We here come to one of Chaucer's best told tales, and one that is most clearly chosen, written, and designed for its place in his unfinished *Tales* and for the pilgrim who tells it, the *Pardoner*. For the *radix malorum est cupiditas*, which the Pardoner tells us is his sole and perpetual theme, is also (not only as a "moral" but as an explicit phrase) embedded in the tale: so that it is difficult to say whether the Pardoner is made to say this because of the tale chosen for him, or the tale chosen because the favourite text of the Pardoner was already selected for the Prologue. The Pardoner's immediate source is, of course, the first epistle to Timothy ch. VI 7–10:...*For the love of money is the root of all evil*...The passage is in fact one of the subsidiary sources of the tale and its medieval presentment. But the *radix malorum* apophthegm is found not only in some of the closer European analogues – e.g. "Treasure in the Tiber", *Originals and Analogues* (Chaucer Society) p. 135: *radice malorum cupiditate affecti* (of the conspirators who think of poisoning their partner).[11] A similar sentiment is found in the oldest and most original oriental source discovered (*Vedabbha Jātaka*). "Truly this passion of avarice is the root of destruction," says the author of this tale, when one of the two remaining robbers went off to get rice cooked in the neighboring village, and into the hearts of both murder came.

But we are here in a quite a different position to that in which a critic of the *Clerk's Tale* finds himself. There we have a known *main* (and indeed for all but a few seldom certain details *sole*) source. [86v] We can there not only (a) first enjoy the tale as Chaucer made it and left it, in itself, and on its own merits or demerits (our main task and obligation to a great writer); we can also (b) amuse ourselves, not without profit, by observing Chaucer at work stanza by stanza and line by line..."Rhyme" is a craft, not all sacred fire and suspiration, but in large parts a plain struggle with a refracting material, sc. both the narrative material *and* the author's own language (as much as a knife on wood or chisel to stone) that cannot ever be wholly successful...

---

[11] W. A. Clouston, "The Robbers and the Treasure-Trove: Buddhist Original and Asiatic and European Versions of Chaucer's *Pardoner's Tale*," in *Originals and Analogues of Some of Chaucer's Canterbury Tales*, ed. F. J. Furnivall, Edmund Brock, and W. A. Clouston (London, Chaucer Society, 2nd series, no. 20, 1872), 415–36.

But here we have no such air. As for the detailed criticism or commentary, we must do our best without crib or parallel. As for the larger criticism: we must decide for ourselves which is "Chaucer's own" – what particular or immediate praise he deserves for this or that turn or feature of the narrative.

The decision will not be easy. Not even as a learned man. For while a great mass of writing from his age (and before it) is preserved in Latin, in French, in English, in Italian (to look no further), much has perished – it is very plain from a consideration of the *Tales* that many things that Chaucer himself *read or heard* have disappeared. It is perfectly possible for Chaucer to have had a *direct source*, even though we can now find none, only remote analogues, which he *could* have "worked up": as in the *Nun's Priest's Tale*, the *Reeve's Tale*, the *Prioress's Tale*, and others. Chaucer was a very well-read man for his day; and doubtless (by our poor standards) in the manner of his day an attentive and retentive man. Stories were in the air: for amusement or edification or both, cropping up as a pastime or in sermons, in full or in brief. It would often be as difficult for a man like Chaucer to say where exactly or when he got this or that story as for a modern "raconteur" – in our weaker day usually limited to a short jest or anecdote – to say where he got his "funny story" with which he raises a laugh after dinner. It does not follow, unless we have close verbal connexions and a direct reference to a source (such as exist in the selections the *Canterbury Tales* from Petrarch), that an "analogue" is in any way immediately connected with Chaucer's version.

Some years ago I heard the jest that about the sickly man who met an old friend looking bronzed and said "How did you manage to get a holiday?" "Holiday? said the other "Oh, that's only because our scullery-window faces south." Now I might have put that down in writing somewhere, and some future researcher into "sources" might derive it from Punch November 5 1947.[12] But he would not be [87r] right. Such stories are in the air, and though someone [*read somehow*] each must have an author at some time (often remote) he can very seldom be detected even in our day, let alone later by the medium of the written records.

Though it is not my immediate point, it is an important point that I may return to later. My version said "scullery-window". The written Punch

---

[12] The cartoon in *Punch* magazine (446 in vol. 213) is captioned, "Holiday? No – but fortunately our kitchen sink faces south." It would not be out of character for Tolkien to hoard a magazine clipping and use it in a lecture several years later. However, it seems likeliest that the cartoon was newly published when he contrasted it with the joke he had heard "some years ago" – in other words, that he first delivered these words in November 1947, not in the 1950s. Further evidence for this is a pencil addition at the top of 87v: 'It used to be said that the Vienna Stock Exchange was the source of most European anecdotes (see review Sunday Times Nov. 19 1950).'

form...said "kitchen sink". That may seem unimportant, since the abstract point (or joke-idea here) are plainly the same *in abstract*. But it is far from unimportant in discussing *derivation*. In real-life *derivation* (as distinct here from mere *classification*) it is precisely the unimportant details (so-called) that are really important. It is the recurrence of these that are the safest evidence in tracking a line of descent. (The *hæftméce* – *heptisax* recurrence in Norse and O.E. is far more important in suggesting a real connexion between Norse and Anglo-Saxon tales of a strong hero wrestling with invading underwater monsters than all other elements in the "plot".)[13] To the bearing of this on *Pardoner's Tale* we will return. One point we may underline at once. Although Chaucer's version of the Tale does not contain it...his line of descent must go back in all probability through a tale *in which that phrase occurs*: *radix malorum est cupiditas*. However many analogues, closer to our *Pardoner's Tale*, are discovered I should look first for that phrase.

But so far as I know up to now, no "analogue" close enough to be the direct or even main source of the *Pardoner's Tale* has been unearthed. And we have to consider Chaucer's observable lines of workmanship in these cases. As a teller (or re-teller) of "tales," Chaucer had not, I think, any taste or indeed any talent for *invention*: primary invention. He liked, when he could get it so, to take a tale already knocked into about the right shape and length for his purpose. So Petrarch's "*mythologia*".[14] That has been the way of many great artists such as Shakespeare, for instance. It is a natural way of narrative poets, whose finest achievements have been in re-telling. So William Morris as a narrative poet – though he had another side as a sheer inventor of unknown worlds and regions: but their power (their virtues and faults) are just different from those of his best retellings in say the *Earthly Paradise*...

[87v] So here I believe that Chaucer had already probably a tale embodying all the main features and machinery of the *Pardoner's Tale* – the localization in Flanders, the drunken revelry, the pursuit of Death, the old churl, the number three of the villains, and so on – though this precise construction is not actually found in any other form...

* * *

---

[13] Tolkien refers to words in Old Norse and Old English, unique to *Grettis saga* and *Beowulf* respectively, which philologists see as evidence that the two narratives draw on a common source.

[14] As the direct source for the *Clerk's Tale*, Petrarch's tale of Patient Griselda went under the Latin title *De obedientia et fide uxoria Mythologia* (1373–74) when translated from Boccaccio's *Decameron* (10.10).

The Parlement of Foules (1948)

Tolkien's first page dated these lecture notes for *The Parlement of Fowles* from January 1948, but their chronology is more complicated. Apparently when Tolkien discovered that he was assigned to teach this dream vision instead of the *Clerk's Tale*, he remembered that he had drafted an introduction and lengthy commentary on its vocabulary when working on his Clarendon Chaucer in the 1920s. So he simply extracted these annotations from his bulky near-200 pages of Clarendon notes, prefaced them with new paragraphs of introduction, and then added a great many supplemental remarks in blue ink on words already glossed for the abortive edition. Later in 1951 when Dan Davin, the Assistant Secretary at OUP, forced the return of his Clarendon Chaucer materials to the Press, Tolkien neglected to include these pages on the *Parlement*. Either he forgot in the heat of the moment, or he worried that he might be assigned to teach the work again and would be caught without ready-made lecture notes. Indeed, the abundance of extra commentary on single words, sometimes requiring new pages, suggests that he might have used these notes in Trinity 1957 when teaching "The Language of Chaucer" (SH 1:532) for which specially compiled teaching materials have not surfaced. Whatever the case, these annotations arrived along a different route to join the Bodleian's Tolkien papers and have the shelfmark MS Tolkien A 38/2, fols. 96–126 (*TLC* 124), unlike the rest of the Clarendon Chaucer notes (MS Tolkien A 39/2). Here we present the prefatory comments which he newly prepared for the 1948 lectures (fols. 96–97r).

* * *

The Parlement of Foules

[96r] *The Parlement of Foules* is now set "for examination" as from the first of this month instead of the *Clerkes Tale*. One wonders what Chaucer himself would have thought of this use of his agreeable and successful little "occasional poem".

I think he would have been tickled – in all senses. That is: *amused* both at the inevitable absurdity of making light verse the subject of "love" and examination at all; and at the choice of this piece in particular for heavy annotation and scrutiny. But at the same time, much *gratified*.

Chaucer thought well of himself; and it is, after all, something to have written things that both in detail and in general effect can still by anybody be thought worth studying after nearly 600 years; and that not a mere lapse of time and change of tongue, for it implies the subsequent competition of some of the greatest writers of verse in recorded history.

Chaucer, indeed, would (I think) have liked our English School, and have been an enthusiastic member of it on all its sides (linguistic and literary). He had a humour that could keep learning in its place (and keep the scholar there too!); and yet he liked learning, and especially learning about literature and its technique and indeed about *language*. He was in fact, within his limits, a thoroughly *literary* man. Both an original poet with the impulse to make things "of his owne" and a living man with an eye for the life of his time – not only the people, but the sky, trees and flowers; he took sustenance from books and from accumulated literary experience. He could have written a good debate between (say) "The Flower and the Roots": the *roots*, rather grubby and earthy, down among the worms, in themselves useless unless they issue in stem, leaf, and blossom; the *flower* doomed very quickly to fade and smell if cut off and stuck in a vase in a cultured room.[15]

Among various sides of his interest, he was concerned for precision and for detail. I think he would have approved more, probably, of our effort after all the centuries to recapture the sound and metre of his lines, and to make as precise as we can [96v] the implications of phrase and word, than (say) to explain the precise reference of his "allegory".

And that is accordingly what (as usual) I propose primarily to do.

Many different kinds of problems are set by different pieces of Chaucer. The *Clerk's Tale*... (whether it attracts still or not, as a story in itself, as a tale of a particular kind, having its own atmosphere) has a value for study because it depends *mainly* and directly on a known and definite single source: of which it is an adaptation. So that through it, apart from reading it as a tale (the first duty), we can see Chaucer at work. And there is profit and pleasure (of a kind) to be derived from the observation of his handicraft in action: we can see him building his stanzas and looking for a rhyme; we can to some extent discriminate between attractions due primarily to stanza and language, and those dictated by the tone and shape that he was deliberately giving to his version of the borrowed story.

But here in the *Parlement of Foules* we have quite a different case. It is not a "tale" at all but an "allegory" – on which more later; and also, as has been said, it certainly "looks like an occasional piece": s.c. a thing composed with

---

[15] The word "useless" is not in the MS but something of the sort seems required by sense.

reference to some definite event. But it is a "composition". It has no direct source; it is not a re-handling or translation of something already more or less shaped as it is in Chaucer. It is (or was) a new thing, but one *composed* of many elements, nearly all of them already old, or well-known. This is no dispraise: the same might have been said of many delectable dishes sent to table by cooks in happier and more abundant days.[16] He says himself:

> *For oute of olde felds as men say*
> *Cometh al this newe corn from yer to yere.*
>
> [*PF* 22–23]

And Chaucer was a skilled cook.

So far then as we get any glimpses of the "workshop" in studying this piece, it will be mainly in observing his solution of odd bits of material to fit in his picture.

[97r] It is my practice to begin with a line by line commentary and leave criticism, analysis, source-hunting, dating, and all such *Chauceriana* to the end – because it is more important, and it does not so much matter if the *Chauceriana* are scamped or omitted (by me). Chaucer has in any case been less well annotated than "researched round" – more talked about or pried into behind his back, so to speak, than examined *viva voce*.[17] The poor results that this can lead to, and too often does, are well illustrated by the *Parlement of Foules*. As is the poem itself, the debate after much wrangling can be broken off without conclusion. So that the student of such lore might well say:

> *And with the shoutyng, whan the song was do…*
> *I wok and othere bokes tok me to.*
>
> [*PF* 693, 695]

For, as you are all well aware, I do not doubt, while the piece may have all the air of an occasional piece with a reference, no one has in fact discovered with certainty to what events if any it does refer, what is its "covert" meaning. To quote the thing itself again:

---

[16] Tolkien speaks in the late 1940s, when rationing and food shortages continued. There is the famous story of the Baltimore doctor who sent C. S. Lewis a ham that became the centerpiece of a celebrated Inkling feast in March 1948 (SH 1:350).

[17] Tolkien alludes to the oral examinations given to Oxford's degree candidates after their written examinations or thesis submissions.

> *How sholde a juge eyther parti leve*
> *For ȝe or nay, withouten any preve?*
>
> [*PF* 496–97]

But "research" of this kind succeeds or fails. It fails if it does not proceed through debate to some conclusion. Fails that is as any critical enrichment of this particular poem, though it may increase knowledge of many things, by the way. The date, the reference of the allegory, are then mere matters of debate. We are left with the poem.

[Here Tolkien's new 1948 preface ends on fol. 97r and leads to his original 1920s headnote for *Parlement of Foules*, already transcribed in our chapter "Editing Chaucer, 1924–28".]

* * *

The Pardoner's Tale (1951–1954)

After starting in Michaelmas 1947, Tolkien returned to lecturing on the *Pardoner's Tale* in Michaelmas 1951 through Hilary 1952, again in Hilary 1953, and yet again Michaelmas 1953 through Trinity 1954. We speculate that many batches from 1947 were salvaged when Tolkien found himself again teaching the *Pardoner's Tale* in 1951–52 and thereafter. The borderline between lecture versions is hazy. The heavy overlay of revisions and additions, together with the variety in handwriting style and writing implement (lead or red pencil; black, blue or red ink or ball-point), all strongly suggest this is material that Tolkien worked on, put away, pulled out, and worked on again, over a significant period. The abundance of materials suggests another instance of the "two square yards" that engaged him obsessively even when not preparing these notes specifically for a new round of teaching.

The scraps of paper that he reused give various indications of dates. Notes on Chaucerian words are jotted on the backs of a memo from Merton College's Estate Bursar dated 26 October 1951 (fol. 106r). But evidently these written-out lectures were still being delivered and developed during the academic year 1953–4 when Tolkien used a Merton College meeting agenda, dated 11 January 1954, from when he was serving as sub-warden. A fragment on the Pardoner's morality appears on the back of a calendar page for 8–14 March 1954 (fol. 107r), labelled by Tolkien "Week 8", the last week of Hilary term.[18] He wrote on these calendar pages with a ball-point pen (making early 1954 his earliest known use of that late 1940s invention) adding many tweaks to his lecture notes and even full new pages (fols. 95v, 97v).

As evidence of further work toward his 1955–56 lectures (see Chapter 6), additional commentary on the Pardoner's character appears on the flip-sides of a memo for *Return of the King* errata and a note of lire ordered for a trip to Italy – both from July 1955 when the Tolkiens father and daughter headed to Venice and Assisi on holiday (SH 1:487-99). More calendar pages (fols. 110v, 172v, 173v) are from October 1955.

Overall, then, these pages represent different periods of teaching, starting with continuation of his original 1947 lectures and perhaps extending as far as his final 1957 lectures on "The Language of Chaucer." The shuffling of different notes for different terms would certainly account for their disorder.

Later continuation of the lecture's opening pages engages in source studies based on W. A. Clouston's "Buddhist Original and Asiatic and European Versions of *The Pardoner's Tale*" (1872), a scholarly work which was mentioned in his 1947 lectures, but which would become the recurrent touchstone for his last revised lectures in 1955-6. Since in Chapter 6 we provide a full transcript of those final lectures, preserved in fair copy, here we give only a brief sample of Tolkien's draft discussion on matters such as story's earliest surviving version in the *Jātaka*.

The later pages of these teaching notes veer unexpectedly to focusing on editorial cruces in the Ellesmere MS by comparing Skeat's received readings with alternative, perhaps authentic readings from other manuscripts, not Ellesmere. This recalls his 25 October 1932 letter to R. W. Chapman (see Chapter 2, page 50) describing himself as "a pettifogging scholar rejoicing in the minute and the intricate, and such games as textual criticism". But it leaves hanging the question of what audience was intended for these intricate discussions befitting an upper-level graduate seminar, not an undergraduate lecture.

We speculate that one member of the audience in the 1954 lectures entitled "*Pardoner's Tale*: The Legend" was Tolkien's youngest son. After Oxford undergraduate studies interrupted by the Second World War, Christopher had completed a B.Litt in 1953 and had just been appointed a University Lecturer.[19] He had a history of attending his father's lectures and would have been especially interested when planning his own edition of the *Pardoner's*

---

[18] June 1954 also finds him examining B. Litt. student F. W. Wyatt on his thesis *Dialogue in Chaucer* (SH 1:456).

[19] Catherine McIlwaine, "Introduction," in *The Great Tales Never End*, ed. Ovenden and McIlwaine, 7–27 at pp. 10, 14, 26.

Tale, which was published four years later.[20] There, he echoes his father's long-standing assertion that the Ellesmere's spellings were those of the fifteenth-century scribe, not the poet (48). He also follows his father in defending departures from Skeat's copy-text when "the overwhelming testimony of the very large number of other manuscripts is against Ellesmere" (52) and when he was confident "Ellesmere is corrupted" (112). Christopher's text provides footnotes indicating where his edition departs from Ellesmere, and his emendations match so precisely those proposed by his father that it is easy to imagine him not only sitting and note-taking through Tolkien's lectures, but actually having these detailed pages at his elbow when making his own editorial decisions.[21] He also probably had his father's Ellesmere facsimile at hand, since his endnotes include comments such as "this is written in the margin of Ellesmere" (108). If editing the *Pardoner's Tale* during the 1950s was in some sense a collaborative enterprise between father and son, it represents an early instance in which Tolkien began one project and Christopher completed it.

After the material we feel is demonstrably from 1947, Tolkien's page-numbering skips six sides of rapid pencil drafting (fols. 88v–90v), which discuss far-off analogues and were perhaps too rough for delivery in a lecture. But he evidently used this material later to create the fair copy which we date to 1955–56; see Chapter 6 and the sample paragraph below.

* * *

Pardoner's Tale

...As I said last time the links between the Oriental and European forms of the story are not known. The roots of Buddhist literature run far back – comparatively: the world of men was already very ancient in the days of Gautama, and Egypt (for instance) was then hoary with antiquity. This literature undoubtedly absorbed and drew into itself much that was older, and much

---

[20] Chaucer, *The Pardoner's Tale*, ed. Nevill Coghill and Christopher Tolkien (London: George G. Harrap, 1958). Christopher also co-edited with Nevill Coghill *The Nun's Priest's Tale* (London: George G. Harrap, 1959) where he was, in a sense, completing his father's unfinished work from his Clarendon Chaucer (*TLC* 275-7). Perhaps we can better imagine father and son discussing the *Pardoner's Tale*, and Christopher reviewing his father's lecture notes while preparing his own edition.

[21] Christopher agreed with his father in rejecting these readings from Ellesmere: *Hoost* (1), *false* (5), *boughte* (7), *gonne to crye* (35), *sire* (78), *ymaked* (94), *fame* (97), and *ther* (244).

that was not begotten or invented in India. The movements of men, and of their cultures and legends, have not moved only from East to West...

> Fol. 91r (numbered in sequence from 87v in the '1947' lecture script) returns to the lectures at hand with a survey of 'Texts': editions such as John Koch's 1902 *Pardoner's Prologue and Tale* as well as specialized resources such as *Specimens of All the Accessible Unprinted Manuscripts of the "Canterbury Tales,"* ed. Julius Zupitza, John Koch, and Frederick James Furnivall (1892–1902). Then 91v explains Tolkien's "philological" approach: "neither verging on the sheer *linguistic* extreme (speech-sounds and their history) nor to the 'literary' extremes in which almost anything but the words said and used in a poem may be studied" before moving on to metre:

...The English Language as a medium of literature (as of verse) is not an easy matter of study, whether studied *historically* in its processes of change, or studied as it was at any given moment (i.e. *synchronically*).

However that may be, I shall still esteem it my function (or duty) to examine this piece chiefly as a *cloth-merchant*, rather than a *tailor* or *dress-maker*.[22] It is a length of very excellent material, English material, that, considering the long time since it was woven, has come down with relatively little damage – not no damage! I mean, I shall pay considerable attention to all linguistic points that arise (if especially those which do not depend for examination and understanding upon the intricacies of sound-change) in working through the text. But I shall do something about the Tale as a Tale, as a work of narrative art...

The whole of this piece is cast in the decasyllabic rhymed couplet. Chaucer was, or made himself, a master of this, in the "easy style" of this measure. He was the first English poet to make any considerable use of it – in fact to discover it capabilities.

It is an easy one to write in English – relatively easy.[23] In so far as it is legitimate to speak of a measure *in the abstract* apart from examples of its particular employment, it is easy because it fits the rhythms, breath-groups and natural word-order of English. Not of course without effort, without care and craft. But with care and a little skill and practice, it can be made to run with very little strain on natural order and idiom....

---

[22] Like his Allegory of the Tower in "*Beowulf*: The Monsters and the Critics", this illustrative tale undercuts his claim in the 1965 "Foreword to the Second Edition" of *LotR*: "But I cordially dislike allegory in all its manifestations."

[23] Tolkien had written his *Mythopoeia* in decasyllabic couplets early in the 1930s (SH 2:822–3).

Continuing to address the work's metre, Tolkien examines several examples of couplets, then remarks upon the poet's "padding" to fill out lines:

[92v] So much for some of the commoner tricks of "padding" or "stuffing" to catch a rhyme or eke a line. In general Chaucer is sufficiently a master of his medium and had sufficient conscience as a craftsman – one much in advance of the general easy-going, easily satisfied custom of his day – not to strain rhythms, word-order and natural usage of the language.... You will not find "strains" like *of which yow toold have I* (530) very frequent in the *Pardoner's Tale*...

Tolkien then turns to Chaucer's word order, giving examples such as "That shewe I first" which reverse what we now consider natural:

This "reversed order" descends from Old English where in natural writing and speech it was much more frequent. It is thus naturally used still in Middle English, quite apart from its metrical convenience; though Middle English speech-feeling was already disturbed and less regular in this point. In modern English apart from a few formulae as "said Thompson", or in graphic style after emphatic initial adverbs like *next, then* (*then came a clap of thunder*), it is unnatural, a literary archaism, a piece of "poetic diction", and even when not unnatural more literary than colloquial.[24]

[93r] But it must again be repeated that Middle English order was not identical with ours, and because (as it were) it retained some older characteristics together with alterations in the modern direction, it was *freer*. Thus there was still a tendency to delay the *verb* or in an analytic verb the participle in a *subordinate sentence*..."

It becomes difficult to sort and classify the lecturer's writings on the *Pardoner's Tale* in MS Tolkien A 13/2, fols. 99–190. In one sense, Tolkien continues his previous discussion on Middle English as a language study with reference to the *Clerk's Tale*, taught only in 1947. But he also returns to discussing sources and analogues. And then, too, he indulges in very detailed editorial choices among manuscript variants of particular words. The following samples begin on fol. 99r:

---

[24] *LotR* features much inversion, signaling older or "higher" modes of speech; and Tolkien ended up having to defend it in letters.

Before we leave the question of words, I must say a little about the "Latin" elements in Chaucer's language. For this purpose the *Pardoner's Tale* is a reasonably good text; but since the question of Latin loan-words is not peculiar to it, nor to Chaucer, but a special feature of the fourteenth century (notably exhibited by Chaucer) I need only be brief.

When is a Latin word Latin – and not French? Well, as you know, this is not a matter in which a hard and fast line can be drawn. The habit of borrowing from Latin, that is direct pillaging of the Latin dictionary, was derived by English from French. (*Not* the knowledge and use of Latin as such!) The reasons for that are part of the history of *French*.

> Tolkien discusses the sound changes that had produced French from Latin, with examples starting with French *œil* < Latin *oculus*, as well as the ongoing French habit of borrowing learned words from Latin – a habit then passed on to English:

[99r] ...the French knew their language *was* Latin (in origin) so that the written form was (for them) in a sense only older, better and less corrupted French: thus you have the basis for the intrusion into *writing* and thence often into *educated speech* of words taken "from the book" – in the more elevated regions of vocabulary: *philosophy, theology, rhetoric, sciences, literary criticism, law, government* and so on, which began as far back as the preserved beginnings of *writing* the Gallic vernacular, but reached a high-tide in France about a century earlier than in England. The French *writing* known to such people as Chaucer was already impregnated with such "Latinisms". The English people of the clerkly class knew Latin as well as the French; and though they knew their own "English" was not Latin, Latin had the same prestige for them, and was also the most readily available source either for "good big rhetorical words," or for "terms" as Mine Host says: for words of the philosophical, theological and technical sphere, which were not possessed by the diurnal colloquial speech. So they imitated the French process with a hearty good will. [99v] The 14th century is the high-tide of this process in England.

> Now Tolkien methodically lists all the Latinisms in the *Pardoner's Tale*, recalling the lists of Chaucer's Latin and French borrowings that he had compiled around 1944 when teaching the *Reeve's Tale* to Navy cadets (Bodleian MS Tolkien A 14/2, fols. 117r-v). He then launches a blistering attack on the impact on English of such Latin borrowings:

[101r] What a legacy of tinkling or trailing words vague in sense and feeling, pretending to a science, a philosophy, a logic which they do not possess... They *start* by being *pretentious*, and end often by being so vague as to be nonsensical or dangerous. As when a group of candidates for "English" could get no nearer to a definition of a "*war of attrition*" than to say it was something to do with "*appeasement*". This is a heavy debt to pay for the apt use (shall we say) by a post or orator who wants a high-flown variation on "wearing away".... [101v] It was a pretentious age (linguistically), and its heirs are linguistically woolly-pated....

[102r] Error, even ludicrous error, must have been a by-product of the spread of such words to persons either unlettered, or with at least no real knowledge of Latin (as still). But the signs of the representation of this in dialogue are infrequent in Chaucer. It is here, of course, not always easy to distinguish between the dramatic bungling of a Chaucerian character (as he depicted it) and the actual bungling of later copyists: some of them evidently very stupid hacks....

> Tolkien promises (fol. 102v) to move on to the actual text but first warns about linguistic "false friends" (familiar-looking words that have changed meaning). Then this relatively continuous passage of lecture script ceases, part-way down the page. On different paper (including the reverses of March 1954 calendar pages, fols. 107 and 109), Tolkien discusses character and morality, asking "How could the Pardoner be tolerated among the Pilgrims?"

[109r] This Pardoner is clearly a rogue, a fraudulent "pardoner" whose bulls and other documents are no doubt as bogus as his relics. But he is not a "fiction": that is to say a piece of anti-Catholic or antipapal propaganda such as might have been invented in the 16th century. Alas, no! There is ample evidence that he represents a class of pernicious and degraded rogues who were actually to be met, all too frequently, in Chaucer's time. Also that Chaucer has in no way overdrawn his description of his character and his tricks and frauds as such, as a picture in itself, by itself.

You did not have to be antipapal to deplore in the strongest terms the existence of such people. Pope Boniface IX in 1390 denounced them, and the grave moral and spiritual harm they did, and desired to have those convicted or such offences imprisoned.

> A new batch of pages (fols. 115–25) finds Tolkien describing the manuscripts of the *Pardoner's Tale* and the editorial methods for establishing the text.

Comments on editorial cruces may represent the latest phase of his work on Chaucer, if they were directed to the prospective *Pardoner's Tale* edition by Christopher (who steadily accepts his father's rejections of various Ellesmere readings):

[115r] Koch's text was based on 55 MSS. These according to Zupitza and Koch fall into *two* main Types subdivisible into 7 groups. This is divergent from Skeat (Vol. IV of his big edition): four types. But a good deal of work has been done on Chaucer's text and the MS authorities since 1902 (date of Koch's edition of the *Pardoner's Tale*). For a summary of the position at present, see Robinson's edition pp. 1001–5.[25] There are 84 MSS or fragments of MSS of the *Canterbury Tales* known to exist, but not all contain the *Pardoner's Tale* or even part of it. There are also 6 early prints: two by Caxton; two by Pynson; one Wynkyn de Worde; one Thynne: they are of negligible value for the text. Greg, for instance, ranks Caxton[1] as of MS authority – being derived, that is, from a lost MS; but if so, it was from a poor MS...

[115v] *Contamination* is naturally a process that obscures the lines of any classification, and opens the door to much debate. By "contamination" is meant the process by which a copyist does not stick entirely to his immediate copy, but makes use (in varying degrees) of another copy, or other copies, that he has by him or can occasionally refer to... This means that in "establishing a text" – that is, in choosing among variants (whether in word, word-order, spelling, or form) what is least corrupted, nearest to Chaucer, or at any rate of the highest extant authority: the readings of A will naturally be preferred, especially those of α, and the agreement of $\alpha\beta\gamma$ will be in most cases decisive – other things being equal.

This also means, or has practically meant, in recent time, that El – the Ellesmere MS – will be taken as the basis of a text of the *Canterbury Tales*...It has also, in fact, brought about an almost [116r] superstitious regard for El. It is printed, there is a facsimile, it is a beautiful well-written legible MS with skilful and well-known little pictures.

But neither regard for El (as, if not quite the oldest extant MS, at least the most careful) nor for type A and the consensus of $\alpha\beta\gamma$ can be applied mechanically.[26]

---

[25] *The Poetical Works of Chaucer*, ed. F. N. Robinson (Boston: Houghton Mifflin, 1933) was establishing itself as the standard edition for classroom study and scholarly citation.

[26] Carleton Brown's review "The Text of *The Canterbury Tales* by John M. Manly and Edith Rickert" made Tolkien aware that the Hengwrt manuscript came closer to preserving Chaucer's original text.

All the MSS or even the oldest members of the groups are separated widely from Chaucer's death (AD 1400) and therefore more widely from his final revision of many parts of the *Canterbury Tales*. Therefore even El, though it may be a specially careful MS based on a good line of descent, is quite inadequate *alone*. How far it may diverge from a supposed "Chaucer" in a special case, severely testing fidelity, I have tried to show by an examination of the text of the "dialect passages" in the *Reeve's Tale* ("Chaucer as a Philologist," *Proc. Of the Phil. Soc.* 1934).[27] Its frequent errors in more straight-forward passages of ME are recognized...

[118v] We cannot rewrite Chaucer or supply the vanished hand, or even the vanished copies that he made or ordered, so all the ingenuity devoted to rearrangement of the fragments of a great Unachieved, are (however fascinating as a private amusement) in the end of little more real service than to make *clear* that Chaucer left the *Canterbury Tales* unfinished and uncoordinated. The agreement of the best MSS makes it at least *highly probable* that the fragments were left more or less in the Ellesmere order (I – X) and that this (in spite of all discrepancies) is the nearest indication we shall ever have of what kind of shape the "map" or plan of tales had taken in Chaucer's mind before he died.

Thus Tolkien rejects the "Bradshaw Shift" of fragments endorsed by the Chaucer Society and followed by Skeat in his editions. Next, on fols. 119–25, Tolkien turns to textual notes, beginning with a long introduction:[28]

[119r] I am now going to comment on the text: *seriatim*. I shall not, of course, translate it, or produce a word by word commentary, as I might with any text in more apparently difficult Middle English, especially one without the wealth of apparatus and assistance now provided for Chaucer. For one thing there is not time – though there is hardly a line (in this or any other part of the *Canterbury Tales*) that could not be made the matter of a note, bearing either on Chaucer and the clearer understanding of what he wrote and meant, or upon the history of English. But I must be selective. So that my notes will *as a rule* not deal with point of *exegesis* where the available notes provide sufficient information and assistance, if I have nothing to add (or subtract)....

---

[27] Tolkien actually wrote '1942'.
[28] Rough outlines for this are on fols. 126–136. Some are on blank sides of proof pages for the *The Life of St George by Alexander Barclay*, ed. William Nelson (London: EETS, 1954), date-stamped 20 August 1953, or of appointment calendar pages for January 1954.

Focusing on manuscript variants on fol. 119v, Tolkien does not get past the first line: "Our *Hoste* gan to swere as he were wood":

> *Hooste*. Nearly all the MSS including the "best" (as El Hg) have *hoost* or *oost*, as in the title. But El (for example) usually writes *hoost*, either where that will scan (as apparently in the General Prologue 327) or where only *hoste* appears to scan (as General Prologue 751). Our present line thus illustrates two points: the treatment of final -ė in certain Old French words; and the difficulty often met of determining the detail of Chaucer's line, amid MS variations, owing to the number of possibilities open to him (and the MSS!) of filling out or compressing a line according to the needs of metre...
>
> [120r] But of one thing we can be fairly certain, and that is that we should *not* print *hooste* as Robinson, Drennan and Wyatt, and even Koch.[29] For all his palaver, Skeat is here quite right, *pace* Koch, to print *hoste*. It is typical of editors to emend *hoost* > *hooste* "for metre". *hooste* appears in no MSS. It is also against the general spelling principles which El usually follows...

Notes follow on textual differences among *Pardoner's Tale* MSS with their philological implications, fols. 121–5, resuming on 137v. Here Tolkien speculates that *gonne to crye*, line 323, should be emended to *gonne crye* (a change from Ellesmere which Christopher later accepted in his edition). From the word *hauteyn*, a troublesome one for Chaucer's copyists, Tolkien launches into an interesting distinction between the Pardoner in the *General Prologue* and the Pardoner in his own *Prologue and Tale* (137v):

> We should at this point consider the description of the Pardoner in the *General Prologue* Though, I think, we shall then conclude (a) that Chaucer did not trouble to bring that into line with the *Pardoner's Tale*. The General Prologue was probably later and more elaborated and visualized. But since, as we shall see 347 ff, the two descriptions of the Pardoner's stock in trade cannot well be equated, there is no certainty that the personal descriptions can either. To my mind in the *Tale* the Pardoner appears as a lustier, more full-blooded rogue than the creature of the Prologue with his long thin pale hair, his pale protruding eyes, his thin (*smal*) bleating voice like a goat, and his hairless face – *I trow he were a gelding or a mare*.[30]

---

[29] Tolkien's students were mostly using the inexpensive textbook of Chaucer's *The Pardoner's Tale*, ed. C. M. Drennan and A. J. Wyatt, 2nd ed. (London: University Tutorial Press, 1937).

[30] Here and in the following lines, Tolkien uses "Prologue" for the General Prologue, not the Pardoner's Prologue.

Such a creature might have exercised a kind of fascination, but would hardly ring out his voice *as round as gooth a belle*. It is true that Chaucer says in the Prologue that *ful loude he song*, but that is quite a different matter from translating *hauteyn* as "loud" in modern English or indeed from translating *loude* of the Prologue by "loud".[31] The words have shifted. In OE *hlūd* and ME *loud* are often used of sounds that we should call "clear" or "shrill" – note the Sumnour bore the *burdoun* or bass part to the Pardoner's song. Note also that *small* does not mean "small" in Prologue but "fine clear – high"... [138r] Well then, if we cannot use the General Prologue safely in elucidating the passage we must deal with it by itself.

Hauteyn must then refer to some quality that the Pardoner thought effective in preaching. Its other uses do not suggest that it was really a word descriptive of *sound*. In any case, would a man say that "he tried hard to have a loud speech"? *Speech* note, not *tone/voice*. I think the Pardoner means that he takes pains to use *lofty* and impressive *imposing* language – so that his hearers will think him a person of power and consequence: indeed *lyk a prelat*....

> The contrasting of the Pardoner's two depictions now turns to the symbols or relics he carries:

[140r] Those in the General Prologue make the Pardoner out no doubt just as great a cheat, but more hypocritical and religious: they appeal to medieval religious sentiment: Our Lady, St Peter, the Cross (possibly represented as containing a tiny fragment of the True Cross), and bones of saints, probably those that were the object of local or contemporary devotion.

Those of the Tale are hardly "religious" at all. They are only slenderly connected with Christianity, and belong rather to the realm of popular superstition and magic. The *magic mitten* is just such, and given no association. The *shoulder-bone of the sheep* is said only to have belonged to a holy Jew, unnamed, and its appeal is rather to the current superstitions about *spatulae* used in magical practices known as "spatulamancy"[32] – though here offered to superstitious country folk as a useful cure for their beasts and themselves.... The appeal is thus to ignorant "uplandish" agricultural superstition – and is not suitable to impress the Pardoner's present audience at all....

---

[31] Tolkien refers to the Pardoner's Prologue 329–31: "Lordynges," quod he, "in chirches whan I preche / I peyne me to han an *hauteyn* speche / And rynge it out as round as gooth a belle."
[32] The *OED* gives the definition "divination by means of the shoulder blade of an animal" but does not cite an attestation earlier than 1652.

The more purely linguistic discussion of forms in various MSS resumes. On fol. 143v, Tolkien reaches the couplet "And who-so findeth him out of swich *blame* / He wol com up and offer in goddess *name*" (385–6) and argues to emend Ellesmere – another change followed by Christopher in his edition:

El here alone has *fame* for *blame*. A good example of the danger of trusting blindly (Drennan and Wyatt's *fame*). For El is clearly wrong and misses the point of the blackmail. It is not those who are free from *public repute* as sinners (*fame*) that will hurry up to offer, but those who are *free from fault* (*blame*). Hardy and notorious sinners the Pardoner cannot blackmail in his way. It is those who fear the whisper – "You see he/she did not make an offering; he dared not or could not; his conscience must be bad" – that he traps...

[159v] 539: Substaunce into Accident. There is no textual question here or linguistic point. But I would pause a moment to say that those notes on this passage are best which are content to point out that there is here a "joke" arising out of the semi-popular knowledge of important philosophic terms – without indulging in half contemptuous references to the "schoolmen", or their subtleties. Subtlety is not necessarily false. The universe in fact seems to be subtle enough in construction (or shall we say pattern) in whatever direction we investigate it. In any case one has to be a rather better philosopher than most (I suppose) of those present, or than any editor of Chaucer to reach a point in which superiority is not ridiculous... There are plenty of parallels in modern half-ignorant or half-jesting use of the terms of various sciences or semi-sciences; but a jester that defended himself against an expert by laughing at his "over-subtle distinctions" would not usually be held to have proved his own superiority. The main point of course is that substantia the underlying "reality" could not be changed, but as it could only be perceived (by the senses) by the "accidents" – of taste, smell, and the like – the complete transformation of these would deceive those dependent (as all of us) on the sense-data. As Skeat says: "Those who partook of the meals so prepared, could not, by means of their taste and smell, form any precise idea of what they were eating. The art is not lost." Oh true Walter! But this is of course in fact to take up a highly "subtle" philosophic position: as to what they were eating – as distinct from taste and smell?

That Chaucer was in fact being topical is possible, but actually the very phrase was culled from his source in Innocent's *De Contemptibus Mundi* – *Alius contundit et colat, alius confundit at conficit, substantiam conuertit in accidens*... But can you tell me why Skeat says "according to Pope Innocent III (*of all people*), the cooks who toil etc."? Why "of all people"? I am mystified.

Innocent III acceded in 1198 (he was thus before St Thomas Aquinas, born 1225). Does this mean either that Popes should not know any technical terms, or that they should not use them casually, or that they should keep their mouths shut – so as not to put their foot in? It is enough to make anyone in occupation of any chair (however lowly compared to that of Peter) frightfully nervous. *But the art is not lost!*...

> The notes then turn at fol. 171r to consider line 713, "An *oold man* and a povre with hem mette", and then the old man's observation (beginning line 722) that even if he walked to India he would find no one willing to swap their youth for his age:

To the identity and function of "the old man," we will learn when we deal with the story... This line cannot be used in any guesses about the nature of "the old man". So far e.g. from supporting any connexion with such "undying" figures of story as Ahasuerus the Wandering Jew, it is against it. For what the old man says is common form (*Inde* used as "limit of the known world") and means "even if I were to go (as I have not) to the ends of the inhabited world, I could not find etc."...

[171v] 729–731. This is imitated from the First Elegy of Maximian... The six elegies of Maximian *De incommodis senectutis* were at one time (especially in the 13th century) one of the books most read by boys learning Latin.... Maximianus belongs to the 7th century and was a friend of Gregory the Great. The elegy here remembered and drawn on is given in Skeat's notes (and Koch). There is it that leaning on a staff Old Age tottering (*mitura*) beats the dull earth with constant stroke... and ('tis said) with wrinkled mouth thus speaks: Take me O mother (*genetrix*), have pity on thy child's woes and deign to cherish tired limbs in thy bosom.... The very ambiguity of the "old man" as just an old (representative) man / as Old Age is present in the source. In fact the Elegy is more than just a source for "Knocking on his mother's gate", but a source of the whole picture which Chaucer seems to have substituted for a different piece of mechanism: the hermit. Of which more anon...."

> Tolkien's promise to discuss the Old Man as a hermit-figure "when we deal with the story" went unfulfilled as fols. 186–90 switch to further remarks on the *Clerk's Tale*. But he was already mining Clouston's *Originals and Analogues* and moving toward identifying the Old Man with the archetypal figure of the *wizard* in his final 1955–56 lectures on the *Pardoner's Tale* which he carefully wrote out in fair-copy – and which we transcribe with annotations in Chapter 6.

5
The Middle English *Losenger*

Tolkien first attended S. R. T. O. d'Ardenne's Liège conference in November 1950 when he delivered, in English, an address explaining the aims of the syllabus of the Oxford English School, perhaps a version of his 1930 article "The Oxford English School" published in *The Oxford Magazine* (SH 3:783). For his next year's appearance, he chose a subject that had also been on his mind for some years. He may have been curious about the word *losenger* first as a schoolboy when reading Chaucer, but he had slighted it in his Clarendon Chaucer glossary with only the brief entry "losengeour, *n*. lying sycophant", and he did not provide any endnote for it in his edition's otherwise over-long commentary. Only in the mid-1940s did he begin exploring the word's complex etymology, as another instance of his "two square yards" of obsessive focus, in ways taking fullest advantage of the philological expertise neglected in his publications during previous years while laboring instead on *The Hobbit* and *The Lord of the Rings*. Concentration on a word understood generally to mean a "lying layabout" probably reflected on some level his own sense of guilt over falling short of academic expectations. Priscilla Tolkien recalled her father was "intensely scrupulous" in his religious standards, which probably merged with his professional standards, whereby he was prone to self-recrimination over the slightest lapse.[1]

"Neck Verse" for the Oxford Dante Society (1947)

In 1945, Tolkien was elected a member of the Oxford Dante Society, which met once a term to enjoy a dinner and hear a paper delivered by a member (SH 3:1235–7). Tolkien's turn for a paper came around in November 1947 at a dinner hosted by Warden Maurice Bowra of Wadham College – famous for complaining "I'm a man more dined against than dining!"[2] He had

---

[1] John Garth, *Tolkien at Exeter College: How an Oxford Undergraduate Created Middle-earth* (Oxford: Exeter College, 2014), 18.
[2] Jan Morris, ed., *The Oxford Book of Oxford* (Oxford: Oxford University Press, 1978), 372. Cf. Shakespeare's *King Lear* 3.2.59-60: "I am a man / More sinn'd against than sinning."

already spent the previous year mulling over his former student Simonne d'Ardenne's draft article on the Old French word *losenge* (SH 1:330). In his own paper, Tolkien found a way to combine his interest in Chaucer's *losenger* with Dante's *lusinga* in the opening canto of *Purgatorio*. His title, "A Neck Verse", referred to a felon's ability to save his neck if he could claim "benefit of clergy" – that is, if he could demonstrate his ability to read and write. Tolkien's script for this talk survives in the Bodleian and thus allows us to examine his early thoughts on this elusive word, as well as catch glimpses of the trajectory for later consideration in his exhaustive – and exhausting – lecture "Middle English *Losenger*". Delivered in Liège in 1951, it was published in *Essais de Philologie Moderne* in 1953, thus representing his last full-scale philological article.

Scull and Hammond (3:1236–7) provide a partial transcript of Tolkien's Dante talk, but they omit his remarks on Chaucer, specifically his reference to *losengeour* in the Prologue to the *Legend of Good Women*. Our transcription from Bodleian MS Tolkien A 13/1 (2) restores this key excerpt. Tolkien had commenced with some humorous references to Sinclair Lewis's *Babbitt* – one literary work which he acknowledged might have suggested to him the word *hobbit* (SH 1:715) – before finally focusing on specific passages from Dante and Chaucer (fols. 173–4).

* * *

It so happened that my attention was caught by a word in the *Purgatorio* and by the attempt to discover what precisely it meant. So in Purg. I, 91–92, I found Cato saying:

> *Ma se donna del ciel ti move e regge,*
> *come tu di', non c'è mestier lusinghe.*

He refers, I suppose, to Vergil's words in particular praising (as Dante elsewhere does) Cato's championship of true liberty… *Lusinghe* is then "flattery" perhaps, but only in the gentlest of its senses, praise not unmerited, yet spoken with a further motive and maybe a little too coloured. But this word brought me of course back to the *losengeours* that I knew at home in 14th century England, and recalled to me a chase that once began after these elusive creatures, so busy about the courts:

> 'For in your court is many a losengeour,
> and many a queynte totelere accusour'

says Alceste the Queen to Cupid in Chaucer's *Legend of Good Women*.[3]

I have pursued this quarry far, far away I fear from Cato and the threshold of Purgatory. Here no doubt our Romance philologists will prick up their ears and other settle to slumber. But do not be dismayed. I know this is an old hunt, and that much has been written on it. The philologists I can only assure that I have pursued most of the matter; and the others that I do not intend slowly to unravel the tangle here and now. I have indeed as Chaucer's Pardoner might say to such a company, already showing sales-resistance:

> I have words and citaciouns in my male,
> As faire as any man in Engelond,
> Whiche were me yeven by the Popes hond.[4]

Or at least they come out of respectable sources and authoritative dictionaries.

But it is only a thread, a main thread of the tangle that I will attempt to exhibit – briefly. A wise word-hunter knows that even in writing, it is difficult to report the chase, or bring back any of the glimpses of wider country that hunter has been given. And this word turns out to be one of specially intricate history, a very brilliant example of the truth that words are not, certainly not in the complex mesh of medieval Europe, such as popular books or fancy may paint them: things with straight linear genealogies... And I do not suppose that *lusinger*, then *lausenger*, *lozenge* would have come into existence, either in form or in meaning, but as a product of the interplay of a given moment between popular Latin and Northern Germanic speech. In that point alone it is interesting, but not wholly singular. If I select it for a note, it is for another reason. Let the cat come out. Let the end of the chase be told first...

We will start at first, however, with Old French *lozenge*, and refuse to be deterred by any of the traps or side-issues that this word may lay for us. Its history has certainly been marked by some curious accidents...

* * *

Tolkien's legible remarks end at the top of fol. 174 and are followed by three smaller pages scribbled over in pencil and ink with hard-to-read notes on this Old French word. These inchoate thoughts would crystalize four years later

---

[3] This quotation comes from Skeat's *Complete Works of Geoffrey Chaucer*, 3:91 (lines 328-29). [Ed.]
[4] These lines are wittily adapted from *The Pardoner's Tale* (*CT* VI, 920–2) where the first line actually reads "I have *relikes and pardons* in my male." Tolkien was simultaneously lecturing on this Chaucer work for the first time at Oxford in Michaelmas 1947. [Ed.]

when Simonne d'Ardenne invited him to deliver a second lecture at the conference in Liège.

When working at the *OED*, Tolkien had resisted the restraints placed upon his philological ambitions for "W" entries such as the one for *wain*, as remarked upon by recent *OED* staffers: "Characteristically, the long etymological note contains a speculation about the ultimate derivation of the word, which Bradley felt obliged to tone down."[5] Some years later Tolkien commiserated with an historical linguist who could not pursue many interesting side-issues due to constraints of space: "Knowing how these little lexicographical chases open vista after vista and one complication after another, we can well believe that much self-denial was practiced to keep notes down to thirteen pages."[6] In 1951, therefore, he welcomed the chance of pursuing the single word *losenger* for thirteen pages freed – though not entirely – from such restrictions. As with other public lectures, his extravagances were constrained by the tyranny of a time-limit – what he described early in the lecture as "the time at my disposal". As an unusually clear indication of his keeping within these limits, we have a handwritten fair copy that looks like his delivery version of the Liège lecture with paragraphs and whole pages crossed out.[7]

Tolkien's Lost Chaucer (224–5) pauses to ponder why Tolkien chose *losenger* from among all the Old English and Middle English words which might have caught his interest over more than forty years as a student of these languages. He had included the word *losengerye* "lying flattery (of a parasite)" in his glossary for Sisam's *Fourteenth Century Verse and Prose*, along with the related words *lorelis* meaning "good-for-nothings" and *loseles* meaning "wastrels". Later he included the word *losengeour* in his Clarendon Chaucer's glossary with the narrow definition "lying sycophant". But he did not draft any endnote on *losengeour* in this student edition and therefore, years later, may have considered this omission as unfinished business. The *OED* had widened the word's unsavoury meanings as "liar", "deceiver", "idler", "unreliable", and "sluggard" (Scottish), all probably influenced by *losel* or "idle wastrel", just as Tolkien himself suggests in his 1951 lecture's concluding paragraph.

---

[5] Gilliver, Marshall, Weiner, *Ring of Words*, 15.
[6] Tolkien, "Philology: General Works" (1927 for 1925), 35.
[7] Bodleian MS Tolkien A 13/1, fols. 6–17. He may have taken the trouble to type up the lecture from this fair copy for the volume's editors and printers, though this typescript does not seem to have survived. He provided such a typescript for his 1953 Ker Lecture "Sir Gawain and the Green Knight" (MS Tolkien 23, fols. 1–42) later published in *Essays* 72–108. The handwritten fair copy, Bodleian MS Tolkien A 13/1, fols. 19–35, preserves many draft pages deleted, as well as others appearing verbatim in the published version.

As early as 1932, he had written to OUP Press Secretary R. W. Chapman fretting about the expectation for him publishing books: "The time is approaching when I...ought to write out of deference to custom and what is expected of professors."[8] As two more decades passed and no books appeared, the year 1951 found him in the position to look upon himself very much as an academic *losel* and *losenger*. The new OUP Assistant Secretary, Dan Davin, who had special responsibility for the Clarendon Press, had demanded the return of Tolkien's Clarendon Chaucer material. This marked the termination of that long-stalled project. Ida Gordon complained to OUP that Tolkien was providing no help with completing her late husband's edition of *Pearl*. He attended meetings of the Early English Text Society painfully aware that his own EETS edition of *Ancrene Wisse* was making no progress and was not even a true edition, but more like a facsimile, complete with his own hand-lettered capitals.

Nor was he feeling successful in his sideline as a fiction-writer (SH 1:395–6, 401–2). A revised text of *The Hobbit* was published in Britain and the United States, but he still had failed to find a publisher for *The Lord of the Rings*, largely because he insisted on its joint publication with *The Silmarillion*, then still in the chaotic state recalled by Rayner Unwin: "I was shown from time to time the serried ranks of box files that contained, as I was told, like beads without a string, the raw material of *The Silmarillion*."[9] Even when his trilogy was in press, he agonized that the authorities of the University would disdain this massive achievement as "an aberration of an elderly professor of philology" (*Letters* 319). And amid so much evidence of non-production, he indulged in a summer holiday with his wife and daughter in Ireland (SH 1:398).

Letter on *faynights* (1951)

As possibly another moment of self-reproach in November 1951, Tolkien responded to some letters in the *Sunday Times* about the word *faynights* that had speculated about its Gaelic or Norman-French origins – wrongly, Tolkien thought. Thereupon he wrote a reply to the letter's authors, Iona and Peter

---

[8] This letter is quoted above in "Oxford University Press Correspondence (1924–51)".
[9] Rayner Unwin, "Early Days of Elder Days", in *Tolkien's "Legendarium"*, ed. Flieger and Hostetter, 3–6 at p. 4.

Opie, in which he traced what he believed was the correct etymology, arriving finally at the Middle English *feine*. One passage refers to Chaucer as follows:

* * *

Here "feign" is used in a curious sense recorded as far back as about AD 1300, and found (once) in Chaucer – "to make excuses, hang back, excuse oneself, shirk (especially, in the earliest uses, in battle)". So in the *Book of the Duchess* 317: *noon of hem feyned to singe* does not mean "none of them pretended to sing" but "none of them refused (or would not try) to sing". In a passage in the *Clerk's Tale* (which neither of the most recent editors have noted)[10] Chaucer even makes this *feyne* transitive: *lords heestes mowe nat been yfeyned*, sc. "lords' commands cannot be treated with a 'fain I'." (a servant is speaking) – or that is what I suspect it really means....[11]:

* * *

Tolkien's letter mentions that he himself had that very day been "puzzling over a curious Chaucer usage" which must be related (SH 1:401), probably *losenger* from his Liège conference paper already delivered in September of 1951, but still on his mind as he prepared it for publication. It is striking that at this time, after years preoccupied with *The Lord of the Rings* and *The Silmarillion*, Tolkien should single out for special commentary both *losenger* "idler, sluggard" and *feyned* "made excuses". As an Oxford professor, he was embarrassed at his neglect of academic writings and sometimes gave voice to it: "Most of my philological colleagues are shocked (cert. behind my back, sometimes to my face) at the fall of a philological into 'Trivial literature'; and anyway the cry is: 'now we know how you have been wasting your time for 20 years.'" (*Letters* 344; see *TLC* 224–5). C. S. Lewis might have been allowed his science-fiction trilogy as well as his *Chronicles of Narnia*, beginning with *The Lion, the Witch, and the Wardrobe* in 1950, but then Lewis, not even a professor but a don busy tutoring undergraduates, had published his scholarly volumes *Allegory of Love* (1936) and *Preface to Paradise Lost* (1942) while nearing completion of his masterful survey *English Literature in the Sixteenth Century Excluding Drama* (1954). His scholarly record put Tolkien to shame.

---

[10] *CT* IV, 529. These two negligent editors were probably Sisam, ed., *The Clerkes Tale of Oxenford* (1923) and Robinson, ed., *Poetical Works of Chaucer* (1933).

[11] SH 1:401 discuss this letter; the transcription is ours from Bodleian MS Tolkien A 18-1, fols. 32r–32v.

"Middle English *Losenger*: Sketch of an Etymological and Semantic Enquiry" (1951/1953)

Tolkien's 1951 conference paper "Middle English *Losenger*" can be seen, then, as a devout Catholic's sly *mea culpa* confessing obliquely his sin of idleness. As early as 1913 he was already confessing to Edith: "I am so dreadfully tempted to sloth."[12] Later, in his 1959 "Valedictory Address", he told his audience: "I must now get out of the chair and finally stand down. I have not made any effective *apologia pro consulatu meo*, for none is really possible" (*Essays* 238). His witty but rather obscure Latin phrase fuses the titles of Cardinal Newman's *Apologia Pro Vita Sua* (an essay defending his religious principles) with Cicero's *De Consulatu Suo* (a poem defending his consulship).[13] What Tolkien meant was that as occupant of two Oxford professorships for a total of thirty-four years, his own conduct was basically inexcusable.

As a student of Classical languages, he knew full well that the Greek *apologia* meant "defence", not "apology". Guiltily aware in 1951 of accusations that he had failed to produce much rigorous scholarship, he offered as his defence the Liège lecture itself, which we might describe as scholarship on steroids, so dense and allusive that it challenges an academic audience to follow his argument even on the printed page. Time and again in his Oxford lectures, he had demonstrated an almost pathological disregard for the needs of his listening audience. On this occasion, his Liège audience was made up of predominantly non-English speakers. One wonders, for example, how many caught his playful allusion "But the course of true etymologies does not run smooth" to Shakespeare's *A Midsummer Night's Dream* (I, 1, 134). As a more challenging instance of willful obscurity, the third paragraph alludes to Heimdallr, the Norse guardian god with nine mothers (a fact mentioned only in two lines from the otherwise lost poem *Heimdalargaldr*). It would seem that Tolkien's aim on this occasion, addressing an "assembly of so much talent and learning", was to demonstrate, as magisterially as possible, that he had mastered his philological resources in the most minute details, even for a paper which his second paragraph described with feigned modesty as "no more than a footnote".

Yet in the greater scheme of things, he was privately aware that the typescript of *The Lord of the Rings* – about which C. S. Lewis ventured, "I would willingly

---

[12] McIlwaine, *Tolkien: Maker of Middle-earth*, 150.
[13] Cardinal Newman had founded the Birmingham Oratory where Tolkien spent much of his youth as an orphan with Fr Francis Morgan as his guardian; see Ordway, *Tolkien's Faith*, 46.

do all in my power to secure for Tolkien's great book the recognition it deserves!"[14] – was sitting on his desk in dire need of a publisher. And he may also have been pondering how "The Voice of Saruman" (*TT* III/10) dramatized a *losenger*'s speech-making at the dark end of the lexical spectrum, with *malicious flattery* (with evil motive) > *slander* > (simple) *lying*, in a chapter which he once considered the best in the book (*Letters* 529).

Our transcription of "Middle English *Losenger*" silently corrects a few misprints, mostly resulting from the errors of French typesetters dealing with a foreign language. Some simple errors like "up-si-de-down" for "upside-down" suggest that Tolkien was not given an opportunity to proofread the galleys. We have also normalized names of contributors and others that are given in uppercase in the proceedings. But we have retained some idiosyncratic punctuation which was probably Tolkien's own. We have also retained the standard phonetic use of square brackets to indicate a sound, such as [s], though we also continue to use them to indicate the original page numbers and other editorial insertions. The conference volume's footnotes, originally numbered anew on every page, have been renumbered sequentially throughout the article. The author's original footnotes are indicated with [Tolkien] whereas our supplementary footnotes, annotating his many arcane references, are signaled with [Ed.]. Tolkien's own two offprints of "Middle English *Losenger*: Sketch of an Etymological and Semantic Enquiry," *Essais de Philologie Moderne (1951)* (Paris: Société d'Édition Les Belles Lettres, 1953): 63–76, are preserved as Bodleian Tolkien VC Pamphs (5) and (6).

* * *

---

[14] *Collected Letters of C. S. Lewis*, Vol. 3: *Narnia, Cambridge, and Joy, 1950–1963*, ed. Walter Hooper (New York: HarperCollins, 2007), 384.

Middle English *Losenger*
Sketch of an Etymological and Semantic Enquiry

It is an honour and a pleasure to be allowed to address this assembly of so much talent and learning; and I am grateful for the permission to make my remarks in English.

The contact (and in various degrees: the blending) of alien languages has been frequent, even in recorded history, in the North-West of Europe, on both sides of *La Manche*;[15] and the struggles and interactions in this area have a special importance, because the languages there developed have in the event become the vehicles of a great culture. These are large matters. To the consideration of them I aim now to add no more than a footnote. What I have to do is to examine afresh one item, one word only, produced by the important events discussed yesterday by Professor Gamillscheg: *the Germanic invasions of Northern Gaul.*[16]

To this word Professor Gamillscheg actually referred. But independently I selected it, the Middle English word (of French origin) *losenger*, because I believe that a fresh scrutiny of its etymology may afford a glimpse (if no more) into the complexities of the contacts of Germanic and Latin in Northern Gaul – even though this interesting, and elusive, not to say treacherous, word has often been studied by scholars of superior learning in the field of Romance philology. I announced this in English or late Middle English form, to indicate that it is principally the Germanic and English aspect of its etymology that I wish to discuss. But the true history of all words is complex: they are all caught in a web of connexions and associations. Few have in fact the straight lineal descent so convenient to Etymological Dictionaries: few spring direct like Athene from the head of Zeus; far more have, like the Norse god Heimdallr, nine mothers. *Losenge* is no exception. And I can only hope in [64] the time at my disposal to indicate a line of argument, and can neither cite all the evidence nor follow all the "red herrings", the false scents, which the treacherous *losengeour* has strewn upon his trail.

It was in Chaucer that I first made the acquaintance of that dubious character the *losengeour*.[17] My earliest enquiries about him were addressed to a

---

[15] *La Manche* (literally "the sleeve") is the name in France and Belgium for the English Channel, hence both in England and on the Continent. [Ed.]

[16] Ernst Gamillscheg had concluded his conference paper with a fortuitous consideration of the forms *laus* and *laudes*; see "La colonisation germanique dans la Gaule du Nord", *Essais de Philologie Moderne (1951)*: 47–62 at pp. 61–2. [Ed.]

[17] Bodleian MS Tolkien A 13/1, fol. 23v preserves an early draft of this passage: "It is in Chaucer that an English learner most often makes contact with language of the past (other than the classical

worthy schoolmaster forty-five years ago;[18] and this was what I was told: "He was a flattering liar, and he was so called because he used the kind of language found on *lozenges*. Now these were panes of glass, and they were commonly used in church-windows to record the virtues of benefactors. But since the benefactors had no virtues, save the possession of money, a man who imitated their style was naturally called a *losenger*". This is more or less Darmesteter's view upside-down.[19] Neither view has the support of evidence. But there are alas! no gulfs of meaning too wide for human ingenuity to bridge, especially the ingenuity of the etymologist in his study.

Nonetheless it must be accounted not the least of the strange accidents of this particular etymological problem that there should exist in Old French two words *losenge*, words of a sound-pattern at once unusual and identical, that cannot be connected at all, except by such fantasies. They are, in fact, (as far as the evidence goes) *not* related at all either in form or sense. The one, which I will call *losenge*[1] is the word with which I am primarily concerned. The other, *losenge*[2], a rhombus, a diamond-shaped figure (especially in heraldry), a small cake or tablet, a pane of glass, exists still in French; and in English, where a form *loseine* (little evidenced in France) has also had a considerable history in the form *losene*, *losen*. But though the etymology of this "red herring", this *losenge*[2], is obscure and difficult, I cannot now be drawn aside to follow it. As I pass it by, I will only comment that here we have an illustration of the fact that even *the closest relationship in sound* may be insufficient to bring two words into effective contact (save in the scholar's study), *by itself*, if the senses, and the normal contexts of use, are too far apart.

To return to *losenge*[1]. Long after the days that I have spoken of, I came back to the passage in Chaucer where I had first [65] met the *losengeour*, in pursuit

---

past) and finds himself confronted with a wealth of strange words, some called Old English, some Old French – from which he may eventually proceed further. *Losengeour* was one of these words that first caught my attention though it was many years before I took up the chase. My earliest enquiries were addressed to a teacher, and concerned the medieval *lozenge*. This was the answer: he was a flattering liar, and he was so called from the lozenge, a pane of glass...used for the recording of the wishes of donors and benefactors to a church." [Ed.]

[18] George Brewerton encouraged his pupils to read Chaucer in the original Middle English. Tolkien was in the Sixth Class under Brewerton at King Edward's School in the spring and summer terms of 1905 (SH 1:13), not 1906 according to the lecture's recollection. John Garth remarked in "The Chronology of Creation: How J. R. R. Tolkien Misremembered the Beginnings of his Mythology," in *Great Tales Never End*, ed. Ovenden and McIlwaine, 89–109 at p. 99: "Tolkien's memory about the circumstances of long-ago writing could be unreliable." [Ed.]

[19] Tolkien probably takes this swipe at Arsène Darmesteter's *Dictionnaire général de la langue française*. See the online entry for *losange*: https://archive.org/details/dictionnairegene02hatzuoft/page/1424/mode/2up. [Ed.]

of another nefarious character, the *totelere*.[20] There in the *Legend of Good Women* one may read lines addressed by Alceste to the God of Love:

> *For in your court is many a losengeour,*
> *and many a queynte totelere accusour,*
> *that taboure in your eres many a thing*
> *for hate or fore jelous imagining.*[21]

The *totelere* has been brought to book elsewhere; for Professor d'Ardenne has studied this creature, his name, and its connexions, in *The Devil's Spout* with a wealth of learning and illustration which (even if I could emulate it) would not on this occasion be possible.[22] Though the *losengeour*, in fact, deserves no less attention.

In any case: who and what was he? What was his function or mischief in the Court of Love? A *flatterer* as the editors and glossaries say (of this passage), or a *slanderer*, a *backbiter*, a *liar*, as the context in this Chaucerian passage (and in many other passages elsewhere in English, French, and Provençal) seems rather to require?[23] And whence came his curious name?

As far as English etymology is concerned, this word is simply referred to Old French, and for the moment we will not consider further the *losengeour* or his fate in mediaeval England. In Old French the English scholar finds not only *losengeour*, and the verb *losengier*, but their source: *losenge*¹. Of this word it is important at once to define the sense, sufficiently to distinguish it from *losenge*², the rhombus. "Flattery", or "malicious flattery", is the definition that would probably usually be given (in English terms). But in fact the sense of this word-group presents itself rather as a "spectrum", ranging from *praise* (exaggerated perhaps, or inappropriate) > *flattery* (with ulterior motive) > *malicious flattery* (with evil motive) > *slander* > (simple) *lying*. A dark line, or break in the continuous shading of the colour, may probably be detected between the third and fourth "bands", between *malicious flattery* and *slander*;

---

[20] Tolkien recalls the endnote in his Clarendon Chaucer from the 1920s: "*totelere* (MS A *totulour*), also spelt *tutelere*. A rare word derived from *totelen*, *tutelen* 'to speak close in the ear, whisper', an 'imitative' word made up in similar fashion to our *tittle-tattle*. Here it is used almost as an adjective 'tittle-tattling'." (Bodleian MS Tolkien A 39/2/2, fol. 60) [Ed.]

[21] Tolkien's quotation from the Prologue to the *Legend of Good Women* (G.328–31) deviates slightly from Skeat (3:91). [Ed.]

[22] S. T. R. O. d'Ardenne, "The Devil's Spout," *Transactions of the Philological Society* 32 (1946), 31–55, focused on the words *tutel* and *tutelin* in the *Ancrene Wisse* from the Corpus Christi 402 manuscript later published by Tolkien for EETS o.s. 249 (1962). [Ed.]

[23] When Tolkien says that *losengeour* had been defined as *flatterer*, he reproduces Skeat's sole definition regarding its use in *The Legend of Good Women* (6:154). [Ed.]

but the last two bands are the broader and more observable. Or in other terms the weight of this sense-range is found rather in *lying* than in *praise*.[24]

[66] This spectrum and range is enough in itself to make one suspect *a priori* that we have here a *semantic* product of *blending*. But the immediate and natural etymological connexion that presents itself is with the derivatives in Old French of Latin *laudem, laudes, laudare*. Especially with O.Fr. *los*, for instance. Since *los* is certainly an Old and early French word for "praise", which was also adopted in Middle English of the fourteenth century, it is not necessary, for the present purpose, to consider at length the precise origin of this form – that is, the source of its [s]: whether it be from the nominative *laus*, under the influence of Church Latin; or from the plural *laudes*. Yet this "irregular" [s] is the second thread in the tangle that malicious chance has woven about the word *losenge*. That this [s] could intrude into the middle of words derived from it is sufficiently shown by the form *aloser* "to praise", whence are derived Middle English *alosen* (and *losen*), and Middle High German *lôsen*. Nonetheless, the combined consideration of (a) the stem-form, (b) the suffix -*enge*, and (c) the "spectrum of senses", should warn one that simple derivation from O.Fr. *los* or *aloser* is unlikely to be adequate, and Romance scholars have in fact in more recent times recognized this.

Words can and often do "deteriorate" in sense. A movement from pure *praise* and *approval* > *flattery* is credible enough. It appears to have occurred in dialectal developments of *aloser*.[25] But in Old French the words *los, aloser*; the more direct derivative [67] of *laudare: loer*, and the word *loenge* (mod. Fr. *louange*), do *not* show this movement. Whereas *losenge* is found at once at the

---

[24] This is, of course, only a summary method of dealing with a complex matter involving many passages in French, Provençal, and English, to look no further. The function of the *losengeour*, especially in the Court of Love, really requires a separate study. But since much is necessarily omitted, it must here suffice to say that according to the *Roman de la Rose* (as in 1034 ff. and other places) his operations were principally *slander* and *base adulation* (even of evil deeds), rather than "flattery", and *slander* was his main business. [Tolkien.] Skeat (1:425) remarked on Chaucer's *Romaunt* (1050): "*losengere*, deceiver, flatterer; see Non. Pr. Ta. B 4516; Legend of Good Women, 352." Skeat's note on *Legend* (3:303) referred readers to the French *Rose* (1033–9): "En sa cort ot maint *losengier*.../ Par devant por eus *losengier* / Loent les gens li *losengier*." [Ed.]

[25] As cited by von Wartburg, p. 210, under "*Laus* lob". It is probably shown also by *lôsen* in MHG in the sense "schmeicheln", verb and noun. As in *Iwein* 7591, also in *Tristan* (Gottfried), *Trojan War* (Konrad), *Meir Helmbrecht*. It is noticeable that this movement is specially (exclusively?) associated with *medial* [s]. It is due rather to the influence of *losenge* than its explication. In *Iwein* 7591 at any rate *âne lôsen* is dependent on the *par losange* of Chrétien. Another quite distinct movement is > fame > notoriety; as in ME *alosed for theft*. But this is neither flattery nor lying. [Tolkien] Walther von Wartburg included *aloser* in a long sub-entry for "*laus* lob" (praise) in volume 5 of *Französisches etymologisches Wörterbuch: eine Darstellung des galloromanischen Sprachschatzes* (Bonn: F. Klopp, 1950), 210. *Iwein* is a Middle High German verse romance by the poet Hartmann von Aue written around 1203 and freely adapted from Chrétien de Troyes' Old French *Yvain, the Knight of the Lion*. [Ed.]

darkest end of the spectrum: its development is hardly to be viewed as a blackening of "praise", but rather as (an occasional) mitigation of "lying".

It would thus certainly be of etymological interest if some other word or words could be found having a more or less similar sound-pattern, but a sense of, say, *mendacity, lying*. The semantic history of *losenge* would then become intelligible.

This was done long ago by Baist.[26] He suggested that O.Fr. *losenge* was connected with ON. *lausung*, and OE. *lēasung, lēasing* "falsehood", "deceit". That is to say that O.Fr. *losenge* was in effect a Germanic loan-word, referable to, say, some such primitive form as **lausinga*, but that its sense-history was largely due to contact on Gallic soil with the local products of Latin *laus, laudare*. This suggestion would appear at a stroke to clarify both the semantic and formal history of *losenge*. It has been very widely, if not universally, adopted. Personally I do not doubt that it contains, but does not exhaust, the truth.

But this word is as treacherous as the *losengeour* himself. It is not so easily to be caught. *First*: the Germanic side needs more careful scrutiny: the situation there is far from clear or simple. And *secondly*: there is another twist in store on the Romance side. On the *Germanic* side the points requiring examination are (1) the sense (2) the form and function of the suffix. The ulterior etymology of Gmc. *laus* is not, for this purpose, of great importance. On the *Romance* side it is the ending *-enge* that presents complications.

The feminine Germanic ending in some such supposed form as **inga* would certainly produce in O.Fr. *enge* (later *ange*). But O.Fr. *enge* could and did have another source, a Romance source: namely *-ēmia* as in *vindēmia* > *vendenge*. At this point the "Germanist" enters a labyrinth. The central question (for the present etymology) is: was there or was there not in Gaul a word *laudēmia* meaning "praise"?

[68] If there was, it would produce in O.Fr. *loenge*.[27] O.Fr. *loenge* certainly existed and exists as *louange*, in the pure sense of "praise", "approval". The forms in Provençal, such as *lauzemia, lausenha* (beside *vendenha*), also appear

---

[26] *Das germanische Suffix* ingô, in *Z. f. R. Ph.*, XXXI, 616. [Tolkien] Gottfried Baist was a German Hispanist and Romance linguist who published his study of the suffix *-ingo* in *Zeitschrift für romanische Philologie* in 1907. [Ed.]

[27] Its precise mode of generation, and its relation to O.Fr. *blastenge* m. (often opposed to *loenge*), **blastemium*, and other words of similar ending (m. f.) I must leave to Romance scholars. The formation is (I suppose) supported by the evidence for *laudemium* in Medieval Latin (whence Provençal *lauzimi*, Span. *laudemio*): though this usually has the legal sense of a payment due to a feudal superior upon the sale of property, the sense of "praise" is also given in the dictionaries. Cf. O.Fr. M.Fr. *los* Fr. *lods*. I here leave aside another curious side-track: that the derivatives of the Gmc. stem *laus* (especially of the causative verb *lausjan*) frequently developed very similar senses: see Lexer s. v. *losunge*. Already in the Gothic Gospel of St. Luke we find *lausjan* used = to exact a tax-payment. [Tolkien]

to confirm the existence of *laudemia. It thus seems probable that we must envisage the following events:

1. A Germanic word of the form *lausing-* f. entered the language of Gaul; it acquired in the North the Gallicized form *lauzenga* (?**lauzendža*), f. "lying," and there made contact with a Romance word **laudenja*, **laudenža*, f. "praise" < *laudēmia*, a word quite unrelated in origin, but of very similar phonetic pattern. The meanings were also originally unrelated, but (unlike the case of *losenge²*) were of similar order and liable to appear in similar contexts. The Romance word was unaffected, or much less affected than the alien, but the alien developed a sense-range derived from the fusion of "lying" and "praise", running from "false accusation" to "false adulation".
2. The same Germanic word in a form *lauzenga* (a form actually frequent in Provençal) made similar contact in the South with *lauzemia, lauzenha*. But later the influence of the Northern form may have been felt also in the South, as was the case with other words of Romance or alien origin.[28]

This, of course, states an intricate matter with undue brevity. Whether it is a reading of the variant forms and textual evidence that commends itself to Romance scholars, is not, however, for [69] my immediate purpose of primary importance. For, *by whatever processes it entered the dialects of Gaul*, and there exerted its malign influence, it is, I think, impossible to deny the intrusion of an alien Germanic word into the *laus-laudare* group in those dialects. Faced with the meanings of *losenge, lauzenga*, and with the similarity in pattern and meaning of such Germanic words as **lausung-*, **lausing-* (the immediate predecessors of Anglo-Saxon *lēasung, lēasing* "lying") no other conclusion is possible.

But if that is so, the affair is not ended, and more remains to be said. It is inadequate and misleading to reduce this event to an etymological statement: "*lausinga* Fränkisch: lüge," as in Meyer-Lübke's dictionary.[29]

All etymological statements, and especially those in dictionaries, are constrained to a brevity that must appear dogmatic. But this compressed statement obscures what is, I believe, the most interesting point of this Germanic word. This point is, perhaps, best brought out by making in opposition a

---

[28] This is not essentially different from an assertion that the Germanic word (as a loan) travelled from North to South at a period sufficiently early for it to retain *au* and *enga*. The *au* of Provençal may, however, have been due to *lauzar* (*laudare*). In any case, in North and South the vowel of the stem is the same in the older and in the adopted words. [Tolkien]

[29] Tolkien cites Wilhelm Meyer-Lübke's *Romanisches etymologisches Wörterbuch* (Heidelberg: C. Winter, 1911) later referenced by him simply as R.E.W. [Ed.]

statement equally succinct and dogmatic: "*lausinga* was not Frankish; it was English." The first gift, perhaps, of *perfidia anglosaxonica* to Gaul.

Of course, if pressed, I should modify this word *English*, first to *Anglo-Saxon*: meaning that type or variety of Germanic speech that eventually became dominant in southern Britain, where it was called English by its speakers; secondly by admitting that Britain was not the place where this Germanic dialect developed its most salient characteristics, nor the only region in which it was (probably) to be found in the Dark Ages. Other titles to fit current speculations might be used; but I will retain for the present purpose the title "Anglo-Saxon", because the etymon **lausinga* shows (a) in the sense of its stem, and (b) in the form and function of its ending, features that are characteristic of actual recorded Anglo-Saxon, and are nowhere else clearly exhibited. In the same way, observing the Old Spanish word *anviso*, *ambiso* "wise, prudent", I should be inclined to reject the etymology of R.E.W. **antevisum*: not so much because that compound did not exist, and had it existed should have meant "*foreseen*" or "seen in front", but because in the area [70] of Indo-European languages concerned the *active* sense of this participial formation is characteristic (a special mark) of the Germanic, not of the Italic or Celtic branches. The exact counterpart is, moreover, actually recorded in Anglo-Saxon *andwīs* "wise, clever".[30]

In this case *Anglo-Saxon* may be regarded simply as giving evidence of a once more widely spread word in Germanic, since Anglo-Saxon shares with Old High German and Gothic several similar formations with the prefix *and(a)*.

But when we wish to choose not among the Indo-European dialects but the Germanic dialects, a similar principle holds good: the use of a feminine ending forming verbal abstracts *ung* varying with *ing* is a feature of Anglo-Saxon, exclusive even of Old Saxon (though probably not of Frisian). The sense of "lying" associated with the stem *laus* is characteristic of Anglo-Saxon to the exclusion even of Frisian.

It is not possible here to discuss the etymology of the Germanic stem *laus*. But there can be no doubt that we have in it a native Common Germanic word, which appears in all the later dialects. Its basic sense was "loose", the implications of which: (a) "not properly fixed, unsteady" on the one hand and (b) "not bound, free", were present in the Common Germanic period. One use is common to all later dialects: the use in compounds, in which *-laus* became virtually an adjectival suffix, "free from, bereft of", as in Gothic

---

[30] *RK* Appendix C lists Andwise Roper as Sam Gamgee's uncle.

gudalaus (gottlos, godless). But the meanings of the simple adjective show in the recorded later languages some dialectal differences.

Gothic *laus*: the characteristic sense is κενός, "void, idle, worthless", though the sense "free from" is recorded.

For *lôs* in Old and Middle High German there is a range of interconnected senses that might be divided thus: "loose": (a) free; (b) bare, devoid, bereft (of); (c) slack, lax, unrestrained – with good implications (such as "gay, sportive") or bad (such as "wanton, impudent"); (d) worthless, frivolous.

Old Saxon *lôs*, at least in the *Hêliand*, is practically limited to use with the genitive in the sense "free from, devoid of". The sense "false" often to *lôs* in *lôs-word*, *lôs-werk* is not [71] in fact present, even contextually.[31] Old Frisian *lâs* has as main senses "loose, free". It may also mean "gay".

Old Norse *lauss* has the characteristic sense "unfixed, unrestrained". Its pejorative trend is to silliness, wantonness, lasciviousness, not to falsehood.

Against this inevitably inadequate sketch (of the older idioms), Anglo-Saxon stands out remarkably, not least in contrast to what are in general its nearest associates: Old Frisian, and Old Saxon. In Anglo-Saxon the suffixed *-lēas*, of course, exists, dissociated from the normal adjective. The use of *lēas*, with the genitive, "bereft of" is also still found, though it is mainly limited to the archaic and special language of verse. But the whole central weight of this extremely common word is thrown on to the sense: "false, feigned, untrue, incorrect". Of this notion *lēas* is the most usual expression. It is the sense of *lēas* in an enormous majority of instances. As a neuter noun *lēas* has the sense "the false, falsehood" only and no other.

The "Anglo-Saxon" development of sense is thus one of those curious aberrations in the use of a common stock of words that may be found to characterize a restricted dialect area, which otherwise shares many features with its neighbours. It is an event in the history of Germanic speech long after its dispersal, but one still far enough back to have had time to dominate almost the whole sphere of the adjective **laus* in this one type of Germanic. The sense-development probably proceeded primarily from the branch "unsteady > unreliable" (rather than from the branch "worthless, frivolous"). For it is worth remarking semantically that this special development is characteristic precisely of Anglo-Saxon, which has abandoned both the ancient stems meaning "true in fact": first prehistorically that represented by *verus*, G. *wahr*;

---

[31] Actually *lôsword* is the counterpart of Gothic *lausawaurdei* (ματαιολογία or κενοφωνία), Old Norse *lausyrði*. It occurs in a moralization on the Parable of the Vineyard, against waste of time in youth. *lôswerk* appears to mean "wicked deeds" generally. [Tolkien] See the Old Saxon epic *Hêliand*, ed. Moritz Heyne (Paderborn: Ferdinand Schöningh, 1866), 259, for gloss of *lôs*. [Ed.]

later the derivative of the verb "to be" (*soþ, sooth*), and has substituted for them the *trēow, true* "the dependable".

There is a further point that may be observed. The earliest [72] derivative of adjectival *laus* was the causative verb *lausjan*. This occurs in all the later languages, and, with or without prefixes, retained its earlier sense "release" (let go, or take away), and did not even in Anglo-Saxon follow the fortunes of the basic adjective. The later derivative verbs were dependent on the later senses of the adjective. It is again only Anglo-Saxon that possessed **lausōn, *lausōjan* > A. S. *lēasian*, which meant simply and only "to tell lies".[32] It is thus only in Anglo-Saxon that the noun **lausungō / *lausingō > lēasung/ing* is "at home", so to speak, since this formation is precisely a verbal abstract requiring or implying the existence of a verb.

This is remarkable and significant. The semantic development of **laus* in Anglo-Saxon is unique; and the occasional appearances elsewhere of a similar sense, or the contextual suggestion of it, offer no real parallel. But the course of true etymologies does not run smooth, unless much is concealed. The existence of *lausung* in Old Norse, usually glossed "falsehood", cannot be passed over; but it may conveniently be dealt with together with the suffix.

The eventually important and productive feminine verbal suffix **ungo/ingo* is of obscure origin. It is not common to the whole Germanic field; but in the so-called West Germanic dialects it became a normal means of forming verbal abstract nouns, primarily from weak verbs. It is not found in recorded Gothic. It is probably historically true to speak of its being "introduced" later into the Scandinavian area; for in Old Norse verbs of the "first weak conjugation" can form abstract nouns with *-ing* (as e.g. the ON. *kenning* from *kenna*, **kannjan*), but other weak verbs do not employ either *ing* or *ung*. The ending *-ung* was used (sparingly) in Old Norse, but it was not associated with verbs. ON. *lausung* must thus be regarded as two distinct words or formations. *Lausung*[1] was an abstract noun belonging directly to the Norse adjective *lauss*; this is well-attested, and meant "looseness", either "being unsettled", or "laxity, lasciviousness": [73] a *lausungar-maðr* was not a liar but a libertine. *Lausung*[2] was a rare word (especially in early documents), a readymade loan from Anglo-Saxon, not associated with the Norse adjective with which it never agreed in sense, meaning "deception, lying". The first is still current in Icelandic; its characteristic alliterative grouping was with *leik*. The second was

---

[32] The equivalents are not found in Gothic or Old Norse, or in Old Frisian. In Old Saxon *lôsôn* was an active verb, more or less the same in sense as *lôsian*. In Middle High German *lôsen*, derivative of OHG *lôsôn*, meant "to be *lôs*", in its various German senses. [Tolkien]

not part of the normal vocabulary, and is not found in modern Icelandic;[33] its characteristic grouping is with *lygi*. The borrowing of *lausung* "deception" probably occurred at widely separated periods: (a) early, as in *lausung við lygi*, "deceit in exchange for lies", occurring only in two adjacent passages of *Hávamál*;[34] (b) much later, as items in the known influence of the specific Anglo-Saxon of Britain upon Norse in the sphere of the Church and the homily: it occurs chiefly in such works as the *Mariu-saga*.[35] The early borrowing is not an isolated event. The early verse of Norse and Anglo-Saxon both show stray examples of the vocabulary proper to the other. Thus two places in the *Elder Edda* offer the only examples in Norse of the sense "bower, woman's room" for *búr* which is characteristic of English, as also is the alliterative collocation with "bright" (see in *björt í búri* "bright in bower", in *Goðrúnarkviða* II).[36] Anglo-Saxon and Norse were never wholly out of touch, and later renewed especially close contact.[37]

From the French problem, then, ON. *lausung* can be set aside, except in so far as it reveals this Anglo-Saxon word for "falsehood" as one of the successful words, characteristic in form or sense of that variety of Germanic, which tended to travel abroad, either earlier or later, like *boat*, or *lord*. If we return to consideration of the suffix, we observe that the variation of *ing* with *ung* in verbal function, in association with a weak verb of the type *lausōn* (cited above), points to Anglo-Saxon, quite apart from the sense. But we must also consider the title *Frankish*. The absence of the variant *ing* from the West Germanic dialects, other than English and Frisian, and therefore [74] from Frankish, is well-recognized and often remarked by Germanic scholars; on this count also *lausinga* is consequently suspect as "Frankish". But there remain the titles *Salfranken* and *Salfränkisch* to play with; although in fact as evidence for *-inga* in Salic Frankisch only such Old French words as *losenge* and *haenge* are usually offered.

If "Salic Frankish" is to mean simply: "the sort of Germanic speech, pure or mixed, that is found to have influenced the Romance language of northern

---

[33] The sense is not recognized by Blöndal. [Tolkien] Sigfús Blöndal's Icelandic-Danish dictionary *Konunglega bókasafnið* (1920–24) remains an essential source for the Icelandic language. [Ed.]

[34] Surviving only in the 13th-century *Codex Regius*, the Old Norse *Hávamál*'s stanza 42 reads: *hlátr við hlátri / skyli hölðar taka / en lausung við lygi*, translated by Tolkien's student W. H. Auden as "Be fair in speech but false in thought / And give him lie for lie." [Ed.]

[35] *Mariu Saga*, ed. C. R. Unger (Christiana: Brögger & Christie, 1871), 910. [Ed.]

[36] Tolkien probably recalled this reference from A. McI. Trounce, "The English Tail-Rhyme Romances: A Romance of *Gaheret*", *Medium Ævum* 1 (1932), 157–82 at p. 171, immediately preceding the first instalment of his own article "Sigelwara Land". [Ed.]

[37] Thus there is a late and isolated example in Anglo-Saxon of *lēasing* in the Norse sense "laxity of morals, lasciviousness", as foreign to the native senses of *lēas* as is *lausung* "deceit" to the Norse senses of *lauss*. [Tolkien]

Gaul", then that is well enough. It matters, at any rate, less in etymology than it may in ethnography whether we mean: (a) that a variety of Germanic (from which also was derived the Anglo-Saxon found in Britain) influenced northern Gaul *independently*, i.e. as the language of elements that did not call themselves "Franks"; or (b) that the sort of Frankish concerned was itself adulterated with linguistic features of this Anglo-Saxon type. The events in the area make either of these processes credible enough, or both.

There exist, however, actual documents which appear to contain a variety of "Frankish" of the adulterated sort supposed. These are the so-called Carolingian Psalms (Wachtendoncks MS), and the Lipsius Glosses.[38] These long labelled "Old Dutch", and other titles, belong according to Mansion and Verdeyen,[39] to the lower Rhineland, or vaguely to the south-east frontier of Low Frankish on the borders of Middle Frankish. They are remarkable in the large number of forms in *inga* which they contain, several having their counterparts only in Anglo-Saxon: e. g. *offringa* (AS. *offring*); *fastingon* "fasting" (AS. *fæsting* "keeping"); *thurofremingon* "consummation" (AS. *freming, fremming*); *losinga* (AS. *lēasing*). It is here also, alone in early documents, that the stem *laus*- has the clear, uncontextual, sense "false, deceitful" outside Anglo-Saxon. In the Glosses *los* is three times equated with *dolosus*, once *losa thing* glosses *falsa*, once *losonga* glosses *dolos*. In Psalm liv *losunga* = *dolus*, and in lxxii appears *losinga* = *dolos*.

[75] The language of these Psalm-fragments is probably not to be taken as representing the language of the Salic Franks or the Merovingians, but it may present a similar sort of language. In all other documents of an early period the sense "false" of *laus; the possession of a verbal abstract **lausung/ing* "deception"; and the variation *ung/ing* in such abstracts are specially characteristic of Anglo-Saxon. Their combined presence in this document (one of its most peculiar features) therefore indicates the admixture in it of elements of the "Anglo-Saxon" type. We meet in Old French also one other word of similar formation which may probably, though less clearly, be attributed to the same type of Germanic. That is *haenge*.[40] With this belongs the indubitably Germanic verb *haïr* "to hate", which also moved southward to Provençal *aïr*.

---

[38] Ed. van Helten, *Die altostniederfränkischen Psalmenfragmente, Die Lipsius'sche Glossen*, Groningen, 1902. [Tolkien]

[39] *L'ancien néerlandais d'après les noms propres*, B.S.L., 26, p. 71 – *Le Flamand* in the *Encyclopédie Belge*, Brussels, 1933. [Tolkien] Joseph Mansion published his piece in *Bulletin de la Société linguistique de Paris*, tome 26, fascicles 1 and 2, no. 79 (Paris: É. Champion, 1925), 67–97, and René Verdeyen published *Le Flamand*. [Ed.]

[40] The modern form *haine* is apparently related to it in the same way as the Middle English loanword *loseine* is related to *losenge*. [Tolkien]

This infinitive points rather to an antecedent Germanic form *hatjan (hatinga) than to the forms haton and hatonga, which are those found even in the Psalms and Glosses cited above. The Anglo-Saxon derivatives of the hatjan-type would be hettan, hetting, of which in fact traces are found in the participial hettend (also Old Saxon hettiand) and in the gloss on-hettinga "persecutions".

In any case, after the formation and establishment in Old French of the word losenge, there remained no parallel to it in colloquial Germanic speech, save in the Anglo-Saxon language of Britain. And although in the passage of time, some hundreds of years, the Anglo-Saxon had proceeded from its ancient *lausingu (acc. sg. lausinga) > læosing > lēasing > lẹ̄sing, their identity was still recognizable. They were equated by those who knew both languages; one result of which was that the O.Fr. losenge was not borrowed but translated by the native equivalent. It was only the derived French verb losengier, and especially the losengeour, with his courtly function, that were adopted. This is well illustrated by a famous passage in the history of King Lear, the first English treatment of a story later made renowned by Shakespeare. To describe what Cordelia thought of the speeches of her elder sisters Wace uses [76] the verb losengier and the noun losenges. Laȝamon, of Arley Regis in Worcestershire, rehandling the passage renders it thus:

> Cordoille iherde þa lasinges
> þe hire sustren seide þon kinge:
> nom hire leaffulne huie
> þat heo liȝen wolden.[41]

This is the earliest recorded renewal of contact (before A.D. 1200). The losengeour had to wait some hundred and fifty years, before he appeared in English, in the courtly francized literature of the fourteenth century. He did not stay long. Words cannot be transplanted without peril. In English the losengeour, once naturalized (and so no longer limited to the literary associations of the Court) made contact with another base creature, a distant etymological kinsman, the losel, an idle wastrel. He fades away as an idle sluggard, and barely survives the Middle Age. The English charge the Scots with lack of humour (a losenge that most nations utter against others); but at any rate the Scots are fond of puns. So that when, in the beginning of the sixteenth century, Gavin

---

[41] Laȝamons Brut or Chronicle of Britain, ed. Sir Frederick Madden, vol. 1 (London: Society of Antiquaries, 1847), 128. See Ency 76–7. [Ed.]

Douglas says that he *lies abed like a losengeour* (perhaps the last recorded use of the word in English language),[42] we may detect the last echo of that *liar* and *slanderer*, who beginning his etymological career in an obscure Germanic dialect of the North-West, ended it in a Scottish pun.

Oxford
                    J. R. R. Tolkien

---

[42] The *OED* cited Gavin Douglas's translation of Virgil's *Æneid* viii. Prol. 178 (1513) – "Thus lysnit I, as *lossingeir*, sic lewidnes to luik" – for the Scottish usage as a "sluggard." [Ed.]

6
The *Pardoner's Tale*: The Story and its Form, 1955–56

The sequence of Tolkien's surviving lectures on Chaucer's *Pardoner's Tale* is a matter of educated guesswork. We can only be certain that the first version began on Bodleian MS Tolkien 13/2 (1), fol. 61, because its opening paragraph is almost identical to the introduction to his lectures on the *Clerk's Tale* which he delivered only once in Michaelmas 1947 and never again. Though not dated by Tolkien (and placed in the fascicle before the text just mentioned), the fair copy of *The Pardoner's Tale: The Story and its Form* in MS Tolkien fols. 39–60 represents what we take to be the last, extended version of his lectures over the three terms Michaelmas 1955, Hilary 1956, and Trinity 1956. Here is some of the evidence. In January 1956, Tolkien complained to Rayner Unwin that he would not be able to work on his *Silmarillion* until the new term's "lectures are in order" (SH 1:509). This would have been the case only if he was preparing new lectures, not recycling those that he had just delivered in 1953-54, as a seasoned professor normally would do. Also the future fantasy author Diana Wynne Jones, who completed her degree in 1956, heard *Pardoner's Tale* lectures in which Tolkien engaged in narrative analysis, not his normal practice of wringing the juice out of individual words.[1]

After his earlier assessment that the *Pardoner's Tale* is "one of Chaucer's best told tales" (MS Tolkien A 13/2, fol. 86), Tolkien's attitude has undergone a complete reversal. "For I do not approve of the *Pardoner's Tale*," he says now. "I like it *evere the longer the wors*".[2] What had happened? We know that he received the galley proofs of *Return of the King* on 5 July 1954, some two weeks after the end of the Trinity term when he had been lecturing for the third time on the *Pardoner's Tale* since becoming Merton Professor (SH 1:450, 458). It seems entirely likely, with Chaucer's story fresh in his mind, that he

---

[1] It is possible that she heard an earlier version of these lectures in Trinity 1954 under the title "*Pardoner's Tale*: The Legend" before Tolkien polished and expanded them in the later fair copy which we transcribe.
[2] MS Tolkien A 13/2 (1), fol. 57v. Tolkien lifted this Middle English phrase from the *Reeve's Prologue* (CT I, 3873), a text that he knew well as editor, critic, performer, and teacher.

had an epiphany when he sat down and revisited the story of Sméagol and Déagol, as well as the quest of Frodo, Sam, and Gollum to Mount Doom, and he suddenly realized that he himself had told the same story in both the two-man and three-man versions rooted in Chaucer's archetypal narrative.

This was a flashpoint. Thereafter he felt compelled to write entirely new lectures in order to subject the *Pardoner's Tale* to narrative investigation with the aim of exposing defects in Chaucer's performance with tacit self-congratulations that his own versions were superior. Here it is easy to recognize Harold Bloom's notion of the Oedipal revolt when newer writers assail the older, established authors – that is, "major figures with the persistence to wrestle with their strong precursors, even to the death".[3] Thus we find Tolkien wrestling with Chaucer to determine who has told the better story. And fittingly, their stories recount men literally wrestling to the death: the Pardoner's three rioters wrestling over the eight bustles of gold in contrast to Frodo, Gollum, and Sam wrestling over the gold Ring in the Crack of Doom.

Tolkien had also changed his opinion about source studies. He had said in his earlier lecture on the *Clerk's Tale*: "The first purpose of his tales was to be tales and to be taken as such without research in his sources or analogues".[4] Now in his chronological survey of archetypal stories, he drew steadily from W. A. Clouston's "The Robbers and the Treasure-Trove: Buddhist Original and Asiatic and European Versions of *The Pardoner's Tale*" (1872),[5] even while reminding his audience that none of these textual versions was in fact an ancient source, because there must have been *older originals*: "They are thus all re-handlings, either by elaboration or often by debasement and reduction, at many removes of older originals that can only be glimpsed through them." Clearly, he wanted to take a deep dive into the earliest recorded versions with confidence that even more ancient versions, though not recorded, lurked behind them: "What indeed do we know of the tales of men in all the lost centuries in the lands we now call Europe?" This bespeaks the steady impulse throughout his philological, editorial, and fantasy-writing careers to search for lost originals. By finding the same

---

[3] Harold Bloom, *The Anxiety of Influence: A Theory of Poetry* (New York: Oxford University Press, 1973), 5. *TLC* 47–52 suggests that Tolkien had staged a prior Oedipal revolt against his scholarly father-figure Walter W. Skeat.

[4] MS Tolkien A 13/2 (1), 5.

[5] Tolkien made no mention of Frederick Tupper's contrary view that "it is clear that the oriental versions could add nothing to the data on Chaucer's source supplied by the occidental versions"; see "*The Pardoner's Tale*" in *Sources and Analogues of Chaucer's Canterbury Tales*, ed. W. F. Bryan and Germaine Dempster (London: Routledge & Kegan Paul, 1940), 415–38 at p. 415. Christopher Tolkien would draw upon Bryan and Dempster for his 1958 edition of the *Pardoner's Tale* (55–60).

moral lesson in stories from Buddhist and Moslem traditions, he also rendered it universal, not specifically Christian.

The care with which he prepared these new lectures is witnessed by much preliminary drafting (Bodleian MS Tolkien 13/2 (1), fol. 72–81), with remarks on the early analogues such as the Buddhist *Jātaka*, the old Italian miracle play of *St Antonio*, and other versions in German, French and Portuguese. He was also sketching preliminary thoughts on the characters: "Thus A is a wise man. By his powers he discovers an ancient treasure (sinister in origin or guarded by evil creatures). He turns away from it." The finished lecture will identify the "wise man" as a *wizard* – and almost certainly Tolkien would have had in mind the wise wizard Gandalf in his own version.

We are fortunate to have a witness to these late lectures on the *Pardoner's Tale* in Diana Wynne Jones, the future fantasy author of works such as *Howl's Moving Castle*. She was also the future wife of the medievalist John Burrow, who was suggested in 1960 as a candidate to complete Tolkien's abandoned Clarendon Chaucer edition (*TLC* 36). Scull and Hammond can be discreet about Tolkien's truancy as a teacher: "On occasion, his Oxford lectures were cancelled" (1:xi). Yet Tom Shippey recalls a longstanding tradition: "In those days, if you had driven your audience away by, say, the third week, you could cancel the rest of the seven-week course *and still get paid*."[6] So Tolkien's notorious defects as a lecturer may have been strategic. These defects figure in Jones's recollections of his lectures on the *Pardoner's Tale*:

> When I was an undergraduate, I went to a course of lectures he gave on the subject – at least, I think that was the subject, because Tolkien was all but inaudible. He evidently hated lecturing, and I suspect he also hated giving his thoughts away. At any rate, within two weeks he succeeded in reducing his substantial audience to myself and four others. We stuck on, despite his efforts. He worked at it: when it did appear that we might be hearing what he said, it was his custom to turn round and address the blackboard.[7]

The persistence of Diana Wynne Jones and her four fellow students may account for odd time-filling digressions onto the *Manciple's Tale* and the *Franklin's Tale* near the end of these lectures, because Tolkien had not expected any students to remain until the term's end. His exasperation may

---

[6] From Tom Shippey's review of Diana Wynne Jones, *Reflections on the Magic of Writing*, in *TLS*, 31 August 2012, 22.

[7] Diana Wynne Jones, "The Shape of the Narrative in *The Lord of the Rings*" (1983), in *Reflections on the Magic of Writing* (Oxford and New York: David Fickling, 2012), 5–25 at p. 5.

also account for the final, weary declaration of defeat in the last sentence: "The tedium which you probably feel in looking up notes to these references is in this case a fair indication that they are in fact a *bore*" (fig. 13).

Undergraduates may have known in advance that Tolkien seldom mentioned storytelling, just single words in single lines, often without telling his audience *which* lines.[8] But Jones persevered precisely because these new lectures addressed Chaucer as a storyteller. Here is what she remembered:

> He started with the simplest possible story: a man (prince or woodcutter) going on a journey. He then gave the journey an aim, and we found that the simple picaresque plot had developed into a quest-story. I am not quite sure what happened then, but I know that by the end he was discussing the peculiar adaptation of the quest-story which Chaucer made in his *Pardoner's Tale*.
>
> As you see, Tolkien did not give away half of what he knew, even about plots, and I suspect he never talked about narrative at all, but it is clear from *The Lord of the Rings* that he knew all about narrative as well. The plot of *The Lord of the Rings* is, on the face of it, exactly the same simple one that he appeared to describe in his lectures.[9]

Not that the surviving script contains everything that Diana Wynne Jones heard. When C. S. Lewis recommended to students that they should attend Tolkien's lectures, he would add "pay particular attention to the extempore remarks and comments he often makes. These are usually the best things in the lecture."[10] There is no mention, for example, of a "woodcutter" in the fair-copy lecture. And the notion that Tolkien's plot in *The Lord of the Rings* was fundamentally the same as Chaucer's did not apparently occur to Jones when hearing these lectures on the *Pardoner's Tale*, but only years later when she had read and reread the trilogy. There is a telling tip-off about Tolkien's caginess on this score. Just before launching upon these lectures in 1955, he had written to Allen & Unwin insisting that *The Return of the King* should be published as planned on 20 October because the next day he was scheduled to deliver his O'Donnell Lecture in Oxford's Examination Schools: "I must hope that a large part of my audience will be so bemused by sitting up late at night before that they will not so closely observe my grave lack of equipment as a

---

[8] This was the undergraduate recollection of Derek Brewer, "Introduction", *A Companion to the Gawain-Poet*, 2; he also recalled Tolkien lecturing only to "a small group of devotees".
[9] Jones, "The Shape of the Narrative in *The Lord of the Rings*", 5–6.
[10] Quoted by Sayer, "Recollections", 21.

lecturer on a Celtic subject."[11] He was joking that publication of the trilogy's final volume would guarantee his audience would have stayed up all night reading it – highly unlikely. But Tolkien probably harboured a similar expectation that his student audience would *not* have been binge-reading the final instalment of his trilogy, or any of its previous two volumes, prior to the start of Michaelmas 1955 when his scrutiny of Chaucer's *Pardoner's Tale* so clearly exposed similarities to his own storytelling. He was also rushing ahead of the 1955–56 BBC radio dramatization of *The Lord of the Rings*, which would have more quickly revealed to listeners the resemblances of his trilogy's core story with the core story in Chaucer's quest narrative.[12]

Tolkien must have enjoyed his private scholarly jest when tracing in Chaucer's archetypal story what he himself had unfolded in *The Lord of the Rings*. When he says about the most primitive archetype's characters, "They must, of course, be at least *two*. They will be represented as friends, companions, or confederates," he would have been mindful of his own two-man version with Sméagol as the friend of Déagol before the Ring turns them into enemies. The archetype continues: "One man will think he has won, and yet in the moment of his wicked triumph when Avarice has led him to treachery and murder, he will die miserably beside the gold." In the long arc of the story, some five centuries after the murder of Déagol over the gold, Gollum in his moment of triumph bites the Ring off Frodo's finger only to stumble to his death in Mount Doom. Gollum being swallowed up by the volcano with his precious Ring resembles one of Clouston's earlier versions of the evil-doer's ending – "the earth opened and swallowed him up and the gold with him". To satisfy readers, Tolkien's scene inside Mount Doom improves upon Chaucer's three-man version of the story, where all three are murderous, by providing what he termed a *eucatastrophe* or "joy of the happy ending" (*Essays* 153; *Ency* 176–7). Only the greedy Gollum dies while the loyal Sam survives along with Frodo, minus his finger because he could not finally let go of the Ring.

There was something else that most of the original undergraduate audience could not have appreciated because they had not yet read *The Lord of the Rings*. Tolkien often engages in psychological "projection" by blaming Chaucer for some of his own faults as a storyteller, discounting his own shortcomings, as it were, while attributing them instead to his fourteenth-century predecessor. No Freudian paradigm from Bloom's *Anxiety of Influence* was

---

[11] *Letters* 330. Christopher Tolkien published this lecture, "English and Welsh", in *Essays* 162–97; see *Ency* 162–3.
[12] See Stuart D. Lee, "A Milestone in BBC History? The 1955–56 Radio Dramatization of *The Lord of the Rings*," in *Great Tales Never End*, ed. Ovenden and McIlwaine, 145–65.

necessary. As a good Catholic, he ought to have taken warning from the Sermon on the Mount: "Why seest thou the mote in thy brother's eye; and perceiveth not the beam in thy own eye?" (Matthew 7:3).[13] For example, Tolkien criticizes the *Pardoner's Tale* as "top-heavy" with much sermonizing about the sins of gluttony, gambling, and blasphemy and "over-elaboration of the previous lives of the *riotours*" before the actual story begins. But he ignores the fact that his own *The Fellowship of the Ring* is also top-heavy, with its "Prologue" explaining at length about Hobbits, pipe-weed, the "ordering of the Shire", the finding of the Ring, and Shire records – all delaying the actual start of the story with Bilbo's birthday party. The 1990 audiobook shrewdly shifts this "Prologue" to follow the conclusion of *The Return of the King*, while Peter Jackson's film adaptation replaces this introduction with Galadriel's monologue tracing the history of the One Ring.

Here are a couple of other instances in which he spots the mote in his brother author's eye but not his own. He castigates Chaucer for Dorigen's lengthy catalogue of suicidal women in his *Franklin's Tale*, but he himself repeatedly indulges his fondness for "Homeric catalogues"[14] – such as Treebeard chanting the vanished place names of Beleriand (*TT* III/4), the companies arriving as reinforcements at Minas Tirith (*RK* V/1), and the naming of warriors who died at the Battle of the Pelennor Fields (*RK* V/6). He abuses Chaucer for employing centuries-old rhetorical devices – "The rhetoric that inculcated this sort of thing was vicious" – and yet he himself was perfectly capable of using to great effect standard devices like *anaphora*, or the repetition of a word at the beginning of successive clauses, as he did at the end of his "Helm's Deep" chapter: "Down through the breach...Down from the hills...Down leaped Shadowfax" (*TT* III/7).

Our edition of these lectures transcribes the fair copy which Tolkien carefully wrote out in blue ink (fig. 12). This was probably a second stage of composition based upon a prior rough draft, perhaps the Trinity 1954 lecture series entitled "The Pardoner's Tale: *The Legend*", since earlier lectures had been entitled simply "The Pardoner's Tale". One page of a prior draft survives in the final gathering (fol. 47r) as evidence of how messy the earlier version must have looked. At some later date Tolkien went back in black ink, pencil, and ballpoint to squeeze extra sentences into available space on the page. Clearly he could not have read aloud all his marginal additions without

---

[13] Quoted by Ordway, *Tolkien's Faith*, 280.
[14] See J. R. R. Tolkien, *The War of the Ring*, ed. Christopher Tolkien (Boston and New York: Houghton Mifflin, 1994), 229, 287, 293, on the Homeric catalogue in *Return of the King* (V/1).

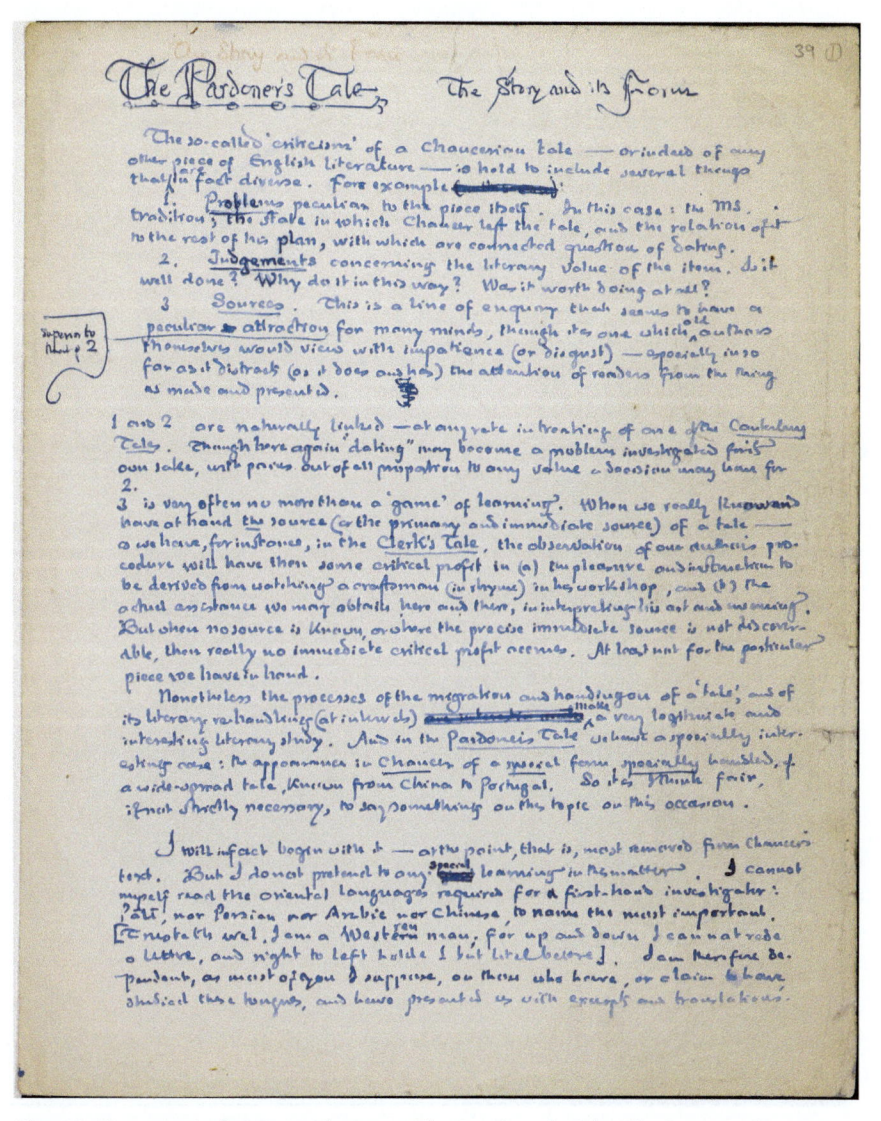

Fig. 12 First page of 1955–56 lectures *The Pardoner's Tale: The Story and its Form* (Bodleian MS Tolkien A 13/2, fol. 39).

disrupting the sense of the surrounding sentences and so losing the main thread of his argument. We insert these into our transcription or present them as footnotes, according to his apparent intention. We occasionally move a parenthetical comment into the footnotes with no warrant except clarity. We also include his other brief afterthoughts written in pencil, red ink, and black ink where they fit best. Throughout, we change his square brackets to

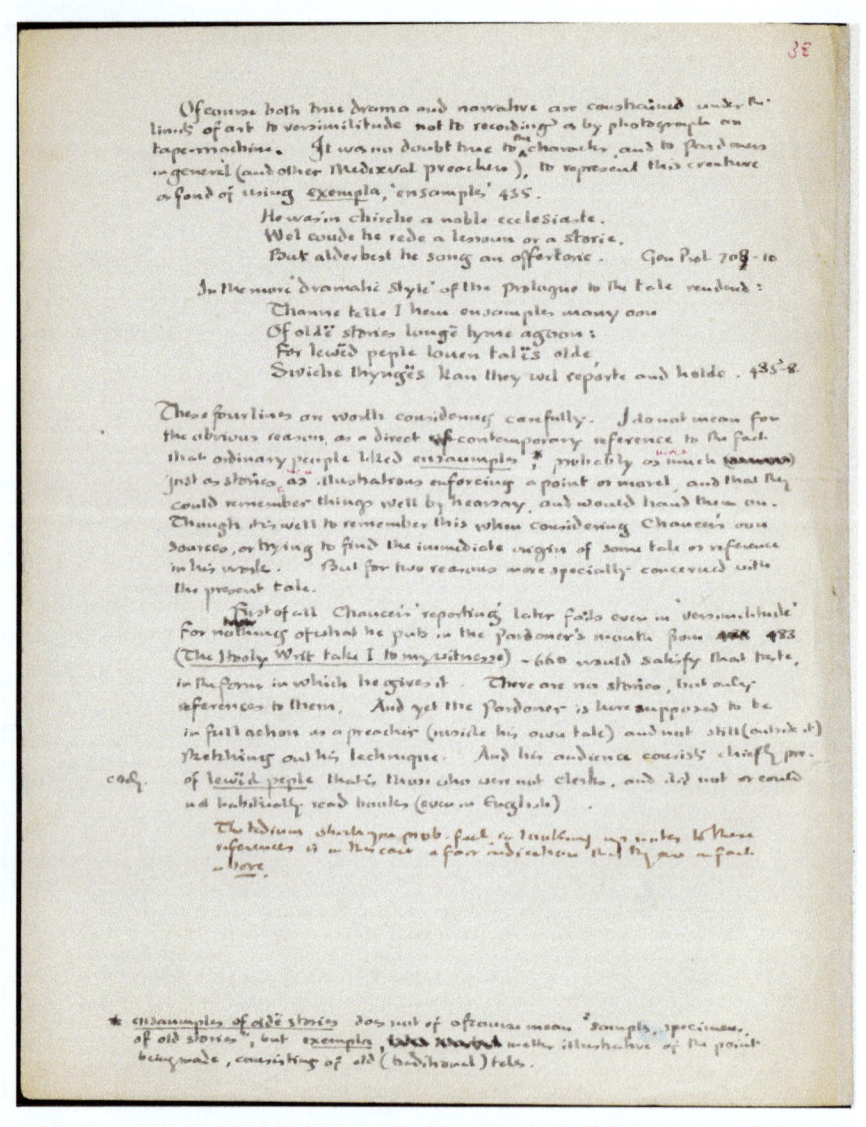

Fig. 13 Last page of 1955–56 lectures *The Pardoner's Tale: The Story and its Form* (Bodleian MS Tolkien A 13/2, fol. 60v).

parentheses (he used them interchangeably), reserving square brackets for our own editorial use. As before, we mark the start of each MS folio in square brackets, but we do not record Tolkien's page numbers.

Tolkien liked to talk about watching "Chaucer in his workshop", and this fair copy gives us a chance to watch Tolkien in his own workshop, still crossing out words and incorporating improvements. He was a tireless reviser. We have nonetheless brought greater consistency to his capitalization and spelling – *oriental* where he sometimes wrote *Oriental* – and we have adhered to a consistent system for single and double quotation marks, which he used almost indifferently. And where he wrote a word such as *top-heavy* variously as *topheavy* and *top heavy*, we have normalized to the currently preferred "top-heavy". Sometimes his careless omissions of articles, pronouns, and helping-verbs have been silently supplied. Other irregularities remain, such as Tolkien's practices of giving a sentence's either/or subject a plural verb and having a compound subject take a singular verb: e.g. "The introduction and setting is sometimes tied up with the central tale."

Our original plan had called for bringing greater correctness to his punctuation, since commas and colons appear in unexpected places or fail to appear in expected ones. It is ironic that he had criticized Skeat for "lavish punctuation" and specifically "a dreadful lot of semi-colons!" because he peppered his text with them, too. But our expert outside readers, John Garth and Catherine McIlwaine, persuaded us that the odd-looking punctuation, including the distracting number of parentheticals, actually helps to clarify Tolkien's sometimes complicated syntax. His many italics and "fright quotes" also signal emphasis for the lecture's oral delivery.

If Tolkien had presented these lectures again in a subsequent academic year, he might have typed up a final-looking revision, as was his common practice. The fact that this handwritten version is the most polished and developed of his various lectures on the *Pardoner's Tale*, however, tends to confirm it as the one dating from 1955–56 when he last taught this Chaucerian work. Lacking a neat typewritten script, we conjecture that the fair copy in Bodleian MS Tolkien A 13/2 (1), fols. 39–60, survives as his last version for public delivery, and therefore it represents "final intentions" to be transcribed just as he wrote it out.

* * *

The Pardoner's Tale: The Story and its Form

[39r] The so-called "criticism" of a Chaucerian tale – or indeed of any other piece of English literature – is held to include several things that are in fact diverse. For example:

1. *Problems* peculiar to the piece itself. In this case the manuscript tradition, the state in which Chaucer left the tale, and the relation of it to the rest of his plan, with which are connected questions of dating.
2. *Judgements* concerning the literary value of the item. Is it well done? Why do it in this way? Was it worth doing at all?
3. *Sources.* This is a line of enquiry that seems to have a peculiar attraction superior to that of 2 for many minds, though it is one which old authors themselves would view with impatience (or disgust) – especially in so far as it distracts (as it does and has) the attention of readers from the thing as made and presented.

1 and 2 are naturally linked – at any rate in treating of one of the *Canterbury Tales* – though here again "dating" may become a problem investigated for its own sake, with pains out of all proportion to any value a decision may have for 2.

3 is very often no more than a "game" of learning. When we really know and have at hand *the* source (or the primary and immediate source) of a tale – as we have, for instance, in the *Clerk's Tale*, the observation of our author's procedure will have then some critical profit in (a) the pleasure and instruction to be derived from watching a craftsman (in rhyme) in his workshop, and (b) the actual assistance we may obtain, here and there, in interpreting his art and meaning. But when no source is known, or where the precise immediate source is not discoverable, then really no immediate critical profit accrues. At least not for the particular piece we have in hand.

Nonetheless the processes of the migration and handing on of a "tale" and of its literary re-handling (at intervals) make a very legitimate and interesting literary study. And in the *Pardoner's Tale* we have a specially interesting case: the appearance in Chaucer of a *special* form, *specially* handled, of a widespread tale known from China to Portugal. So it is I think fair, if not strictly necessary, to say something on this topic on this occasion.

I will in fact begin with it – at the point, that is, most removed from Chaucer's text. But I do not pretend to any special learning in this matter. I cannot myself read the oriental languages required for a first-hand investigator: Pālī nor Persian nor Arabic nor Chinese, to name the most important. (*Trusteth wel, I am a Westren man; for up and down I cannot rede a lettre, and right to left holde I but litel betere.*)[15] I am therefore dependent as most of you, I suppose, on those who have, or claim to have, studied these tongues and have presented us with excerpts and translations.

[39v] These one may use – with appropriate *distrust*. Bitter experience, in following the trail of such good folk, when it leads to languages one knows something of, teaches one that excerpts and (compressed) translations are often deceptive, and only of limited usefulness. They were made as a rule by people who did not know what you would be looking for, and often did not appreciate what is important. Too commonly they think "plot" is more important than casual detail.[16] And of course they may make mistakes.

Here is an example.[17] We shall have occasion later to refer to the Buddhist story in Pālī the 48th *Jātaka*. In the nub of that tale, corresponding generally to Chaucer's *Pardoner's Tale* lines 796–830, the text apparently runs more or less so: "those two men deftly carried off that wealth and hid it in a thicket near a village, and one remained guarding it, sword in hand, while the other took some rice and went off to the village to get it cooked. *Truly this passion of avarice is the root of destruction.* For the one who was guarding the wealth said to himself, 'When my fellow returns…' as he plans to murder him."

I am not now commenting on the obviously close connexion at this point between the Eastern tale and ours. This is my point. One of the three scholars who first pointed out the connexion – the second, Mr Francis[18] – thought that the text went with the moral apothegm *inside* the murderer's soliloquy. A very interesting point, if true. Indeed he calls the robber "a veritable oriental Pecksniff!"[19] And we, unless helped by other orientalists, might well be led astray into thinking especially that there was a tone of hypocrisy about the

---

[15] Tolkien makes a humorous adaption of the Parson's disclaimer "But trusteth wel, I am a Southren man / I can nat geste *rum, ram, ruf* by lettre / Ne, God wot, rym holde I but litel bettre" (*CT* X, 42–4), joking about the fact that he cannot read vertically like Chinese or right-to-left like Arabic.

[16] Which is by no means true if you are trying to trace actual descent and derivation. Thus a re-teller may make grave alterations in plot and yet keep (just because it was not important, but was there) some casual detail (such as the name of a minor character) and so reveal his indebtedness. [Tolkien]

[17] Tolkien draws steadily upon Clouston's "The Robbers and the Treasure-Trove: Buddhist Original and Asiatic and European Versions of *The Pardoner's Tale*" (1872), 415–36. Skeat 3:439–44 summarized these analogues.

[18] The actual first was that very great scholar, a giant among our academic ancestors, Dr Richard Morris [Tolkien, in parentheses]. Cilli 210–16 records more than two dozen scholarly volumes by Richard Morris that figured in Tolkien's reading, the most important of them perhaps his and Walter W. Skeat's *Specimens of Early English* (1898) used as an Oxford textbook when Tolkien was an undergraduate. Tolkien's "Celtic Library" included ten volumes by Morris notably three copies of his edition of *Sir Gawayne and the Green Knight*.

[19] Seth Pecksniff, an unctuous English architect whose insincere behavior made his name synonymous with hypocrisy, appears in the Dickens novel *Martin Chuzzlewit*. Clouston, 421n, had quoted Francis from *The Academy* 1883 where the robber was called "a veritable Oriental Pecksniff." Skeat's bibliography 6:393 included H. T. Francis, *The Vedabbha Jātaka Translated from the Pālī and Compared with Chaucer's "The Pardoner's Tale"* (Cambridge: J. Palmer, 1884).

tale from the beginning. Here in the oldest version is a villain denouncing the very vice he suffers from. *But it is not so.*

So that all that I can honestly offer is a process of vicarious digestion: a perusal of material and reflection upon it, both of which are open to us all. But *ars longa vita brevis!*[20] If you find anything that I have to say either useful or interesting, any clue in a labyrinth, it is all I can hope. But do not think that I am giving you anything more than can be found in the obvious places, in (say) vol. III of the large edition of Skeat, or in F.N. Robinson (if you care to pursue his bibliographical references),[21] or in such works as *Chaucer: Originals and Analogues* (Chaucer Society).

* * *

We have first of all a very elaborate story found in Buddhist literature among the *Jātakas* or "Birth-stories." The thread upon which these stories are strung is the belief in "reincarnation."[22] An ordinary mortal does not remember his previous existences at all, but a Buddha remembers them all.[23] And Gautama (the Buddha), according to tradition, used his knowledge of his own and other men's previous lives for purposes of instruction. 550 stories of his own previous existences were supposed to have been collected immediately after his death. It is the 48th (in Fausböll's edition of the Pāli text), the *Vedabbha Jātaka*, which resembles the *Pardoner's Tale*.[24] It is, even if the oldest existing written form of the story, also the most elaborate.

There are also other Eastern stories presumably derived from this *Jātaka* (or from other older or allied forms). There are decrepit forms which have passed with Buddhism to Tibet and China. There are other more interesting forms in Persian and Arabic. I know of no *proof* that these have in fact travelled back (westward) out of India. They may depend on ancient [40r] Persian (Aryan) forms that remained further west when part of the Aryans penetrated northern India. In any case, they are given an Islamic setting and have no trace of the specifically Buddhist setting (which does not affect the actual tale).

---

[20] This proverbial Latin phrase, going back to Hippocrates, was paraphrased by Chaucer in the first line of his *Parlement of Foules*: "The lyf so short, the craft so long to lerne."

[21] Robinson, ed., *Poetical Works of Chaucer* (1933), 834.

[22] Tolkien devised his own concept of reincarnation for Elves who were slain and then reborn (SH 2:811–14). Later in the 1950s he drafted *Reincarnation of Elves* discussed by Christopher in *Morgoth's Ring*, 363–6, and presented by Carl F. Hostetter in Tolkien's *The Nature of Middle-earth*, 246–66.

[23] Tolkien at one time imagined reincarnation of the Dwarf Fathers as with the Elves (*War of the Jewels*, 204), and each of these reincarnated kings, particularly Durin the Deathless, recalled his previous lives in *The Peoples of Middle-Earth*, ed. Christopher Tolkien (Boston and New York: Houghton Mifflin, 1996), 383.

[24] See V. Fausbøll, ed., *Buddhist Birth Stories, or Jātaka Tales*, trans. T. W. Rhys Davids (London: Trübner and Co., 1880).

The link between the Western (European) versions and the Eastern is, so far as I know, lost. How soon this tale was known in lands adjacent to areas of Greek and Latin speech can only be guessed. My own guess is that it was very early – i.e. not a result of the Crusades, but of much earlier movements, such as the conquests of Alexander. Indeed it is my guess that the reasons why the Epistle to Timothy fits in so curiously well, and why St Paul's language in the source-passage is so pictorial (indeed so suggestive of a story) is that he himself had in fact at the back of his mind this story, or one much like it. St Paul was after all a native of Asia Minor.

This is the text of 1 Timothy ch. vi, 7–10:

οὐδὲν γὰρ εἰσηνέγκαμεν εἰς τὸν κόσμον, δῆλον ὅτι οὐδὲ ἐξενεγκεῖν τι δυνάμεθα· ἔχοντες δὲ διατροφὰς καὶ σκεπάσματα, τούτοις ἀρκεσθησόμεθα. οἱ δὲ βουλόμενοι πλουτεῖν ἐμπίπτουσιν εἰς πειρασμὸν καὶ παγίδα [τοῦ διαβόλου not in all Greek texts][25] καὶ ἐπιθυμίας πολλὰς ἀνοήτους καὶ βλαβεράς, αἵτινες βυθίζουσιν τοὺς ἀνθρώπους εἰς ὄλεθρον καὶ ἀπώλειαν· ῥίζα γὰρ πάντων τῶν κακῶν ἐστιν ἡ φιλαργυρία [cf. Gothic *failugeiro*] ἧς τινες ὀρεγόμενοι ἀπεπλανήθησαν ἀπὸ τῆς πίστεως καὶ ἑαυτοὺς περιέπειραν ὀδύναις πολλαῖς.

Nihil enim intulimus in hunc mundum: haud dubium quod nec auferre quid possumus. / Habentes autem alimenta et quibus tegamur, his contenti simus. / Nam qui volunt divites fieri, incidunt in tentationem et in laqueum diaboli, et desideria multa et nociva, quæ mergunt homines in interitum et perditionem. / *Radix enim omnium malorum est cupiditas*: quam quidam appetentes erraverunt in fide, et inseruerunt se doloribus multis.

For we brought nothing into this world, and it is certain that neither can we carry anything out. / And having food and raiment, let us be therewith content. / But they that will be rich fall into temptation and a snare [of the devil], and into many foolish and hurtful lusts which drown men in destruction and perdition. / *For the love of money is the root of all evil*; which while some coveted after, they have erred from the faith and pierced themselves through with many sorrows (rather *pains*; Lattey *pangs*; Gothic *sairam*).[26]

[40v] This is of course for Europe the primary source and text. Symbolic (pictorial), and therefore story-making, elements are present or latent in

---

[25] Tolkien amends the received Greek text here and above by inserting δῆλον. He had started learning the language at King Edward's School where he attended the Head Master's classes on the Greek New Testament (SH 2:621–2).

[26] Cuthbert Lattey was one of the general editors of *The Westminster Version of the Sacred Scriptures*, a Catholic project that included the New Testament in four volumes published between 1913 and 1935. The parallel passage of Timothy I 6:10 from the Gothic Bible ends, "galaubeinai jas sik silbans gaþiwaidedun *sairam* managaim", where Gothic *sair* means 'pain'.

it – whether it partly derives from a story or is only the germ of one. Thus the Greek has not mere *cupiditas* but φιλαργυρία, thus introducing beyond the abstract vice of covetousness the symbol of the precious metals.[27] And of those desiring *money* (silver), it is said that they fall into a trap or snare (in some texts: of the Devil). These two elements combined were alone enough to beget a story – about gold or silver lying unguarded as the bait of a trap (of the Devil) – to illustrate the perils of the lust for wealth. But the story was already made.

I will begin now with some remarks on this story intended to illustrate the growth of stories about an "incident" in general, as well as to exhibit this example in particular. I will start, therefore, without reference to any particular recorded form.

The core or essential, central, part of a "story" has as such no reality or literary life. It does not matter whether it is an abstraction from actual particularized stories, or is just a piece of generalized observation from life. It is in this state just a piece of potential material (from the point of view of story-making) and it must be made particular again, reincarnated in person, time, and place if it is to "come alive" again.

But when this has been done, then it becomes alive and potent: it has "character". And as long as it is handed on *in story form* (i.e. not reduced once more to a dried seed of apothegm or reflection) that character will tend to cling to it. A later teller or writer will not easily undo the older one's work, nor easily obliterate or wholly transmute its character and air. A later writer will attempt these things at his peril, even if he be Chaucer or Shakespeare. (Neither *The Clerk's Tale* nor *The Merchant of Venice* are wholly successful in transmuting into "realistic" terms the symbolical and indeed "fairy-tale" character of the underlying stories[28] – not even though both had previously passed through other (Italian) hands working in the same direction.)

The "core," of course, often has a latent character of its own: I mean it is by its nature comic, or satirical, or fantastic, or mysterious, and so on. The one we are dealing with belongs to the large and ancient class of the "moral" or the *wise*: whose point lies in indicating a matter of morals or of prudence. Like

---

[27] Note the Gk for *cupiditas* "love of money" is here φιλαργυρία, containing the more pictorial word ἄργυρος silver, *minted* money. [Tolkien in red ballpoint at the foot of the page.] Chaucer's rioters find eight bushels of new-minted coins. [Ed.]

[28] Tolkien had thought deeply about "fairy-tales" in his 1939 lecture "On Fairy-Stories" (*Essays* 109–61). Here he singles out Chaucer's tale of Patient Griselda because it was a set text for examination, as he complained when lecturing on it along with the *Pardoner's Tale* in 1947 (MS Tolkien A 13/2, fol. 5). He himself had adapted the fairy-tale ending of Shakespeare's *Merchant of Venice*, where Portia and her husband Bassanio invite his friend Antonio to live with them at Belmont, by having Frodo invite his friend Sam with wife Rose Cotton to live with him at Bag End (*RT* VI/9).

the fables associated with the name of Æsop; for instance the dog and his reflection in the water. In consequence the first thing to note is that however much it may develop, the *teller* will aim at instruction and assume the mantle of wisdom: he will *preach*.[29]

[41r] Here is the core. Let us see how far its development can be, as it were, foreseen from its inherent nature, more or less independent of place and time.

Two men find an unguarded or ownerless treasure. The effect on them is disastrous for it wakes greed in their hearts, and they kill one another – and so neither of them enjoy any of it at all.[30]

As such it is hardly effective. It could be cast into a beast-fable form, and then the parallelism, and the need to do the simple work of transferring its application to human affairs would give it a little more interest. But we are following a line of development that did not go that way. The incident was turned into a tale about people. Several different things will then – more or less inevitably – happen to it: not, of course, necessarily in this order, nor indeed *seriatim* at all. A "setting" must be devised: to *account for the treasure* and *the way in which it was found*. Since the story could be many thousands of years old, and yet be still in a time when things held *beautiful* (such as gold or silver or jewels) were hoarded and coveted, and indeed derived much of their worth (*sc.* exchange value) from that esteem, and the desire of possession which they aroused, the "treasure" will take the shape of precious metals or gems.

But the teller of a tale with a "moral" has by that act already placed himself upon the seat of Wisdom, as a teacher, so that the setting will partake of the morality. We are dealing with the ῥίζα τῶν κακῶν, *radix malorum*,[31] but it must have a soil. Among the first, then, of the improvements or refinements, we may expect attention to be given to *finders*. They will not be allowed just to light on the treasure, like innocents falling by the mere malice of fate into a trap or men catching a disease as unawares. Thus two new elements (directed toward enhancing the inherent *moralitas*) are likely to come in:

(a) The *finders* will be wicked men, or at least of such a sort that they catch the disease by predisposition: so that their fate is not merely "exemplary" to those outside the tale but "just" within it.[32] (Thus Chaucer's

---

[29] Last three words added in red ballpoint.

[30] See *Tolkien's Lost Chaucer*, 259–61, on how Tolkien had already developed this "core" in his story of Déagol and Sméagol finding the Ring.

[31] The root of evils. [Ed.]

[32] NB: This element is still in Chaucer's tale. The Devil has *permission* to tempt the Riotour to murder – because of his past evil life [Tolkien]. Added in blue ballpoint in the left margin with, in red ballpoint, curlicues above and below, a pointing hand, and asterisks. [Ed.]

lines *For-why the feend fond hym in swich lyvinge / That he hadde leve him to sorwe brynge*:[33] though cast in mediaeval Christian terms, may come down from a long way back, and are in any event but the making more explicit of a primary implication of the early "setting.")

(b) Probably (if less certainly and inevitably) the finders will be *warned* – and neglect or scorn the warning. Why? Because this feature *inside the story* will give a moral tale much greater force as between *teller* and *audience* outside it.

[41v] So the story begins to take shape, growing outwards from within like a seed. But it cannot develop thus abstractly unaffected by soil and climate. The account of the *treasure* and of its *origin*, or at least the explanation of how it was open to the finders to claim, will be done in terms of time and place of the story-teller, and of his tastes and beliefs – and these features will consequently be specially liable to variation and alteration. So also (if less so) will be the characterization of the finders and their evil dispositions which lay them open to cupidity. But we can follow them a little further.

They must, of course, be at least *two*. They will be represented as friends, companions or confederates. Why? Well, partly for simple mechanical reasons: it is the simplest and most obvious way of explaining their joint discovery. Partly, as further growth from the *moralitas*, in this way their fall under the influence of cupidity is enhanced, is made more shocking. Thus, if they are represented as *professional thieves* (one of the most obvious devices for the purpose even in a very remote and "primitive" time),[34] they will likely be under some bond to one another. (The finders are "sworn brothers" in Chaucer. A special reason is given for this in his version; but the feature of the bond of confederacy is in itself most probably a very ancient one.)

There now enters another element. A "wise man". In a sense he represents the teller of the moral story, put inside the tale. But his place in the machinery is to *warn* the finders. Therefore he must already *know about the treasure*. At the least he must know what it is, and where it is at the moment lying – but he *may* know more than that: he may know about its nature and origin. And a reason must be given for two things: (a) why he tells the finders about it, (b) why he himself eschews it.

---

[33] *Pardoner's Tale* (*CT* VI, 847–8).
[34] Tolkien's "On Fairy-Stories" (*Essays* 124) also placed the word "primitive" in quotation marks to indicate that he used the adjective in no pejorative sense.

The first (a) is a matter of mechanism, and liable to vary. It will depend a good deal on the way in which the *finders* are depicted. Thus, if they are "thieves", an obvious device is to make them extract the knowledge from the sage by threats or violence, e.g. "ransom". The insolence of the "riotours" to the *old cherl* in Chaucer (though his tale has here been given an unnatural twist away from its essential line) is undoubtedly a relic of some such feature. For (b) the reason given will be one of *wisdom* (prudence or morality) – inevitably: since this tale is from its seed upwards of that nature.

There is no need, of course, for us to consider this tale as an item in a chain whether of Buddhist birth-stories or of Christian pilgrims. Indeed we must forget that, and consider rather what else is likely to be done to it, while it was told as a single tale in its own right. In that case, it is likely to be further "tied up" interiorly, and rounded off.

[42r] One "tying up" likely to occur – though not inevitable – relates to the *treasure*. The mode will naturally depend much on time and place and current beliefs. Thus in "primitive" times we meet often the association of what we should call *wisdom*, mere prudential wisdom, or on a more religious plane "moral teaching", with powers of foresight, occult knowledge, and even control over physical things such as we should loosely call "magic" or (in hagiographical legends) "saintly" power. The "wise man" is apt to be also a *wizard*.[35] In such an atmosphere, he is quite likely to become even closer connected with the treasure, as its discoverer or even producer; and will take on a mythological or saintly stature while the treasure itself will become "magical" or "demonic".

(In Chaucer's version that relationship is left wholly unexplained. But this need not be a primitive trait, indeed clearly is not.[36] But the lying of a heap of gold under a tree is, by its very lack of explanation, mysterious. And the fact that it consists of coins of pure gold, round as if new-minted, derives evidently from a form of story in which the gold had a strange, unnatural origin.)[37]

As for the "rounding off" – a process more nearly approaching the inevitable: it is we might say "almost inevitable" that the "wise man" will return to

---

[35] See *Tolkien's Lost Chaucer*, 260–1, on Gandalf as the "wise man" apt to be a wizard of saintly stature. "Gandalf is not, of course, a human being," Tolkien wrote in 1954; "I would venture to say that he was an incarnate 'angel' – strictly an ἄγγελος" (*Letters* 298). Tolkien's 1954 account of *The Istari* offered "wise" and "wizard" as translations of the Quenya word *istar*; see *Unfinished Tales of Númenor and Middle-earth*, ed. Christopher Tolkien (Boston and New York: Houghton Mifflin, 1980), 388.

[36] Last four words added in red ballpoint.

[37] This sentence, from "derives evidently from...", is marked in red ballpoint with two vertical lines and a pointing hand. E. C. Clark, "Notes on the Roman and Early English Law of Treasure Trove", *Archaeological Journal* 43 (1886), 350–7, explained how an ownerless treasure legally belonged to the King and withholding it was a crime punishable by death. [Ed.]

the scene of the catastrophe. And just as he himself represents the story-teller inside the tale, so there will now come in an "inside audience" to whom he can speak and draw the moral conclusion. This audience (in the "atmosphere" sketched above) is likely to be made a disciple (or several) of the saintly wise man himself. But since they are introduced to learn his wise summing up at the end, they are likely to be mentioned earlier in the tale.

So the tale acquires a powerful or ominous setting. But we have yet to consider the mechanism of the essential incident. So far we have been considering rather the treasure and what are in a sense excrescences, outgrowths from this. Let us now jump on again to the *finding*. As soon as the treasure is discovered, the problem of its use and *division* arises; for this is the heart of the matter, that must lead to the disaster. The problems are now just simple problems of effective procedure and "mechanism". The parties are each to kill the other. How is this to be most naturally and convincingly achieved, and with best narrative effect? The latter will mean (in such a tale) also the most moral effect – the clearest exhibition of *baseness* on part of the finders, to show forth the corrupting power of "treasure".

[42v] We shall not get, then, a sudden violent quarrel: knives drawn on the spot. It can happen, but it is not very convincing to make two combatants (still less two groups of combatants) kill one another. Also a sudden quarrel is not so shocking – it is more on the hungry animal plane, and does not exhibit human baseness, corruption through *thought*. Let us think of something better. *Poison!*

You can see the story-teller who thought of this – and it was very long ago: it comes into the oldest versions – you can see him patting himself on the back. It is so base, and so sinister. And, even mechanically, how it will improve the narrative at the centre. One man will think he has *won*: and yet in the moment of his wicked triumph, when Avarice has led him to treachery and murder – he will die miserably beside the gold.[38]

Excellent, but the *poison* will further define the story. It brings in *food* and *drink*. It creates at once a village or town nearby – which appears in nearly all but the most truncated and debased versions.

* * *

---

[38] Early on, Tolkien had devised how his story's "one man" would "die miserably beside the gold" in this 1939 plot note: "At that moment Gollum – who had seemed to reform and had guided them by secret ways through Mordor – comes up and treacherously tries to take the Ring. They wrestle and Gollum *takes Ring* and falls into the Crack." See Tolkien, *The Return of the Shadow: The History of the Lord of the Rings, Part I*, ed. Christopher Tolkien (Boston and New York: Houghton Mifflin, 1988), 381.

The story thus has grown to what we may perhaps call its "typical shape."

(1) There is A, a Wizard or Sage. By his powers he discovers a great treasure – probably sinister in origin, made or guarded by evil spirits. He will have nothing to do with it. He instructs his disciple-companion B to beware of it. (Here, probably at a very early stage, a form of words was used that later had considerable effect on the story: for example A to B, "That which you see is as perilous as a venomous snake" or "That is a snare"[39] or "There death lies hid.") A variant of this opening could be connexion of A (or B) with the treasure, as its actual maker or producer. But this is perhaps not the oldest device, though it appears with variations in many oriental forms, as we shall see. It is never entirely happy, since it requires special motivation or leaves the treasure-making a piece of meaningless "magic" that detracts from the moral. Thus in the Buddhist version the *wisdom* is transferred from the *wizard* A to the *disciple* B (the Buddha in an earlier existence), and the *wizard* becomes an (unwise) magician with an astrological power of producing a rain of precious things at certain junctures. In Persian and Arabic when "Jesus son of Mary" occupies the place of A, there is special machinery to account for [43r] the making by "power" of the treasure, but its abandonment, so as (by purpose or chance) to be a temptation to finders, is not satisfactorily motivated or explained.

(2) There are some wicked men C, D – whose previous lives (e.g. as thieves) predispose them to disastrous cupidity; but they are close friends, and bound to one another by vows of fellowship. They come by, and meet the wise man A (and/or his disciple B), and are warned against the sinister treasure. (Here the same formula is used again, or is first used, denoting the treasure in ominous or riddling terms as a "serpent" or as death – or a *trap* or *snare*.)[40] But the evilly disposed men scorn the sanctity of A, and pass on to find the treasure. The machinery here varies: the scorn of C, D is often enlarged to make them actually force A to lead them to the treasure. He then passes on and leaves them.[41]

---

[39] In the main text "That is a snare" was added in red ballpoint. When Bilbo first offers the Ring to Gandalf for safekeeping, the wizard recoils, "No, don't give the ring to me" (*FR* I/1). Gandalf reacts even more violently when later offered the Ring by Frodo: "I dare not take it, not even to keep it safe, unused." (*FR* I/2). He then instructs his disciple Frodo about its evil powers.

[40] The words "or a *trap / snare* ?" were added in red ballpoint.

[41] As Chaucer's *cherl* still does. Only in debased and stupid forms do the villains (C, D) kill the wise warner, as in the German form of the story by Hans Sachs (cited by Clouston). For it is of the *essence* of the story that A should by his wisdom *escape*, while C and D perish. [Tolkien]. He refers to Clouston, 434. [Ed.]

(3) As soon as C, D find the treasure, the evil spell of Avarice begins to work; but at first they plan amicably how best to deal with their good fortune. They perceive at once that the treasure must be *guarded* until it can be got away (secretly). An immediate need is for food and drink. (It is also a frequent motive that they wish to celebrate their luck.) They draw lots, and D goes *to a nearby town or village* to get what is required. (This often includes means of transport.) He takes some small part of the treasure to use in purchase.

(4) As soon as they are separated, Avarice begins its deadly work. D thinks of the treasure left in C's hands, and as he goes, plots to get rid of C on his return: he resolves to poison D's share of the food and drink. But C looking at the treasure begins to regret that it must be divided, and resolves to slay D as soon as he comes back.

It is at this point that C is likely to be divided into two C/E. In any case it is notable that the number involved in the central catastrophe is – apart from the ancient Buddhist version – usually *three* (less often four). [43v] I have suggested that the number was enlarged to *three* for narrative reasons: most of all to make certain and effective the murder with weapons of D on his return. In any case where three are concerned, it is always *two* that remain behind, even though D has often a lot to do.

The introduction and setting is sometimes "tied up" with the central tale, by making B, the companion of A, neglect his master's instruction, and remain by the treasure, which is then found by *two* travellers who dispute the ownership with him. But this is probably not old or original, but a product of the fact that B becomes a foolish or wicked companion in order that A should produce treasure as a test.

(5) The story then proceeds to the prepared catastrophe.[42] D returns and is at once murdered by C (and E).[43] C (and E) feast and drink, and in the moment of triumph succumb and die beside the treasure. (Here a formula frequently occurs in Europeans versions: *which remained free and ownerless as it was at first. The gold does not die.*)

(6) To wind up: A comes back to the scene of the catastrophe and draws the moral. It was at this point, I suggested, that the disciple B came in: since

---

[42] Tolkien's "On Fairy-Stories" (*Essays* 153) coined the word *eucatastrophe* as a contrast to a tragic ending: "the joy of the happy ending: or more correctly of the good catastrophe, the sudden joyous 'turn.'" *The Lord of the Rings* ends with a eucatastrophe when Frodo and Sam, as part of the three-man version, are snatched from death after completing their unselfish quest.

[43] E is a third wicked man in some versions of the story, who remains with C and the treasure. See footnote to the paragraph above.

dialogue is most effective, with "A to B" representing *inside the story* the teller and his audience outside it. Thence B was transferred also to the beginning. (In many versions, whether by later truncation and reduction, or by descending from more primitive shapes, B is absent altogether.)

It is here, if anywhere, that moral reflections (on the processes of cupidity; on the death by treachery of those who plot it; on the wicked dispositions that make men more prone to cupidity and to follow its lead into wickedness) should come in.

[44r] Now there is nothing in all this to fix it definitely in any part of the world. It requires, of course, what might be called archaeologically "an advanced state of culture", in which precious things (metals and gems) are already hoarded,[44] and arouse *greed* since they are valuable (*sc*. can be exchanged for goods and pleasures) and *acquisitiveness* since they are held desirable in themselves. Not to mention the use of *poisons*. But such a state was reached many thousands of years ago, so long ago that the story could, even before the Christian Era, have travelled "hence out of Ind" and back (or *vice versa*) several times.[45]

The fact therefore that the oldest known version (and one already fully elaborated, indeed already altered for a special purpose) is *Indian* and *Buddhist* is no proof that this tale arose in India and spread thence westward. To say no more the Sanscrit language and its descendants, the primary vehicle of Buddhist literature, is not indigenous to India but entered from the northwest, leaving behind peoples of very close connexion in language (and in religion and myth) in the wide lands between, right up to the borders of what we now name Europe. *Buddhism*, and therefore the roots of its literature, go back to a time that seems to us ancient; but the world of men was already very old in the days of *Gautama*: Egypt was (for instance) hoary with antiquity, and the Mesopotamian world hardly less. Buddhist literature undoubtedly absorbed and drew into itself much that was far older, whether "Aryan", or indigenous to non-Aryan India; but we need to detect in tales that find in it their analogues something of its special impress, before we can assert that a wide-spread tale came *out* of (Buddhist) India, and not from some even older centre.

---

[44] But are all the better "instruments" for the revelation of greed since the foundation of their value is partly *aesthetic*. You could not buy things with gems or even with gold if men had not thought them *per se* desirable. Thus "treasure" attacks the human mind at two vulnerable points at once: *greed* for pleasure and physical satisfactions; and acquisitiveness, *desire to possess*. [Tolkien]

[45] Probably Tolkien alludes to lines from the Old Man's speech in the *Pardoner's Tale* (CT VI, 721–2): "for I ne can nat finde / A man, though that I walked into Inde."

Whether that is the case in this instance I cannot judge. That the tale is "moral" shows nothing: it is so by its nature. That the moral it inculcates, or one that it can inculcate, is a feature of Buddhism – contempt of worldly riches – shows no more. It is a feature of most "higher" moral or religious spheres above the level of mere prudence. And in fact (as we shall see) the actual moral drawn in the Buddhist *Jātaka*-story is against "trying to take improper advantage over others". The wise disciple (after the death of the foolish wizard) takes the treasure and uses it properly "in alms and righteous acts". But the association with a supreme [44v] figure in the function of A-B (in the *Jātaka*-story B is Gautama himself) may be held to be a special feature reflected in the association in the Islamic area with Jesus son of Mary (as a saintly figure of wisdom and power), and in Europe occasionally with Christ and his disciples.

* * *

The study of tales and their migrations and transformations, and the collection of analogues, is a pursuit in itself, and quite a different business from the consideration of a given, shaped and placed story and the tracing, if possible, of its direct descent. This is well illustrated by another Chaucerian story, the *Manciple's Tale* of the tell-tale crow. Here the collectors of analogues provide us with a mass of excerpts from, and references to, the vast stores of oriental stories about talking and tell-tell birds.[46] But these are really all beside the point. Doubly. First because even if there is any lineal connexion (going into a remote past) between such things and Chaucer's tale, the oriental "analogues" are quite different in tone, setting, and purpose.[47] Secondly because we know Chaucer's direct source in this case. His *direct* tale-source is Ovid, the briefly told story of *Phebus* and *Coronis* and how the white and sweet-voiced *corvus* became a black croaking bird. This he has told with his characteristic blend of pedantry and satiric humour (and contrived to spoil the story at its crisis) and our consideration of his art, and its virtues and defects, depend on no oriental analogues.[48]

---

[46] Clouston, "The Tell-Tale Bird: Latin Source, Other European Versions, and Asiatic Analogues of Chaucer's *Manciple's Tale*," in *Originals and Analogues*, 437–80. Skeat 3:501 mentions Clouston but focuses on Chaucer's immediate source Ovid's *Metamorphoses* with further reference to Gower's treatment in his *Confessio Amantis*.

[47] They might for example be independent products of human fancy proceeding from such common data as unfaithful lovers (or wives) and various kinds of birds that can imitate human speech. Parrots in any case are not Crows or Ravens. [Tolkien]

[48] Unless it be in the fact that the unfaithful woman (nameless) is called Phebus' *wife* and the centre of the story (in spite of mythological description of Phebus at the beginning and his godlike power at the end) is thus given more of the air of stories of this type that are not Ovidian. [Tolkien]

So it might be, if we had a direct source for the *Pardoner's Tale*. But since we have not, we may in this case be excused for going far afield and for scrutinizing (as far as we have time) some of the versions: for only so shall we be able to guess at what Chaucer himself has done, and be able (tentatively) to accord him praise or blame. Yet let the *Manciple's Tale* warn us again (as I have already said) that the contacts of Orient and Occident are ancient, and did not begin with the Crusades or Venetian trade! What indeed do we know of the tales of men in all the lost centuries in the lands we now call Europe? Such as we know that come to us from the ages before the Christian Era are largely Greek – and the Greek world (notably that of its legends) was as much of the "Near East" as of Europe. But centuries [45r] before the Hellenized oriental Phoenician letters were used to write down any of our barbaric tongues, the ships of the Phoenicians and the Greeks had crept west and north; and trade had passed up the great Scythian rivers to the Baltic. Europe has never been cut off from Asia, for the simple reason that it is essentially a part of it. Or coming later: we must not forget the "oriental" Jews, already widely settled in Europe in the Dark Ages.

* * *

For any further consideration of the story in Chaucer's *Pardoner's Tale* we must, I fear, have actually before us the Buddhist story that I have referred to so often: the *Vēdabbha Jātaka*.

On this Clouston gives in *Chaucer: Originals and Analogues* (Chaucer Society 1888) C. H. Tawney's translation in full – which he calls (illegitimately I think) "Buddhist Original" – from *Pāli*.[49]

It should of course be present to the mind of my audience, and my part should be to make a few comments or points in it notable (for our purposes). But that is hardly to be expected. Nonetheless though short it is too long for recitation *in extenso*, since it is remote from Chaucer and the Pardoner, our primary business. I will therefore present a much reduced and "potted" form.[50] The danger of using potted forms, to which I have before referred, may in this case be reduced, since I am not just offering a précis of the essentials of a story blind, but am aware (or think I am) of the points of special interest for our enquiry.

---

[49] Clouston, 418–22. [Ed.]
[50] Tolkien's disdain for "potted" summaries returned in his 1959 "Valedictory Address" (*Essays* 224): "I would always rather try to wring the juice out of a single sentence...than pot a poet in a paragraph." The *OED* traces back to Boswell's *Life of Johnson* the dismissive sense "put into a short and easily assimilable form; condensed, summarized, abridged."

There is a brief "potting" in Drennan and Wyatt's edition. This would be (barely) adequate if it did not make some curious errors – the chief of which is to say that at the end "the Buddha points the moral much as does the Pardoner".[51] Which is quite misleading. The *Pardoner's Tale* comes (as not unusually in Chaucer, whose tales tend to be top-heavy, and this one especially so) to an abrupt end, whereupon the Pardoner rather than pointing a precise "moral" of his story, utters a general imprecation:

> *O cursed synne of all cursednesse* etc. 895–903.[52]

But the Buddha's "moral" is this:

> "He who desires advantage unseasonably is afflicted;
> The men of Chedi slew Vedabbha, and they all themselves perished."[53]

Which is very different. For "unseasonable" or improper desiring of advantage, overreaching others, is only, as it were, *one* part of the more complex vice of *cupiditas*, or rather φιλαργυρία, while the final treacherous baseness of the poisoner and murderer are not specially alluded to at all.

[45v] Very well. The "Buddhist original" not only contains the cited "moral" near the end, but *begins* with it. For *Gautama* is lecturing an obstinate member of his brotherhood, and revealing to him how in a previous incarnation he (the disciple) had been the *Vedabbha Brāhman* who brought death on himself by his own folly. At that time *Gautama* had been a student under him "studying the sciences".

He tells that long ago in the reign of King *Brāhmadatta* in Benāres, there was a Brāhman who knew a spell called *Vedabbha* (hence his name the Vedabbha Brahman). It was an astrological spell of "priceless efficacy", for at a certain position of the moon, he could cause a rain of the seven kinds of precious things to fall from heaven. The Brāhman set out one day with his disciple on a journey to the Kingdom of Chedi. They were waylaid by 500 Sending Thieves: so called because if they captured two prisoners they sent one away to get a ransom and held the other. The disciple was sent, and said

---

[51] Tolkien cites C. M. Drennan and A. J. Wyatt's student edition of the *Pardoner's Tale* (London: University Tutorial Series, 1937), 30, as part of its "potted" survey 29–31.

[52] Tolkien quotes Drennan and Wyatt instead of Skeat's *O cursed sinne, full of cursednesse* (*CT* VI, 895).

[53] Clouston, 422.

to the Brāhman that he would be back soon, and warned him not to use his spell, though the appropriate time was approaching.

The thieves bound the Brāhman, and when the moon rose he yielded to the temptation to release himself quickly from affliction and repeated the spell. A rain of treasure came from heaven. The thieves collected it and started off. The Brāhman followed them. But another band of 500 thieves took the first band prisoners; and to secure their release, the latter said: "If you desire wealth, seize this Brāhman, for he made a rain of treasure fall from heaven."

Accordingly the second 500 let the first band go, and seized the Brāhman and demanded wealth. But the Brāhman said that he could not do so, until the moon was in the right position again, in a year's time. Impatient and angry the thieves cut the Brāhman in two, and left his body by the road; then they pursued the first band and fought with them and slew them all. Then they themselves were divided into two bands and fought, until half were slain on each side. And so it went on until only two remained.

Now those two "deftly carried off" all the treasure and *hid it in a thicket near a village*. There one remained to guard it, while the other took some rice and went off to the village to get it cooked. "*Truly this passion of avarice is the root of destruction*" (auctor!),[54] for the one [46r] on guard resolved to kill his companion with a sword as soon as he came back; while the other resolved to put poison in the rice for his fellow to eat. But on his return the other at once cut him in two, and threw his body into a thicket. Then he ate the rice and fell dead on the spot. Thus because of the treasure all these men perished.

But the disciple after a day or two returned with the ransom. He did not find the Brāhman where he had left him, but saw wealth scattered about, and so knew that against his advice the spell had been used. He went along the road, and found his master's body, which he burned on a pyre. Further on he found 500 men lying dead, and then 250, and so on, until at last he saw only two corpses: a thousand slain all save two; and he wondered where the last two thieves were. Following the tracks he came at length to the thicket, saw the heap of treasure done up in bundles, and the man lying dead upon a plate of rice, and found the cast-away body.

Then he exclaimed: "Disregarding my advice, my teacher lost not only his own life but caused the death of a 1000 men. Truly those who unseasonably and wantonly pursue their own advantage meet, as he, with utter ruin." This reflection he put into verse:

---

[54] The Latin word *auctor* can mean an authoritative pronouncement. [Ed.]

"He who desires advantage unseasonably, he is afflicted;
The men of Chedi slew Vedabbha, and they all themselves perished."

The woods resounded to his utterance, and the sylvan deities applauded him as he set forth the moral lesson contained in the stanza. Then he "deftly removed the wealth" to his own house, and continued the rest of his life giving alms and doing other righteous acts, and when he died he attained heaven.

The *Jātaka* ends with the Master (Gautama) revealing to the obstinate brother of his community that on that occasion, the obstinate brother was the Vedabbha Brāhman and he himself was the pupil.

* * *

Though I have considerably abridged Tawney's translation, I have given the *Jātaka* more fully than usual, because *if we are to consider it at all*, we must get something of its tone and style, and must at least glimpse its excrescences and elaborations.

Even set out thus abbreviated I think you will agree that it is absurd to call it *the Buddhist original*. The *Jātaka* is certainly not the *original* of anything, but a late version specially elaborated (I should say irrationally and even "unseasonably" elaborated) and specially shaped and altered for a particular purpose and setting, quite as much as Chaucer's version is adapted to its particular setting. It certainly contains, if in [46v] altered or diffused form, all the elements of the primary full-grown tale (as I sketched it), and in this exaggerated form or something like it, may have been the source of other forms directly connected with Buddhism (e.g. versions or relics of versions found in Tibet and China).[55] But behind it must lie a much simpler form, from which other tales, further west, may well be independently derived.[56]

The alterations which this *Jātaka* has undergone are probably of two kinds: those due to particular use and purpose; and those due to place and culture.

As a *Jātaka* it is one of a huge series of 550 stories all supposed to be memories of his previous incarnations related by the Buddha, each for a purpose of instruction. The story can (as can each of the *Canterbury Tales*) be taken by

---

[55] For instance a (debased) Tibetan version cited by Clouston (op. cit.) in which 500 robbers, very hungry, find the carcass of an elephant, and divide into parties of 250, one to cut up and cook the meat, the other to fetch water. Each party uses poison. [Added by Tolkien in left margin, referring to Clouston, 431-2.]

[56] Originally, as usual in blue ink, Tolkien wrote "a much simpler and more rational form" and ended the sentence with "from which other tales, further west, are derived". The final phrasing was made by successive emendations in red ballpoint and then black ink.

itself, yet its setting affects the turning of the tale (as it does some of the *Canterbury Tales*, notably the *Pardoner's Tale*).

Thus: the Master is lecturing an obstinate disciple, and the *primary* moral becomes entangled with a warning against the *obstinate refusal of good advice* – as the *Pardoner's Tale* becomes entangled with reflections on the sins of gluttony and blasphemy. For, if I am right in defining the presence of A(B) *inside* the story as a representation of teller and audience outside it, then any change in these will be likely to be reflected in the A(B) within the story. Thus by an effective stroke (for the purpose) the situation of A + B is here altered, so that their positions are reversed: inside the story the function of wisdom and warning is transferred to B (the disciple). Outside it is the disciple who is now superior. The warning against the treasure in pictorial language given by A to B becomes "diffused" to a mere warning against using a spell, or producing (by magic) a treasure that will cause the user's death. But it is the introduction of this "obstinacy" motive that makes this elaborated *Jātaka* form top-heavy – somewhat again, as Chaucer's form is, with its over-elaboration of the previous lives of the *riotours*. For the obstinacy must lead to death, and so the treasure begins to work too soon, as it were; and we have to have machinery for that, and so we are presented with the "sending thieves".[57]

These and other points (such as the elaboration of the ending, the revisiting of the scene of final catastrophe) are due largely [48r] to particular purposes. To place and culture (India and Ceylon) are no doubt due the gross exaggerations of nearly all the details – (absurd and distasteful to Western taste). The incredible spell and rain of the seven kinds of precious things – in southern Buddhist lists: gold, silver, pearls, all precious stones, lapis lazuli, diamonds, and coral; the two great bands of robbers and their slaughter, and so on. (This very "unoriginal" feature is not found in any of the versions given or cited by Clouston, except the debased Tibetan form referred to above.)

That even in "Buddhist" literature the situation, as regards A and B, at the beginning, was once much simpler (and so much nearer to Western forms) is suggested by one of *Avadánas*, or Indian tales and apologues, which is cited by Clouston from the French translation of S. Julien (Paris 1859) out of *Chinese*.[58] "One day the *Buddha*, journeying in the province of Prasirajit, saw a place where a treasure had been deposited by someone…Buddha said to *Ananda*: 'Do you see that venomous serpent?' 'I see it,' replied Ananda. But

---

[57] The sentence "The warning against the treasure" is highlighted with a vertical line in blue ink. The entire paragraph stands between two horizontal lines in black ink. Drafting for it is preserved on fol. 47r, a page torn from an exam booklet.

[58] Clouston, 432, cited Stanislas Julien's *Les Avadánas*, 3 vols. (Paris: Benjamin Duprat, 1859).

there was a man walking behind Buddha, and he went to look at the serpent. When he saw the precious things, he railed at Buddha for a fool." The story then proceeds differently, but the man was brought to misery and torture by the treasure. (Here we have the germ of the formula in European versions used by the wise man A who calls the gold *Death* – a point that proved of great importance in determining the story's heredity.)[59]

In one point the *Jātaka* form remains primitive. The final catastrophe – the old "core" of the story – remains simple: just two men, guard-murderer and messenger-poisoner. Coming at the end of a long series of murders and slaughter it is not specially effective. Their murder of one another is hardly impressive: we are numbed before we come there. This point alone is sufficient to show that this Pālī *Jātaka* is not an "original". It is indeed the end of one over-grown branch from which no further growth could be expected. In its withering and debasement we should in fact expect the two original unhappy victims to be forgotten – as in the debased story of 500 hungry robbers and the elephant (Tibet) alluded to above. It is from older, simpler forms that C, D will become C, E + D – whether this be due to "realism," the storyteller's keeping his eye on the final catastrophe and its probabilities (as I suggested), or to the tendency for tales (especially those of symbolic or moral import) to adopt the number three. Neither "realism" [48v] nor the simple story triad can be expected from a tale that has already substituted (for either of them) a kind of formal arithmetic of division. And, incidentally, one that does not work. For you cannot, in fact, continually divide 500 by 2 and have at last 2 remaining. When 250 fought 250 and on each side half are killed, the next battle would be between 125 a side, but the result would be 62½ remaining in each team, and the fraction would continue to get more refractory – you would end up with 125/128 a side (I believe).[60]

*   *   *

With these continually bisected sides (and corpses), ending in the poor little poisoned figure on its plate of rice, we may take leave of the *Jātaka*.

If we turn to other versions we shall find one thing common to them all. *They are all late in record*. Few in fact are anterior, in point of text, even to Chaucer's date. They are thus all rehandlings (either by elaboration, or as often by debasement and reduction) at many removes of older originals that can only be glimpsed through them. They are only examples of the kinds of

---

[59] This parenthetical sentence is a later addition in blue ink.
[60] Tolkien had puzzled out the arithmetic in the left margin of fol. 46r.

forms this story could take, and the types of treatment of its essential features. None are "originals", either in the case of the eastern versions as representing the story that came to Europe, or in the case of European versions, as representing the story that reached Chaucer's eye (or ear). Indeed, preliminary deductions to be made are that (a) different types of developments were current in the nearer East and that (b) more than one form reached Europe.

In dealing (briefly) with the other oriental variants cited by Clouston and others, I do not think it is necessary to give versions of the comparative fullness of my "potting" of Tawney's translation of the *Jātaka*. There were good reasons for dealing more carefully with that – among them, destruction of the claim that it is (or is even like) the "original". All we now want is to find variants which exhibit features which are characteristic of the European lines of development.

[51r][61] These are not difficult to find, and actually we do not need to have recourse to the "Buddhist original" for any of them – except the one curious detail: the comment in the middle of the tale (just before the final catastrophe) *truly this passion of avarice is the root of destruction*. Though Drennan and Wyatt do not even trouble to include it in their "potting", it seems to me that most interesting detail in the whole *Jātaka*. Its presence there might be accident, but that seems to me unlikely. More likely the line of descent to Chaucer (though not from the *Jātaka* itself, but from its source) leads through a series in which the *radix malorum* formula was present.[62]

Coming westward (to Persia) the version given most fully by Clouston is a mediæval one (in our terms). That is, it is a re-handling of the story by a Persian mystic (Sūfī) and poet Ferīdu'd Dīn 'Attar of the 12th century, who made it into a poem, as an item in his *Book of Calamities* (*Kitab-i Masībat Nāma*). He was called 'Attar (the word we have in *attar* or *otto* of roses) because he had once been a dealer in perfumes. I do not attempt to reproduce the doubtless reduced version given by Clouston (apparently itself from a German metrical translation by Dr F. Rückert who published it in 1860).[63]

---

[61] On fol. 49r (torn from an exam booklet) Tolkien jotted a memo about the Islamic stories that he would go on to discuss, with the comment, "Elaboration at upper end then recurs at upper end," and the disconnected words "Jesus / loaves / confession / gold / forms of death".

[62] It is here that we see the comparative uselessness of "potted" versions. Thus we might have only Drennan and Wyatt to depend on, and then would not know that a formula so curiously similar to St Paul was present in the *Jātaka*. Similarly, even in using the material provided by Clouston we can only be certain of its absence in those versions (few) that he has given fairly fully.

Also it would be important to know, as I do not, if Tawney's translation is strictly accurate and literal (and not for instance influenced by St Paul!) in using the word *root*. [Tolkien]

[63] The Orientalist and poet Friedrich Rückert (1788–1866) published "Eine persische Erzählung" in *Zeitschrift der Deutschen Morgenländischen Gesellschaft* 14 (1860), 280–7. Tolkien lifts his paraphrase from Clouston, 423–6.

The points of interest are these:

It begins "Jesus, from whom beamed light, came into a village, and an evil man was his path-fellow".

Jesus is made the author or producer of the treasure, which is gold only. The machinery to explain this is fairly elaborate. Jesus has three loaves; he eats one, gives one to his companion, and one remains. The companion eats this, while Jesus has gone to get water. Jesus returning asks what has become of the loaf and the companion denies all knowledge of it. Jesus then displays an extraordinary pertinacity (or so it would seem to us) in discovering what had happened to the loaf or (perhaps more fairly said) in extracting a confession from the thief. He performs two miracles – taking the man by the hand and walking with him over the sea; killing a roe-deer and eating it, and bringing it back to life from the bones (like Thórr in the house of the Bóndi[64]) – then [51v] conjures the man (by the might of God by whom these marvels were done) to tell what he knew, but the man is obdurate. A third miracle and trick-test is therefore performed. Jesus after "pure and sweet prayer" turns three mounds of earth into *pure gold*. And he said, "One is mine, one is thine, and the third is for the one who secretly ate the bread." The man then at once confessed that he had eaten it.

Jesus then rejects the gold, and parts with his evil companion, for he desires him no longer. Sorrowfully he goes away.

Two men come by, see the gold, and quarrel with the first, who now claims all as his own. After long debate the three at last agree to share in equal parts. They are weary and hungry after the long debate. One says: "I will go to town and get bread." The others agree gladly. The one comes to the town, buys bread, eats some himself, and then puts *poison* in the rest, desiring all the gold for himself. The other two made a covenant to kill him and share the gold in halves. At that moment the one returned, and they killed him at once, but themselves died as soon as they ate the bread.

Jesus son of Mary returned to the spot, and saw what had happened, and said, "If this gold remains here, untold numbers will perish because of it." He then after prayer turned the gold back to dust.

* * *

---

[64] Tolkien recalls the legend of Thórr in *Hymiskviða* or "Hymir's Poem" from the *Poetic Edda*. Six editions and glosses of the *Edda* were among the books of his Celtic Library. His "On Fairy-Stories" discussed Thórr as the deification of thunder, but with a personality surpassing the natural phenomenon (*Essays* 123–4).

Now the "First Arabian Version" (*sic*) which Clouston gives (from unknown source)[65] is, I think, clearly *not* – as Clouston thought probable – derived from 'Attar, but from a form of the story lying behind 'Attar, which it preserves still in more original and rational form. I will therefore postpone comment on the "Persian Version" till we have seen what the "Arabian" has to offer.

Jesus is again made author of the *gold*. His companion is a *Jew*. The machinery of the loaves is similar (except that they hold bread in common, and the Jew had actually contributed two of the three loaves). Jesus performs several miracles, and the Jew persists in declaring that there had been only two loaves. Jesus then makes three mounds of earth into three blocks of gold; and the Jew confesses and claims two blocks. Jesus gently rebuked him for lying, gave him all three and went away; but he returned and warned [52r] the Jew, who was trying in vain to remove the blocks, to have nothing to do with them. "They will cause the death of three men. Leave them, and follow me." He did so.

Three travellers now pass by, and find the gold with great joy. They agree each to take a block. But they cannot carry them, so they agree that one should go to the town for carts, and for food. One goes off, but the other two plot to kill him on return. Murder comes into the mind also of the other, and he buys food and poisons it. The moment he comes back the two beat him to death. They then eat the food and fall down and die.

Jesus and the Jew soon after pass along the same road and see the three men lying dead beside the gold. Jesus exclaims: "This will be the end of the covetous who love gold!" He then raised the three men to life, and they confessed their guilt and repented and became his disciples. But the Jew persisted in his avarice, and as he still struggled to carry off the blocks, the earth opened and swallowed him up and the gold with him.[66]

* * *

Common to both is the setting with "Jesus son of Mary" taking the place of A (the Wise Man) and also acting as the producer of the fatal treasure – which is *pure gold* (as usual in all versions as we go westward). Both have the same machinery[ ] to account for this.

---

[65] Clouston derived it from an 'Account of the Virgin Mary and Jesus Christ according to the Arabian Writers' contributed to *The Orientalist*, vol. I, pp. 46–7 (Kandy, 1884), for which the contribution unfortunately gave no authority. [Tolkien.] See Clouston, 426. [Ed.]

[66] This version approximates Mount Doom's chasm swallowing Gollum and the gold Ring with him (*RK* VI/3).

The use of the figure of Jesus for this purpose is probably Islamic.[67] And it is usually assumed that, when the Buddhist story travelled westward and reached the regions of Islam, his figure was substituted for that of the Buddha, since his combination of sanctity (and moral purpose and instruction) with power (derived from Almighty God) made this natural. I am not convinced of this, though my opinion in such a field is of no great value. It seems to me that the story could later and independently have been attributed to a great historical figure, as A the Wise Man. And in any case it is hardly credible that either of these above-mentioned versions could have come from the story as found in the Pāli *Jātaka*.

[52v][68] Both are derived from a form in which the device of making A-B actually produce, and not merely know about, the treasure had been hit upon. But the whole situation and machinery is wholly different from that of the *Jātaka*. Indeed it has the air of being hit upon quite independently, for it is related to the interior of the story (which is not the case in the *Jātaka*). Thus it clearly depends on a version in which there are already *three* partners in the final scene, for there are *three* heaps or blocks of gold, and from that flows the device of the *three* loaves in the "prologue". That Jesus says at the end (of the Persian variant) that if the gold remains it will cause "the death of untold numbers" might possibly be an echo of the greater slaughter in the *Jātaka*; but it is said after the final catastrophe, and need have no such origin.

Of course these variants are late and must have themselves a long history behind them, and show both over-elaborate excrescence, and forgetfulness. The miracles and the machinery leading up to the making of the gold have grown out of hand, and are unoriginal (as of course is the anti-Jewish satire in the Arabic variant) while on the other hand neither say anything of the past history of the *finders*: they appear just as travellers, accidentally caught in a snare, with scant justice.

---

[67] Islam has never entirely lost the character of a Christian (unitarian) heresy, which is indeed its origin. In consequence "Jesus the Messiah" occupied in its traditions a special place as a sacred (if not divine) figure combining both sanctity and power. The air of the Gospels, however much garbled, can then be felt in stories about him. In the Persian story above cited he is called Saviour-Guide. Even when in fact his "miracles" are in form but pieces of folklore "magic," they are not performed without moral purpose and are usually the result of prayer, and attributed to God. They are specially frequently miracles of *recalling to life* or *healing*. He was thus a very appropriate figure to replace *Gautama*. [Tolkien]

[68] From the top of this page, Tolkien's handwriting improves markedly, perhaps simply indicating a resumption after a pause (not necessarily a long one), but perhaps suggesting that he was now considering getting his script typed or even published.

Of the two the Arabic version is I think (as I said above) the better. In the Persian variant the gold, having served its purpose in forcing a confession is just left, and the travellers are accidentally involved. The device of making the disciple of the A-B setting become one of the *three* C-D-E who murder one another is notable. A curious feature of the Arabic variant is that it seems to be blending a variant in which this was so, and one in which it was not: one in which the Jew remained with the gold and quarreled with the new-comers, and one in which he was just a disciple of Jesus and the recipient of his warning: "*this gold is death*" – here made more matter-of-fact and merely prophetic of the actual catastrophe: "this gold will cause the death of three men." But in any case, in this variant the actions of Jesus as the Wise Man A are less casual and purposeless. The gold is not left unguarded without thought, and the unfortunates caught in the snare are healed and given a chance of confession and repentance. This is much more satisfactory (as a miracle-story), but is undoubtedly a product of later working-up, and quite a late development – not unconnected with the satire on Jews, for the Jew persists in avarice and perishes.

Other simpler variants (in Persian and Arabic) are referred to in Clouston, in which, as far as can be determined from his brief notes, Jesus is not connected with the origin of the treasure, and is only concerned to discover the disaster after its occurrence and to moralize upon it. One of these appears in *Book of the Thousand and One Nights* (Burton's "Supplementary Nights," vol. I, p. 250).[69]

[53r] Actual links between these (vaguely) oriental variants, and those found in Europe are *not* in fact, it seems, extant, though there is not really any greater gap between the European variants and the "Islamic" than there is between those and the Buddhist.

Turning to the European things only *three* of those given, or summarized, in *Originals and Analogues* seem to me here worth again summarizing.

---

[69] I do not know why Clouston should assert that a story of this form in a Latin translation (of a Persian text unknown) by Warner (Leyden 1644), "may be considered a link between European versions and the Buddhist original", or if so why so important a document was not set out more fully. However it appears to have contained a formula which resembles one in many European variants – that the treasure after causing the death of men remained itself unaffected. See citation by Clouston, *Analogues*, p. 426 footnote. Jesus seeing the dead bodies says: *Hæc est conditio mundi! Videte quomodo ternos hosce tractaverit et ipse tamen post eos in statu suo perseveret. Væ illi qui petit mundum ex mundo!* [Tolkien.] The Latin translates as "This is the condition of the world!.See how the world treated these three men, and yet after them it itself proceeded on in its own way. Woe to him who will seek the world from the world!" The reference to Sir Richard Burton is lifted from Clouston, 428. Clouston's 426 footnote refers to the Orientalist and manuscript-collector Levinus Warner's *Proverbiorum et Sententiarum Persicarum Centuria* (Leiden, 1644). [Ed.]

I will refer first to the "old Italian Miracle Play", because this retains an oriental ("Near East") setting in *Damascus*.⁷⁰ In the play the spirit of *Avarice* tempts St *Antonio*. First he places a silver dish in his path, and St Antonio walking in the desert finds it, perceives its evil origin, and scorns it. Avarice then tries a great heap of gold, and again fails.

Meanwhile two *robbers* (*Tagliagambe* and *Scaramuccia*) meet. Business is bad. Tagliagambe has not a groat left. Scaramuccia has just been robbed at a fair (in Reggio!). They join forces. Then they fall in with an old friend *Carapello*, and make an agreement to share all spoils equally.

By orders of the Devil (*Satanasso*) fiends beat and wound Antonio; but he is comforted by Jesus. Being healed, Antonio walks in the desert again and meets the three robbers, and counsels them *to turn back from death, which lies in their path.*⁷¹ They scorn him as a madman and go on. They find the gold and laugh at the silly hermit who called the gold *Death*.

The robbers draw lots, for one of them to go to *Damascus* for food and wine, and scales to weigh the gold. *Scaramuccia* set out, but on the way thinks how foolish he has been to leave the others with the gold. He purchases *ratsbane from an apothecary*,⁷² and much food and wine, which he poisons. Meanwhile Tagliagambe and Carapello have plotted together to murder him on his return. They do so. Then they sit down to dine, and praise Scaramuccia's taste in wine; but in the midst of their triumph and plans for spending the treasure, the poison works and quickly kills them.

Avarice is delighted and reports to *Satanasso*, who promises him a crown in Hell as a reward, since though failing with St Anthony he has after all succeeded in ensnaring three souls instead of one. An angel closes the play, bidding the audience to take warning by the catastrophe.

[53v] In the transference of this tale to the Christian "background" St Antony the Hermit was a very suitable figure to take the place of A, the

---

⁷⁰ Clouston gives in summary form the plot of this (or the part relative to our enquiry), from D'Ancona's *Rappresentazione Sacre*, vol. ii, p. 33ff. No dates are given. Very oddly, Clouston says: "I suppose the holy hero of this play is the St Anthony," *sc.* of Padua (born in Lisbon 1195, died in Padua 1231). This is clearly *not* so (originally at any rate), the "hero" being the much earlier St Anthony, the hermit of the desert, after whom St Anthony of Padua (who was christened Ferdinand) avowedly took his name in religion. St Anthony the Hermit lived to be 105, being born in 251, and dying in A.D. 356. He was a native of Upper Egypt and became a solitary (famous for the temptations which he endured). In 305 he founded the first "monastery" or community of hermits in the Thebaïs. He was revered and renowned in the West as well as the East, especially since he took the Catholic side against the Arians at the Council of Nicæa. [Tolkien]

⁷¹ This line is marked by a pointing-hand symbol in the margin. [Ed.]

⁷² Tolkien underscored these words first in black and then in red, for special emphasis. As he points out later, the details of *ratsbane from an apothecary* are identical to Chaucer's version in the *Pardoner's Tale* (CT VI, 851–4).

Wise Sage, in the setting. But though this transference and substitution could have taken place without *intervention of Islam* (occurring indeed before that heresy came into being) the arrangements in the miracle play seem to show later alteration. That is: St Anthony has replaced B "the disciple", and then usurped the function of A. Since Jesus is still in another version (to be treated next) retained as A with unnamed disciples, it would seem likely that that was the situation in (at least one main line of) the earlier "Christian" variants. But in none that are cited by Clouston does Christ appear as a *"magician"*, however benevolent, nor is he connected with the *origin* of the gold. The treasure is evil, explicitly or implicitly – an instrument of *temptation*. It is this no doubt that drew the hermit Anthony into the plot, renowned as he was for resisting the temptations of the Evil One. In the play Christ therefore appears only in relation to Anthony and without any connexion with the main story.

It is also notable that the play is the only "European" variant cited that includes any explanation of the *origin* of the gold at all. And it is not difficult to see why this part of the tale should have been reduced and disappeared. For if the treasure is to be of its nature evil, and an instrument of the Devil, whereby the dreadful workings of *cupiditas* are exemplified, then actually no special "origin" is required. Any treasure found "ownerless" will do.

This miracle play therefore (whatever its actual date) must be held to contain archaic features and to preserve unusually well the general form of a main line of the story's development in Europe – in spite of its alteration of the function of Christ and Disciple. The formula *radix malorum* does not (it seems) actually occur in it – for *Avarice* has become personified, and made the actual producer of the gold.

In this version one perceives clearly that the only function of the *third* finder – who is actually later added to the primary pair – is to assist in the murder of the companion sent to buy food, and to make certain of his death (without injuring those who are to die of poison).

The story is still linked with the "East" by the figure of Anthony, the references to the *desert* and the city of Damascus; and by the appearance in it still (if without original function) of the figure of Christ.

Links with Chaucer are seen in the warning that "Death lies in the way" and in the scorn of the wicked men; and still more curiously and cogently (and just because it is an unnecessary detail) in the purchase of *rat-bane from an apothecary*.

[54r] Another variant. This is in point of record a late document, though it would seem an ill-told and clumsy abbreviation of a tale much older. This is

the version in *Lo Ciento Novelle Antike* cited from a printed edition of 1525. (It was Tyrwhitt who first pointed out its resemblance to the *Pardoner's Tale*.)[73]

Christ was walking in a wild country with his disciples when they saw shining by the way some piastres made of fine gold (*doro fine*). They wondered why he did not stop, and they cried: "Lord, let us take this gold, which will relieve us of many needs!" But Christ turned and reproved them, saying: "You desire the very things that rob our kingdom of the greater part of men's souls. That this is true you will learn as we come back."

A little later two companions (dear friends) found the gold and were delighted, and by agreement they went (sic! *andaro*, but an error) to the nearest village to fetch a mule; the other remained on guard. But hear now the evil deeds that ensued from the wicked thoughts that the Enemy put into them. The one returned with the mule and said to his companion: "I have eaten in the village, and you must be hungry. Eat these two nice loaves, and then we will load up."

The other replied: "I have no great desire to eat at the moment; let us load up first!" Then they began to load the mule, and when they had nearly finished, one stooped to tie the pack-saddle, and the other treacherously ran him through from behind with a sharp knife and slew him. Then he took one loaf and gave it to the mule. The other loaf he ate himself. The bread was poisoned; so he and the mule fell dead before they could stir from that place – *but the gold remained free as at first*.[74]

Our Lord passed by on that same day with his disciples, and showed to them the warning example which he had foretold.

* * *

This is a clumsily reduced form. (I mean in the actual Italian cited: I have translated most but not all of it.) Though now mishandled it appears to derive from a form in which the main tale was fully told (including the growth of evil thoughts in the hearts of finders, once dear friends, here only barely referred to) and the final murder scene was recounted with dramatic detail and some suspense.

It is notable in only having *two* finders; but whether that is an archaic feature or a product of reduction later is not clear. The poor mule indeed seems

---

[73] Clouston does not summarize this Italian analogue, but Skeat does (3:439–40), and Tolkien would have found the Bodleian's copy (perhaps the same used by Tyrwhitt) of *Ciento Nouelle Antike*, ed. Carlo Gualteruzzi (Bologna, 1525) so that he could pedantically quote the Italian *doro fine* and note the error *andaro*.

[74] Exactly the same formula occurs at the end of the next variant cited. [Tolkien]

partly to have replaced one of the three finders that perished. There is no origin given for the gold. Though there is a warning given and a moral drawn at the end, *no warning* is given to the finders; and nothing is said of their previous life (to explain the treachery of "dear friends"). There are *no names* of place or person (other than Christ).

* * *

[54v] A third Italian variant (translated and a little reduced from the text given in *Originals and Analogues*, which is drawn from) *Libro di Novelle et di bel Parlar gentile*, Fiorenza 1572, p. 86: novella lxxxii.

A hermit was walking one day through a wild country, and he came to a great hidden cave and there had a mind to rest; but as he entered he saw a great shining, because much gold lay there. As soon as he was aware of that, he left in haste and ran *through the desert* as fast as he could go.

As he was running the hermit encountered three great robbers who were in that wild place to rob any who passed that way, but had never discovered that the gold was there. Out of their hiding they saw the hermit running, though no one was pursuing him, and they were somewhat alarmed; but they stopped him and asked why he was fleeing in this fashion, at which they were much amazed. "My brothers," said he, "*I am fleeing from Death*, who is behind, pursuing me."

But they, seeing neither man nor beast, said: "Show us who is pursuing you and bring us to where she (sc. *Morte*, fem.) is." Then the hermit said: "Come with me, and I will show her to you." But all the same he begged them not to go. They insisted, however, and being unable to dissuade them, and fearing them, he guided them to the cave, and said: "Here is Death, who was pursuing me!"

But the robbers at once saw that it was gold that lay there, and they were in high glee; and they bade the good man farewell, *and he went off on his own business (per i fatti suoi)*.[75] But they remained behind, making fun of his simplicity; and they began to debate what they should do.

And one said: "*It seems to me that, since God has sent us this high good fortune*,[76] we should not depart from here, unless we carry away all this treasure." And another said: "No, let us do thus: let one of us take a little of it, and go to the town and sell it, and so buy bread and wine and what is needful to us."

---

[75] Cf. Pardoner's Tale 749, *old cherle* says: *I mote go thider as I have to go*. [Tolkien]
[76] Cf. Pardoner's Tale 779. [Tolkien]

To this all three agreed. The crafty Devil, desirous as ever of doing all the evil that he can, put it into the heart of the one that went to the town for the provisions: "When I am in the town" (said he to himself) "I will eat and drink as much as I need, and then I will provide myself with such things as I now require; and next I will poison what I bring to my companions – so that when they are both dead, I shall be master of all the treasure; and it is, I deem, so great that I shall be the richest man in all this country." And even so he did. He took all the food that he needed and poisoned the rest, and so brought it to his companions. But while he [55r] went to the town, if he had evilly plotted to kill his companions, so that all should be his, they had no better thought for him, and they said one to another: "As soon as this companion of ours comes back with the bread and wine, and the other necessaries, we will kill him, and then we will eat what we wish, and this great treasure will be between us two only, and we each shall get more."

Now the one who had gone to the town returned, and as soon as they saw him they leaped upon him and slew him. And when they had killed him, they ate of the food that he had brought, and as soon as they were filled they both fell down dead. Thus all three died and did not possess the treasure. Even so God paid the traitors; for they went after Death, and in this manner they found it (her) as they deserved. But the wise man (*saggio*) safely fled from it (her), *and the gold remained free as at first.*[77]

This version is better told than the previous one, and less reduced – though it certainly appears to be a reduction of a longer tale. The part of the "wise man" is now played only by the hermit (become nameless); and there is no origin recounted for the gold – though placing in a secret cave comes nearer to explaining it than just letting it appear by the way. The hermit is possibly derived from an earlier St Anthony: the word *diserto* is actually once used, though there are no *names* at all in this version of persons or places.

The point of chief interest with regard to the *Pardoner's Tale* is the play with the word *Death*. It would appear from the "moral" at the end that more was originally made of this earlier than now is found at the meeting of the robbers and the hermit. At that point this version as it stands is now confused (blending more than one treatment?); but it would seem that the robbers were at an

---

[77] This formula occurs in identical form in the variant previously cited, also in similar form in others referred to by Clouston. [Tolkien.] The tale of the three murderous robbers who die, with their gold left behind in a cave, may have lurked in the back of Tolkien's mind when devising *The Hobbit*'s episode of the Three Trolls with their gold left behind in a cave after being turned to stone. Instead of suffering temptation, Thorin's dwarves wisely bury the pots of gold in case they might return and claim the treasure. Only on their homeward trip do Bilbo and Gandalf retrieve the gold without any hint of greed. "Share and share alike!" says the wizard (359). [Ed.]

earlier stage made to take Death as a person's name, and vowed to attack him (her), much as in Chaucer's treatment.

* * *

There is another curious variant cited in *Originals and Analogues*. It is in point of record of about the same date as those above cited; but seems to descend from quite a different line – a later importation of a corrupt Eastern version? It is certainly far more oriental in tone, in spite of mention of the *Tiber*, than the others. It has little or no connexion with the line of development seen in Chaucer, except only that it actually contains the formula *radix malorum* etc. For which reason I give the gist. It is in Latin. (The text in *Originals and Analogues* is drawn from Morlini's *Novellæ*, Paris reprint, 1799, of Naples edition of 1520).[78]

"A wizard (*magus*) by the revelation of spirits in magical whispers learned that a treasure lay hid in the Tiber in a certain cave. And when it was found, since he saw a great mound of coins (*sicla*), by the common vote" – no clear indication is given of why there were so many persons or whence they came – a part of the companions went to the nearby town to purchase good food and drink, and other things. But the others meanwhile built a large fire and guarded the treasure. When, however, they reached town, *radice malorum cupiditate affecti* they resolved to kill their confederates with dire poison [55v] and rob them of their share in the treasure. That being agreed, they feasted in an inn, and drank deeply, and so delayed for some time. Their companions in the Tiber, waiting for them and suffering hunger, complained bitterly of their delay; and they swore to Jove that, when they did return from the town, they would rob them of life and share in the treasure. Thus they conspired against one another...[79] The first party returned with abundant provision: skins of wine, chickens, fish, sausages, and so on. The others came to meet them and attacked them at unawares and killed them all. Then they prepared a great feast with all the poisoned victuals; and they sat down and swilled and guzzled, but hardly had they risen from table when *they were overtaken by death* (*morte preuenti*). They lost their lives, even as their companions had, and there under the water (*sub elemento*) dead and buried they remained.

This is a curious (and textually corrupt) form. It has evidently omitted or forgotten much. It has an oriental tone, is only barely "moral" in implications, and is not religious or "Christian". What happened to the *magus*, or what part he played after receiving information from the spirits, is not told. Where

---

[78] Skeat 3:442–3 reprints the story from Morlini's Latin *Novellae*. [Ed.]   [79] Tolkien's ellipses.

I have said "town", on each occasion the Latin has *oppidum seu castellum* – which suggests conflation. Rome is not mentioned in spite of the Tiber (though Rome is the scene in some non-Italian variants). The expression *morte preuenti* suggests that "fleeing from death" may possibly originally have appeared in this form also. Points of interest for Chaucer are the actual use of *radix malorum* (without *omnium*) etc., rather clumsily dragged in – seeming to show that the formula was in the older form used for this potted version, and there made more integral. Also the *gluttony*: much more is made of the food and the preparation of the feast than I have entered above.

* * *

There are, it appears, various versions in other European languages. Clouston briefly cites examples from German, French, and Portuguese.[80] None appear in point of written source to be older than (or as old as) the *Pardoner's Tale*; and none bring us any closer to Chaucer than the Italian tale of the Hermit. A form very close to this is found (according to Clouston) in *two* German works by Hans Sachs, written in 1547 and 1555; but the only notable point about these is that the author makes the robbers kill the hermit when he warns them that the treasure is Death, because they think he is making fun of them. A reasonable "realistic" touch, likely enough to happen – but ruinous of the essence of the story (as "realistic" touches applied to symbolic tales often are), which should exhibit the escape from death of wisdom, and the destruction of the unwise who fall into the snare of avarice.

[56r] It may also be noted that *most* variants (nearly all apparently) make the finders men who were *already rascals*; and their number is usually *three* (sometimes four). In a Portuguese version (briefly cited from the *Orto do Sposo* of Frei Hermenegildo 14th century) the scene is in Rome: four robbers open a grave there and find in it much treasure of silver, gold and jewels, and one takes the finest gold cup to pay for food in the town. But the treasure is usually gold (money) as in Chaucer.[81]

A French version of the 15th century ends with a formula which we have already met: "Thus we may understand how things of earth are death to those who know not how to use them well; for a hundred men may damn themselves for an inheritance, and the inheritance remain in its place to this day. It is the golden stone that does not die." (This Clouston derives from M. Paulin Paris, *Les Manuscrits français*, tome iv, p. 83, citing a treatise upon Scripture

---

[80] Clouston, 434–5. [Ed.]
[81] Tolkien cites the Portuguese and French versions from Clouston, 435.

of the 15th century "blaming the vices and praising the virtues". Is this related to 1Timothy vi?)

*　*　*

If we now pass from all these "analogues" to Chaucer's version, we shall see that (even allowing for a considerable amount of alteration for his special purpose by Chaucer himself) his tale is not *directly* connected with any particular version that we have encountered or that (so far as I know) has yet been found.[82]

The following points were characteristic of Chaucer's version – that is of the version he used or had in mind (though he may, of course, have known more than one).

1. (a) The "origin of the treasure" was not made explicit. (b) It was lying unguarded in a wood. (c) But it was of gold, minted. (Probably there were eight bushels of it.)
2. An old man, venerable, wise (and godly), discovered it or knew of it.
3. (a) There were *three* men of *evil life* who met the old man, (b) and were warned against *Death*,[83] but nonetheless (because they insisted) were directed to the treasure; and (c) *the old man passed on.*
4. One of the "shrews" exclaims on their good fortune, and proposes that they shall draw lots, to see who shall go and get food and wine so that they can be at ease until they can decide how and whether to move the treasure.
5. *One* man went to the nearby town or village and bought food and also bought *rat-bane* from an *apothecary*. The *two* left behind plot to murder the *one*. (This comes first in Chaucer.) The Devil puts evil thoughts into the heart of the one as he goes to town.
[56v] 6. The story contained, or was related explicitly to, the text from I Timothy vi *radix malorum* etc.

---

[82] Most of the peculiarly reminiscent points: e.g. rat-bane / apothecary / exclamation on Fortune / old hermit-like man / *radix malorum* agree more nearly than any with *Italian version*. [Added by Tolkien at the bottom of the page, perhaps at the same time as the words (also in black ballpoint) at the end of the paragraph: "or that (so far as I know) has yet been found".]

[83] Here (I think) a narrative artist, such as Chaucer was, would ask at once: "Why should they *insist* on seeing *Death*?" Hence would come in (possibly from a different source) the town of the *plague* or Black Death. [Added by Tolkien in black ballpoint in the left margin. The parentheses around "and godly" and the emphasis under "Death" were added in pencil.]

There is no revisiting of the scene of murder by anyone "inside the story", but that may be due to its curious setting; for the Pardoner, himself a character in a fiction though outside the inner tale, is the enunciator of the text and the moral commentator.

The story was probably *nameless*: no place or character had specific names. But Chaucer puts it (vaguely) in Flanders.[84]

None of the versions cited above contains all these points. One – the curious unnecessary precision about *eight bushels* – appears nowhere else, but is more likely to have been repeated than invented. (A large number of other numerals will scan in line 771, and though some manuscripts read the more stereotyped VII or *seuen*, the fact that two of these have *an seuen* seems to show this an alteration of VIII.)[85] Though the nearest analogues are from Italy there is nothing in Chaucer's tale to connect his version definitely with Italy except *floryns* (from Florence) 770, 839, which, as we have seen, is not decisive.[86]

Leaving aside elaborations and shifts of balance, which we will consider later, Chaucer has altered this version in one marked point – the character and function of the *venerable old man*. Otherwise he has left the plot and details alone. Though we may suspect that he also made one other (more legitimate) alteration: the three finders are, when "shrews" (as is usual) professional *robbers or thieves*. They appear in Chaucer as *riotours* – men who passed their life in gluttony, drunkenness, lechery, and gambling. Their "economics" are not explained; but they are plainly not imagined as getting the money for their debauches from highway-robbery.

This latter alteration – for so it probably is – is legitimate: for it explains equally well mechanically, and with more *moral* force, how the "shrews" then succumbed to temptation to treacherous murder. And it makes a much better link with the Pardoner (or too good a link!) giving him several other sins to glance at in his sermon.[87]

This alteration is probably actually due (as often in Chaucer, when we can catch him in his workshop, or guess at his procedure) to blending other sources with his tale. The key to these is probably to be found in *Flaundres* 463.

---

[84] No doubt due to its source or subsidiary source. [Added by Tolkien in black ink. The sentence about Flanders was added in black ballpoint.]

[85] Eight was probably deliberately chosen because it is not equally divisible by 3 but only 2. [Added by Tolkien in black ballpoint in the left margin.]

[86] The original *florin* was a gold coin struck in Florence from 1252 to 1533, but during the fourteenth century, some 150 European authorities minted their own copies of the florin, hence an international currency of exchange. Edward III ordered coining the English *floryn* in 1344. [Ed.]

[87] But its probable "reason" is to explain the pursuit of "Death" as a person. It would occur naturally to anyone who had experienced the plague or Black Death. A quarrelsome drunkard in his cups is more convincing as the sort of fool who would take Death literally. [Added by Tolkien in black ink in the left margin.]

[57r] On the inappropriateness (as it seems to me) of the opening *In Flaundres whilom was a compaignye of yonge folk* I will touch later. But this localization – of which nothing more is made (and which is very unsuitable to 662–701)[88] – is probably derived from the same source as much of the elaboration (or over-elaboration) of the early part of the tale.

Long ago Miss K. Petersen in a monograph *On the Sources of the Nonne Prestes Tale* (Boston 1898), p. 100 note, drew attention to the probability that in the *Pardoner's Tale* Chaucer shows evidence of having used the *Liber de Apibus* of Thomas de Cantimpré (born c. 1210), a Dominican of Flanders.[89] This book is a collection of moral stories for the use of preachers. It contains a tale whose beginning resembles the beginning of the *Pardoner's Tale*: it concerns a "company of young people that led a wild life" in *Brabantiae partibus*, and are led to see by their horrible blasphemies "they rend our Blessed Lord's body in pieces". Two other stories have features reminiscent of the *Pardoner's Tale*: one mentions *Flanders* and refers to dancers and wicked revels, and treats of an impious man suddenly struck down for his impiety;[90] in another, a mysterious person appears to revellers (but turns out be the devil himself, which is not the case with Chaucer's *cherl*).

Flanders is a perhaps not inappropriate setting for a background of gross revelry and gluttony. Whether it was this setting that also drew in the "death" – the plague or pestilence – is not easy to determine.[91]

* * *

Chaucer's alterations then – mostly consequent upon the use to which he put the story, and the working up of it into a complex whole together with the sketch of the Pardoner and his preaching – are probably these.

---

[88] Parentheses were added in red ballpoint and the phrase about unsuitability was (later?) struck out in pencil.

[89] Kate O. Petersen, *On the Sources of the Nonne Prestes Tale* (Boston: Radcliffe College Monograph, No. 10, 1898), cites Thomas de Cantimpré's *Bonum Universale de Apibus* from around 1259. This work addressed the anti-Semitic "blood libel" whereby Jews were accused of ritual murders of Christians; by contrast, Chaucer's three rioters re-crucify Christ himself by swearing upon his tortured body: "Our blissed lordes body they to-tere; / Hem thoughte Iewes rente him noght y-nough" (*CT* VI, 474–5). Three sentences later, Tolkien quotes this first line in translation. [Ed.]

[90] This might be the *olde felawe of youres* suddenly slain by Death as he sat drunk on the bench, 672 ff. [Tolkien]

[91] David Wallace, "In Flaundres," *Studies in the Age of Chaucer* 19 (1997), 63–91, identifies the nation's medieval reputation: "Flemings were famous drunks" (80). David Nicholas, *Medieval Flanders* (New York: Longman, 1992), 305–7, reports that Flanders suffered worse from bubonic plague *after* the initial pandemic of 1348–49.

The supposed teller of the tale (outside the inner tale of the gold) becomes the Pardoner, and he takes on any moralizing functions of wise man and disciples inside the story.[92]

The rascally finders are changed from "thieves" to young *riotoures* sunk in drunkenness, gluttony, lechery, and gambling.[93] The scene of their "riot" is casually laid in *Flanders*.

An entirely new motive is introduced, at least nothing resembling it is found elsewhere: the "shrews" *go to seek Death*, but this is not the Death that lies in gold or treasure, but Death personified (somewhat confusedly) as a *privé theef* who slays people with a spear, especially at the moment, when (apparently) a pestilence is raging. That this element has been attracted by the use of *deeth* = pestilence (as in Black Death), and the use of *deeth* in the warning against the gold, seems clear. It is I think an unfortunate elaboration detracting from the function of the original tale at its centre.[94]

Another major change is in the character and function of the *old man*: the *cherl*. He, of course, [57v] descends from the *Hermit* – as he from the Wise Man A (+ disciple B). His function was to discover the gold, to meet the "shrews" and both direct them to it and warn them against it (as being Death); and above all to *exhibit wisdom*, freedom from worldly desires and cupidity, which by scorning the gold, and fleeing from it and its baneful influence, thus *escaped Death*.

Chaucer has altered this. We may say so with some confidence for we know that main source from which he drew the *cherl*, and his speech, the *Elegies of Maximian*. (See notes to 721 ff.)[95] At this point Chaucer has been clever – whether successfully so or not is another matter. Having already sent his shrews out *pursuing Death*, before ever they heard a word from the old man, he now establishes a contrast between young reprobates seeking Death as an enemy, and an aged man (really Old Age in individualized form) who wants death, but Death will not touch. (The ultimately unanalyzable confusions we are landed in cannot be made more simple.) But he still has to work the

---

[92] So the reflection on the permission of the Devil to tempt a man already of evil life, 847 ff. [Tolkien]

[93] A commonplace of moral instruction. See Frère Lorens (1279). Thus in DM transl Morris p. 51. Which curiously diverges into a consideration of hypocrisy. [Tolkien.] The allusion is to Lorens d'Orléans' influential *Somme le Roi* (c. 1279), translated by Dan Michel into Middle English as *Ayenbite of Inwyt*, which was edited by Richard Morris, EETS o.s. 23 (1866); Tolkien's copy is the Bodleian's Tolkien VC 188. [Ed.]

[94] The last sentence is an addition in pencil, inked in black.

[95] Tolkien refers to notes in Skeat (5:287–8): "Professor Kittredge, of Harvard University, informs me that ll. 727–733 are imitated from the first Elegy of Maximian…" Skeat then quotes ten lines in the original Latin.

mechanism, necessary to the tale, by informing the shrews where Death is to be found – under a tree nearby! If he wanted Death, why not go there himself? He could have led the men there and got himself killed by them. With that aside the Chaucerian version breaks down even as allegory – in spite of the art that he has expended on its texture at the surface.

*　*　*

I suppose we may now proceed to some consideration of Chaucer's tale as he left it and we read it – to answer, that is, that hackneyed question of the Schools: Consider in some detail the *art* of the Pardoner's Tale.[96] If this point seems to some over-long delayed, I will say that I do not think anything less than I have said as preliminary would be adequate preparation. If the question seems hackneyed, then at least I hope my answer to it will not seem so.

For I do not approve of the *Pardoner's Tale*. I like it *evere the longer the wors*.[97] As so much of Chaucer's work, it has a surface finish and attraction but does not support examination or long familiarity. It exhibits both his art and some of his defects.[98] Whether wrong or right, that is not a hackneyed opinion. I would wager much that whenever that question has been set the examiner has expected praise (more or less undiluted) to result. Do not therefore (should you find yourself faced with such a question) rashly disappoint him. *Rashly* I say. For, of course, received opinions are safest, for those who have none of their own, or cannot remember texts and evidence. But heterodoxy is *not* (in Schools) perilous for those who can state a case.

[58v] Very well. I do not think that Chaucer did all things well. In this case I think he did much that was ill. But analytic and destructive criticism is rightly suspect – it is far too easy, at any rate far easier than writing a tale in verse.[99] Even a narrative that is in fact (as rarely) well told and well constructed can be "guyed" by the malicious. Let us then be or try to be strictly fair, and make at the outset the most generous allowances and handsomest admissions.

It cannot be for nothing that so many people have admired this Tale – really meaning, of course, the whole complex from the *Words of the Host*; and should have called it "striking" or "impressive" and the like. It is not for

---

[96] The undergraduate Tolkien began his own examinations for the Honour School on 10 June 1915 and sat for his Chaucer paper the next day with "ten miscellaneous questions about Chaucer's poetry and prose" (SH 1:73).
[97] Tolkien quotes *Reeve's Prologue* (*CT* I, 3873).
[98] Tolkien wrote "specious surface finish" and "gravest defects" but bracketed *specious* and *gravest* in pencil, then struck them out in black ink.
[99] A pencilled hand points to this passage from the margin.

nothing – though the habitual posture of praise before an established great author will account for something, and attack on the corruptions of the mediæval church for more, of many critics' expressed pleasure. But Chaucer is a good performer (of course), he has style, his writing is (as a rule) line by line artful and lively. On this count much of the Tale is in fact very readable, but certainly not all.[100]

And of course the old tale is given a dramatic setting. It is specially (and perhaps more than any other of the *Canterbury Tales*) integrated with the delineation of the supposed teller; so much so that it is all mixed up with talk and self-exhibition and flows into it and out of it. It is legitimate in such circumstances that it should be in many ways altered to fit this situation. It ends abruptly (as Chaucer's tales are apt to do), as if he had expended so much energy (or too much) on the beginning that he had barely breath to stay the course. Yet that – at least the abrupt ending – is well enough as things are. So much of what was in, or could be in, the tale itself is now transferred to the teller, the Pardoner. And as for the management of the tale itself, after the sudden and auspicious beginning *In Flaundres whilom was a compaignye* 463 to somewhere around 480, we may allow that to be accommodated to the Pardoner.

All that, and possibly more, is true. And yet! Perhaps I am setting too high a standard, but only so can one distinguish *alpha* performances when one meets them.[101] An *alpha* performance will not only have this surface finish, this style, this management of words at the immediate point of contact, this readableness, but it will endure familiarity, it will survive (even be enhanced) by scrutiny and analysis. It will answer the questions that reflective criticism may discover to ask. Now I do not think the *Pardoner's Tale* can endure that treatment. It won't really bear examination or thinking about. It is clever, at this or that point, but not successful as a whole.

[58v] Let us set aside the *Words of the Host* and the *Prologue*, to which rather different criteria should be applied. *Heer bigynneth the Pardoners Tale*. Let us begin there.

If we do, I think there are several different kinds of criticism (I mean adverse criticism) that could be preferred against the piece. Let us take the simplest and most obvious first – all the more because it is applicable to much else of Chaucer's narrative verse.

---

[100] "…but certainly not all" is an addition in pencil, inked in black.
[101] Tolkien refers to the Oxford system of grading examination papers with letters of the Greek alphabet – alpha, beta, and so forth.

The thing is top-heavy. There are about 530 lines given to the actual story. But after its swift pictorial opening *In Flaundres* etc. there are nearly 200 lines (much more than a third) before anything happens. And why is this? Because at line 480 *syngeres with harpes, baudes, waferores / Whiche been the verray develes officers* the Pardoner slides off into a sermon against drunkenness and gluttony, and then against gambling, and then against blasphemy, with exempla and Scriptural texts.[102] We have *Lot, Herod*, a citation of *Seneca*, an apostrophe on gluttony, *Adam*, a citation of St Paul, a diatribe against elaborate cooking, then the comic *Sampsoun* passage (and a topical allusion to the frauds of the London wine-trade: well enough in their way), a swift reference to victories in the Old Testament done in abstinence and prayer, *Attila, Lamuel* (Lemuel).[103] Enough? No. *Now wol I you defenden hasardrye*, more "learned" references, and so to *Stilbon* (for Chilon), *King Demetrius* and the King of the Parthians; and so to blasphemy, with citation of St Matthew, of Jerome, and of the Commandments. And at last at 661, we return to *Thise riotours of which I telle*... And all this *nihil pertinet ad rem*.[104] The story that is to be told is not concerned with any of these things. The connexion of it is *not* with the story of what is to befall the "shrews", *nor* how it befell them, but with their past life. And that past life has been altered, *made to fit it*, not the intruded matter to fit the tale. And note it is inside the tale, interrupting it, not outside as moral prologue or epilogue.[105]

"Yes, yes" it may be said, "but this is part of that accommodation of the main argument of the tale to the teller you spoke about. This is dramatic. This shows you the Pardoner." To that I would rejoin it is too like a transcript to be tolerable. The Pardoner may have been so used to machine-preaching with stock exempla and texts that they were liable to ooze out, and spoil any tale he had to tell, but a much smaller and swifter sample would have been preferable. Or a different placing of the matter. And anyway [59r] I fear this sort of stuff is quite as *much like Chaucer himself* as it is like the Pardoner.[106] You may make the dramatic plea to excuse him, and it may on this occasion appear to have some force. For Chaucer *devised things on purpose to give him a chance of*

---

[102] John M. Bowers, "'Dronkenesse Is Ful of Stryvyng': Alcoholism and Social Violence in Chaucer's *Pardoner's Tale*," ELH 57 (1990), 757–84, explores the tale-teller's personal obsession with drinking in order to account for this lengthy sermonizing.
[103] Tolkien added the words "done in abstinence and prayer" in the margin in black ink.
[104] This Latin legal phrase means "nothing pertains to the matter". [Ed.]
[105] The last two sentences are highlighted with a vertical line in red ballpoint.
[106] In pencil, a hand points to this passage from the margin and "much like Chaucer himself" is underlined.

writing just so. He liked doing so.[107] He was perfectly capable of doing so, without any kind of excuse, even in defiance of a dramatic propriety which he himself feels. Had the teller of the tale been someone quite different, not a professional preacher at all, you would probably have had much of this homiletic interlude anyway, though maybe interspersed with apologies. For Chaucer was a "*man textuel*" to a fault.[108] And even when he knows this, and is actually presenting to us a teller who is *not* so, he makes the mistake of saying so!

Observe the Manciple and his Tale. It is a short tale badly told. And the teller – "*but for I am a man noght textuel*," he says, "*I wol noght telle of textes never a deel*" 235; but he has, and not at all appositely. And again 316 (after another) "*But as I seyde, I am noght textuel*" as a prelude to a string of them. And what does this stuff profit us or the tale? It does not profit us, for we see not the Manciple in all this so much as Chaucer struggling with a vice. It does not profit the tale which is ruined. So little attention is given to it or its own nature and force that its supreme moment of pathos, the last words of *Coronis* to *Phebus*, is bungled hopelessly.

> *Et dixit, "Potui poenas tibi, Phoebe, dedisse,*
> *Sed peperisse prius: duo nunc moriemur in una."*[109]

So Ovid. It was the knowledge that his lover Coronis was with child that caused the sudden violent revulsion in Phoebus.

Thus Chaucer:

> *And in his ire his wyf thanne hath he slayn.*
> *This is th'effect, ther is namoore to sayn;*
> *For sorwe of which he brak his mynstralcie,*
> *Both harpe, and lute, and gyterne and sautrie.*

Could it be worse?
And could even effectual characterization of the teller justify such stuff?

* * *

---

[107] The words we italicize in these last two sentences are underlined in black ink.

[108] Chaucer's Manciple denies with false modesty, "for I am a man noght textuel" (*CT*, IX, 236), quoted by Tolkien in the next paragraph. [Ed.]

[109] Clouston, 439-40. Ovid's *Metamorphoses* II:608-9 is quoted and translated by Edward Wheatley, "The Manciple's Tale", in *Sources and Analogues of "The Canterbury Tales"*, ed. Robert M. Correale and Mary Hamel, vol. II (Cambridge: D. S. Brewer, 2005), 754-5.

It was a pedantic and rhetorical age, with a palate in general too cloyed to appreciate simplicity in narrative, and addicted (to the point of vice) to illustration and citation at second third or even further hand. In this respect at least Chaucer did not rise superior to his time, but was among the most addicted: as were a man to smother all his meats with condiments and sweets, or smoke between all the courses! And there is an attitude that seems to think that when it has been indicated that the Manciple's Tale proceeds according to *Rhetoric* that is enough defence. It is as if when finding a heraldic "leopard" amongst a set of drawings of real animals one was told that it was drawn according to the laws of heraldry.[110]

[59v] But this is a small poor thing. Let it go. Leave it to the people who delight to find that the "rules of Rhetoric" are observed, and think that thereby a narrative is praised.[111] Yet you will find the same again, or worse, on more important occasions.

Observe the Franklin and his Tale. Or rather do not observe the Franklin, for there is really only the same old Chaucer (or same old fourteenth-century rhetoric) behind the mask as ever, whether it fits him ill as the Manciple or more nearly as the Pardoner. Observe the Tale.

Now this is a story old and far-spread out of East to West, like that told by the Pardoner; but it is a happy moral story, beautiful and graceful. And to judge by its setting *In Armorik that called is Britayne* it had reached Chaucer in the form of a "Breton Lay", to which it owed its touch of magic (not essential to the story), and so probably in a tale told with some limpidity and straightness such as that which still gives to the corrupt text of *Sir Orfeo* its singular charm.[112] But consider how the *Franklin* is made to tell it – a country squire devoted to the pleasures of the table. At least consider this one point. Turn to the central point. The simple kind and blameless Dorigen finds herself trapped. It is the nub of the story. In the moment of her amaze and despair she cries out against Fortune that has snared her, so that she has only two choices: death or dishonour.

---

[110] The last sentence is added in black ink.
[111] The last sentence is inserted in pencil, then inked in black.
[112] Tolkien had glossed *Sir Orfeo* for Sisam's *Fourteenth Century Verse and Prose*, 13–31; he edited the text in 1944 for his cadet students (two copies from the Academic Copying Office, Oxford, survive in the Bodleian); and he made a Modern English verse translation, probably also in 1944, edited for publication by Christopher in *Sir Gawain and the Green Knight, Pearl, and Sir Orfeo* in 1975.

> But nathelees, yet have I levere (to) lese   1360, R p. 142[113]
> My lif than of my body to have a shame,
> Or knowen myselven fals, or lese my name;
> And with my deth I may be quit, ywis.

Enough?

> Hath ther nat many a noble wyf er this,
> And many a mayde, yslayn hirself, allas!
> Rather than with her body doon trespas?

Quite enough!
But no! You are now going to get 90 lines more of the simple Dorigen's reflections.

> Yis, certes, lo, thise stories beren witnesse,

and out they troop, examples mainly of women who committed suicide to avoid being ravished or after it – nearly all of which are in fact *off the actual point* for Dorigen was in no danger of being ravished; but was caught in a *rash promise*. Nonetheless we must have them, and do not ask either where the Franklin learned them, or still less Dorigen: the 30 tyrants of Athens and the daughters of Phido (11 lines); the 50 maidens of Sparta (7); the tyrant Aristoclides and the maiden Stymphalis (8); Hasdrubal's wife at the siege and sack of Carthage (6); Lucrece and Tarquis (4); the [60r] seven maidens of Miletus when it was taken by the Gauls; after which Dorigen asserts that she could still tell more than a thousand stories "*as touchynge this mateere / Whan Habradate was slayn, his wyf so deere.*" But not Dorigen really of course, nor the Franklin; for Chaucer is mounted on his hobby-horse and has forgotten them, and has still a long canter to go. We have to endure 13 more examples, no more apposite than the others, including Penelope (singularly inappropriate since she had contrived herself a form of promise which she had under control) and Portia wife of Brutus![114]

The rhetoric that inculcated this sort of thing was vicious. But at least more effort could have been made to equate the examples more closely with the

---

[113] Tolkien later added in pencil the line references to the *Franklin's Tale* (*CT* V, 1360-3, 1364-6, 1367, 1399) in F. N. Robinson's *Works of Geoffrey Chaucer*, second edition (Boston: Houghton Mifflin, 1957), 142.

[114] The parenthetical comment, from "since she had contrived", is added in pencil and inked in black.

story – or if that was not possible, the "ornament" might have been eschewed.[115]

Many editors and commentators seem to think that when they have shown that the disposition of a Chaucerian piece and its parts are in accordance with the Art Rhetorique of the age they have put him beyond the reach of criticism, and put out of court the complaint of the un-rhetorical.[116] But it is unnecessary to remind members of this School, perhaps too far swung the other way into disrespect of learning and its tradition, that what the dons of one age teach the dons of another will ridicule.

And I have perhaps been unfair in selecting one of the grosser examples of this pedantry, in a specially inappropriate setting. Let us return to the Pardoner.

The obvious defence of this Tale (that is the whole thing with its immediate setting in the Words of the Host, the Prologue in the mouth of the Pardoner himself, the Tale and its digressions, and the final quarrel-scene) is that it has not only the literary purpose of providing one more tale for the great Series, but the purpose of delineating the character of the Pardoner himself. A character that stirred the imagination of Chaucer to a kind of curious interest, such as that with which a naturalist might study some odious or noxious creature of bizarre shape and colouring and strange if disgusting habits. And this character-drawing has really replaced the story-telling as prime object – as the prologue of the Wife of Bath far outgrew in art and interest her tale (which is not particularly distinguished).[117]

To that anyone will agree. But let us beware then of applying falsely the criteria of true drama acted on the stage to literary-work of this kind, led astray by the word "dramatic", which if it is legitimately used (for lack of a better) for the dialogue and reported speech of narrative works, is nonetheless always dangerous.[118]

[60v] Of course both true drama and narrative are constrained under the limits of art to verisimilitude not to recording as by photograph or

---

[115] This is the last paragraph written in blue ink. From here, the text is in the same black ink used for inserts elsewhere in the manuscript.

[116] Tolkien probably had in mind John M. Manly, *Chaucer and the Rhetoricians* (London: Proceedings of the British Academy, 1926).

[117] In pencil, a hand points to this passage from the margin. Tolkien clearly found much interest in the *Wife of Bath's Tale*, with its opening descriptions of the Elf Queen and her dancing ladies (like his own dancing Lúthien) as well as the disenchantment of a land where fairies have vanished, anticipating the departure of his own Elves from Middle-earth; see *TLC* 249–54.

[118] This paragraph is marked with a vertical pencil line. Tolkien wrote "legitimately used...*to* the dialogue", where *to* is clearly an error for *for*; we have also added parentheses for clarity. Tolkien knew something about "drama acted on the stage" since he had performed in various student productions, notably the cross-dressing role of Mrs Malaprop in Sheridan's *The Rivals*, as well as dressing up as Chaucer and performing the *Nun's Priest's Tale* in 1938 and the *Reeve's Tale* in 1939; see *SH* 2:315–17.

tape-machine.[119] It was no doubt true to the character, and to pardoners in general (and other mediæval preachers), to represent this creature as fond of using *exempla*, "ensamples" 435.

> He was in chirche a noble ecclesiaste.
> Wel coude he rede a lessoun or a storie,
> But alderbest he song an offertorie.   Gen. Prol. 708–10

In the more "dramatic style" of the prologue to the tale rendered:

> Thanne telle I hem ensamples many oon
> Of oldë stories longë tyme agoon:
> For lewëd peple louen talës olde,
> Swiche thyngës kan they wel reporte and holde.   435–8

These four lines are worth considering carefully. I do not mean for the obvious reason, as a direct contemporary reference to the fact that ordinary people liked *ensaumples*,[120] probably more just as stories than as illustrations enforcing a point or moral, and that they could remember things well by hearsay, and would hand them on. Though it is well to remember this when considering Chaucer's own sources, or trying to find the immediate origin of some tale or reference in his work. But for two reasons more specially concerned with the present tale.[121]

First of all, Chaucer's "reporting" later fails even in "verisimilitude". For nothing of what he puts in the Pardoner's mouth from 483 (*The Hooly Writ take I to my witnesse*) to 660 would satisfy that taste, in the form in which he gives it. There are no stories, but only references to them. And yet the Pardoner is here supposed to be in full action as a preacher (inside his own tale) and not still (outside it) stretching out his technique. And his audience consists chiefly precisely of *lewïd peple*, that is those who were not clerks, and did not or could not habitually read books (even in English).

The tedium which you probably feel in looking up notes to these references is in this case a fair indication that they are in fact a *bore*.

---

[119] Sayer, "Recollections of J. R. R. Tolkien," 23, introduced Tolkien to his tape-machine in 1952, when he recorded the riddle scene from *The Hobbit* and some favourite prose sections from *The Lord of the Rings* (SH 3:1129).

[120] *ensaumples of oldë stories* does not of course mean 'samples, specimens, of old stories', but *exempla*, matter illustrative of the point being made, consisting of old (traditional) tales. [Tolkien]

[121] After the convolutions of the last two sentences, Tolkien finally completes his opening formulation "I do not mean for the obvious reason" with "But for two reasons…"

7
Valedictory to Chaucer, 1959

Almost from his arrival at Oxford as Professor of Anglo-Saxon and his first meeting with C. S. Lewis in 1926 – when they sized each other up from opposite sides of the Language *versus* Literature split within the English Faculty (*TLC* 71–2) – Tolkien had waged a campaign to expand and strengthen the Language side. In 1930 he went public with his argument when *The Oxford Magazine* published "The Oxford English School", really a manifesto. In this he shrewdly enlisted Chaucer to his cause, because the author was revered as the father of English poetry and his *Canterbury Tales* stood as the traditional starting point for English literature. He argued that this literary giant needed his poetry rescued by language experts from amateurish appreciation: "Chaucer should be recovered for such students as a mediæval author, and part of his works become once more the subject of detailed and scholarly study."[1] As the decades passed, however, and even after recruiting Lewis to support his cause, Tolkien watched the steady undermining of his position.[2]

His last salvo came on the occasion of his retirement in 1959 with his "Valedictory Address", delivered to a packed hall at Merton College, when he again brought forward Chaucer as a major ally to his cause. He recalled Professor Walter Raleigh's lectures on "Chaucer and his Contemporaries", and he revisited his steady insistence (for example in his 1938 letter to John Masefield) that Chaucer occupied a mature mid-point in English literary history rather than standing as a "fumbling beginner". A telling moment, indeed a shocking one, came when he invoked imagery of the trench warfare, which he had known personally at the Battle of the Somme, to dramatize his account of these faculty skirmishes.

The Bodleian's Tolkien archives contain a surprising number of notes, drafts, and typescripts (with carbon copies) indicating that a great deal of care and attention went into this summation of his career.[3] It became one of the

---

[1] J. R. R. Tolkien, "The Oxford English School", in *The Oxford Magazine* 48 (1930), 778–82 at p. 782.
[2] See Shippey, "Fighting the Long Defeat: Philology in Tolkien's Life and Fiction", in *Roots and Branches*, 139–56.
[3] The lecture's handwritten drafts can be consulted in MS Tolkien 23, fols. 43–179.

Tolkien on Chaucer, 1913–1959. John M. Bowers and Peter Steffensen, Oxford University Press.
© John M. Bowers and Peter Steffensen 2024. DOI: 10.1093/oso/9780192848888.003.0008

last instances of the "two square yards" to which he devoted his obsessive energy. The better-known version was published in *Essays* (224–40), but we have chosen to reprint selections from the first-published version in the 1979 memorial volume *Tolkien: Scholar and Storyteller*.[4] Christopher remarked about the alternative versions: "there were many copies of this lecture, and since I made available the text for that volume I have come upon another to which my father made a good many alterations (without in any way changing the argument): these changes are incorporated in the text printed here" (*Essays* 4). We preferred this earlier-published version partly because it was the first published and partly because it preserves punctuation closer to Tolkien's habitual usages. We have inserted as footnotes some variant readings from Christopher's slightly different version. Our excerpts begin eleven pages into this earlier printing of his farewell lecture, where Tolkien continued considering the English School's title of "Language and Literature".

* * *

Excerpts from "Valedictory Address to the University of Oxford" (1959)

But whatever may be thought or done about the title of our School, I wish fervently that this abuse in local slang of the word *language* might be for ever abandoned! It suggests, and is used to suggest, that certain kinds of knowledge concerning authors and their medium of expression is unnecessary and "unliterary" the interest only of cranks not of cultured or sensitive minds. And even so it is misapplied in time. In local parlance it is used to cover everything, within our historical range, that is mediaeval or older – except "Chaucer and his Contemporaries".[5] It thus contrives to smear some of the tar not only on Mediaeval philology but also on Mediaeval literature. Except of course Chaucer. His merits as a major poet are too obvious to be obscured; though it was in fact Language, or Philology, that demonstrated, as only Language could, two things of first-rate literary importance: that he was not a fumbling beginner, but a master of metrical technique; and that he was an

---

[4] J. R. R. Tolkien, "Valedictory Address to the University of Oxford, 5 June 1959", in *J. R. R. Tolkien: Scholar and Storyteller*, ed. Mary Salu and Robert T. Farrell (Ithaca and London: Cornell University Press, 1979), 16–37 at pp. 26–7 and 29–30. Reprinted with permission.

[5] Tolkien recalls Professor Sir Walter Raleigh's lectures, which he attended in 1914 and which we discuss in Chapter 1.

inheritor, a middle point, and not a "father".[6] Nonetheless, it is in the backward dark of "Anglo-Saxon" and "Semi-Saxon" that Language, now reduced to bogey *Lang*, is supposed to have his lair. Though alas! he may come down like Grendel from the moors to raid the "literary" fields. He has (for instance) theories about puns and rhymes! (26–27)

* * *

...Let us glance again at Chaucer, that old poet out in the No-man's land of debate. There was knifework, axe-work, out there between the barbed wire of *Lang* and *Lit* in days not so far back. When I was a young and enthusiastic examiner, to relieve the burden of my literary colleagues (at which they loudly groaned), I offered to set the Chaucer paper, or to help in reading the scripts. I was astonished at the heat and hostility with which I was refused. My fingers were dirty: I was *Lang*.

That hostility has now happily died down; there is some fraternization between the barbed wire. But it was that hostility which, in the reformed syllabus of the early thirties (still in essentials surviving), made necessary the prescription of *two* papers dealing with Chaucer and his chief contemporaries. *Lit* would not allow the greedy hands of *Lang* to soil the poet. *Lang* could not accept the flimsy and superficial papers set by *Lit*. But now, with the latest reform, or mild modification, that comes into force next year, once more Chaucer is presented in one common paper. Rightly, I should have said. But alas! What do we see? "Candidates for Courses I and II may be required to answer questions on language"![7]

Here we have hallowed in print this pernicious slang misuse. Not "*his* language", or "*their* language", or even "the language of the period"; just "language". What in the name of scholarship, or poetry, or reason, can that here mean? It *should* mean, in English fit to appear in documents of the University of Oxford, that certain candidates may be asked questions of general linguistic import, without limitation of time or place, on a paper testing knowledge of the great poetry of the Fourteenth Century, under the general heading "English Literature". But since that is lunatic, one must suppose that something else is meant.

---

[6] *Essays* 234 continues: "Not to mention the labours of Language in rescuing much of his vocabulary and idiom from ignorance or misunderstanding."
[7] Christopher adds a note of explanation: "Courses I and II: options in the English School at Oxford allowing the student to concentrate on earlier periods. These courses, taken by relatively few, are largely *Lang*; while Course III, taken by the great majority, is very largely *Lit*." (*Essays* 240)

What kind of question can it mean which no candidate of Course III need ever touch? Is it wicked to enquire, in paper or *viva voce*, what here or there Chaucer really meant, by word or form, or idiom? Is metre and verse-technique of no concern to sensitive literary minds? Must nothing in any way related to Chaucer's medium of expression be ever allowed to disturb the cotton wool of poor Course III? Then why not add that only Courses I and II may be required to answer questions that refer to history or politics or religion?[8]

The logical result of this attitude, indeed its only rational expression would be this direction: "Courses I and II may be expected to show knowledge of Chaucer in the original; Course III will use a translation into our contemporary idiom."[9] *But*, if this translation, as may well happen, should at any point be erroneous, this may *not* be mentioned. That would be "language". (29–30)

* * *

For all the celebration and provocation in 1959, this was not in fact Professor Tolkien's farewell to teaching at Oxford. When C. L. Wrenn went on sabbatical leave, Tolkien stepped in to lecture on *Beowulf* in Michaelmas 1962 and on *The Freswæl* in Hilary 1963 (SH 1:630, 636). The latter is the "Finnesburg Fragment", upon which he had lectured repeatedly since the 1920s, and these teaching notes would be posthumously edited along with supporting material by Alan Bliss as *Finn and Hengest*, published in 1982 (SH 2:433-7).

---

[8] The sentence ends differently in *Essays* 237: "…to history or politics, to astronomy, or to religion?"
[9] The phrase "our contemporary idiom" appears as "contemporary English" in *Essays* 237.

Coda
Tolkien on Chaucer's *Retracciouns*

This book began with the view that scholarship is another form of autobiography. Two years before his retirement, we find Tolkien taking a particular interest in Chaucer's *Retracciouns*, a brief text found at the end of all complete manuscripts of the *Canterbury Tales*. In it, Chaucer employed formulas of the confessional to repent of his "translacions and endytinges of worldly vanitees" (Skeat 4:644), simultaneously using the occasion to list his major works so that they would not be forgotten or misattributed by a posterity of future readers. We wonder whether Tolkien was indirectly fretting about the future of his own works such as *The Silmarillion* not then published and not likely to be published during his lifetime.

Tolkien was prompted to consider this text after being contacted by Przemyslaw Mroczkowski, a Polish professor who had met him and other Inklings while spending a year in Oxford.[1] Professor Mroczkowski was asking advice for a review which he had drafted on the second edition of F. N. Robinson's *Works of Geoffrey Chaucer*, newly published in 1957, and which he hoped to publish in the *Times Literary Supplement*. Tolkien's overall interest is not surprising since, as Tom Shippey reminds us, he had always defined his professional duties primarily in terms of editing.[2] In addition to embarking on Clarendon editions of *Sir Gawain*, *Pearl*, and Chaucer, his 1934 article "Chaucer as a Philologist" emphasized the implications for future editors of the *Canterbury Tales*, and his undergraduate Chaucer lectures of the 1940s and 1950s steadily paused to consider editorial cruces. The initial typescript of Professor Mroczkowski's review survives, with Tolkien's extensive corrections and suggestions written in pencil and red ink, between lines and into the margins, even on the backs of some pages. Mroczkowski's draft

---

[1] Łukasz Neubauer, "The 'Polish Inkling': Professor Przemyslaw Mroczkowski as J. R. R. Tolkien's Friend and Scholar", *Mythlore* 39 (2020), 149–76.

[2] Tom Shippey, "Tolkien as Editor", in *Companion to J. R. R. Tolkien*, ed. Lee, 41–55. His final lectures on the *Pardoner's Tale* had made specific reference to Robinson's first edition of 1933, with a later side note alluding to the second edition of 1957.

review begins with consideration of the *Retraccioun*, quoted here in Tolkien's revised version:

> Lovers of Chaucer are inclined to read the troublesome passage at the end of the *Canterbury Tales*, the author's *Retractation*, with dismay and too single a mind. They take the gloomy view of the adviser or confessor who near the end of the poet's career appealed to him for a repudiation of so much which he had called forth to life.[3]

In his accompanying letter, Tolkien focused almost exclusively on Chaucer's *Retracciouns*, a text which he had previously found no occasion to discuss at any length because it was not included in his Clarendon edition or in his Oxford lectures.

A Chaucerian as well as a Python, Terry Jones makes three points about *Retracciouns* that are worth keeping in mind as we read Tolkien's remarks. Like St Augustine's *Retractationes*, Chaucer's was actually a survey rather than a rejection of the author's own literary output; the only work Chaucer approved by title was his prose translation of Boethius' *Consolation of Philosophy*; and in the increasingly hostile pursuit of Wycliffite heretics around 1400, many men such as his longtime friend Sir Lewis Clifford were forced to retract publicly their prior religious views.[4] Thus Chaucer's *Retracciouns* sounds like a confession, almost from the grave, safeguarding posthumously his writings from future allegations of blasphemy and heresy, but also reminding future readers which were his authentic literary works.

Here are Tolkien's remarks from his cover letter:

* * *

I think the first paragraph (first 19 lines) is involved, and in places obscure, or unnecessarily controversial, and hardly concerns a review of "Robinson". All that it really amounts to is: "We should have suffered a great loss, if Ch's works had not survived – a reflection aroused by his *retracciouns* – but in inheriting his works, or so large a part of them, we have inherited not only delight, but a burden of enquiry and scholarship."

---

[3] The Morgan Library now owns the corrected typescript (MA 7958.1), the accompanying letter (MA 7958.3), and additional handwritten notes by Tolkien (MA 7958.2). Quoted with permission. Tolkien did not change here the oddly modernized title *Retractations*.

[4] Terry Jones with Robert Yeager, Terry Dolan, Alan Fletcher, and Juliette Dor, *Who Murdered Chaucer? A Medieval Mystery* (New York: St. Martins Press, 2003), "Did Chaucer Repent", 319–29.

The question of the *retracciouns* is a special one, and need not be debated, unless in consideration of any remarks or views of "Robinson" on this topic. I think, for myself, that the question is here misrepresented. The words do not read to me like a document composed under duress from any confessor! (The confession alluded to is in the hoped future, not in the immediate past.) The force of *revoke* is probably misunderstood – since it refers to *nameless* works, or to books of *forgotten* titles, it cannot have been an instruction to executors; and the picture of the fire in the chamber is unreal. The chief point that I should deduce is that copies of his works had long escaped from Chaucer's control!

If the *retracciouns* are to be mentioned at all, I should advise a simplification, somewhat in this style:

"Lovers of Chaucer, coming upon his *retracciouns*, may well be dismayed at the thought of the losses that they would have suffered, if by *I revoke* the poet had intended an instruction for the burning of the guilty works, and if his wishes had been carried out. *Troilus and Criseyde* (first named) would have disappeared, many of the *Canterbury Tales*, and other things now prized. But the occasion and purpose of the 'revocation' need not be debated; for the works of Chaucer have in fact survived, and, though short no doubt of his complete output, they remain a large bequest to posterity. English letters have from Chaucer's hand received a great inheritance, which may be likened by one surveying it, to *a lusty plain habundant of vitaille*.[5] There many succeeding generations have found an almost inexhaustible variety of human situations and environments, lit by the glamour and touched by the peculiar pathos which are associated with the name Chaucer. Yet like all great inheritances, this one has laid upon his heirs burdens and responsibilities."

Personally I should omit the *retracciouns* and merely begin by saying something of this sort:

"Though doubtless less than his complete output – for even the poet himself could not remember all the things that he had written, and time and the destructive hands of men have certainly since exercised a random and uncritical censorship – the "works of Chaucer" that have survived are a massive bequest to English letters. In their extent and variety, they might be likened to *a lusty plain* etc...."

* * *

---

[5] The *Clerk's Tale* (*CT* IV, 59) thus describes Walter's realm in Lombardy. Tolkien in his lecture on the *Clerk's Tale* had paused to wonder: "But what of *lusty*? What precisely did Chaucer mean to imply by *lusty playne* 59?" (Bodleian MS Tolkien A 13/2, fol. 15v).

Professor Mroczkowski's review, dutifully entitled "A Lusty Plain, Habundant of Vitaille", was in fact published in the *Times Literary Supplement* and began as Tolkien suggested: "Lovers of Chaucer, reading the troublesome passage at the end of the *Canterbury Tales*, the author's 'Retractation,' are usually dismayed…"[6]

Tolkien's sympathetic appreciations of Chaucer here (so different from his recent harshness about the author's *Pardoner's Tale* in his 1955–56 lectures) can perhaps be read as late-career reflections upon his own future reputation as author of *The Hobbit* and *The Lord of the Rings*. His remarks about works not surviving may reflect specifically his own anxieties in 1957 when *The Silmarillion* (and much more!) remained unpublished and therefore subject to similar loss at the whim of "time and the destructive hands of men". Tolkien had previously reflected upon these vicissitudes when drafting his Clarendon Chaucer notes on the Prologue to the *Legend of Good Women*, where the poet had listed his works to date, including works that have not survived. About his "balades, roundels, virelays" (*Legend* line 411) Tolkien wrote, "It seems certain that a great many 'minor poems' of this sort written by Chaucer are now lost altogether." About the work called *Wreched Engendring of Mankinde* (line 414), he concluded, "It has perished entirely", and about the English rendering of Origen's *De Maria Magdalena* (line 418), he added gloomily, "No trace of it is left".[7] In the *Retracciouns*, Chaucer lists his love lyrics ("many a lecherous lay") as well as his *Book of the Leoun*, works of which Tolkien could also have said that they had "perished entirely".

After so many years of engaging with Chaucer, even impersonating him on the stage in 1938 and 1939, Tolkien at the end of his career may have developed a warmer sense of literary kinship, without any Bloomian antagonism toward his poetic father-figure. The *Beowulf* poet and the *Gawain* poet had provided biographical blanks. But Chaucer had left enough life records, and had projected his personality into his poetry steadily enough, to afford a medieval mirror in which Tolkien could catch glimpses of himself as an author with his own late-life concerns for literary posterity.

During the years from his retirement in 1959 until his death in 1973, Tolkien found only more reasons to worry about his unpublished writings, even as lesser works such as *Leaf by Niggle* and *Lay of Aotrou and Itroun* had

---

[6] The anonymous review appeared in *TLS* (13 June 1958), 327.
[7] Bodleian MS Tolkien A 39/2/2, fols. 63–4. Line references for the *Legend of Good Women* are to what Skeat calls the A-text and Robinson the G-text.

appeared, albeit in somewhat out-of-the-way venues.[8] He did manage to see into print his long-delayed EETS edition of *Ancrene Wisse* in 1962, but he failed to deliver other long-promised publications such as his *Pearl* translation and, even more burdensome for the creator of Middle-earth, his disorganized and gap-filled *Silmarillion*. The Coda of *Tolkien's Lost Chaucer* suggested that both authors relied hopefully upon their sons as literary executors – Thomas Chaucer especially for the unfinished *Canterbury Tales* and Christopher Tolkien for the *Silmarillion* as well as his *History of Middle-earth*.[9] Such a prospect would have given special meaning to Tolkien's 1957 reflection on Chaucer's *Retracciouns* quoted above: "Yet like all great inheritances, this one has laid upon his heirs burdens and responsibilities."

---

[8] Tolkien, "Leaf by Niggle", *The Dublin Review*, 216 (January 1945), 46–61, and "The Lay of Aotrou and Itroun", *The Welsh Review* 4 (1945), 254–66.

[9] *TLC*, "Fathers and Sons", 269–77, describes Thomas Chaucer overseeing posthumous production of Ellesmere, as well as other deluxe manuscripts of the *Canterbury Tales*, and Christopher publishing the twenty-five volumes of his father's works (recently updated by Catherine McIlwaine, "Christopher Tolkien: Bibliography", in *Great Tales Never End*, ed. Ovenden and McIlwaine, 206-09).

Works Cited

Adams, Michael. "Phantom Dictionaries: The Middle English Dictionary before Kurath". *Dictionaries: Journal of the Dictionary Society of North America* 23 (2002), 95–114.
Ælfric's Lives of the Saints. Ed. and trans. Walter W. Skeat. EETS o.s. 76, 82, 94, 114 (1881, 1885, 1890, 1901).
Allen, Hope Emily. *Rolle Richard, Hermit of Hampole and Materials for His Biography*. New York: Modern Language Association, 1927.
Ancient Laws of England. Ed. Benjamin Thorpe. London: Eyre and Spottiswoode, 1840.
The Ancren Riwle: A Treatise on the Rules and Duties of Monastic Life. Ed. James Morton. London: Camden Society, 1853.
Anderson, Douglas A. "'An Industrious Little Devil': E. V. Gordon as Friend and Collaborator with Tolkien". In *Tolkien the Medievalist*, ed. Chance, 15–25.
Arthour and Merlin: nach der Auchinleck-Hs. Ed. Eugen Kölbing. Leipzig: O.R. Reisland, 1890.
Bacon, Sir Francis. *Essays*. London: Oxford University Press, 1902.
Barbour, John. *The Bruce*. Ed. Walter W. Skeat. EETS e.s. 11, 21, 29, 29, 55 (1870, 1874, 1877, 1889).
Bertolet, Craig E. "The Anxiety of Exclusion: Speech, Power, and Chaucer's Manciple". *Studies in the Age of Chaucer* 33 (2011), 183–218.
Bishop Percy's Folio Manuscript: Ballads and Romances. Ed. John W. Hales and Frederick J. Furnivall. 3 vols. London: Trübner, 1867–68.
Blake, N. B. "The Northernisms in *The Reeve's Tale*". *Lore and Language* 3 (1979), 1–8.
Blodgett, James E. "William Thynne". In *Editing Chaucer*, ed. Ruggiers, 35–52.
Bloom, Harold. *The Anxiety of Influence: A Theory of Poetry*. New York: Oxford University Press, 1973.
Bowers, John M. "'Beautiful as Troilus': Richard II, Chaucer's Troilus, and Figures of (Un)Masculinity". In *Men and Masculinity in Chaucer's* Troilus and Criseyde, ed. Tison Pugh and Marcia Smith Marzec. Cambridge: D. S. Brewer, 2008, 9–27.
Bowers, John M. "Chaucer after Retters: The Wartime Origins of English Literature". In *Inscribing the Hundred Years' War in French and English Cultures*, ed. Denise Baker. Albany: State University of New York Press, 2000, 91–125.
Bowers John M. "'Dronkenesse Is Ful of Stryvyng': Alcoholism and Social Violence in Chaucer's *Pardoner's Tale*". *ELH* 57 (1990), 757–84.
Bowers, John M. "Durin's Stone, Ruthwell Cross, and *Dream of the Rood*". *Tolkien Studies* 20 (2023), 9–28.
Bowers, John M. *Chaucer and Langland: The Antagonistic Tradition*. Notre Dame, Indiana: University of Notre Dame Press, 2007.
Brewer, Derek. "Introduction". In *A Companion to the* Gawain-*Poet*, ed. Derek Brewer and Jonathan Gibson. Cambridge: D. S. Brewer, 1997, 1–21.
Brown, Carleton, ed. *Religious Lyrics of the XIVth Century*. Oxford: Clarendon Press, 1924.
Brown, Carleton. "*The Text of the Canterbury Tales* by John M. Manly and Edith Rickert". *Modern Language Notes*, 55 (1940), 606–21.

Burrow, J. A. "Elvish Chaucer". In *The Endless Knot: Essays on Old and Middle English in Honor of Marie Borroff*, ed. M. Teresa Tavormina and R. F. Yeager (Cambridge: D. S. Brewer, 1995), 105–11.

Carpenter, Humphrey. *J. R. R. Tolkien: A Biography*. 1977; Boston and New York: Houghton Mifflin, 2000.

Catholicon Anglicum: An English-Latin Wordbook Dated 1483. Ed. Sidney J. H. Herrtage and Henry B. Wheatley. EETS o.s. 75 (1881).

Chance, Jane, ed. *Tolkien the Medievalist*. London: Routledge, 2003.

Chaucer. *The Canterbury Tales of Chaucer*. Ed. Thomas Tyrwhitt. 5 vols. London: T. Payne, 1775–78.

Chaucer. *The Clerkes Tale of Oxenford*. Ed. Kenneth Sisam. Oxford: Clarendon Press, 1923.

Chaucer. *The Complete Works of Geoffrey Chaucer*. Ed. Walter W. Skeat. 6 vols. Oxford: Clarendon Press, 1894.

Chaucer. *The Nun's Priest's Tale*. Ed. Kenneth Sisam. Oxford: Clarendon Press, 1927.

Chaucer. *The Nun's Priest's Tale*. Ed. Nevill Coghill and Christopher Tolkien. London: George G. Harrap, 1959.

Chaucer. *The Pardoner's Tale*. Ed. C. M. Drennan and A. J. Wyatt. 2nd ed. London: University Tutorial Series, 1937.

Chaucer. *The Pardoner's Tale*. Ed. Nevill Coghill and Christopher Tolkien. London: George G. Harrap, 1958.

Chaucer. *The Poetical Works of Chaucer*. Ed. F. N. Robinson. Boston: Houghton Mifflin, 1933.

Chaucer. *A Six-Text Print of Chaucer's Canterbury Tales: In Parallel Columns from the Following MSS 1. The Ellesmere: 2. The Hengwrt 154; 3. The Cambridge Univ. Libr. Gg. 4.27; 4. The Corpus Christi Coll., Oxford; 5. The Petworth; 6. The Lansdowne 851*. Ed. Frederick J. Furnivall. 8 vols. London: Chaucer Society, Trübner, 1869–77.

Chaucer. *The Works of Geoffrey Chaucer*. Ed. F. N. Robinson. 2nd. ed. rev. London: Oxford University Press, 1957.

Chaucer's Poetry: An Anthology for the Modern Reader. Ed. E. T. Donaldson. New York: Ronald Press, 1958.

Christopher, Joe R. "Tolkien's Lyric Poetry". In *Tolkien's* Legendarium, ed. Flieger and Hostetter, 143–60.

Ciento Nouelle Antike. Ed. Carlo Gualteruzzi. Bologna, 1525.

Cilli, Oronzo. *Tolkien's Library: An Annotated Checklist*. 2nd ed. rev. Foreword by Tom Shippey. Afterword by Verlyn Flieger. Edinburgh: Luna Press, 2022.

Clouston, W. A. "The Robbers and the Treasure Trove: Buddhist Original and Asiatic and European Versions of Chaucer's *Pardoner's Tale*". In *Originals and Analogues of Some of Chaucer's Canterbury Tales*, ed. F. J. Furnivall, Edmund Brock, and W. A. Clouston (London: Chaucer Society, 2nd series, no. 20, 1872), 415–36. Also "The Tell-Tale Bird: Latin Source, Other European Versions, and Asiatic Analogues of Chaucer's *Manciple's Tale*", 437–80.

Cook, Albert S., ed. *A Literary Middle English Reader*. Boston: Ginn & Co, 1915.

Cossio, Andoni. "Addenda: One Middle English Manuscript and Four Editions of Medieval Works Known to J. R. R. Tolkien and What They Reveal". *ANQ: A Quarterly Journal of Short Articles, Notes and Reviews* (2021), 1–8.

Cursor Mundi: A Northumbrian Poem of the XIVth Century. Ed. Richard Morris. EETS o.s. 57, 59, 62, 66, 68, 99, 101 (1874–93).

Dan Michel's Ayenbite of Inwyt or Remorse of Conscience. Ed. Richard Morris. EETS o.s. 23, (1866).

D'Ardenne, S. T. R. O. "The Devil's Spout". *Transactions of the Philological Society* 32 (1946), 31–55.

D'Ardenne, S. R.T. O., ed. *The Katherine Group edited from MS Bodley 34*. Paris: Société d'edition Les Belles Lettre, 1977.

D'Ardenne, S. R. T. O., ed. *Þe Liflade ant te Passiun of Seinte Iuliene*. EETS o.s. 248 (1961).

Davis, Norman. Review of Bennett's *Chaucer at Oxford and at Cambridge*. *Review of English Studies*, n.s. 27 (1976), 336–7.

Deanesly, Margaret. *The Lollard Bible and Other Medieval Biblical Versions*. Cambridge: Cambridge University Press, 1920.

Drout, Michael D. C. "J. R. R. Tolkien's Medieval Scholarship and its Significance". *Tolkien Studies* 4 (2007), 113–76.

Eden, Bradford Lee. "The 'Music of the Spheres': Relationships between Tolkien's *The Silmarillion* and Medieval Cosmological and Religious Theory". In *Tolkien the Medievalist*, ed. Chance, 183–93.

Ekwall, Eilert. *The Place-Names of Lancashire*. Manchester: University of Manchester Press, 1922.

The Ellesmere Chaucer Reproduced in Facsimile. Ed. Alex Egerton. 2 vols. Manchester: Manchester University Press, 1911.

The English Works of Wyclif. Ed. F. D. Matthew. 2nd ed. rev. EETS o.s. 74 (1902).

The Equatorie of the Planetis edited from Peterhouse MS 75.I. Ed. Derek J. Price with linguistic analysis by R. M. Wilson. Cambridge: Cambridge University Press, 1955.

Everett, Dorothy. "Chaucer's 'Good Ear'". *Review of English Studies* 23 (1947), 201–8.

Ferré, Vincent. "The Son behind the Father: Christopher Tolkien as a Writer". In *Great Tales Never End*, ed. Ovenden and McIlwaine, 53–69.

Fitzgerald, Jill. "A *Clerkes Compleinte*: Tolkien and the Division of Lit. and Lang." *Tolkien Studies* 6 (2009), 41–57.

Flannery, Mary C. "The Case for the Defence: New Evidence Suggests that Geoffrey Chaucer May Be Innocent of Rape". *TLS*, 21 October 2022, 18.

Flieger, Verlyn, and Carl F. Hostetter, eds. *Tolkien's Legendarium: Essays on The History of Middle-earth*. Westport and London: Greenwood Press, 2000.

Gamillscheg, Ernst. "La colonisation germanique dans la Gaule du Nord". In *Essais de Philologie Moderne (1951)*. Paris: Société d'édition Les Belles Lettres (1953), 47–62.

Garth, John. "The Chronology of Creation: How J. R. R. Tolkien Misremembered the Beginnings of his Mythology". In *Great Tales Never End*, ed. Ovenden and McIlwaine, 89–109.

Garth, John. *Tolkien at Exeter College: How an Oxford Undergraduate Created Middle-earth* Oxford: Exeter College, 2014.

The "Gest Hystoriale" of the Destruction of Troy. Ed. George A. Panton and David Donaldson. EETS o.s. 39 and 56 (1869 and 1874).

Gilliver, Peter. *The Making of the Oxford English Dictionary*. Oxford: Oxford University Press, 2016.

Gilliver, Peter, Jeremy Marshall, and Edmund Weiner. *The Ring of Words: Tolkien and the Oxford English Dictionary*. Oxford: Oxford University Press, 2006.

A Glossary of the Old Northumbrian Gospels (Lindisfarne Gospels or Durham Book). Ed. Albert S. Cook. Halle: M. Niemeyer, 1894.

Gordon, E. V., and C. T. Onions. "Notes on the Text and Interpretation of *Pearl*". *Medium Ævum* 1/2 (1932), 126–36.

Gower, John. *The English Works of John Gower*. Ed. G. C. Macaulay. EETS e.s. 81 and 82 (1900 and 1901).

Hall, Joseph, ed. *Selections from Early Middle English*. 2 vols. Oxford: Oxford University Press, 1920.
Halliwell, James Orchard. *A Dictionary of Archaic and Provincial Words, Obsolete Phrases, Proverbs, and Ancient Customs from the Fourteenth Century*. 2 vols. London: John Russell Smith, 1847.
Hammond, Eleanor Prescott. *Chaucer: A Bibliographical Manual*. London: Macmillan, 1908.
Havelok the Dane. Ed. Walter W. Skeat. EETS e.s. 4 (1868).
Hêliand. Ed. Moritz Heyne. Paderborn: Ferdinand Schöningh, 1866.
Honegger, Thomas. "Tolkien's 'Academic Writings'". In *Companion*, ed. Lee, 27–40.
Horobin, Simon C. P. "Chaucer's Norfolk Reeve". *Neophilologus* 86 (2002), 609–12.
Horobin, Simon C. P. "J. R. R. Tolkien as a Philologist: A Reconsideration of the Northernisms in Chaucer's *Reeve's Tale*". *English Studies* 2 (2001), 97–105.
Hostetter, Carl F. "Editing the Tolkienian Manuscript". In *Great Tales Never End*, ed. Ovenden and McIlwaine, 129–44.
Hostetter, Carl F. "*Sir Orfeo*: A Middle English Version by J.R.R. Tolkien". *Tolkien Studies* 1 (2004), 85–123.
Hulbert, James R. *Chaucer's Official Life*. Wisconsin: Collegiate Press, 1912.
Jones, Diana Wynne. "The Shape of the Narrative in *The Lord of the Rings*". In Robert Giddings, ed. *J. R. R. Tolkien: This Far Land*. London: Vision, 1983, 87–107. Rpt. in Diana Wynne Jones, *Reflections on the Magic of Writing*. Oxford and New York: David Fickling, 2012, 5–25.
Jones, Terry. *Chaucer's Knight: The Portrait of a Medieval Mercenary*. London: Eyre Methuen, 1980.
Jones, Terry, with Robert Yeager, Terry Dolan, Alan Fletcher, and Juliette Dor. *Who Murdered Chaucer? A Medieval Mystery*. New York: St. Martin's Press, 2003.
Jordan, Richard. *Handbuch der mittelenglischen Grammatik*. Heidelberg: Carl Winter, 1925.
Joseph of Arimathie: The Romance of Seint Graal. Ed. Walter W. Skeat. EETS o.s. 44 (1871).
King Alfred's West-Saxon Version of Gregory's Pastoral Care. Ed. Henry Sweet. EETS o.s. 45 and 50 (1871).
King Horn: A Romance of the Thirteenth Century. Ed. Joseph Hall. Oxford: Clarendon, 1901.
Knox, Philip. "The 'Dialect' of Chaucer's Reeve". *Chaucer Review* 49 (2014), 102–24.
Kolve, V. A. *Chaucer and the Imagery of Narrative: The First Five Canterbury Tales*. Stanford: Stanford University Press, 1984.
Kolve, V. A. *The Play Called Corpus Christi*. Stanford: Stanford University Press, 1966.
Krapp, G. P., ed. *The Junius Manuscript*. London: Routledge, 1931.
Langland, William. *Piers the Plowman in Three Parallel Texts*. Ed. Walter W. Skeat. 2 vols. Oxford: Oxford University Press, 1886.
Larsen, Kristine. "Sea Birds and Morning Stars: Ceyx, Alcyone, and the Many Metamorphoses of Eärendil and Elwing". In *Tolkien and the Study of his Sources*. Ed. Jason Fisher. Jefferson NC and London: McFarland & Co., 2011, 69–83.
Layamon's Brut. Ed. Joseph Hall. Oxford: Clarendon, 1924.
Lee, Stuart D. "Manuscripts: Use, and Using". *Companion*, ed. Lee, 56–76.
Lee, Stuart D. "A Milestone in BBC History? The 1955–56 Radio Dramatization of *The Lord of the Rings*". *Great Tales Never End*, ed. Ovenden and McIlwaine, 145–65.
Lee, Stuart D., ed. *A Companion to J. R. R. Tolkien*. Oxford: Wiley Blackwell, 2014.
Lewis, C. S. *The Allegory of Love*. London: Oxford University Press, 1936.
Lewis, C. S. *Collected Letters of C. S. Lewis*, Vol. 3: *Narnia, Cambridge, and Joy, 1950–1963*. Ed. Walter Hooper. New York: HarperCollins, 2007.

Lewis, C. S. *English Literature in the Sixteenth Century Excluding Drama*. Oxford: Clarendon Press, 1954.
Lewis, Warren. *Brothers and Friends: The Diaries of Major Warren Hamilton Lewis*. Ed. Clyde S. Kilby and Marjorie Lamp Mead. San Francisco: Harper & Row, 1982.
Libri Psalmorum Versio Antiqua. Ed. Benjamin Thorpe. Oxford: 1835.
The Life of St. Cuthbert in English Verse. Ed. Joseph Thomas Fowler. Durham: Surtees Society Publications, no. 87, 1891.
Life of Saint Katherine. Ed. Eugen Einenkel. EETS o.s. 80 (1884).
Ðe Liflade of St. Juliana. Ed. Oswald Cockayne. EETS o.s. 51 (1872).
Lloyd, Richard J. *Northern English: Phonetics, Grammar, Texts*. Leipzig: Teubner, 1899.
Loomis, Laura Hibbard. "Chaucer and the Breton Lays of the Auchinleck MS". *Studies in Philology* 38 (1941), 14–33.
Lounsbury, Thomas R. *Studies in Chaucer: His Life and Writings*. 3 vols. New York: Harper, 1892.
Ludus Coventriae or The Plaie Called Corpus Christi. Ed. K. S. Block. EETS e.s. 120 (1922).
Lydgate, John. *Lydgate's Fall of Princes: Part I*. Ed. Henry Bergen. EETS e.s. 121 (1924).
McIlwaine, Catherine. "Christopher Tolkien: Bibliography". In *Great Tales Never End*, ed. Ovenden and McIlwaine, 206–09.
McIlwaine, Catherine. "Introduction". In *Great Tales Never End*, ed. Ovenden and McIlwaine, 7–27.
McIlwaine, Catherine. *Tolkien: Maker of Middle-earth*. Oxford: Bodleian Library, 2018.
Manly, John M. *Some New Light on Chaucer*. New York: Henry Holt, 1926.
Manly, John M., and Edith Rickert, eds. *The Text of the Canterbury Tales Studied on the Basis of All Known Manuscripts*. 8 vols. Chicago and London: University of Chicago Press, 1940.
Manning, Robert, of Brunne. *Handlyng Synne*. Ed. Frederick J. Furnivall. EETS o.s. 119 and 123 (1901 and 1903).
Marie de France. *Fabeln*. Ed. Eduard Mall. Halle: Max Niemeyer, 1898.
Mariu Saga. Ed. C. R. Unger. Christiana: Brögger & Christie, 1871.
Mawer, Allen. *Place Names of Northumberland and Durham*. Cambridge: Cambridge University Press, 1920.
Meyer-Lübke, Wilhelm. *Romanisches etymologisches Wörterbuch*. Heidelberg: C. Winter, 1911.
Minot, Laurence. *The Poems of Laurence Minot*. Ed. Joseph Hall. 3rd ed. Oxford: Clarendon, 1914.
Mirk, John. *Mirk's Festial: A Collection of Homilies*. Ed. Theodore Erbe. EETS e.s. 96 (1905).
Moir, James, ed. *The Actis and Deidis of the Illustere and Vaiȝleand Campioun Schir William Wallace Knicht of Ellerslie by Henry the Minstrel Commonly Known as Blind Harry*. Edinburgh: William Blackwood, Scottish Text Society, nos. 6, 7, 17 (1889).
Morris, Jan, ed. *The Oxford Book of Oxford*. Oxford: Oxford University Press, 1978.
Morris, Richard, and Walter W. Skeat, eds. *Specimens of Early English, Part II*. Oxford: Clarendon, 1873.
Mroczkowski, Przemyslaw. "A Lusty Plain, Habundant of Vitaille". *TLS*, 13 June 1958, 327.
Neubauer, Łukasz. "The 'Polish Inkling': Professor Przemyslaw Mroczkowski as J. R. R. Tolkien's Friend and Scholar". *Mythlore* 39 (2020), 149–76.
Nicholas, David. *Medieval Flanders*. New York: Longman, 1992.
The Northern Passion: Four Parallel Texts and the French Original. Ed. Frances A. Foster. EETS o.s. 145 and 147 (1913 and 1916).

An Old English Miscellany Containing a Bestiary, Kentish Sermons, Proverbs of Alfred, Religious Poems of the Thirteenth Century. Ed. Richard Morris. EETS o.s. 49 (1872).

Ordway, Holly. *Tolkien's Faith: A Spiritual Biography*. Elk Grove Village IL: Word on Fire Academic, 2023.

The Orygynale Cronykil of Scotland by Androw of Wyntoun. Ed. David Laing. 3 vols. Edinburgh: Edmonston and Douglas, 1872-79.

Ovenden, Richard, and Catherine McIlwaine, eds. *The Great Tales Never End: Essays in Memory of Christopher Tolkien*. Oxford: Bodleian Library Publishing, 2022.

The Owl and the Nightingale. Ed. John Edwin Wells. Boston and London: Heath, 1907.

The Owl and the Nightingale. Ed. and trans. J. W. H. Atkins. Cambridge: Cambridge University Press, 1922.

Pearsall, Derek. "Thomas Speght (ca. 1550-?)". *Editing Chaucer*, ed. Ruggiers, 71-92.

A Poem on the Evil Times of Edward II. Ed. Charles Hardwick. London: Percy Society, 1849.

Pollard, Alfred W., ed. *English Miracle Plays, Moralities, and Interludes: Specimens of the Pre-Elizabethan Drama*. Oxford: Clarendon Press, 1909.

The Promptorium Parvulorum. Ed. A. L. Mayhew. EETS e.s. 102 (1908).

Queen Elizabeth's Englishings of Boethius. Ed. Caroline Pemberton. EETS o.s. 113 (1899).

Raleigh, Walter. *The English Novel: A Short Sketch of its History from the Earliest Times to the Appearance of Waverley*. London: John Murray, 1894.

Rickert, Edith. "Thou Vache". *Modern Philology* 11 (1913-14), 209-226.

Robert of Gloucester. *The Metrical Chronicle*. Ed. William Aldis Wright. 2 vols. London: Eyre and Spottiswoode, Rolls Series 86 (1887).

Rolle, Richard, de Hampole. *English Prose Treatises*. Ed. George G. Perry, EETS o.s. 20 (1866).

Rolle, Richard, de Hampole. *Psalter Translated by Richard Rolle of Hampole*. Ed. H. R. Bramley. Oxford: Clarendon, 1884.

The Romance of William of Palerne. Ed. Walter W. Skeat, EETS e.s. 1 (1867).

Ruggiers, Paul G., ed. *Editing Chaucer: The Great Tradition*. Norman, Oklahoma: Pilgrim Books, 1984.

Ryan, John S. "J. R. R. Tolkien's Formal Lecturing and Teaching at the University of Oxford, 1925-1959". *Seven: Journal of the Marion E. Wade Center* 19 (2002): 45-62.

Salu, Mary, and Robert T. Farrell, eds. *J. R. R. Tolkien, Scholar and Storyteller*. Ithaca and London: Cornell University Press, 1979.

Sayer, George. "Recollections of J. R. R. Tolkien". *Mythlore* 21 (1996), 21-5.

Scull, Christina, and Wayne G. Hammond. *J. R. R. Tolkien Companion and Guide: Revised and Expanded Edition*. London: HarperCollins, 2017: Vol. 1: *Chronology*; Vol. 2: *Reader's Guide, Part I: A-M*; Vol. 3. *Reader's Guide, Part II: N-Z*.

Sedgefield, W. J., ed. *An Anglo-Saxon Verse-Book*. Manchester: University of Manchester Press, 1928.

Sedgefield, W. J., ed. *King Alfred's Old English Version of Boethius' De Consolatione Philosophiae*. Oxford: Clarendon Press, 1899.

Seinte Marherete: The Meiden ant Martyr. Ed. and trans. Oswald Cockayne. EETS o.s. 13 (1866).

Shippey, Tom. "Fighting the Long Defeat: Philology in Tolkien's Life and Fiction". In *Roots and Branches*, 139-56.

Shippey, Tom. "'A Fund of Wise Sayings': Proverbiality in Tolkien". In *Roots and Branches*, 303-19.

Shippey, Tom. Review of Diana Wynne Jones, *Reflections on the Magic of Writing*. *TLS*, 31 August 2012, 22.

Shippey, Tom. *The Road to Middle-earth*. Rev. ed. Boston and New York: Houghton Mifflin, 2003.
Shippey, Tom. *Roots and Branches: Selected Papers on Tolkien*. Zollikofen, Switzerland: Walking Tree Publishers, 2007.
Shippey, Tom. "Tolkien's Academic Reputation Now" (1989). In *Roots and Branches*, 203–12.
Shippey, Tom. "Tolkien as Editor". In *Companion*, ed. Lee, 41–55.
Sir Eglamour: A Middle English Romance. Ed. A. S. Cook and Gustav Schleich. New York: Holt, 1911.
Sir Tristrem. Ed. George P. McNeill. Edinburgh: William Blackwood, Scottish Text Society, no. 8, 1886.
Sisam, Kenneth. "MSS Bodley 340 and 342: Ælfric's *Catholic Homilies*". *Review of English Studies* 7 (1931), 7–22.
Sisam, Kenneth, ed. *Fourteenth Century Verse and Prose*. Oxford: Clarendon Press, 1921.
Small, John, ed. *English Metrical Homilies from Manuscripts of the Fourteenth Century*. Edinburgh: William Paterson, 1862.
Smith, A. H. *The Place-Names of the North Riding of Yorkshire*. Cambridge: Cambridge University Press, 1928.
Smith, M. Bentinck. *The Language and Metre of Chaucer*. London: Macmillan, 1901.
Sources and Analogues of Chaucer's Canterbury Tales. Ed. William Frank Bryan and Germaine Dempster. Chicago: University of Chicago Press, 1941.
Stenström, Anders. "*The Clerkes Compleinte* Revisited". *Arda* 6 (1990 for 1986), 1–13.
Stevenson, W. H. "Some Old-English Words Omitted or Imperfectly Explained in Dictionaries". *Transactions of the Philological Society* 23/3 (1897), 528–42.
The Story of Genesis and Exodus. Ed. Richard Morris. EETS o.s. 7 (1865).
Stratmann, F. H. *A Middle-English Dictionary*. Rev. Henry Bradley. Oxford: Clarendon Press, 1891.
Strohm, Paul. *Chaucer's Tale: 1386 and the Road to Canterbury*. New York: Viking, 2014.
Sweet, Henry, ed. *Anglo-Saxon Reader in Prose and Verse*. Oxford: Clarendon, 1879.
The Tale of Gamelyn from the Harleian MS No. 7334, Collated with Six Other MSS Ed. Walter W. Skeat. Oxford: Clarendon, 1884.
Ten Brink, Bernhard. "Die Vocale". In *Chaucer's Sprache und Verskunst*. Leipzig, 1884, 7–63.
Thomas, Mary Edith. *Medieval Skepticism and Chaucer: An Evaluation of the Skepticism of the 13th and 14th Centuries of Geoffrey Chaucer and His Immediate Predecessors – An Era That Looked Back on an Age of Faith and Forward to an Age of Reason*. 1950; rpt. New York: Cooper Square Publishers, 1971.
Tolkien, J. R. R. "*Ancrene Wisse* and *Hali Meiðhad*". *Essays and Studies* 14 (1929), 104–26.
Tolkien, J. R. R. *The Battle of Maldon, together with the Homecoming of Beorhtnoth*. Ed. Peter Grybauskas. London: HarperCollins, 2023.
Tolkien, J. R. R. *Beowulf: A Translation and Commentary*. Ed. Christopher Tolkien. Boston and New York: Houghton Mifflin, 2014.
Tolkien, J. R. R. "*Beowulf*" *and the Critics*. Ed. Michael D. C. Drout. Tempe: Arizona Center for Medieval and Renaissance Studies, 2002.
Tolkien, J. R. R. "Chaucer as a Philologist: *The Reeve's Tale*". *Transactions of the Philological Society* (1934), 1–70. Reprinted with author's corrections in *Tolkien Studies* 5 (2008), 109–71.
Tolkien, J. R. R. "The Devil's Coach-Horses". *Review of English Studies* 1/3 (July 1925), 331–6.
Tolkien, J. R. R. "English and Welsh" (1955). In *Essays*, 162–97.

Tolkien, J. R. R. "The Homecoming of Beorhtnoth, Beorhthelm's Son" (1953). *Poems and Stories*. Boston and New York: Houghton Mifflin, 1994, 75–109.
Tolkien, J. R. R. 'The Lay of Aotrou and Itroun'. *The Welsh Review* 4 (1945): 254–66.
Tolkien, J. R. R. "Leaf by Niggle". *The Dublin Review*. 216 (January 1945): 46–61.
Tolkien, J. R. R. *The Legend of Sigurd and Gudrún*. Ed. Christopher Tolkien. Boston and New York: Houghton Mifflin Harcourt, 2009.
Tolkien, J. R. R. *The Letters of J. R. R. Tolkien*. Ed. Humphrey Carpenter and Christopher Tolkien. 1981; Boston and New York: Houghton Mifflin, 2000.
Tolkien, J. R. R. *The Letters of J. R. R. Tolkien: Revised and Expanded Edition*. Ed. Humphrey Carpenter and Christopher Tolkien. London: HarperCollins, 2023.
Tolkien, J. R. R. "Middle English *Losenger*: Sketch of an Etymological and Semantic Enquiry". In *Essais de Philologie Moderne (1951)*. Paris: Société d'édition Les Belles Lettres (1953), 63–76.
Tolkien, J. R. R. *The Monsters and the Critics, and Other Essays*. Ed. Christopher Tolkien. 1983; London: HarperCollins, 2006.
Tolkien, J. R. R. *Morgoth's Ring: The Later Silmarillion, Part I*. Ed. Christopher Tolkien. Boston and New York: Houghton Mifflin, 1993.
Tolkien, J. R. R. *The Nature of Middle-earth: Late Writings on the Lands, Inhabitants, and Metaphysics of Middle-earth*. Ed. Carl F. Hostetter. London: HarperCollins, 2021.
Tolkien, J. R. R. "The Oxford English School". *The Oxford Magazine* 48 (1930), 778–80.
Tolkien, J. R. R. *The Peoples of Middle-Earth*. Ed. Christopher Tolkien. Boston and New York: Houghton Mifflin, 1996.
Tolkien, J. R. R. "Philology: General Works". *Year's Work in English Studies*, 4 (1924 for 1923): 20–37; 5 (1926 for 1924): 26–65; and 6 (1927 for 1925): 32–66.
Tolkien, J. R. R. "The Reeve's Tale: Version Prepared for Recitation at the 'Summer Diversions' Oxford: 1939". Rpt. *Tolkien Studies* 5 (2008), 173–83.
Tolkien, J. R. R. *The Return of the King*. 1955; Boston and New York: Houghton Mifflin, 1988.
Tolkien, J. R. R. *The Return of the Shadow: The History of the Lord of the Rings, Part I*. Ed. Christopher Tolkien. Boston and New York: Houghton Mifflin, 1988.
Tolkien, J. R. R. Review of *Hali Meidenhad: An Alliterative Prose Homily of the Thirteenth Century*, ed. F. J. Furnivall, EETS o.s. 18 (1922). TLS, 26 April 1923, 281. Rpt. *TLS* 30 June 2017, 34.
Tolkien, J. R. R. "Sigelwara Land". *Medium Aevum* 1 (1932), 183–96, and 3 (1934), 95–111.
Tolkien, J. R. R. *The Silmarillion*. Ed. Christopher Tolkien. 1977; London: HarperCollins, 2008.
Tolkien, J. R. R. *Sir Gawain and the Green Knight, Pearl, and Sir Orfeo*. Ed. Christopher Tolkien. London: George Allen & Unwin, 1975; rept. New York: Ballantine Books, 1980.
Tolkien, J. R. R. "Some Contributions to Middle-English Lexicography". *Review of English Studies* 1 (1925), 210–15.
Tolkien, J. R. R. *The Story of Kullervo*. Ed. Verlyn Flieger. Boston and New York: Houghton Mifflin Harcourt, 2016.
Tolkien, J. R. R. *The Two Towers*. 1954; Boston and New York: Houghton Mifflin, 1988.
Tolkien, J. R. R. "Valedictory Address". In *Essays*, 224–40. A slightly different version was printed in Salu and Farrell, eds., *Tolkien, Scholar and Storyteller*, 16–32.
Tolkien, J. R. R. *The War of the Jewels*. Ed. Christopher Tolkien. Boston and New York: Houghton Mifflin, 1994.
Tolkien, J. R. R. *Unfinished Tales of Númenor and Middle-earth*. Ed. Christopher Tolkien Boston and New York: Houghton Mifflin, 1980.

Tolkien, J. R. R., ed. *Ancrene Wisse: Edited from MS Corpus Christi College Cambridge 402*. Intro. N. R. Ker. EETS o.s. 249 (1962).

Tolkien, J. R. R., and E. V. Gordon, eds. *Sir Gawain and the Green Knight*. Oxford: Clarendon Press, 1925.

Tolkien, John, and Priscilla Tolkien. *The Tolkien Family Album*. Boston: Houghton Mifflin, 1992.

Tolkien, Priscilla. "A Personal Memory". In *Great Tales Never End*, ed. Ovenden and McIlwaine, 46–52.

The Towneley Plays. Ed. George England and Alfred W. Pollard. EETS e.s. 87 (1897).

Trevelyan, George Macaulay. *England in the Age of Wycliffe*. 2nd ed. London: Longmans, Green, 1899.

Trounce, A. McI. "The English Tail-Rhyme Romances". *Medium Ævum* 1 (1932), 87–108, 168–82; 2 (1933), 34–57, 189–98; and 3 (1934), 30–50.

Unwin, Rayner. "Early Days of Elder Days". In *Tolkien's* Legendarium, ed. Flieger and Hostetter, 3–6.

Vices and Virtues. Ed. Ferdinand Holthausen. London: Oxford University Press, 1888.

Wallace, David. "In Flaundres". *Studies in the Age of Chaucer* 19 (1997), 63–91.

The Wars of Alexander: An Alliterative Romance. Ed. Walter W. Skeat. EETS e.s. 47 (1886).

Wartburg, Walther von. *Französisches etymologisches Wörterbuch: eine Darstellung des galloromanischen Sprachschatzes*. Bonn: F. Klopp, 1950.

Wheatley, Edward. "The Manciple's Tale". In *Sources and Analogues of The Canterbury Tales*. Ed. Robert M. Correale and Mary Hamel. Vol. II. Cambridge: D. S. Brewer, 2005, 749–73.

Windeatt, B. A. "Thomas Tyrwhitt (1730–1786)". In *Editing Chaucer*, ed. Ruggiers, 117–43.

Wright, Joseph. *English Dialect Dictionary*. 6 vols. London: Henry Frowde, 1898–1905.

Wright, Thomas, ed. *The Political Songs of England from the Reign of John to That of Edward II*. London: Camden Society, 1839.

Wyld, Henry Cecil. *A Short History of English*. London: John Murray, 1914.

Yeager, R. F. "John Gower's French". In *A Companion to Gower*. Ed. Siân Echard. Cambridge: D. S. Brewer, 2004, 137–51.

York Plays. Ed. Lucy Toulmin Smith. Oxford: Clarendon, 1885.

Ywain and Gawain. Ed. Gustav Schleich. Leipzig: E. Franck, 1887.

Index

Note: Because Tolkien's writings are unusually heavy with references to Middle English texts and earlier English scholarship, our index is necessarily selective. We do not record all twenty-nine references to *Cursor Mundi*, for example, or all sixty-six citations of Walter W. Skeat.

Adam the scribe 39, 71, 82, 107, 111, 114, 119
Æsop 281
allegory 17, 68, 70, 71, 74, 84, 231, 233
Allen & Unwin 270
Alliterative tradition 3, 41, 66, 89, 102–5
anaphora 272
Ancrene Riwle / Ancrene Wisse 46, 100, 148, 250, 327
andwis / Andwise, Sam Gamgee's uncle 260
Anne of Bohemia 74, 84
Anthony the Hermit, Saint 300–1
Aristotle 86, 87
Auden, W. H. 16

Bacon, Sir Francis 17, 70
Battle of the Somme 30, 319
Beowulf 24, 50, 176, 322
Beren and Lúthien 37
Bestiary 140
Bilbo 64 n.33, 71 n.44, 84 n.79, 272, 285 n.39, 304 n.77
Bloom, Harold, *Anxiety of Influence* 268, 271–2, 326
Boccaccio, Giovanni 28, 87, 93, 220
Boethius, *De Consolatione Philosophiae* 29, 56, 77, 81–3, 88, 151, 216, 324
Bowers, John M., *Tolkien's Lost Chaucer* (*TLC*) 1, 28, 34, 42, 56, 61, 178, 249, 327
Bowra, Warden Maurice 246
Bradley, Henry 30–1, 249
Bradshaw Shift 241
Bratt, Edith 10, 20, 28
Brewer, Derek 25, 270 n.8
Brewerton, George 14, 255 n.18
Brown, Carleton 45, 215 n.2

Brutus 81
bugle 64
Burrow, John 55, 269
Burton, Richard 176
buskes / busshe 42, 43, 58

Carpenter, Humphrey 16, 42
Catholic 1, 19, 239, 252, 272
Chapman, R. W. 41, 49, 51, 234, 250
"Chaucer in his workshop" 58, 84, 232, 274, 276, 308
Chaucer, Geoffrey:
    Alliterative tradition 3
    Astrolabe 90–1
    balades, roundels, virelays 65, 326
    Boece 29, 56
    Book of the Duchess 71–3, 74, 251
    Book of the Leoun 326
    Canterbury Tales 3, 91, 114
    Clerk of Oxford 99
    Clerk's Tale 1, 36–7, 216, 231, 251, 268
    Compleint to his Empty Purse 80–1
    Compleynte unto Pité 27, 70–1
    Former Age 43, 77–8
    Franklin's Tale 9, 315–16
    Friar's Tale 96, 141
    Gentilesse 79–80
    Knight's Tale 2, 18, 43, 75, 86, 89, 104, 155
    Lak of Stedfastnesse 80
    Legend of Cleopatra 3, 54–5, 66, 87–90, 102, 103, 104, 255
    Man of Law's Tale 72, 83
    Manciple's Tale 139, 288–9, 314–15
    Merciles Beaute 78
    Miller's Tale 99
    Monk 99

340 INDEX

Chaucer, Geoffrey (*cont.*)
   Monk's Tale 55, 93, 176
   Nun's Priest's Tale 1, 3, 45, 66, 176
   Pardoner, character of 239, 242, 248
   Pardoner's Tale 1, 9, 39, 215, 235
   Parlement of Foules 27, 38, 68, 73–7, 216
   Parson 100, 105
   Plan of the *Tales* 100–1
   Prioress 39–40, 96–9, 182
   Prologue to the *Canterbury Tales* 91–102
   Prologue to the *Legend of Good Women* 83–7
   Reeve's Tale 1, 38, 98, 101–2, 106–214
   Reeve's Tale, Tolkien's experimental edition 184–214
   Retracciouns 5, 323–5
   Romaunt of the Rose 68–70
   Shipman 100
   Sir Thopas 149–50
   Squire 95
   To Rosemounde 78
   Troilus and Criseyde 9, 23–30, 82, 111, 119, 162, 214, 325
   Truth 78–9
   Wife of Bath's Prologue 181
   Wife of Bath's Tale 79
   Wordes unto Adam His Owne Scriveyn 39
Chaucer, Lewis 90
Chaucer, Thomas 19, 327
"Chaucerian incubus" 41, 50
Classical names 70–71, 88–9
Clouston, W. A., "The Robbers and the Treasure-Trove: Buddhist Original and Asiatic and European Versions of Chaucer's *Pardoner's Tale*" 227, 234, 268, 289, 293, 295, 297, 299, 306
Coghill, Nevill 176
Craigie, William 30
Cursor Mundi 121 n.38, 128, 130, 138, 148 n.90, 157, 159, 171
Cuthbert, Saint 164–5, 171, 185

D'Ardenne, S. R. T. O. (Simonne) 4, 25 n.34, 183, 246, 249
   "The Devil's Spout" 256
   Katherine Group edited from MS Bodley 34 155 n.121

Ðe Liflade ant te Passiun of Seinte Iuliene 25 n.34, 183
Dan Michel, *Ayenbyte of Inwit* 46 n.13, 100 n.125, 310 n.93
Dante 29–30, 75, 82, 87, 246–7
Davin, Dan 52–5, 56, 177, 230, 250
daysies 84–5
Deanesly, Margaret 216
Donaldson, E. T. 172 n.178
Douglas, Gavin 265–6
Drennan, C. M., and A. J. Wyatt, eds. Chaucer, *The Pardoner's Tale*. 242, 244, 290, 295
Drout, Michael 1, 8, 56

eagles 76
Elder Edda 263
Elizabeth I 82
Ellesmere *Canterbury Tales* 4, 7, 34, 56, 119, 156, 161, 178, 215, 223, 234–5, 240, 241, 244
Elrond 22
"elvish Chaucer" 80–1
Equatorie of the Planetis 6–7
eucatastrophe 29–30, 271, 286 n.42
Everett, Dorothy 103
Exeter College 9, 10, 18
Exodus 51, 141, 142, 149, 152

fabliau 3, 101, 106, 112, 116, 162, 184
Faramir and Éowyn 28–30
feigned history 17
Ferīdu'd Dīn 'Attar 295
fer in the north 38, 116, 185, 189
Fingal 15
Finn and Hengest 50, 322
Flanders 229, 308
Frodo and Sam 14, 183, 268, 271
Furnivall, Frederick J. 31, 109, 236
   Hali Meidenhad 25 n.35, 36
   Handlyng Synne 124 n.45
   Six-Text Print of Chaucer's *Canterbury Tales* 34, 109

Gamelyn 114 n.25, 122 n.42, 144
Gamillscheg, Ernst 254
Gandalf 29, 269, 283 n.35, 285 n.39, 304 n.77
Garth, John 275
Gautama (Buddha) 235, 278, 287–8, 290

geen/gaan 55, 56, 117, 121, 129, 161, 172–5
Gibbon, Edward 81
Gilliver, Peter 32
Gimli and Galadriel 29
gniden/gnodded 43, 59, 77–8
Gollum 183, 268, 271
Gordon, E. V. 35, 42
Gordon, George S. 16, 35, 41, 42, 45, 46, 52, 106
Gordon, Ida 250
Gower, John 27, 72, 85, 86, 87, 92–3, 97
grey eyes 1, 94, 98–9, 182, 187

Hali Meidenhad 3, 25, 36–37, 155 n.121
Hammond, Wayne G., and Christina Scull 7, 247, 269
Havelok 15, 141, 149, 151, 152, 170
Heimdallr 252, 254
Hêliand 261
Henry IV 79, 80, 81
Henry the Minstrel (Blind Harry) 153
heterly 55, 58, 60, 89, 102–3, 155
Hobbler/Hobbit 68–9 n.36
holly 75–6
Homeric catalogue 73, 75, 272
Honegger, Thomas 107
Hulbert, James 17

Indo-European 38, 77, 260
Innocent III, Pope 244–5
Isidore of Seville, Saint 76

Jackson, Peter 272
James I of Scotland, *Kingis Quair* 27
Jātaka 227, 269, 277, 278, 288, 289, 292, 294, 295, 298
Jesus, son of Mary 285, 288, 296, 297–8
Jews 289, 299, 309 n.89
Jones, Diana Wynne 267, 269–70
Jones, Terry 216, 324
Jónsson, Finnur 49

Kalevala 15–16, 28, 116 n.28
Katherine Group 12, 25, 46 n.13, 108, 155 n.121
Kentish dialect 10, 11, 35, 77
Kolve, V. A. 6, 22
  Chaucer and the Imagery of Narrative 22
  Play Called Corpus Christi 22

Latin 9, 14, 24, 36, 56, 73, 82–3, 88, 90, 183, 216, 221, 226, 238–9, 252, 254, 257, 279
Leeds University 2, 6, 16, 35–6
Lewis, C.S. 6, 66, 183, 252–3, 270, 319
  Allegory of Love 29, 41, 251
  Chronicles of Narnia 251
  English Literature in the Sixteenth Century 251
  Lion, the Witch, and the Wardrobe 251
  Preface to Paradise Lost 251
Lewis, Sinclair, *Babbitt* 247
Lewis, Warren 119 n.33, 215
Lollardy 19
Lollius 24
Loomis, Roger Sherman 35
losengeour/losenger 1, 4, 86, 246, 247, 249, 250, 251, 255
Lounsbury, Thomas R. 17
Lydgate, John 78, 80, 90, 145

Manly, John M., and Edith Rickert 107, 108, 165
Masefield, John 3, 176–8
Maximian 245, 310
McIlwaine, Catherine 180, 275
Merton College 6, 18, 233, 319
Merton Professor 4, 16, 37, 41, 215, 267
Middle English Dictionary 40, 47
Milton, John 105, 211
Minot, Laurence 158 n.136, 164, 171
minstrel 72, 103, 116 n.28
Miracle Plays 22
Moore, Samuel 40, 147
Morse code 64
Mroczkowski, Przemyslaw 323, 326
music of the spheres 74

Navy cadets 4, 27, 106, 178–83, 238
New English Dictionary 30, 109, 113; see also *Oxford English Dictionary*
Nicholas of Lynne 91
Nichol Smith, David 41, 45, 51, 66
Northern dialect 2, 11, 12, 20, 61, 102, 106, 107, 108, 112, 114, 115, 122, 123, 137, 158, 161, 177, 184, 185, 208

Oedipal revolt 17, 268
Opie, Iona and Peter 250–1

Ormulum 46 n.13, 141, 151 n.107, 170
overthwert 64–65
Ovid 72, 75, 77, 288, 314
Oxford Dante Society 4, 246–8
Oxford English Dictionary (OED) 2, 30–5, 249
Oxford Mail 3, 177, 178
Oxford's Summer Diversions 3, 106, 176–8, 181, 184

Pearl 5 n.6, 69–70, 163 n.144, 250, 323, 327
Pecksniff, Seth 277
Petersen, Kate O. 309
Petrarch 220, 221, 222, 223, 229
Philological Society 31, 51, 55, 107, 110
Phoenician letters 289
Piers Plowman 49 n.20, 80, 139, 150, 160, 168
potted story 289–90, 295 n. 62, 306
Price, Derek J. 6–7
Promptorium Parvulorum 75, 116, n.26, 139, 140, 146, 149, 152, 160
Punch (1947) 228–9
Purgatory/*Purgatorio* 4, 75, 87, 247, 248

Ragnar Loðbrók 90
Raleigh, Walter, Merton Professor 23, 24, 29, 319
  Chaucer and his Contemporaries, lectures 2, 15–23, 319
reincarnation 278
Rhodes Scholar 10, 35
Richard II 74, 80, 84
Rickert, Edith 79
Riders of the Mark 12
Robinson, F. N., Chaucer editor 83 n.78, 101 n.126, 103, 108, 240, 242, 278, 323–5
Role, Richard, of Hampole 152
Romance of the Rose 64, 73, 75, 79, 82, 97, 151
Royal Society of Literature 110
Ruthwell Cross 1 n.1, 143

Sachs, Hans 306
Sawles Warde 36, 140 n.65, 148 n.91, 155 n.121
Sayer, George 1–2, 6, 66

scholarship as autobiography 1, 323
Scogan, Henry 79
Scull, Christiana, and Wayne G. Hammond (SH) 1, 3, 4, 5–6, 9, 16, 23, 25, 28, 35, 36, 38, 177, 178, 180, 183, 216, 230, 234, 246, 247, 250, 251, 267, 269, 322
Shakespeare, William 90, 229
  King Lear 246 n.2, 265
  Merchant of Venice 280
  Midsummer Night's Dream 252
Shippey, Tom 108, 111 n.17, 147 n.87, 166 n.153, 178 n.188, 269, 323
Sir Gawain and the Green Knight 16, 22, 23, 24, 28, 35, 36, 42, 44, 45, 61, 64, 89, 115, 155, 180, 323, 326
Sir Orfeo 4, 9, 180–1, 315
Sisam, Kenneth 10, 18, 35, 37, 42, 43, 45, 46–8, 52, 54, 55–6, 106, 181, 223
  Clerkes Tale, edition 37, 41
  Fourteenth Century Verse and Prose, edition 35, 61, 102 n.130, 113 n.20, 152 n.112, 162 n.139, 249
Skeat Prize 18
Skeat, Walter W. 3, 4, 11, 17, 24, 37, 41, 43, 44, 55–6, 58, 75, 78, 96, 129, 139 n.63 (*Piers* edition), 141, 153, 162 n.139, 163–65 (on Strother), 172, 173, 175, 178, 180, 182, 185, 215, 234, 235, 241 (Bradshaw Shift), 244, 245 (Maximian), 275 ("a dreadful lot of semi-colons!") 278
  Northern dialect in *Reeve's Tale* 12, 102, 106–7, 112 n.18, 162 n.139
  Works of Geoffrey Chaucer, edition 10, 23, 29, 33–4, 43
slik 126, 132, 143, 154, 170–1, 193
Sméagol and Déagol 183, 268, 271
spatulamancy 243
Speght, Thomas, Elizabethan editor 17 n.13, 33
Spenser, Edmund 27, 75, 211, 214
Stratford at Bow 39, 96–7
Strother 38, 101–2, 106, 163–4

Tatlock, John S. P. 33
Ten Brink, Bernard 15, 24, 63
Thomas à Becket 95

Thomas, Mary Edith 34–5
Thousand and One Nights 299
Thynne, William, Elizabethan editor 33, 63, 71, 90, 240
Times Literary Supplement (*TLS*) 3, 6, 25, 35–7, 323, 326
Timothy 1 vi.7–10 227, 279, 307
Tolkien (biopic) 2
Tolkien, Christopher 20, 107, 109, 183, 234–5, 240, 244, 320, 327
  Silmarillion, editor 7
Tolkien, J. R. R.:
  Athrabeth Finrod Ah Andreth, Boethian dialogue 81 n.73
  "*Beowulf*: The Monsters and the Critics", lecture 23, 29, 108
  Beren and Lúthien 20
  "Chaucer and the Alliterative Tradition" 102–5
  "Chaucer as a Philologist", article 106–75, 110–75
  "Chaucer's Use of Dialect", lecture 10, 106
  "Chaucerian Grammar" 4, 107, 180–1, 183, 201–14
  Clarkes Compleinte 36
  Clerk's Tale, lecture 216–24
  "Devil's Coach-Horses" 36
  "does not support examination or long familiarity" Tolkien on *Pardoner's Tale*, 1955 311
  Fellowship of the Ring 272
  Hobbit 20, 247, 250, 304 n.77, 326
  "I don't approve of the *Pardoner's Tale*" 311
  "Introduction on Language" (*TLC*) 41–2
  Lay of Aotrou and Itroun 326
  Leaf by Niggle 326
  Letter on *faynights* 250–1
  "Light as Leaf on Lindentree" 37
  Lord of the Rings 5, 17, 20, 23, 107, 146, 183, 250, 251, 252, 270, 271, 326
  "Middle English *Losenger*", conference paper 2, 4, 7, 15, 31, 38, 246, 247, 252–66
  Middle English Vocabulary 35, 36
  "Neck Verse", lecture 246–8

  "odious or noxious creature of bizarre shape" Tolkien on Pardoner, 1955 317
  "On Fairy-Stories", lecture 29
  "one of Chaucer's best told tales" Tolkien on *Pardoner's Tale*, 1947 227
  OUP *Selections* Correspondence 42–55
  "Oxford English School", newspaper article 246, 319
  Pardoner's Tale, 1947 lecture 224–9
  Pardoner's Tale, 1951–54 lectures 233–45
  Pardoner's Tale: The Legend, 1954 lectures 234
  Pardoner's Tale: The Story and its Form, 1955–56 lectures 5, 267–318
  Parlement of Foules, 1948 lectures 230–3
  perfectionist 2, 34, 66
  "Philology: General Works", *Year's Work in English Studies* 3, 38–40
  Return of the King 5, 234, 267, 270, 272
  Selections from Chaucer's Poetry and Prose 1, 3, 25, 27, 34, 38, 41–105, 43, 48, 57, 58, 67, 103, 216
  Selections Glossary 3, 12, 41, 43–4, 45, 46–7, 55–6, 61–6, 246, 249
  Selections Notes 3, 7, 45, 46, 47, 48, 50, 55, 61, 66–105, 107, 109, 177
  "Sigelwara Land", two articles 49 n.19, 51
  Silmarillion 5, 7, 15, 37, 250, 251, 267, 323, 326–7
  "Some Contributions to Middle-English Lexicography", article 25, 36
  "The Language of Chaucer" 1913 10–15
  "Valedictory Address" 5, 25, 252, 319–22
Tolkien, Michael 44
Tolkien, Priscilla 19, 90 n.100, 246
"top-heavy" (*Pardoner's Tale*) 272, 275, 290, 293, 313
tragedy 22, 29–30, 87
Trevisa, John 102, 113, 162 n.139
tulle 166–70
"two square yards" 2, 3, 66, 176, 233, 246, 320
Tyrwhitt, Thomas 2, 34, 126 n.50, 302

Unwin, Rayner 250, 267

Vache, Philip de la 79
Valentine's Day 76

West Midland dialect 12, 25
wizard/wise man 245, 269, 283, 285, 288, 294, 297–9, 304, 305, 310

Wrenn, C. L. 322
Wright, Joseph 9, 10
Wycliffite 19, 35, 140, 216–17, 324
Wyld, Henry Cecil 116, 173 n.181

York Plays 142, 147, 148 n.90, 167, 169, 171